SUNY series, Alternatives in Psychology
Michael A. Wallach, editor

Between Conviction and Uncertainty

Philosophical Guidelines for the Practicing Psychotherapist

Jerry N. Downing

State University of New York Press

Cover concept by Mark A. Lutterbie

Published by
State University of New York Press, Albany

For information, address State University of New York Press,
State University Plaza, Albany, N.Y. 12246

Production by Michael Haggett
Marketing by Patrick Durocher

Library of Congress Cataloging-in-Publication Data

Downing, Jerry N., 1943–
    Between conviction and uncertainty : philosophical guidelines for the practicing
psychotherapist / Jerry N. Downing.
        p. cm. — (SUNY series, alternatives in psychology)
    Includes bibliographical references and index.
    ISBN 0-7914-4627-1 (alk. paper) — ISBN 0-7914-4628-X (pbk. : alk. paper)
        1. Psychotherapy—Philosophy. I. Title. II. Series.

RC437.5 .D68 2000
616.89′14′01—dc21
                                                                                    99-051479

10 9 8 7 6 5 4 3 2 1

To my Mother and Father—
Whose lives have taught me about uncertainty

Contents

Tables

Acknowledgments

The writing of this book would not have been possible without the generous support of colleagues, friends, family members, and institutions. I must begin with Michael and Lise Wallach, who served as my mentors over twenty-five years ago at Duke University. Since that time, they have remained as valued colleagues and friends who have added much to my professional and personal life. Without their unflagging enthusiasm for this topic, their steady insistence that I take the time to write, and their incisive commentary on the manuscript which resulted, this project, quite simply, would never have come to fruition.

Peter Gilford has been a faithful companion in the attempt to define the philosophical and moral terrain of contemporary psychotherapy. Lucy Lutterbie, who understands well the wonders and horrors of the academic life, has unstintingly supported my decision to revive scholarly goals which had long been dormant. They are included with a group whom I especially thank for reading and critiquing all or parts of the manuscript: Naomi Brown, Lisa Harrison, John Tennant, and Lori Varlotta. While not all of the other individuals, including many predoctoral psychology interns and postdoctoral fellows, who encouraged my interest in these ideas can be mentioned here, I want to single out the contributions of Marie Ali, Michael Carey, Jessica Drew, Tanya Russell, Jeff Sandler, Jane Slaughter, Suzanne Slyman, Kim Smith, Jim Thomas, and Cathie Todd.

Work on this piece extended over several years while I was also functioning as a full-time psychologist and Training Director in the

Counseling Center at the University of San Francisco. I thank Barbara Thomas, Director, and my colleagues at the Center for their understanding of my occasional periods of preoccupation and/or general testiness. I am especially grateful to Carmen Jordan-Cox, Vice President for Student Affairs, who granted a three-month sabbatical during which I was able to focus my attention exclusively on this project.

At USF, Rebekah Bloyd's editing skills led to improvements in the initial drafts of the manuscript, and Kristen Angel's computer expertise was essential to reformatting the tables. The comments of the readers for the State University of New York Press were extremely helpful to making needed revisions of the argument. My gratitude also goes to Jane Bunker, Michael Haggett, Patrick Durocher, and the other editors and staff of the State University of New York Press who were instrumental in guiding this book through revision, production, and distribution.

Finally, I appreciate the forbearance of my brother, Bill Downing, and my sister-in-law, Mary Bachman, who consistently encouraged my efforts to complete this work—even when they would have preferred to talk about something else.

Introduction

It is reasonable to ask—as most publishers outside of this series might—why a book with "philosophy" as its focus would be addressed primarily to the "practicing psychotherapist." It is my hope that the themes of this book will appeal not only to those who have specific interests in theoretical and philosophical psychology, but also to the more typical busy clinician, clinical supervisor, or clinical trainee. Indeed, it is my belief that the question of the solidity of the knowledge base of our field cannot be confined to occasional academic debates. Rather, it is a question which we as therapists live out daily in our moment-by-moment interactions with clients, and that living-out occurs with or without our awareness.

For example, consider a therapist who makes an interpretation to a client of the sort, "When you talk about your girlfriend, I am reminded of what you have told me about your mother." What assumptions are behind this interpretation? By "assumptions" I am not referring to the content of the interpretation. For the purposes of this book, it would not matter if the interpretation were cognitive-behavioral rather than psychodynamic in nature. It would not even matter if an experientially oriented therapist objected to the very notion of interpretation, claiming that therapists should ignore theory and remain closer to the client's own language. Whatever therapists' theoretical orientations, and however we relate to the question of interpretation, certain assumptions are being made. These assumptions concern how we define our own view of reality and its associated truth value, how we define the client's view of reality and its truth value, and how we propose to bridge those two realities. It can be argued that assumptions of this kind are at least in part philosophical in nature.

I believe that some urgency surrounds the task of beginning to acknowledge and clarify the philosophical assumptions on which everyday, routine psychotherapeutic practice is built. The question is not just epistemological: What can we know? It is also ethical and moral: What are the implications of the gap between what we can know and what we must assume? These moral implications loom even larger if we as therapists fail to acknowledge that such a gap exists, and function in society from a position of acting as if our theories and methods are seamlessly aligned with that which is right and true.

Although it can be argued that the crucial intellectual and moral dilemmas of psychotherapy practice are largely philosophical in nature, the goal of linking these two domains represents a considerable challenge. Erwin (1997) suggests that, until recently, philosophers have written relatively little about psychotherapy. I would add that clinicians could justifiably complain that much of the existing literature is too far removed from the practical issues of psychotherapy practice. Moreover, while an increasing number of psychologists and psychotherapists are interested in translating philosophical concepts to the clinical realm (Miller, 1992), such interests have not as yet entered the mainstream. Consequently, most psychotherapists are never formally exposed to philosophical thinking during their academic and clinical training or subsequent professional careers.

I have approached the task of making philosophical thinking more accessible to clinicians by attempting to order, clarify, and synthesize a great deal of sometimes complex and even confusing material. Philosophical terms (e.g., "philosophy of science," "epistemology," and "realism") and psychological terms (e.g., "constructivism" and "narrative"), which are glossed over in the introduction and chapter 1 and which might be unfamiliar to some readers, will be defined at appropriate points in the text. Further, in structuring an argument, I have attempted to remain guided by an objective of developing a more tangible, applied approach to heady theoretical and philosophical questions. By reviewing and reformulating the debates within contemporary philosophy and academic psychology that are of most relevance to psychotherapy, I hope to provide clinicians with tools of analysis which can then be applied to their own practices.

Despite these good intentions, the dual audience to which the book is directed means that both philosophically minded readers and more clinically oriented readers may each have their own moments of frustration. While the former group, which certainly includes some therapists, might expect a discussion which is as theoretically complete and philosophically sophisticated as possible, many practitioners would undoubtedly prefer a presentation which is quite focused, readily intelligible, and clinically pragmatic.

It is one of the themes of this work that psychotherapy practice is best conceived in dialectical terms, and the notion of a tension between opposites seems to apply to the argument itself. In the best of all worlds, this book would be both more philosophically and theoretically complete and more clinically accessible and pragmatic. However, I have found that these objectives, beyond a certain point, are not mutually compatible. Moving too far toward the one pole would begin to take the argument too far away from the other. In the end, it was necessary to make choices which balanced the argument between those poles, and these choices were most influenced by two considerations. While I wanted the philosophical and theoretical analyses of psychotherapy to be suitably comprehensive and intellectually sound, I have also attempted to present this information within clear, coherent frameworks (e.g., tables 1, 2, & 3) which can be grasped by readers with no philosophical background. In addition, I wanted the practical implications of these analyses to accurately reflect the complex moral issues which inevitably confront psychotherapy practice.

Therefore, I anticipate that the tension which is inherent in this argument might be experienced by potential readers as follows: Some philosophically minded readers may find the theoretical and philosophical analyses at certain points to be *less* complete or sophisticated than they would wish and some clinically oriented readers might find them at times to be *too* comprehensive or complex. Specifically, chapters 2–4 may test the patience of some clinicians. I believe that this material is crucial to the development of a philosophical framework for psychotherapy, but I also want to assure the persistent reader that it will be framed in a more clinically accessible and pragmatic form in chapters 5–7.

Before moving to a brief review of the individual chapters, it is fitting to offer two other clarifications for the clinical reader. First, as will be examined in chapter 1, one of the perplexing developments of our field today is the very proliferation of psychotherapeutic theories and methods. It is not my intention to add to that ever growing supply of theoretical views; rather, my goal is to provide a means by which therapists might examine and critique the assumptions on which their existing theoretical orientations rest. At most, therapists will be encouraged to add to their repertoire of epistemological positions, not to their stock of psychological theories and therapeutic methods. If there is a psychological theory being proposed here, I hope that it falls within the tradition pioneered by George Kelly (Maher, 1969), constituting a "theory about theories."

Second, as the main title of the book suggests, the exploration which is undertaken here is not one which results in a final psychological or philosophical position which would somehow deliver therapists from conceptual ambiguity and personal discomfort. Concluding that therapists can never operate from a position of assuming that we have some "truth" to offer to the client would resolve much of the ambiguity and tension inherent in our societal role—a resolution which is perversely similar to that provided by assuming that we always can impart that same "truth." It will be argued that therapists not only must learn to *doubt more radically* than is thought imaginable from the traditional stance towards practice ("realism") but also must often acknowledge a need to *believe more fully* than is deemed acceptable by either of the current, conflicting, critical stances toward practice ("empiricism" and "social constructionism" / "constructivism"). At best, a psychotherapist whose practice is epistemologically sound and morally grounded must continue indefinitely to live out a dialectic between conviction and uncertainty which is altogether congruent with answering the "perilous calling" (Sussman, 1995) of this profession.

Given the thrust of this argument, a skeptic might contend that it is a bit misleading to promise that the book will provide "philosophical guidelines" for psychotherapy practice. Certainly, the clinical marketplace today is inundated with guideline books, ranging from treatment manuals to less structured "how to" approaches. As a rule, clinical guidelines are expected to be quite concrete, to offer direction, and to reduce ambiguity. While the philosophical guidelines which are gradually developed in chapters 5 and 6 and then made more explicit in chapter 7 do provide direction and are illustrated at various points with clinical examples, they necessarily remain rather abstract in nature. Worse yet, they actually increase the ambiguity of the psychotherapeutic enterprise! After arguing that practitioners should become more dialectical and pluralistic in their approach to psychotherapy, the remainder of the book's last chapter explores what is likely to impede one's ability to move in the recommended direction.

Therefore, clinicians who expect conventional guidelines for practice may be disappointed by what is offered here. In fact, the secondary title of the book is paradoxical: It is meant to capture something of the essential tension between philosophical awareness and clinical application. To understand these "philosophical guidelines" is to acknowledge that certain intellectual and moral dilemmas are intrinsic to the practice of psychotherapy—and that the most that one can do is to remain vigilant and aware. Moreover, these guidelines suggest that we as clinicians will often of necessity remain unaware of the moral implications of our theories and methods, and at other times we will wish that we could be less aware—that is, we will feel as if it is "just too difficult" to practice a morally situated approach to psychotherapeutic knowing. For a profession that is ostensibly dedicated to self-knowledge, these are difficult realizations, and I sit with them no more comfortably than any other clinician. Yet, if we are truly to serve the welfare of the client, then nothing could be more important than recognizing the intellectual and moral vulnerabilities which we face daily as practitioners, despite the personal and professional unease this recognition may engender.

Chapter 1 selectively reviews the historical, comparative, empirical, and theoretical literature on psychotherapy from the vantage point of the metatheoretical question, "What do therapists know?" While many different identities have historically been associated with the practice of "mental healing," one particular identity, that of "scientific healer," has been most instrumental in establishing the conceptual ground and the social legitimacy of Western psychotherapy. Since this identity rests most firmly on the assumption that the knowledge provided to clients is objective and valid, the review focuses particularly on the scientific status of psychotherapeutic theories and methods.

Chapter 2 shifts the question from what therapists *do* know to what they *can* know through a selective examination of positions associated with both the philosophy of science and "postmodern" philosophy. This review proposes four philosophical positions which are of most relevance to psychotherapy practice: realism, sophisticated realism, sophisticated relativism, and anti-realism. Anti-realism is further articulated in relation to Rosenau's (1992) categories of "affirmative" and "skeptical" postmodernism, which are associated, respectively, with the philosophical problems of relativism and nihilism. Postmodernists endeavor either to dismiss or reframe these problems, and such attempts, based largely on philosophical hermeneutics and neopragmatism, are also explored in some detail.

Chapters 3 and 4 trace the implications of the previous chapter for the questions of the function and range of theory in personality psychology and psychotherapy. Regarding the question of *function*, when

Thomas Kuhn's (1970a) approach to the history of science is conceptualized as a psychological theory about the behavior of scientists, a par-
allel can be drawn to the theories of certain personality psychologists,
especially those of Carl Rogers and George Kelly. This analysis converges on the generalization that theories of personality and psychotherapy serve the opposing functions of *revealing* a particular
interpretation of reality while simultaneously *restricting* the range of
potentially valid, alternative interpretations.

It is then argued in chapter 4 that the contrast between realism and
anti-realism in philosophy holds promise for encompassing a wide *range* of
theoretical assumptions and methods associated with contemporary psychotherapeutic practice. On the one hand, the realism pole includes both
those therapeutic approaches which assume the possibility of objective
truth (for example, classical psychoanalysis and behaviorism) and those
which reject objectivism but hold out the possibility of other forms of truth
(phenomenological and transpersonal therapies). On the other hand, the
anti-realist pole corresponds to a variety of constructivist, narrative, intersubjective, and social constructionist therapies which may reject the notion
of therapeutic truth altogether. The complex relationship between constructivism and hermeneutics, as well as the frequent inconsistency between
the therapist's stated philosophical position and his/her actual experience
and behavior, represent important subthemes of the chapter.

Chapter 5 reorients the discussion of the previous two chapters to
the issue of translating abstract theoretical and philosophical positions
into the concrete experience of the theorist or therapist. The construct
of *lived* modes of knowing is introduced as a way of anchoring philosophical positions to the cognitive, affective, and behavioral (interpersonal) experience of the therapist. Not only does this construct move the
discussion from philosophical analysis to psychological application, but
it also addresses the discrepancy between theory and behavior which has
long plagued the psychotherapy research literature (Kiesler, 1966). From
this perspective, it is expected that therapists' inner experience and outer
behavior will at times deviate from the theoretical positions which they
hold, since modes of knowing, unlike general philosophical and psychological positions, are fluid phenomena. Further, since modes of knowing
can exist at different levels of awareness, therapists may be unaware
when they are operating from within a given mode and, therefore, may
not acknowledge the possible discrepancy between that mode and their
stated orientation to practice.

The therapist modes of knowing (and their associated philosophical
positions) which are introduced in chapter 5 include: Realist (realism);

Representational (sophisticated realism); Perspectival (sophisticated relativism); Dialogical (affirmative postmodernism); Critical (limited skeptical postmodernism); and Nihilistic (unlimited skeptical postmodernism).

Chapter 6 then provides detailed referents for these lived modes of knowing, describing the characteristics of each along the dimensions summarized in table 3 of chapter 5. The goal of this analysis is to provide readers with a sufficiently rich and textured account as to allow them to recognize these modes of functioning within their own or others' therapeutic approaches. Thus, this chapter models the exploration of questions such as the following: "What is the experience of functioning in a Representational mode of knowing in actual therapeutic interaction with a client? What is it like when I shift to a Realist mode? How do I define my role with the client when I am in a Dialogical mode? Is it possible to practice therapy from a stance of Nihilistic knowing? Can psychotherapy be practiced in the absence of any Realist functioning whatsoever?"

While the previous chapters have attempted to provide therapists with a conceptual scheme through which they might identify and describe their own and others' changing philosophical assumptions, the final chapter turns to the question of recommendations for practice. Building on the prior analyses, it is argued that one's philosophical assumptions, whether implicitly or explicitly held, cannot be disentangled from the moral issues inherent in clinical practice.

The notion of therapist "ethics," as defined by professional organizations such as the American Psychological Association, is first expanded to include a "moral" dimension related to philosophical awareness. A holistic, dialectical approach to clinical practice is then recommended which establishes the complementary relationships among the six modes of knowing and encourages therapists to find value in each. At different moments of interaction with one's client(s), a therapist's capacity to move among different philosophical positions can serve as a set of checks and balances.

For example, the Realist mode of knowing appears to be a pervasive aspect of human functioning. It can be one manifestation of the therapist's empathic connection with the client and often serves as a vehicle for conveying new understanding to the client. Yet, left unchecked, this way of knowing can lead to an uncritical and even self-serving approach to therapy practice. Shifting from this mode to one which takes a hypothetical stance and examines empirical evidence, recognizes the constructed nature of theoretical terms, assumes the intersubjective nature of knowing, or stresses the sociopolitical context of therapeutic interventions can provide necessary balance. Further, this dialectical approach emphasizes the value of balancing the positive claims of the first five modes of knowing with the negative claims of a Nihilistic experience of knowing. By coming into contact with our own limits as human beings, therapists—like clients—may experience moments of acute anxiety, tension, confusion, and uncertainty. Yet, this brush with the existential givens can serve as the ultimate corrective to the occupational hazard of overvaluing our theories and methods.

In addition to a recognition of the dialectical nature of psychotherapeutic knowing, the recommended approach is "epistemologically pluralistic" and balances "conceptual thought" with "direct experience" and "knowing" with "being." These characteristics are summarized by borrowing terms associated with Kuhn (1970a) and Feyerabend (1970) and framing them in relation to the moral dimension of psychotherapy practice. Thus, in the natural sciences, as in lay psychology, the "normal" component of knowing (conviction) tends to dominate and is periodically disrupted by a "revolutionary" or "philosophical" component (uncertainty). Psychotherapists also have strong needs for belief, certainty, and legitimacy which manifest through the implicit and explicit positions which we hold, whether these positions are reputedly "scientific," "humanistic," "hermeneutic," or "postmodern" in their philosophical and theoretical assumptions. However, as is documented in chapter 7, the consequences for clients can be devastating if this normal component is allowed to rule one's approach to psychotherapy.

Therefore, it is concluded that psychotherapists must aim for a higher standard of philosophical awareness than has characterized the natural sciences. This requires going against our human inclinations by struggling to balance, on a daily basis, the normal component of our functioning with philosophical knowing. From the experience and recognition of an ongoing dialectic between *necessary conviction* and *radical uncertainty*—a dialectic which is not resolvable by a philosophical, theoretical, or therapeutic position of any kind—a morally situated psychotherapy can emerge.

Chapter 1

Challenges from the Psychotherapy Literature:
What *Do* Therapists Know?

In an evaluation of the current status of psychoanalytic thinking, Stephen Mitchell (1993) includes a chapter similar in title to this one and concludes that a "crisis in confidence" exists within analytic circles today. He contends that psychoanalysis was historically characterized by an assumption that there was a single theory which represented "scientific truth." But, today

> there are many psychoanalytic schools, each with claims to an exclusive possession of objective truth. . . . It is hard to imagine a time when any one theoretical perspective will demonstrate such compelling reasonableness and truth that proponents of the others will change ranks, and psychoanalysis will once again be whole. (p. 45)

Further, he proposes that this change in thinking within psychoanalysis parallels intellectual trends in the larger culture and has involved a shift "not on the level of theory but on the level of metatheory: theory about theory" (p. 42). That is, one can discern and comprehend this shift in thinking in the analytic community only by stepping back from the concrete, multitudinous changes in psychoanalytic theorizing and asking what they imply for the question, "What does the analyst know?"

Mitchell's characterization of psychoanalysis anticipates some conclusions which could be reached for the general field of psychotherapy, and his focus on "metatheory" parallels the strategy which I will employ here. Since the literature on psychotherapy is so vast and unwieldy, it is important in a work of this kind to approach it from a particular, limited vantage point. Therefore, those aspects of the historical, comparative, empirical, and theoretical literature on psychotherapy which are reviewed were selected because of their direct bearing on the metatheoretical question, "Now what does this tell us about what therapists really know?"

THE PROLIFERATION OF THERAPEUTIC THEORIES AND METHODS

It would be no surprise to the practicing clinician, who is constantly bombarded by flyers in the daily mail touting seminars on new therapeutic techniques and strategies, to find the following conclusion supported by the literature: Mitchell's observations about the proliferation of theory and method in psychoanalysis apply to the field of psychotherapy as a whole. The number of therapeutic alternatives available in this field has increased dramatically within the relatively short period of less than 40 years. London (1986) cites Harper (1959) as describing 36 "systems" of psychotherapy, Parloff (1976) as counting 130 "titles" but only 17 distinct modalities, and Herink (1980) as cataloging more than 250 non-redundant types of treatment (p. 42). More recently, Karasu (1992) estimates that there are over 400 types of therapy, a number more than ten times that of Harper's original formulation.

Of course, these numbers may be inflated to some unspecified degree because there is disagreement over exactly what should be called a therapeutic theory or method. Certainly, the higher estimates encompass a variety of ways of defining therapy including the traditional approach of naming the school/theoretical stance (cognitive therapy or narrative therapy) as well as the newer strategy of counting approaches which represent a specific problem or population (sex therapy or substance abuse therapy), a specific modality (family therapy or group therapy), or a specific technique (hypnotherapy or relaxation training). In addition, London (1986), pointing to usages such as "Horticultural Therapy" and "Poetry Therapy" (p. 42), suggests that "there are more psychotherapies than there used to be because the boundaries of what can legitimately be called psychotherapy have shifted radically, and the taxonomy of treatments has had to shift with them" (p. 43).

Debates about criteria for inclusion, however, should not detract from the agreement which has been reached about the larger issue. There has been a virtual explosion in theories and methods by which one might conduct psychotherapy, and it is directly related to the guiding question of this chapter. Whether or not one would see this proliferation of theory and method as adding to our collective knowledge about psychotherapy, it appears to have the opposite impact on the individual level. It can be experienced as a constant din of claims that something *newer* and *better* has been discovered which *must* be added to the repertoire of any responsibly informed therapist. Prochaska and Norcross (1994) write: "A healthy diversity has deteriorated into an unhealthy chaos. Students, practitioners, and patients are confronted with confusion, fragmentation, and discontent. With so many therapy systems claiming success, which theories should be studied, taught, or bought?" (p. 1).

HISTORICAL AND COMPARATIVE APPROACHES TO PSYCHOTHERAPY

It is interesting to juxtapose the current proliferation of therapeutic systems with historical and comparative views of the definition of psychotherapy and its identity as a cultural institution. Reviews (Kiev, 1964; Bromberg, 1975; Ehrenwald, 1966, 1976a; Frank, 1973; Frank & Frank, 1991) of the history of mental healing, broadly considered, underscore that Western psychotherapists are not the first socially sanctioned mental health practitioners to assume that cultural role:

> If mental healers were to be summoned to the patient's bedside in the order of their appearance in history, the magician or medicine man would be the first one to answer the call. He[1] would be followed by the philosopher-priest of various religious denominations, who would, in turn, yield his place to the scientifically oriented psychotherapist. (Ehrenwald, 1976b, p. 17)

Different views of the causation and amelioration of mental distress are associated with each of these identities and include "the religiomagical, the rhetorical, and the empirical or naturalistic" (Frank & Frank, 1991,

---

[1] Throughout the text the reader is asked to judge seemingly sexist language in quoted matter in relation to the prevailing standards when the passage was written.

p. 3). The cause and cure of mental distress are found in the spiritual domain by the former and in the physical and psychological domains by the latter. "Rhetoric" is historically associated with the combination of a philosophical and naturalistic outlook, such as that of the ancient Greeks, who saw the role of the rhetorician as one of exerting a kind of moral influence on the listener through facilitating the adoption of "noble" beliefs (pp. 65–66).

Jerome Frank has been so impressed with the parallels among religiomagical healing, religious revivalism and cults, thought reform, the placebo effect in medicine, and Western psychotherapy that his classic study (1961) of comparative psychotherapy, and its subsequent revisions (Frank, 1973; Frank & Frank, 1991), define "psychotherapy" broadly enough to encompass all of these manifestations. For Frank, all of these psychotherapies involve a special relationship between a socially sanctioned healer and a sufferer, where the healer attempts to modify the sufferer's thoughts/beliefs, feelings, and behaviors. Thus, all psychotherapy represents an attempt at "persuasion," whether the healer's influence is direct or indirect, unacknowledged or acknowledged.

Ehrenwald (1976c) suggests that healers as diverse as magicians and shamans in preindustrial societies, demonologists in the European Middle Ages, Mesmer in eighteenth-century France, and the Christian Scientist Mary Baker Eddy in nineteenth-century America probably all had a "modicum of success" in their attempts to heal sufferers (pp. 571–572). This observation offers a clue to understanding the proliferation of Western psychotherapies, described in the last section. Perhaps all of these psychotherapies, like their historical predecessors, have a "modicum of success" in improving the lives of clients who are seen and, therefore, find at least a temporary niche in the therapeutic marketplace. While the empirical evidence for this proposition will be examined in the next section, stating it here provides some context for the historical/comparative approach.

Indeed, the comparative work of Ehrenwald and Frank represents an early and, especially in Frank's case (Weinberger, 1993), influential statement of what has come to be known as the "common factors" approach to psychotherapy. Both are interested in addressing two intriguing questions. What does it mean that there have been a series of quite different approaches to mental healing which have occurred across different cultures and times? And, what does it mean that so many different approaches to psychotherapy have been produced in our own culture and time?

Ehrenwald and Frank bring conceptual order to a vast number of contradictory observations through making a simple assumption: All of these historical modes of healing and all of the contemporary approaches to psychotherapy are characterized by certain common elements which contribute to their success on both the individual and societal level. Frank and Frank (1991) propose that the following four factors appear in all forms of psychotherapy, whether the practitioner is a shaman, a psychoanalyst, or a behavior therapist:

> An emotionally charged, confiding relationship with a helping person (often with the participation of a group). . . .
> A healing setting. . . .
> A rationale, conceptual scheme, or myth that provides a plausible explanation for the patient's symptoms and prescribes a ritual or procedure for resolving them. . . .
> A ritual or procedure that requires the active participation of both patient and therapist and that is believed by both to be the means of restoring the patient's health. (pp. 40–43, italics omitted)

The "myth" and "ritual" prescribed by the therapist not only must fit with the client's beliefs and expectations to the extent that "faith" and "hope" are awakened but also must provide specific learning which will allow the client to make concrete changes in areas such as emotional expression, sense of self-efficacy, and behavior.

It is important to note that Frank's analysis is more textured and subtle than it may appear in this brief summary. He does not simply reduce psychotherapy to "faith" or the placebo effect, and he is not saying that "training in any particular theory or technique is superfluous" or that "anything goes" in psychotherapy (Frank & Frank, 1991, p. xiv). In fact, he acknowledges that it is valuable for therapists to have in their repertoire a variety of theoretical / methodological approaches which can accord "with the patient's personal characteristics and view of the problem" (p. xv).

The historical / comparative approach to psychotherapy represents a serious challenge to the thinking of most clinical practitioners, undermining many assumptions about what is known. While it is generally presumed without question that Western psychotherapy is a unique approach to dealing with human problems, these historians of the field argue that there are vestiges of religiomagical healing and rhetoric in present-day practice. Worse yet, Ehrenwald (1976c) suggests that it may be more difficult than is generally assumed to demonstrate "conclusively the superiority of scientific psychotherapy over its primitive forerunners" (p. 573).

Frank further jostles our assumptions by taking to task our cherished theories of personality and therapeutic change. He refers to such theories as "myths," not because they invoke spirits or supernatural powers, but because: "(1) they are imagination-catching formulations of recurrent and important human experiences; and (2) they cannot be proved empirically. Successes are taken as evidence of their validity (often erroneously), while failures are explained away" (Frank & Frank, 1991, p. 42).

It might be more accurate to say that therapeutic failures or disconfirming observations in the psychotherapy field do not lead to the displacement of old theories but to the generation of new theories. When Carl Jung and Alfred Adler began to see a different way of conceptualizing human problems that better described their own experience and was seemingly more effective with their patients, then two new theories took their place alongside Freudian theory. The same process has continued unabated up to the present time and is no doubt a major contributor to the proliferation of theory and technique in psychotherapy.

Further, Frank emphasizes the *function* rather than the *content* of therapeutic theories, and this emphasis leads to the clarification of another puzzle of the therapeutic field. Returning to an earlier assumption that therapies must have some success with at least some clients to survive in the marketplace, a focus on theoretical content might lead to the faulty conclusion that all of the different accounts of therapeutic change are somehow "equally true." Shifting to a comparative analysis highlights a factor which crosscuts the different theories and which is no doubt a universal need of human beings. From this perspective, the function of theory is to provide new meanings for the client, and this function is independent of any one theory or technique.

Framing this same point in the context of psychotherapeutic interpretation, Frank (1973) would contend that interpretations need not be true to benefit the client, they need only be plausible (p. 224). Plausible interpretations serve many functions including: (*a*) demonstrating the therapist's understanding and concern, (*b*) evoking emotional release, (*c*) providing reassurance, and (*d*) giving the client a new set of meanings for self-understanding. Thus, Frank's thinking is similar to that of Spence (1982), who argues that interpretations work, not because of their "historical truth," but because of their "narrative truth." Both of these accounts provide an explanation for the widely observed phenomenon that clients in different therapies often produce dreams, free associations, or insights that conform to the particular theoretical leanings of the therapist they happen to be seeing (Ehrenwald, 1976c, p. 573).

The impact of the historical and comparative literature on the question "What do therapists know?" can be summarized by turning to the issue of therapist identity in contemporary America. Bromberg, writing in 1975, offers an observation which in the context of subsequent developments seems prescient: "The present scene in this country represents virtually a recapitulation of the entire history of the art and science of mental healing" (p. 347).

On the one hand, the majority of psychotherapists who practice in the United States, and presumably the majority of clients who seek psychotherapy, associate its practice with the tradition of medical or "scientific" healing. This includes therapists who are empirically oriented and identify specifically with a "scientist-practitioner" model of practice. It also includes therapists who intentionally or unintentionally don the mantle of science through the seemingly scientific nature of their theoretical language, their therapeutic methods, or the locale of their practice. "Secular therapies typically take place in a therapist's office, a hospital, or a clinic. Many of these sites carry the aura of science" (Frank & Frank, 1991, p. 41). This identity for the therapist is congruent with many current societal expectations—including those stated and enforced by the managed care industry, state licensing boards, and professional organizations—where objectivity and accountability are seen as defining sound practice.

On the other hand, there are a significant number of psychotherapists, and pockets of consumers of psychotherapy, who embrace a nonscientific identity for psychotherapy, including identities associated with the prehistory of Western psychotherapy. An informal sign that some therapists are returning to a religiomagical identity is given by the directories which have appeared in many urban areas and guide prospective clients to "alternative" therapists and healers. While this trend may be more developed in the San Francisco Bay Area than in some other parts of the country, a local directory (*Common Ground*, 1996) advertises approaches such as "Alchemical Hypnotherapy," "the Animal Imagery Circle," and "Phoenix Rising Yoga Therapy." A relatively mainstream expression of the same trend is represented by the development of "Transpersonal Psychology" as a branch of the field with its own membership, annual conference, and journal. While not all transpersonally oriented theorists and therapists reject science as a way of knowing, many are interested in investigating (Lukoff, Turner, & Lu, 1993) and applying (Waldman, 1992) spiritual/religious healing practices.

Other movements within the American psychotherapeutic community seem to embrace neither a scientific nor a religiomagical identity and represent a return to what Frank would call "rhetoric." While it's doubtful that many therapists of this persuasion would embrace his term as a description of their philosophy and practice, they might identify more readily with his characterization of this approach to psychotherapy as "the transformation of meanings" (Frank & Frank, 1991, chap. 3). This redefinition moves psychotherapy from a natural science, intent on discovering facts, to a kind of "human science" (Giorgi, 1970)—or even to a form of "moral discourse" (Cushman, 1993)—concerned with the question of how individual and culture intersect to create meaning and being. While such a formulation may ignore some important points of difference among the various psychotherapies emphasizing a rhetorical approach, it is broadly descriptive of psychotherapists who champion either an older ("humanistic-existential") or a newer ("social constructionist," "hermeneutic," or "narrative") alternative identity for therapeutic practice.

Like the proliferation of theoretical theories and methods outlined in the last section, these contrasting identities for the psychotherapist are another reflection of the confusion and upheaval surrounding the status of psychotherapeutic knowledge. At the very moment that external forces are pushing psychotherapy to become more accountable and to justify its societal value on empirical grounds, internal challenges to a strictly scientific and empirical agenda are increasing in both number and credibility. These two contrary trends are certainly visible within the American Psychological Association (APA), as some of its recent publications would attest. For example, this organization's Division of Clinical Psychology has established a special Task Force to respond to the cultural press for empirically validated treatments. It has proposed criteria for choosing treatments on this basis, drafted lists of specific treatments which meet these criteria, and emphasized the importance of the dissemination of this information to clinical psychologists and training programs (Task Force on Promotion and Dissemination of Psychological Procedures, 1995). Further, given that this effort has been inspired in part by the fear that legal and managed care guidelines for the treatment of psychological disorders will come to be dominated by psychiatry and psychopharmacology (Barlow, 1996), the Task Force recommendations could also have future implications for health care policy, third party payers, and reimbursement.

Meanwhile, APA's flagship journal, the *American Psychologist,* has been peppered during recent years with pieces that critique a singularly empirical approach to questions of method, identity, and social value. Three of the many such articles include a suggested identity for the clinical psychologist as that of "metaphysician-scientist-practitioner" (O'Donohue, 1989), a proposal for "multiplicity" in the research methods on which clinical practice and training are built (Hoshmand & Polkinghorne, 1992), and a recommendation that a "constructive relationship" between religion and psychological science be established (Jones, 1994).

THE EMPIRICAL LITERATURE ON PSYCHOTHERAPY

To this point, a review of the literature has demonstrated considerable confusion in the general field of psychotherapy, marked by a proliferation of theories and methods and by contrasting identities for the psychotherapists who hold those theories and practice those methods. As Mitchell (1993) documents for the subfield of psychoanalysis, during such periods of disagreement and chaos, it is not unusual for the principals to turn to empirical research with the hope that "the facts" will dispel the confusion. Of course, this is the very strategy recommended above by the APA Task Force, and from the standpoint of those who would advocate a reformulated identity for psychotherapy, it is not without its illusions and biases. However, bracketing that objection for now, let us see how psychotherapy researchers themselves might respond to the question, "What do therapists know?"

Research on Psychotherapy Outcome and Its Interpretation

More than 40 years after Eysenck (1952) threw down the gauntlet, challenging therapists to prove the effectiveness and value of psychotherapy, a consensus has been reached by psychotherapy researchers. The editors and authors of the standard reference in this area, *Handbook of Psychotherapy and Behavior Change* (4th ed.) (Bergin & Garfield, 1994a), are largely in agreement: Psychotherapy "works"! There is evidence that clients in psychotherapy as a group show improvement which is both "statistically significant" and "clinically meaningful," and these gains exceed those of comparable clients receiving placebo or control treatments (Lambert & Bergin, 1994, pp. 180–181).

However, while there is robust data attesting to the efficacy of the different psychotherapeutic approaches which have been studied to this point, it has been much more difficult to establish differences in outcome among these methods. For example, Sloane, Staples, Cristol, Yorkston, and Whipple (1975) found no overall difference between brief psycho-dynamic and behavior therapy with a general outpatient population. The massive NIMH Collaborative Depression Study (Elkin et al., 1989; Imber et al., 1990) produced more complex results, but no real differ-ences between interpersonal psychotherapy and cognitive-behavioral therapy were found. Lambert and Bergin (1994) summarize the avail-able data by indicating that no therapy is clinically superior across the board with "moderate outpatient disorders," but that

> behavioral and cognitive methods appear to add a significant increment of efficacy with respect to a number of difficult prob-lems (e.g., panic, phobias, and compulsion) and to provide use-ful methods with a number of nonneurotic problems with which traditional therapies have shown little effectiveness (e.g., child-hood aggression, psychotic behavior, and health-related behav-iors). (p. 181)

Although the outcome measures used by researchers are a popular critical target of surveyed clinicians (Morrow-Bradley & Elliott, 1986), the data regarding psychotherapeutic outcome, for the most part, are not in dispute. However, ambiguities and disagreements abound when interpretations of the meaning of these data are offered.

One of the most popular and influential interpretations of the very minor differences in outcome among different therapeutic approaches was made by Luborsky, Singer, and Luborsky (1975). These reviewers borrowed a line from the Dodo bird in *Alice in Wonderland*, and pro-claimed that "Everybody has won and all must have prizes." This "Dodo bird" conclusion was later supported by meta-analytic studies (e.g., M. L. Smith, Glass, & Miller, 1980) and has become something of a truism of the field (Stiles, Shapiro, & Elliott, 1986): All psychothera-pies produce largely similar outcomes.

When Norcross (1995) and Beutler (1995) were invited to partici-pate in a journal section on "myths of psychotherapy," both cited the above conclusion as one of their pet peeves. Norcross points out that—of the 400 plus different therapies supposedly in existence—only "7 or 8" therapeutic approaches have been studied extensively (p. 500). Therefore, from his perspective, it is a mistake to assume that all psy-chotherapies are equivalent when most psychotherapies have not yet been systematically researched. Both also object to the "uniformity myths" (Kiesler, 1966) implicit in the conclusion that all psychothera-pies are equivalent. The first assumes that all therapists of the same orientation are equivalent in effectiveness, and the second assumes that there are no important client differences which might lead to differential outcome. Norcross suggests that the latter assumption "defies clinical reality," since experienced therapists do not believe that "all things work equally well for all patients" (p. 502), and Beutler cites empirical work in support of this view. Thus, the question for Norcross and Beutler is not the general one of whether psychotherapy works, but the specific one of how different therapies and therapists match with different client problems and characteristics.

It is important not to lose sight of one point which can bring some clarity to the above-mentioned dispute. The disagreement here is really a restatement of the contrast between "common" and "specific" factors in psychotherapy, and the question really isn't whether one or the other exists. Even those who have been most influential in espousing a common factors view (Frank & Frank, 1991; Garfield, 1980) acknowledge the existence of specific factors. The issue, therefore, involves relative emphasis and whether the individual theorist sees psychotherapy research and practice advancing most surely through a focus on similarities or differences.

This theme is echoed in a second popular interpretation of the outcome literature, offered by Bergin and Garfield (1994b). They identify a general trend in the field, not unrelated to the "equal outcomes phenomenon," toward eclecticism in theory and practice. If the major therapeutic schools do not produce substantial differences in outcome, then perhaps it makes most sense to rethink one's commitment to a single viewpoint and consider some other theoretical or empirical strategy which fits better with the available data and might in time improve outcome.

Norcross and Newman (1992) document this development, indicating that many therapists now prefer the term "integrationism" over "eclecticism," since the latter still has a negative (unsystematic) connotation for many practitioners. They see three popular approaches to integration, two of which reiterate the contrast between specific and common factors. Beutler and Clarkin (1990) and Lazarus (1992) are exponents of *technical eclecticism,* which eschews traditional theory and focuses on matching specific intervention to specific problem / client. The *common factors approach* has previously been illustrated through the work of Jerome Frank and seeks to identify the core ingredients of successful therapy. *Theoretical integrationism* is a more ambitious attempt to combine two or more therapeutic approaches, with the expectation that the best aspects of each might contribute to a more powerful, comprehensive approach. Wachtel and McKinney (1992), with their interest in bringing together psychodynamic, family systems, and behavioral theories, represent an example of this integrationist tactic.

Implications of Outcome Data for the Validity of Theories

What do these data on outcome tell us about the validity of the theories which lie behind the different therapeutic methods that have been studied? Protter (1988) comments on the position within psychoanalysis which confuses a "theory of the mind" with a "practice of treatment" and which assumes, therefore, that "the theory can be proven true by the therapy curing" (p. 499). He and others (Grünbaum, 1984; Holzman, 1985) argue that this conclusion is unwarranted, and the same can be said of any like conclusions which might be drawn from the general outcome data on psychotherapy. Research on outcome is not designed to answer the question of "why" or "how" a given psychotherapy works, only that it does so compared to no treatment. As Frank illustrated with his common factors theory, change in the client could be due to countless influences, many of which might have very little to do with what the theory of therapy predicts.

Interest in discovering the actual variables that produce change in psychotherapy is pursued not through outcome research but through "process research," which "is even more complicated than the research on outcome" (Garfield & Bergin, 1994, p. 10). A brief account of research on the behavioral technique of systematic desensitization will both emphasize this point and illustrate what is known about the validity of theoretical rationales.

Wolpe (1958) developed the theoretical rationale for systematic desensitization, which he called "reciprocal inhibition," by applying animal research to the human level. Conditioned avoidance could be established in cats by pairing electrical shock and some neutral stimulus—for example, the cage where the cats normally would feed. This reaction could be deconditioned by feeding the cat at some distance from the cage and then gradually bringing the food nearer to the cage, but never increasing the proximity faster than the fear reaction was dissipating. Wolpe reasoned that the positive response of eating inhibited the negative response of fear because the two were physiologically incompatible: It is impossible to be afraid and relaxed simultaneously.

He then devised the method of systematic desensitization, which combines training in relaxation with exposure in imagination to a hierarchy of fear situations, for humans suffering from conditioned fear reactions (phobias). Clients are not taken to the next step in the fear hierarchy until they can become relaxed in the presence of the present hierarchy item. As they move through the imagined situations, they are also encouraged to begin confronting a comparable level of their fears in real-life situations. Improvement in clients' fear and avoidance is then seen as confirming Wolpe's theory: The deep muscle relaxation acts as an inhibitor of autonomic arousal and thereby suppresses the fear response, allowing clients to approach the phobic situations.

"Until recently, systematic desensitization . . . has been the best known behavioural therapeutic procedure" (Emmelkamp, Bouman, & Scholing, 1995, p. 69), and it has been extensively studied through outcome and process research. However, this research has often produced surprising findings, and Leitenberg (1976) suggests that "almost every aspect of the systematic desensitization procedure has at some time been experimentally demonstrated to be unessential" (p. 131). For example, it has been found that neither a hierarchy nor relaxation training are critical to obtain positive results. Over time, Wolpe's theoretical rationale was rejected, and it was concluded that this procedure in all likelihood is effective "because it indirectly encourages patients to expose themselves to actual feared objects" (p. 133). In fact, "exposure" is the principle on which most behavioral treatments for fear and panic rest today (Barlow, 1988).

This research underscores the fallacy of equating the success of a treatment with the validity of its theoretical rationale. Moreover, congruent with Frank's viewpoint, an invalid theoretical rationale can still be instrumental in producing positive outcome. Leitenberg (1976) observes that "patients believe the rationale of systematic desensitization" (p. 132), and this belief, combined with success in reducing anxiety in session, makes it more likely that they will try confronting their fears in real life. Frank and Frank (1991) suggest that this kind of therapy is not without its persuasive elements as well, since "its ritual persuades patients to remain in actual or imagined contact with the phobic situation long enough for the fear to subside" (pp. 55–56).

Finally, it should not be concluded that the new principle of "exposure" itself answers all questions about a theoretical rationale. In fact, it is not really an explanation or a "theory of therapeutic action" but merely "an observation of a common procedure in many treatments" (Barlow, 1988, p. 286). While Sweet, Giles, and Young (1987) contend that cognitive and behavioral methods are the treatment of choice for anxiety disorders, they confess that they appear to "provide their efficacy through as yet mysterious channels, which are the subject of much controversy and debate" (p. 55).

If it is this laborious to establish the crucial aspects of theory behind a simple behavioral technique, imagine the difficulty in establishing the validity of the theoretical rationales behind more complex therapeutic procedures such as those based on object relations theory, self psychology, or even cognitive therapy. Silberschatz (Persons & Silberschatz, 1998) observes that "little is known about basic mechanisms of change in psychotherapy," and that existing outcome research often ignores this question by incorporating the *presumed* crucial ingredients of change— the therapeutic technique and the implicit or explicit theory which grounds it—into the treatment manual (p. 128). It is for this reason that Bergin and Garfield (1994b, pp. 821–822) are seeing a turn away from work on the "macro" level (What is the nature of personality or therapy?) to research work guided by "minitheories" (What aspects of the therapeutic alliance are crucial to positive outcome? Do cognitive methods add to the effect of relaxation in reducing panic?).

Implications of the Empirical Literature for Clinical Practice

In sum, Bergin and Garfield (1994b) characterize current trends in the field by emphasizing an advance toward "empiricism," "eclecticism," and "minitheories" accompanied by "a steady decline in strict adherence to traditionally dominant theories of personality and therapeutic change, such as the behavioral, psychoanalytic, humanistic, and other major approaches" (p. 821). Omer and London (1988), whose review declares an "end of the systems' era" in psychotherapy, agree with this general conclusion.

Have Clinical Practitioners Become More Empirically Oriented?

While it is obvious that these observations are quite descriptive of many developments in the theoretical and empirical literature on psychotherapy, are they equally applicable to clinical practice? Bergin and Garfield (1994b) believe that they are, and assert that "psychotherapy research has had a profound effect on how the major traditional orientations to therapy are being construed" (p. 824). They note that behavior therapists have become more cognitive and cognitive therapists have become more behavioral and that research is one of the factors influencing this change. They also see the influence of research on the decreasing impact of the nondirective experiential (client-centered) approach and on the increasing definition of psychodynamic approaches as "more eclectic, abbreviated, and specifically targeted" (p. 824). Finally, they perceive a fundamental change in the psychodynamic assumption that interpretation, especially transference interpretation, is the key to therapeutic change, and they believe that this revision "has been brought about largely by careful therapy research" (p. 824).

A variety of social, economic, political, and cultural factors have shaped theory and practice in American psychotherapy over this century (Cushman, 1992; VandenBos, Cummings, & DeLeon, 1992) and it seems naive to weight one factor, research, so heavily in producing the changes which Bergin and Garfield catalog. Further, in some instances they overgeneralize the impact of circumscribed empirical developments, and their comment about a general shift in the centrality of psychodynamic interpretation is a good case in point. Although they later specify that their statement about psychodynamic therapy refers only to certain—not all—manual-driven brief psychodynamic therapies, the question then arises if it makes sense to claim an empirical "trend" when the referent is so restricted. Interestingly, a transformation of the meaning and use of interpretation within the larger field of psychoanalysis and psychodynamic therapy appears to be well underway today, but it reflects metatheoretical influences, not specifically empirical ones (Mitchell, 1993).

Other observations which could be made about the field also fit less well with the hypothesis that empiricism is greatly influencing practice. Garfield and Bergin (1994) themselves acknowledge "the surprising increase in the number of different forms or orientations in psychotherapy" (p. 6), a development which goes counter to the trend toward both empiricism and eclecticism. By definition, when new therapies come on the scene, they are untested and typically assert some unique viewpoint. Gold (1993), reflecting on how developments in psychotherapy have historically emerged, suggests that new therapies have often incorporated "ideas and methods from the social and natural sciences, from medicine, philosophy, theology, and literature" (p. 6). Relative newcomers to the therapy arena such as the narrative (Parry & Doan, 1994), constructivist (R. A. Neimeyer & Mahoney, 1995), and intersubjective (Orange, 1995) perspectives have all been influenced by philosophical views imported from the larger culture, and some of these philosophical positions are inclined to question the very foundation on which much of the current research in psychotherapy is based.

Norcross (1995) was quoted earlier as asserting that "only 7 or 8" of hundreds of therapeutic approaches have been studied extensively, and he adds: "Neurolinguistic, Jungian, existential, and Ericksonian therapies, for example, have never been subjected to rigorous testing, to my knowledge" (p. 500). Surely, practitioners of these approaches, like those of scores of other therapies, are continuing to practice their therapeutic approaches in the absence of confirming outcome data. If Bergin and Garfield are correct in assuming that client-centered therapists have decreased in numbers in some direct relationship to the "poor effect sizes" generated by their approach in meta-analytic studies, then they would no doubt be the first school of therapy to disband based on disappointing empirical results!

In addition, the argument that empirical work is having a direct and significant impact on clinical practice contradicts the existence of a considerable gap between the data which researchers produce and the information which practitioners value and utilize (Morrow-Bradley & Elliott, 1986; Cohen, Sargent, & Sechrest, 1986; Talley, Strupp, & Butler, 1994; Goldfried & Wolfe, 1996). The first study cited above consisted of a mail survey of psychologists belonging to the Division of Psychotherapy of APA. About half of the respondents ranked direct experience with clients as their primary source of information for conducting psychotherapy, and another 32% identified a variety of other nonresearch activities (theoretical / practical books, the experience of being a client, supervision-consultation, and practical workshops / conferences) as their primary source. Only 4% of the sample ranked empirical books / articles as their primary source, with another 6% ranking psychotherapy research presentations as most important. When respondents were asked what information they utilized when faced with difficult cases, only 24% reported that they turned to psychotherapy research.

Cohen et al. (1986) were interested in obtaining more extensive information about psychologists' attitudes toward research than a mail survey might provide, and they conducted an interview study. Although their sample of child psychologists was small (N=30), the psychologists' rankings of information sources were similar to the results previously described and to those obtained by Cohen in a prior national mail survey of psychologists. Research articles and books were ranked lowest among potential information sources for conducting therapy, discussions with colleagues were ranked highest, and workshops on clinical practice, theoretical books / articles on clinical practice, and "how-to" books / articles on clinical practice were intermediate. Interviews indicated that written material would not be enough to encourage therapists to adopt a "positively evaluated treatment": Specific training, including some direct interpersonal contact (workshop, supervision), would be required. Further,

> the psychologists stated that it would be difficult for them to
> provide a treatment modality that was not consistent with their

clinical style and personality, even a modality that had been shown by research to be effective. Variables related to clinical style and personality seem to us to have been underemphasized in the dialogue on psychotherapy research use. . . . Given the personal meaning attached to being psychodynamic or behavioral, it is unlikely that a positively evaluated psychotherapy will be readily adapted if it is inconsistent with a clinician's theoretical (and often personal) identity. (p. 204)

Beutler, Williams, Wakefield, and Entwistle (1995) found clinicians to be more interested in research than is often thought, and unquestionably more interested in research than researchers are interested in clinical writings. But clinicians are "discriminating readers" of research who "generally read research from the vantage point of his or her own, usually very personal, clinical experience, embracing research findings that support what he or she already holds true and disregarding findings that do not" (p. 991).

The above studies were conducted with psychologists, who represent the mental health specialty which historically has most identified its training with empirical research. It is likely that the gap between research and practice would be even larger if therapists trained in other programs—for example, social workers, counselors, nurses, and psychiatrists—were studied.

Have Clinical Practitioners Embraced Eclecticism,
Ending the "Systems' Era"?

The observation that eclecticism is now the dominant orientation of therapists, resulting in the end of the era of theoretical systems, is also a complex issue, and the relevant data can be interpreted differently, depending on one's emphasis and purpose. Jensen, Bergin, and Greaves (1990) summarize 25 studies conducted between 1953 and 1990 on the theoretical orientations of clinicians, and the percentage of those endorsing an eclectic orientation varied widely: findings ranged from 19% to 68%, with the latter figure obtained by the authors. Variations in the data have been summarized by estimating that between one-third and one-half of American psychotherapists endorse an eclectic orientation (Arnkoff & Glass, 1992).

Milan, Montgomery, and Rogers (1994) studied psychologists listed in the National Register of Health Service Providers in Psychology to determine if some of the predicted shifts in theoretical orientation had occurred during the 1980s. Samples were taken from the 1981, 1985, and 1989 editions of the Register, during which time registrants could identify up to three orientations, in order of preference, from a list of eleven. The percentage of psychologists selecting eclecticism as their primary orientation actually declined slightly from 1981 (43.3%) to 1989 (39.1 %). There was a significant increase in those identifying with a rational emotive-cognitive orientation (2.9%–1981; 6.8%–1989), a significant decrease in those endorsing an existential-humanistic orientation (9.0%–1981; 6.4%–1989) and little change in those endorsing behavioral (7.4%–1981; 8.9%–1989), psychoanalytic (14.6%–1981; 14.2%–1989), and interpersonal (10.3%–1981; 11.9%–1989) orientations. The authors note that approximately 90% of the respondents during the sampled years identified secondary or secondary and tertiary orientations, and these data certainly indicate a strong willingness to entertain alternative frameworks.

Norcross, Prochaska, and Farber (1993) report a 1991 random survey of psychologists in the Division of Psychotherapy allowing a comparison with data previously collected on this division in 1981 (Prochaska & Norcross, 1983). Like the study summarized above, they did not find an increase in those endorsing an eclectic/integrative orientation over the 10 year period (30%–1981; 29%–1991). Surprisingly, they found that the psychodynamic / neo-Freudian (18%–1981; 21%–1991) and psychoanalytic (9%–1981; 12%–1991) orientations each rose somewhat in popularity over the decade. In summary, they found about one-third of the respondents endorsing an eclectic-integrative orientation, about a third identifying with some variation of a psychodynamic orientation, and the remaining third distributed across behavioral, cognitive, systems, and various humanistic orientations.

Therefore, from these data, one could emphasize that one-third to one-half of clinical practitioners are primarily eclectic in orientation or one could stress that one-half to two-thirds of clinical practitioners still strongly identify with a particular therapeutic framework. More importantly, this disagreement in emphasis may obscure one similarity between the two groups: Eclectic therapists are not necessarily any more empirically grounded than their colleagues who endorse a single orientation. While psychotherapy researchers may see an eclectic orientation as the modal, informed response to what is known about psychotherapy outcome, the adoption of that orientation is not itself based on empirical factors. Although it stands to reason that flexibility in theory and technique would produce a better outcome—given that clients and problems may be differentially responsive—outcome data of this kind are not yet available. Thus, Lambert (1992) concludes that, "despite the openness of eclectic theorists to knowledge derived from clinical practice and basic research, the eclectic approach has not yet produced a distinguishable body of research that supports its claims of superior efficacy" (p. 119).

Something *is* known of the most popular combinations of orientations chosen by eclectic therapists and how these have shifted over time. A study of psychologists done by Garfield and Kurtz (1977), and updated by Norcross and Prochaska (1988), found that the "modal combination" of the 1970s was behavioral-psychoanalytic (25%). For the 1980s sample, 32% of the respondents endorsed combining cognitive therapy with some other modality (behavioral, humanistic, or psychoanalytic). Jensen et al. (1990) found that dynamic, and then systems orientations were chosen most frequently by eclectic psychiatrists, social workers, and marriage and family therapists, while eclectic psychologists chose cognitive, and then dynamic orientations. Yet, beyond identification with these broad labels, it is not known how eclectic therapists came to choose these particular combinations of orientations or what specific techniques are selected from them: It is not known what eclectic therapists actually *do* in practice. Garfield and Bergin (1994) admit that "the use of the term *eclectic* does not have any precise operational meaning beyond the general definition of selecting from diverse sources what is considered best for the individual case" (p. 7).

Returning to the question of a general movement of the field to an eclectic orientation, evidence definitely supports the conclusion that many clinicians have moved away from "strict adherence" to a single theoretical / therapeutic framework. Nonetheless, many therapists also continue to identify with unitary frameworks, and it is not clear that the end of the era of theoretical systems is at hand. Milan et al. (1994) conclude that the behavioral, interpersonal, and psychoanalytic orientations "continue as powerful forces in contemporary clinical psychology," and that the cognitive orientation is now joining this elite group (p. 400). Norcross et al. (1993), when they combine primary and secondary theoretical orientations, report that 70% of their respondents endorse some form of neo-Freudian orientation leading them to conclude that psychoanalysis is experiencing "a revival or a resurgence . . . with an interpersonal twist" (p. 697). Lazarus (1990), in an introduction to a clinical exchange over issues confronting eclectic and integrationist therapists, indicates that "the integrative therapy movement . . . has had little impact in many quarters, and prominent clinicians are still inclined to adhere to a single or unitary perspective" (p. xiv).

Summary: What Does the Empirical Literature
Add to the Clinician's Knowledge?

So, has further clarification of the question "What do therapists know?" resulted from this sometimes tedious excursion into the empirical literature on psychotherapy? Obviously, I agree with psychotherapy researchers that practicing psychotherapists should be familiar with this literature—or else it would not have been included in this review. However, I also understand why many clinicians contend that existing research has provided less new and usable information than researchers might assume, and I will support that statement in relation to five components of the clinician-literature interaction:

First, it is enormously difficult to conduct research in the area of psychotherapy, and the work of researchers to establish the efficacy of psychotherapy represents a monumental achievement. Yet, since it is something of an occupational necessity, clinicians—aside from moments of doubt—have always assumed that "psychotherapy works."

Second, evidence which supports the conclusion that different psychotherapies—when applied to a heterogeneous outpatient population—are generally equivalent regarding outcome may be surprising to clinicians, just as it has been to researchers. However, it is unclear what implications should be drawn from these data by the practicing clinician. Should therapists who are wedded to a given theoretical framework see it as reassuring that their approach has produced positive outcome, or should they be distressed that other approaches also received confirmation? What does the existence of "common factors" imply for the work of clinicians who practice within a single orientation? Based on their meta-analytic study of psychotherapy outcome, M. L. Smith, Glass, and Miller (1980) propose that "one of the paradoxes of psychotherapy . . . may be that although all therapies are equally effective, one must choose only one to learn and practice" (p. 185). It is likely that the great majority of practicing psychotherapists and clinical trainees, as well as many other psychotherapy researchers, would find this conclusion to be both baffling and unsatisfactory. Indeed, the therapists surveyed by Morrow-Bradley and Elliott (1986) were most critical of "research that treats all therapists or all responses by therapists as interchangeable" thereby obscuring crucial differences (p. 193, table 5).

Third, the difficulty clinicians experience in utilizing research findings about common factors reflects a larger issue which was previously reviewed. Based on their own experience with clients, their theoretical commitments, and their personal identity and style (Morrow-Bradley & Elliott, 1986; Cohen et al., 1986; Beutler et al., 1995), clinicians will extract from research that which "fits" and leave the rest. This attitude bewilders many researchers, who believe that "psychotherapy should be regarded as a professional activity, to be based, therefore, more on scientific information than on personal inclination" (Cohen et al., p. 204). The desires of researchers notwithstanding, material reviewed in the next section of the chapter will suggest that personal and subjective factors play a significant role in both theory construction and theory use. Therefore, Crits-Christoph (1996) believes that the focus should be on training the next generation of clinicians in empirically validated treatments rather than on attempting to retrain existing practitioners. He views many of the latter as having "rather firm attachments to a given approach" which means that they "may not be especially open to learning new approaches, particularly if there is no major incentive for them to do so" (p. 263).

Fourth, assume for a moment that psychotherapists could fulfill the wildest dreams of researchers and become completely objective, that is, empirically oriented, to the point of being willing to base their practices entirely on the available evidence. What guidance in formulating a practice could the literature provide?

Turning first to the literature on common factors, empirically oriented eclectic psychotherapists would find that their choices are rather limited and confusing. They could embrace a common factors framework, such as that of Garfield (1992), which is broad enough to ground practice, but which lacks empirical confirmation (Lambert, 1992). Or they could choose one of the "minitheories" which has been empirically supported, for example, the work of the Vanderbilt group on the therapeutic alliance (Henry, Strupp, Schacht, & Gaston, 1994). However, they would find that therapists trained in this approach did not necessarily improve their therapeutic relationships and in some cases worsened them (p. 502). Even if the training problem could be overcome with this or another minitheory, the eclectic therapist might reasonably wonder if such an approach is sufficiently broad to provide the foundation for a comprehensive clinical practice.

Eclectic clinicians interested in incorporating research on "specific factors" into their practice would also find that the empirical literature can provide only limited direction. Again, *models* of "technical eclecticism" (Lazarus, 1992) and "systematic eclectic psychotherapy" (Beutler & Consoli, 1992) are available, but they have not as yet received significant empirical support (Mahalik, 1990; Lambert, 1992). If clinicians in search of guidance turned their attention from these integrative models to empirically generated *guidelines* for practice, they would discover considerable disagreement in the contemporary literature. That is, the wisdom of modeling psychotherapy research on "clinical trials" in psychopharmacology (e.g., Elkin et al., 1989) and the validity of proposed lists of "empirically-validated psychological treatments" (e.g., Task Force on Promotion and Dissemination of Psychological Procedures, 1995) represent hotly debated issues in the field today. Indeed, several recent journal issues have been devoted in part (Glass & Arnkoff, 1996; Kazdin, 1996a; Kendall, 1998) or in full (Rainer, 1996; VandenBos, 1996) to this controversy. It is not possible to summarize the pros and cons of this debate here, and the interested reader is referred to Persons and Silberschatz (1998), who highlight some of the salient issues. Instead, I will describe a moderate position which an eclectic therapist, who is interested in incorporating empirically supported, specific factors into his/her practice, might adopt after reviewing these materials.

This position would hold that empirically *supported*—not validated—treatments (Garfield, 1998) have been established for a *limited* number of client problems. Further, there is as yet no consensus regarding the treatments and disorders which would be included in this grouping. Bergin and Garfield (1994b) confine themselves to the generalization that cognitive and behavioral therapies are more effective with "severe phobias (e.g., agoraphobia and panic), compulsions, tension headaches, insomnia, and other health-related dysfunctions" (p. 824). Other lists (Task Force on Promotion and Dissemination of Psychological Procedures, 1995; DeRubeis & Crits-Christoph, 1998) are more ambitious and add other disorders (e.g., bulimia) and treatment modalities (e.g., IPT—interpersonal therapy, for depression), while specifying more precisely the nature of certain cognitive and behavioral interventions (e.g., exposure and response prevention for obsessive-compulsive disorder).

Roth and Fonagy (1996) provide a review of the psychological disorder *x* intervention literature which is both more extensive and more critical than the APA Task Force approach. In his forward, Kazdin (1996b) indicates that "the book conveys the limitations of current research. How we currently conceive of treatment and treatment evaluation may be limited and not provide the sorts of answers we need to guide clinical services" (p. vi). However, Chambless (1996) clarifies that the Task Force does not intend for any list of treatments that it proposes to be regarded as "mandated" in relation to training—much less in relation to the issues of clinical practice or reimbursement, which she contends their report did not attempt to address (p. 230). Moreover, the treatments that are listed should be thought of as "examples" of those which meet specified empirical criteria, and the composition of any list of such treatments should be expected to change as further data become available.

Even for those clinical problems where there is some consensus regarding efficacy—for example, the treatment of panic disorder with exposure or exposure plus cognitive restructuring—at least two limitations must be addressed by the clinician who would consider adding this intervention to his / her repertoire (Stricker, 1996). First, studies that establish efficacy of treatment based on the methodology of randomized controlled trials may not predict actual effectiveness (clinical utility) of treatment in the field. Second, protocols that were established in controlled research must often be modified to fit the demands of clinical reality, including factors such as comorbidity, the quality of the therapeutic alliance with this specific client, cultural background, or unexpected crises.

Goldfried and Wolfe (1996) believe that these problems in translation can be lessened through a strengthening of the collaboration between researchers and clinicians. For example, they cite a journal issue (Wolfe, 1995) which attempts to bridge the gap between the research literature and the treatment of panic disorder with agoraphobia under naturalistic (clinical) conditions. After a review of the relevant literature, four cases are presented, and all of the clinicians initially based their interventions on the accepted empirically supported approach to managing panic symptoms and agoraphobic avoidance. However, once the symptoms had diminished, each clinician then proceeded somewhat differently to address other aspects of the case, such as predisposing personality or interpersonal factors. Persons (Persons & Silberschatz, 1998) describes this strategy as one of linking empirical guidelines for practice with an "idiographic (individualized) case formulation" (p. 128).

Shoham and Rohrbaugh (1996) summarize the current status of empirically based clinical practice simply by quoting the authors of the Task Force report themselves—who indicate that clinicians must continue to rely on "clinical judgment" in making treatment decisions about the individual case (p. 199). Roth, Fonagy, and Parry (1996) propose a more formal model wherein the clinician's experience guides the use of empirically derived treatments. For example, if the clinician judges a given case to be "normative," an empirically supported protocol might be followed initially. The decision to provide an alternative treatment or to modify a protocol can only be based on clinical judgment which encompasses an "integration of skills training, theoretical knowledge, and past clinical experience, as well as acquaintance with the research literature" (p. 51). Finally, Shapiro (1996) underlines that the absence of adequate research regarding a given psychotherapeutic approach should not be equated with ineffectiveness, and Roth, Fonagy, and Parry (1996) caution against public policies which might prematurely restrict practice to empirically supported treatments since such guidelines also "could stifle innovation and development" (p. 43). They point out that it is unlikely that we would have seen many of the therapeutic innovations of the past thirty years, including the development of cognitive therapy, if clinicians had been restricted to practicing the "narrow range of behavioral techniques, effective but of limited application" (p. 41), which represented our "validated" treatments of the 1960s.

Fifth and consequently, it is not possible for a therapist, however well intentioned, to base a comprehensive approach to practice only on the existing "facts" which have been established by researchers, and it can be argued that this will *never* be possible. Materials reviewed later in this chapter and in the following chapter will address the issue of the impossibility of a strictly objective or empirical approach to any human activity, including psychotherapy, but for now I will support this conclusion from within the empirical framework itself.

Both eclectic and single-orientation therapists base their practice on some complex combination of prior training experiences, direct experience with clients, further developments in the research and theoretical literature, personal style and identity, and existing theoretical rationales. All psychotherapists, whether they swear allegiance to a single theory, mix-and-match theories, integrate theories, or choose technique over theory, employ such theoretical rationales in their day-to-day work with clients. The simplest behavioral techniques, for example, systematic desensitization, have historically included a theoretical rationale, and, in this case, it was later discredited by researchers. Yet, because it was believed by therapist and client alike and had implications for behavior change, this invalid rationale nonetheless contributed to positive outcome.

I suspect that most therapists would be surprised and dismayed to hear that these theoretical rationales, which constitute the glue holding the therapy experience together, have received virtually no empirical confirmation by researchers. Given the powerful confirmations which clients provide for these rationales on a daily basis, Mitchell (1993) observes that "psychoanalysts have traditionally been confident, even sometimes complacent, about the truth of their own theoretical convictions" (p. 41), and the same conclusion could be drawn for psychotherapists considered more globally. Shapiro (1996) cites the example of process research on the cognitive therapy of depression and concludes that the "evidence that even well-researched methods achieve their effects via the mechanisms posited by their instigators is not over-whelmingly strong" (p. 257). Therefore, in this important regard, the current empirical literature supports Jerome Frank's earlier assessment of the status of theoretical rationales in psychotherapy: They remain largely unproven, and they do not easily lend themselves to disproof.

SUBJECTIVE FACTORS IN THEORY CONSTRUCTION, SELECTION, AND USE

Garfield (1992), commenting on contemporary training in psy-chotherapy, contends that it usually relies either on an intensive involve-ment with a single orientation (e.g., psychoanalysis or cognitive therapy) or on a haphazard exposure to perhaps a dozen different orientations. He is critical of both approaches and of a tendency which can accom-pany either:

> In some cases the view is presented that students simply need to select the form of therapy that appeals to them and "run with it." Although it is important that the therapist get some feelings of satisfaction when engaged in psychotherapy, the satisfaction should result from helping the patient improve and not from other considerations. (p. 196)

Lazarus (1993) is incensed by the "subjectivity" and "bias" he sees in current practice when therapists hold too rigidly to theoretical orienta-tions and asserts that any course in the philosophy of science would make it clear to all "that acceptable ideas are those that can be tested empirically" (p. 675).

Garfield and Lazarus, like the hypothetical psychotherapy researchers mentioned in the summary of the last section, surely do not believe that they are asking too much. They simply want therapists to base their theories and interventions on that which will lead to improve-ment in the client, while minimizing or eliminating their own personal and subjective contributions to the psychotherapeutic exchange. Mate-rials in this section will attempt to demonstrate that the issue of subjec-tivity is more complex and insidious than these views might imply.

Subjective Factors in Theory Construction

Atwood and Stolorow (1993) provide a fascinating account of the personal, subjective factors which shaped the theoretical constructs of Sigmund Freud, Carl Jung, Wilhelm Reich, and Otto Rank, and Cushman (1995) does the same for Melanie Klein. These authors employ a case history method where psychobiography is utilized to explicate the connection between personal life and theoretical achievement. Because of the psychological, political, and legal difficulties of his later years, Reich's story most dramatically illustrates the usefulness of this perspective toward theory construction.

Atwood and Stolorow (1993) describe Reich's work in relation to three thematic elements that in turn influence the theoretical constructs which he generated: (*a*) the degree of life adjustment or healthy functioning is measured by the degree of sexual expression; (*b*) the expression of healthy sexuality is constantly suppressed and distorted by the character defenses, which reflect the internalization of antisexual death forces; and (*c*) he, Reich, must join this conflict on the side of championing the life forces over the death forces (p. 104).

Reich (1933a / 1949) initially pursued his work within the traditional confines of psychoanalysis and during this period generated theoretical constructs ("character armor") and therapeutic methods ("character analysis") that continue to have an impact on therapeutic thinking and practice today. Atwood and Stolorow (1993) emphasize that the above-mentioned themes were already present in Reich's early work: the patient's suppressed sexual-biological nature leading to maladjustment or unhappiness; the character armor, which represented the means of suppression; and, the role of the therapist, which was to liberate the patient's sexuality and facilitate free, spontaneous emotional expression (pp. 105–106).

Given his emerging view, it is not surprising that Reich (1933b/1973) soon shifted his attention from the mechanisms of suppression in the individual to their origins in society and then to the need for social reform. He reasoned that political and economic forces, acting through socialization processes in the family, were ultimately responsible for sexual repression, and for a period had hopes for a socialist revolution. Eventually, he became discouraged about the possibility of political reform, and—after he was expelled both from the Communist Party and the International Psychoanalytic Association—his interests shifted to biological research.

The above developments portend the most controversial and, ultimately, tragic phase of Reich's (1948 / 1973) life and theorizing. He became interested in cell biology and believed that he had identified two particles which corresponded on the microscopic, cellular level to the forces of life and death. This work eventually was integrated both with his prior views of sexuality and his newfound interest in cancer. Reich found that cancer patients inevitably suffered from an inhibition of sexual expression, and he hypothesized that this repression led to the generation of negative particles—which could be opposed by positive particles that emitted life-giving "orgone energy." He later came to think of the Earth and its atmosphere as itself a living organism that emitted free orgone, which could be concentrated through an "orgone energy accumulator." His work and claims in this area led to a lengthy investigation by the Food and Drug Administration and, in the end, he was arrested and put in prison, where he died of a heart attack.

Atwood and Stolorow (1993), basing their information on a biography written by his third wife and on his own autobiographical sketch written at age 22, then link Reich's theoretical preoccupations with quite personal elements of his own life story (pp. 111–117). He grew up on a farm in Austria and his family included his mother and father, and a brother, Robert, who was three years his junior. During early childhood, the boys were educated at home by their parents, and Wilhelm much preferred the gentler approach of his mother to the strictness of his authoritarian father, who used physical punishment or withdrawal of attention for mistakes or lapses of concentration. Reich describes himself as having a much closer relationship with his mother, who, given the historical period and context, understandably deferred outwardly to her husband.

All of this changed dramatically at age 13 when Reich discovered that his mother was having an affair with one of his tutors. He writes in his autobiography what it was like to hear their lovemaking, and how his earlier positive feelings for his mother were replaced by a confusing mixture of anger, abandonment, excitement, and sympathy for his father. Despite the latter, he did not reveal his knowledge until some time later when the father accused his wife of a sexual indiscretion with another man. While she was not guilty in this particular instance, Wilhelm confessed what he knew of her prior liaison. After the confession, they heard a moan from the next room and he soon learned that his mother had tried to commit suicide by taking poison. Although she survived this attempt, the next months were marked by her husband's unremitting anger and abuse, and she attempted suicide on two subsequent occasions, succeeding at last with the third attempt. Despite denying any intense grief at the time of her death, in later years Reich idealized his mother while his attitude towards his father became quite negative.

Atwood and Stolorow (1993) believe that these events and their emotional impact set the terms for Reich's subjective experience of the world, and that this experience then shaped the cast of his theoretical thinking:

> If it is assumed that in betraying his mother's unfaithfulness the young Reich was acting out of an identification with his father's authoritarian and sexually restrictive values, then the reasons for his subsequent life of struggle against sexual repression begin to become clear. Since in acting on the basis of a narrow code of sexual morality he was responsible for the death of the one person he loved above all others, an immense burden of pain and guilt must have been generated. What could be a better way to atone for his fateful act of betrayal than devoting himself to the eradication of all those values and ways of thinking which had motivated him? (pp. 114–115)

The authors do not attempt to provide a definitive explanation for Reich's later deterioration to a delusional state, wherein his theoretical constructs were imposed on the universe as a whole. However, they convincingly demonstrate how both his clinical interests and observations and the specific psychological constructs he generated to account for those observations are directly related to his own subjective experience and personal struggles.

> Reich's metapsychological view of the personality in terms of the dialectics of the sexual life energies and the antisexual death forces we found to be the product of his subjective interpretation of his mother's suicide, for which he felt responsible. Through his eventually delusional reification of the omnipresent, all-enveloping orgone energies, which carried the imago of his reactively idealized mother, he undid the terrible trauma of her death and magically restored her to life. (p. 174)

The thrust of psychobiographical work of this kind is not to undermine the possible validity or usefulness of the theoretical constructs which have emerged from a theorist's personal experience of the world (Atwood & Stolorow, 1993, pp. 9–11). In fact, schools of therapy would not exist if the founder, through direct experience, did not touch upon some important feature of the human condition which somehow speaks to others, including both other therapists and their clients. However, psychobiography can provide clues to understanding the emergence and consequent functioning of these therapeutic schools.

Based on this analysis of Reich's life, which is representative of those provided for the lives of Freud, Jung, Rank, and Klein, assume for a moment that the following generalization can be made. Many of those who have formulated new theories or founded therapeutic schools have been motivated at least in part by a need to articulate and resolve some personal issue or conflict. Granting this assumption, it is not surprising that there are so many different schools of psychotherapy, and that this proliferation continues up to the present—since human experience is so diverse and complex and lends itself to myriad, plausible interpretations. Possibly, it is the gift of each founder of a school of personality or psychotherapy to capture some facet of human experience so thoroughly, vividly, and compellingly that the reader, student, or client who comes in contact with that account finds something new and fresh revealed in themselves and leaves the encounter feeling fundamentally transformed.

If it is the theorist's genius to take the raw material of the personal or subjective and mold it into a form which opens up new vistas for others, then the limitations of any theoretical system are implicit in that same personal, creative act. Atwood and Stolorow (1993) are interested in just those aspects of the emerging theory that constrain vision and produce rigidity and turn their attention particularly to "reified metapsychological superstructures" (p. 11). Such concepts posit "hypothetical energies, forces, and structures" which are taken to be a true description of reality (p. 168)—but, in actuality, these constructs can neither be validated nor invalidated (p. 11). Examples include Freud's drive theory, Jung's concept of the collective unconscious, and Reich's notion of orgone energy. Atwood and Stolorow see these concepts as reflecting some struggle in the theorist's experience and as performing "functions analogous to those of character defenses. Through such reifications, each theorist's solutions to his own dilemmas and nuclear crises became frozen in a static intellectual system that, to him, was an indisputable vision of objective reality" (p. 175).

This is to say that the great innovators in the field of personality psychology and psychotherapy have generally shown a tendency to confuse the idiosyncratic with the universal. Although they have touched on something in their subjective experience which can bring clarification and understanding to the lives of *some* others, they then frame their discovery in a conceptual scheme which decrees not only that it applies to *all* others, but also that it actually represents *"the One True Meaning"* and provides *"the One True Method"* (Omer & Strenger, 1992, p. 253).

Subjective Factors in Theory Choice and Use

While few of us in the psychotherapy field will develop far-reaching theories of personality and psychotherapy, all of us face choices regarding the theories and therapeutic orientations that will guide our daily practice. These critical moments in a therapist's development provide the same opportunity for the influence of subjective factors as has been established above for the generation and construction of theories.

Barton (1974) offers an existential-phenomenological approach to the comparison of the therapeutic systems of Freud, Jung, and Rogers. He convincingly takes the same hypothetical client through three different therapy experiences, underlining how differently both therapist and client experience the world from within each theoretical / therapeutic framework. A significant component of his approach entails an analysis of the factors that predispose a therapist to choose a particular approach to theory and therapy.

One can sidestep the question of whether potential therapists necessarily have adjustment problems which are beyond the normal range, and simply assume that they "may be self-selected for their sensitivity to certain kinds of human distress" (Frank & Frank, 1991, p. 165). Barton (1974) gives his own frame for this observation in suggesting that potential therapists generally are "reflective" and are attracted to the field because of an investment in having certain psychological questions answered and certain personal issues clarified (p. 6). The specific nature of those questions and issues, combined with personal factors such as individual style or personality and social factors such as the particular role models who are available and their prestige, will then predispose the budding therapist to gravitate to one or more specific therapeutic frameworks.

Once novice therapists enter into training, other social forces are brought to bear that increase the likelihood of their internalizing the theoretical constructs and therapeutic methods of the given school or approach. Not the least of these influences is the therapist's own personal therapy (p. 7). Although depth psychology training programs are traditionally associated with this component of training and do often regard the trainee's personal therapy as conceivably the most decisive element of training, personal therapy within any therapeutic framework can have a powerful impact on the trainee's personal experience, beliefs, and theoretical commitments. Through the therapy—whether Jungian, object relations, cognitive, control mastery, or eclectic in nature—the trainee learns to look at the world from a particular vantage point and understands the *value* of doing so. Thus, when trainees find that their relationships improve or that their anxiety diminishes or that their general outlook on life becomes more integrated and coherent, these personal changes can serve as potent validations of the theory and method. When trainees find similar positive changes are occurring with their clients, just as the approach would predict, then their faith in the theoretical stance and method is further strengthened.

In addition, while some doubts are tolerated by the training program and therapeutic community in question, challenges to the core assumptions of the approach are usually discouraged, dismissed, or treated as "resistance." The trainee learns rather quickly that there are ways of experiencing, behaving, and verbalizing which receive praise and reward from the mentors, and those that are greeted with a raised eyebrow, silence, or even rebuke. The urge to belong to the community, especially to the inner circle of the group, may be strong and may effectively overcome whatever doubts or reservations the trainee brought to the training.

Jerome Frank sees some advantages to such training, since detailed knowledge of the theory and practice of at least one therapeutic system will probably give the trainee a sufficient sense of competence to inspire the client's confidence (Frank & Frank, 1991, p. xiv). Barton (1974) agrees with this assessment but, like Frank, also indicates how this kind of training can instill a personal belief system which is quite resistant to modification:

> When this approach to training combines with the student therapist's inner reasons for moving toward psychotherapy, a rigidification of therapeutic theories occurs. The therapist now learns to live out a certain salvation code. . . .
>
> After some years of training and experience, the practitioners of a particular therapy orientation have so well outlined and fundamentally packaged a world that they become virtually immovable by any other point of view. They now live out a particular world view as outlined by their specialist subculture, whether analytic, behavioristic, client-centered, rational-emotive, direct-analytical, Gestalt, or whatever. (pp. 7–8)

MORAL AND POLITICAL DIMENSIONS
OF THERAPY PRACTICE

It could be argued that the subjective factors implicated in theory construction, choice, and use outlined above are most descriptive of theorists who identify with a particular school of therapy. In some sense, this is exactly the argument of the eclectic therapists, Garfield and Lazarus, which began this section. If only therapists would constrain their penchant for grand theorizing, pay more attention to the outcome data, and become willing to adapt their approach to the specific needs of the client and the problem, then subjective factors in therapeutic practice could be minimized if not eliminated.

There is a history of dissent within American psychology and psychiatry, however, which charges that psychotherapy is inherently subjective in nature. Psychotherapy can never attain the status of an objective practice because the social, political, and moral values of the therapist are inevitably transmitted to the client through the therapeutic exchange. Therefore, this critique does not exempt any approach to therapy (single orientation *vs.* eclectic) or any modality of therapy (individual *vs.* family *vs.* group) from its argument. In fact, the current professional agenda of attempting to establish the empirical ground for psychotherapy in order to ensure more effective, objective treatment— goals which are not unrelated to bolstering the stature of psychotherapy in a marketplace demanding results and emphasizing "managed care"— is seen from this perspective as itself a political act (Gilford, 1996). More "effective" therapies would simply solidify the role of psychotherapy as a means of social control, and more "objective" treatment would signify the intensification of a process of "mystifying" (Laing, 1967) the public. Through this mystification, the moral and political dimensions of psychotherapy would be hidden ever more skillfully beneath a veneer of objective data and scientific respectability.

This dissenting position first made a significant appearance within the larger field of mental health in the 1960s and early 1970s, and was stimulated by two different intellectual and cultural developments. Intellectually, it was marked by an interest in reflecting on psychological and psychiatric practice from the standpoint of other social sciences, especially the disciplines of political theory, social psychology, and sociology (Goffman, 1961; Szasz, 1960; Scheff, 1966; D. Cooper, 1969; Ryan, 1976; Rosenhan, 1973; Ingleby, 1972). Culturally, it was swept along by a general increase in political awareness and activism associated with the emergence of a "counterculture" which, when directed toward the mental health professions, manifested variously as "anti-psychiatry" (D. Cooper, 1971; Laing, 1972; Boyers & Orrill, 1971) in Britain and as "radical psychiatry and radical psychology" (P. Brown, 1973) or "radical therapy" (Ruitenbeek, 1972) in the United States.

All of these intellectual and cultural movements shared the view that the mental health professions had ignored the larger social / political / economic context in which their theories had arisen and in which their practices were currently being applied. While much of the critique was addressed to issues surrounding the diagnosis and institutionalization of those labeled "mentally ill," more routine psychotherapy was also typically characterized as a means of supporting the "status quo" of the society (Halleck, 1968; Braginsky & Braginsky, 1974).

Although such thinking had some impact on the diagnosis and treatment of severe mental disorders—for example, the move to de-institutionalization (Marx, Test, & Stein, 1973) was no doubt accelerated by sociopolitical analysis—its effect on psychotherapeutic practice was negligible. Accordingly, "radical" therapy quickly disappeared from view, but a feminist analysis of psychology and mental health practice, which parallels many of its tenets, was born in the same era and has followed a different course. Naomi Weisstein's (1968 / 1993) "Psychology Constructs the Female" and Phyllis Chesler's (1972) *Women and Madness* set the terms for a feminist critique of psychology and therapy that continues to grow in influence today. Moreover, feminism was soon joined by two other like-minded developments in the field: multiculturalism and social constructionism. A forceful overview (Sue & Sue, 1990) of the "politics" of counseling the "culturally different" first appeared in 1981 and was followed by Gergen's (1985) documentation of the social constructionist movement in "modern psychology."

Although feminism, multiculturalism, and social constructionism certainly represent different traditions and have their own agendas regarding reform, they have one important commonality. All three assume that the very institutions which promise to study and ameliorate human problems—the social sciences, including psychology, and counseling and psychotherapy, respectively—may actually end up *harming* those who are studied or helped. In either instance, this harm results from a failure of our theories, research methods, and practices to adequately situate our work with others in a historical-political-cultural context.

Unlike the radical mental health movement, each of these perspectives is exerting an important influence on current practice. Feminist therapy has existed as a recognized orientation within the field since the

1980s. While multiculturalism has perhaps had a greater impact thus far within "counseling" as opposed to "psychotherapy" circles, its sway over all mental health training and practice will only increase as U.S. society continues to become more multiracial and multicultural. Of late, the social constructionist approach has also been applied quite explicitly to an understanding of psychotherapy, and the most complete and textured argument of this kind is found in the work of Philip Cushman (1990, 1991, 1992, 1993, 1995). Since my goal here is to substantiate that psychotherapy necessarily is a subjective enterprise with moral and political elements, I will utilize Cushman's argument as an illustration and will begin by placing it in some context.

Ryan (1976), building on the sociological perspective of C. W. Mills (1959), makes a distinction between approaches to social issues which are "exceptionalistic" *vs.* "universalistic" in their explanations and interventions. For example, the social problem of unemployment can be viewed from either an exceptionalistic ("private troubles") or universalistic ("public issue") framework. If unemployment is seen as the problem of an individual or of a small group of individuals, then it is the exception and not the norm, and steps to explain and remedy it must be taken on an individual level: It is a private trouble. However, if unemployment is widespread, and perhaps concentrated in a particular social class or ethnic group, then it would be crucial to shift to a viewpoint which recognizes it as the norm and not the exception: It is a public issue. Ryan suggests that the application of exceptionalistic explanations and solutions to problems which are more universal in nature is an ideological process that can be called "Blaming the Victim" (pp. 18–19).

Cushman (1990) agrees with these earlier social critics and their contemporary variants (e.g., Prilleltensky, 1989), who see psychological thinking as morally and politically dangerous just to the extent that it blindly applies exceptionalistic explanations and interventions to what are at base universal human problems. Whether the problem is teenage unemployment or depression in women, if the true causes of the condition are to be found primarily in the surrounding sociopolitical context, then directing attention exclusively to that which is largely individual and internal is at once a political and moral act—and one which serves to maintain the societal status quo. Cushman extends this formulation considerably, however, through a historically informed analysis of how universal human problems shift with different social-economic-political conditions and how psychotherapeutic fashions shift accordingly—always offering to relieve human suffering, while actually replicating the very conditions that have created that suffering.

Cushman (1990) offers the concept of the "empty self" as a description of the isolation, lack of direction, psychic emptiness, meaninglessness, interiority, and longing for fulfillment which is endemic to late twentieth-century middle-class America. He traces the roots of this empty self primarily to two conditions: (*a*) social and historical factors connected with the breakdown of cultural traditions, community, and close interpersonal relationships; and, (*b*) economic factors associated with the need of modern capitalism to ensure that the populace will continue consuming nonessential goods.

How does psychotherapy attempt to come to the aid of this empty self? Unfortunately, by finding the causes of the problem within that very self. While the bias to locate problems within the self is obvious in early versions of psychodynamic theory and therapy, Cushman (1992, 1995) points out just how difficult it has been for psychotherapy to move away from this stance, even when theorists and therapists have attempted to become more "humanistic" and "interpersonal" in their approaches.

For example, Wallach and Wallach (1983) underline that humanistic psychologists such as Maslow and Rogers, despite their avowed interest in promoting fundamental personal and societal change, for the most part continue to frame the change process either in terms of the individual (pursuing "self-actualization") or the small group (establishing facilitative conditions for change). There is really no humanistic vocabulary or method for addressing social, political, or economic problems, unless one assumes that "society is run as a therapeutic session or an encounter group where feelings of equality and community arise as part of the healing process" (Prilleltensky, 1989, p. 799).

Similarly, while D. W. Winnicott, the object relations theorist, and Heinz Kohut, the self psychologist, each modify psychoanalytic thinking in the direction of emphasizing the relational aspect of human functioning, "they both located the significant transformative events that create the self within the individual" (Cushman, 1992, p. 52). Even family therapy, which in some varieties attempts to shift the focus from the individual to the functioning of the family as a system, typically "does not take its analysis into the realm of history and culture" (p. 56).

Accordingly, Cushman (1995) insists that psychotherapists should give up the image of psychotherapy as a neutral, objective activity and acknowledge its political and moral dimensions. He emphasizes here that the problem is not that psychotherapists have *"failed"* to be objective, but rather that they have *"tried"* to be objective, and have even gone so far as to claim that they have *"accomplished"* that goal (p. 287).

However, he also concedes that this admission places psychotherapy and psychotherapists in a "contradictory position" in contemporary society (p. 287). On the one hand, psychotherapy, through its theory and practice, usually serves as just another way of temporarily soothing or filling the empty self and thereby plays an important role in maintaining the conditions that have created this core problem.

> On the other hand, there is also a morality implicit in some psychotherapy practices that offers an alternative to the status quo. . . . For instance, mainstream practices often stipulate that patients must be treated with respect, listened to and understood, granted the privilege of confidentiality, and protected from a dual relationship with the therapist that would cause financial, ideological, or sexual exploitation. These practices demonstrate a morality contrary to that which is implicit in capitalism's unyielding allegiance to the profit motive and the era's omnipresent commodification of relational life. . . .
>
> Psychotherapy, therefore, implicitly puts forward various moral ideas that often *conflict* with one another. Although the overall practice of psychotherapy is conducted within an individualist and consumerist moral frame, it also challenges, or at least undermines, that frame. (pp. 287–288)

Cushman (1995) later acknowledges that it is questionable if any approach, including the stance which he recommends, is fully adequate to the task of resolving the political and moral contradictions inherent in psychotherapy practice (pp. 329–331). This question will be further explored when the assumptions and methods of social constructionist and hermeneutic therapies are examined in chapters 4 and 6.

SUMMARY

This review of the psychotherapy literature has approached the same question—"What do therapists know?"— from many different angles, and each time a similar conclusion has been reached. The last sections answered the question by emphasizing that subjective and sociopolitical factors in theory construction, choice, and implementation are a seemingly inescapable component of therapeutic practice. Adding that conclusion to those which have preceded it, the following image of psychotherapy as a field of knowledge begins to emerge. The very foundation of psychotherapeutic practice is undermined by its vulnerability to historical, conceptual, empirical, political, and moral challenges. Consequently, the knowledge it provides is presently much further removed from any ideal of psychological "truth" than the great majority of its practitioners and clients might assume.

Chapter 2

Challenges from Philosophy: What *Can* Therapists Know?

A review of the general literature on psychotherapy reveals a field marked by such a diversity of theories, practices, and identities as to border on the chaotic. Moreover, the attempt to rein in the anarchy through an appeal to psychotherapy outcome and process research has not greatly impacted practice. Not only are the majority of clinicians disinclined to heed the findings and advice of researchers, empirical research has not yet advanced to the point of providing clear guidelines for a comprehensive clinical practice. Finally, even in a perfect world characterized by adequate research and cooperative clinicians, subjective factors cannot be eliminated from an endeavor which necessarily straddles the scientific, personal, moral, and political domains.

The present state of psychotherapy theory and practice is reminiscent of a conclusion reached by Sigmund Koch for the general field of psychology. Koch (1959–1963) edited a mammoth study of the status of this discipline, a project which extended to some eighty scholars and six volumes, and later observed:

> The idea that psychology—like the natural sciences on which it is modeled—is a cumulative or progressive discipline is simply not borne out by its history. . . . I think it is by this time utterly and finally clear that *psychology cannot be a coherent science,*

or indeed a coherent field of scholarship, in any specifiable
sense of coherence that can bear upon a field of inquiry. (1969,
p. 66)

Therefore, he has suggested the renaming of psychology as *"the psychological studies,"* which will refer to a heterogeneous collection of subdisciplines "some few of which may qualify as science, whereas most do
not" (1993, p. 902).

It would be premature to assume that this characterization of the
status of scientific psychology will necessarily hold for the applied field
of psychotherapy. Still, it is helpful to realize that Koch was asking the
same question that has directed the present inquiry: His mandate was to
guide an assessment of what psychologists know. After a hundred years
of the existence of their discipline, what cumulative knowledge had
emerged? When the answer to that question appeared to Koch to be
largely disappointing, it is also useful to recognize the mode of analysis
which helped him to understand this outcome. With his interest and
skills in philosophical analysis, Koch (1959, vol. 3) could propose that
the dead end that had been reached was in large part the result of an
unexamined and outdated philosophy of science that had been guiding
much of empirically oriented American psychology: "Psychology was
unique in the extent to which its institutionalization preceded its content
and its methods preceded its problems" (p. 783, italics omitted).

Can some coherence be brought to the chaos of the psychotherapy
field by turning away from the theories and methods of its practitioners
and toward philosophical modes of analysis? Cushman's social constructionist argument, cited in the last chapter, contends that psychotherapeutic theory and practice cannot be disentangled from
philosophical questions. Miller (1983), O'Hanlon and Wilk (1987),
O'Donohue (1989), Tjeltveit (1989), Messer (1992), Hanna (1994),
Held (1995), Orange (1995), and Woolfolk (1998), representing a variety of theoretical positions in the field, also emphasize the importance of
examining the relationship between psychotherapy and philosophy.

What then are the philosophical presuppositions which, often invis-
ibly, support contemporary psychotherapy practice? I will propose an
answer to that question over the next three chapters and will begin with
a review of the philosophical literature. Because of the specifically philosophical content of this chapter, it is appropriate to preface it with several caveats. I am trained as a psychologist, not as a philosopher, and my
purpose in turning to the philosophical literature is directed by a pragmatic interest in clarifying the theory and practice of psychotherapy.

Accordingly, the philosophical positions which have been singled out for review have been chosen on the basis of their potential for providing a kind of mapping of what clinical practitioners currently assume. The strategy of reducing the available positions in the philosophical literature to a limited set of categories of most relevancy to contemporary psychotherapy, while ignoring much of the attendant debate about these positions, is in the interest of this pragmatic goal. That debate is largely focused on the question of what is the "true" or, at least, the "more true" philosophical position. Since there is obviously no consensus within philosophy regarding what is true, and since I will later argue that all of the categories have some relevancy to the work of psychotherapists, I have the luxury of bracketing this question. The debate over truth is included in the review only to the extent that it clarifies a progression in the development of the positions—that is, how does one position critique, reject, or build upon the prior position? In addition, some of the contrasts and terms used to structure the review and summarize the positions do not strictly follow philosophical usage. All of this is to say that I make no claims that a professional philosopher would find the following review to be complete, convincing, or entirely fair.

RELEVANT PHILOSOPHICAL TERMS AND TRENDS

The definitions of philosophical terms provided below are intended only as an introduction for the reader, and further clarification will occur as the chapter unfolds. Although this brief characterization of trends in the philosophical literature is intended to serve primarily as a rough overview of the field, it also provides some context for the decision to emphasize certain positions in the more extensive review which follows.

A good, short definition of *philosophy* describes it as "thinking about thinking" (Honderich, 1995, p. 666), and the various branches of philosophy are defined by the subject matter or questions to which this reflective thinking is applied. Questions about the knowledge base of psychotherapy direct this review particularly to the branch of philosophy known as *epistemology*. It refers to the "theory of knowledge," and is "concerned with the nature of knowledge, its possibility, scope, and general basis" (p. 242). As the title of this chapter indicates, epistemology presumably allows us to set the conditions about what can be "known."

Because of the great technical success of science in understanding and transforming the natural world, laypersons and philosophers alike have generally assumed that it may represent the surest approach to attaining valid knowledge. Therefore, a specialty of the general field of epistemology has become known as the *philosophy of science,* and, given the scientific aspirations of psychotherapy, it is specifically relevant to this study.

Many philosophers of science are trained as philosophers, but some first began their career as scientists (Thomas Kuhn; Michael Polanyi) and later turned to philosophy as a way of reflecting on the nature of science and the status of its methods and findings. In either case, the contrast between scientist and philosopher of science might be likened to the contrast between an artist and a critic. The critic does not create art but offers a commentary on the work produced by others. Within the philosophy of science, that commentary is directed specifically to questions about the "justification" and "objectivity" of one's claims to knowledge (Honderich, 1995, p. 809).

Although many laypeople probably equate the study of philosophy with *metaphysics,* its definition, status, and usefulness within philosophy have always been debated (Honderich, 1995, p. 556). It can be characterized as the "most abstract and in some views 'high-falutin' part of philosophy, having to do with the features of ultimate reality, what really exists" (p. 556). The term apparently originated in the second half of the first century B.C. when it was used to describe those writings which followed "physics" in the catalog of Aristotle's works (p. 556). Because of the nature of those writings, the term is now associated with speculative philosophy, for example, the grand philosophical systems of Aquinas, Descartes, Hegel, or Kant. Following this usage, H. Smith (1989) defines metaphysics simply as "a worldview that provides a sense of orientation" (p. 18). One branch of metaphysics, *ontology,* focuses specifically on the question of "being," including the issues of "existence" and the nature of the categories which structure reality (Honderich, 1995, p. 634). It is also used in a more technical sense "to refer to the set of things whose existence is acknowledged by a particular theory or system of thought: it is in this sense that one speaks of 'the' ontology of a theory" (p. 634).

Throughout this century, interest in metaphysical and ontological questions waned, particularly in American and British philosophy. H. Smith (1989) suggests that the last important attempt to construct a metaphysical system, "a logical, coherent scheme of ideas that would blueprint the universe" (p. 8), was Whitehead's (1957) *Process and*

Reality, originally published in 1929. Historically, philosophers of science in particular have been disparaging of metaphysics, since its questions do not lend themselves to methods associated with ensuring objective knowledge. However, in recent years there has been a "modest revival" of interest in metaphysical and ontological questions by professional philosophers (Honderich, 1995, p. 634), spurred in part by the recognition that the natural sciences themselves are not exempt from their own implicit metaphysical assumptions (O'Donohue, 1989) and "ontological schemes" (Honderich, p. 634).

Postmodernist philosophy can be loosely described as a contemporary trend which mounts "an attack on truth. . . . A critique of the very possibility of objectivity" (Lawson, 1989, p. xi). Both traditional epistemology and metaphysics are taken to task because they attempt to fix the nature of reality in accord with a foundational method or a systematic world view, respectively. These are impossible goals because the human observer cannot be eliminated from the epistemological equation: Knowledge claims are always influenced by expectations and beliefs bearing the mark of history, culture, and power.

Although some postmodernists embrace a *hermeneutic* approach, the two philosophical positions also have their differences. Philosophical hermeneutics also challenges the hegemony of scientific or objective knowing, but, unlike postmodernism, it does not necessarily reject the possibility of scientific truth. Traditionally, hermeneutics is associated with the study of texts (the Bible), and is defined as the "art of interpretation" (Honderich, 1995, p. 353). In the hands of thinkers like Wilhelm Dilthey and Hans-Georg Gadamer, philosophical hermeneutics aims "to expand the number of disciplines in which truth claims could be made" (Woolfolk, 1998, p. 135). Thus, the human sciences, which presumably include psychology and psychotherapy, place understanding or meaning at the center of philosophical inquiry and can make their own claims to (nonobjective) truth.

From these postmodern and hermeneutic stances, there is no neutral vantage point from which one might assign objective meaning, because all understanding is historically and subjectively situated and necessarily involves some "prejudice" (Gadamer, 1975). While most postmodernists would apply this statement to all systems of knowledge, including the natural sciences, many hermeneuticists would focus its application to the human sciences. In either case, more traditional philosophers are horrified by this abandonment of the search for a method or foundation which would guarantee objectivity, because of the looming specter of multiple, relativistic conceptions of knowledge (Harris, 1992).

A FORMULATION AND REVIEW OF
PHILOSOPHICAL POSITIONS

If psychotherapy is presumed to be a scientifically grounded practice, then it would follow that the philosophy of science would contribute most to a clarification of its status. However, not all psychotherapists claim a scientific identity for their approaches, and not all contemporary philosophers prize science. To do credit to the conflicting views within both fields regarding the possibility and desirability of an objective, scientific foundation for knowledge, a balanced review would include not only dissenting positions within the philosophy of science, but also postmodern accounts which quite literally attempt to "dismantle truth" (Lawson & Appignanesi, 1989).

In turn, a consideration of the philosophy of science and its postmodern alternatives necessarily places epistemology at the center of any review of philosophical positions of relevance to psychotherapy, and this emphasis has several advantages. For example, the current movement toward outcome research, managed care, and therapist accountability, as well as the contrary trend toward critiquing "objectivity" in psychotherapy from a sociopolitical and moral standpoint, both represent forms of the epistemological question "What is psychotherapeutic knowledge?"

One could also argue that the field of psychotherapy historically has been preoccupied, in a largely unproductive fashion, with matters of ontology. Since the nature of being can be defined in countless ways, a focus on this question leads directly to the proliferation of theories and therapies which was noted in the last chapter. Just as Jung and Adler dissented from Freud's approach to defining being or reality, the rapid generation of new theories and therapies continues up to the present. Much of the subsequent discussion in the literature then concentrates on offering compelling arguments in support of one or another particular view of reality. It can be fascinating to debate whether human reality ultimately is best construed in relation to biological drives, object relations, intersubjective experience, or hermeneutics, and representative arguments of this kind are presented in chapter 4 in some detail. However, the following review is designed to ensure that these debates do not overshadow the epistemological questions which underlie the practice of psychotherapy.

Finally, emphasizing epistemological issues in this review serves the pragmatic goal of providing the reader with a structure which can readily link philosophical positions with the function (chapter 3) and range (chapter 4) of theories of psychotherapy. By contrast, there is no available analysis of ontological positions within philosophy—for example, see Erwin's (1997) critique of Stephen Pepper's well-known "world hypotheses"—which would offer a comparably comprehensive and relevant framework for contemporary psychotherapeutic theory and practice.

Nevertheless, questions of epistemology and ontology are always related, and their interaction is fundamental to an undertaking that inescapably depends on both the knowing *and* being of the psychotherapist. Therefore, this relationship, including its more complex manifestations, will continue to be explored throughout the text. While I believe that an epistemological emphasis best clarifies the philosophical questions confronting psychotherapy, this approach does not mean that important ontological issues will be ignored.

Differing positions in the philosophy of science and postmodern thought could be formulated in relation to several contrasts which exist in the philosophical literature—for example, realism *vs.* anti-realism (Honderich, 1995, pp. 746–748; Held, 1995), objectivism *vs.* relativism (Bernstein, 1983), foundationalism (Honderich, 1995, p. 289) *vs.* antifoundationalism, and representationalism *vs.* anti-representationalism (Rorty, 1991). My own formulation combines elements of several of these contrasts, having realism and anti-realism at its poles, and modifications of realism and relativism intermediate between those poles.

The realist pole of this formulation defines a position regarding knowledge which corresponds to Bernstein's notion of objectivism / foundationalism and Held's view of realism. Bernstein (1983) acknowledges that his concept of "objectivism" is more inclusive than the standard usage and is "closely related to foundationalism" (p. 8). It is assumed "that there is or must be some permanent, ahistorical matrix or framework to which we can ultimately appeal in determining the nature of rationality, knowledge, truth, reality, goodness, or rightness" (p. 8).

Bernstein (1983) sees a strong tendency within Western philosophy to associate the potential loss of this indisputable ground for knowledge with what he calls the "Cartesian Anxiety" (p. 16). This is not to imply that this project begins with Descartes, but simply that both the quest for groundedness and the motivation behind it appear so clearly in his work.

Reading the *Meditations* as a journey of the soul helps us to appreciate that Descartes' search for a foundation or Archimedean point is more than a device to solve metaphysical and epistemological problems. It is the quest for some fixed point, some stable rock upon which we can secure our lives against the vicissitudes that constantly threaten us. The specter that hovers in the background of this journey is not just radical epistemological skepticism but the dread of madness and chaos where nothing is fixed, where we can neither touch bottom nor support ourselves on the surface. (p. 18)

Thus, this position reduces the question of knowledge to an "Either / Or": Either we find a secure foundation for our knowing and being, or "we cannot escape the forces of darkness that envelop us with madness, with intellectual and moral chaos" (p. 18).

Although Bernstein can mount an argument for equating "objectivism" with the kind of foundationalism that is characterized above, it is a confusing usage for those of us who are accustomed to the narrower meaning of objectivism within the sciences, which he himself cites. For example, if Bernstein's expanded usage is accepted, then it would be reasonable to say that even a subjectivist—who assumes that a secure, although subjective, foundation for knowledge is possible—is an objectivist. Consequently, I will refer to the quest for a secure starting point or framework as "foundationalism" and restrict the meaning of "objectivism" to a specific foundational approach insisting on objective knowledge obtained through empirical means.

Within this framework, *realism* represents a form of foundationalism which makes the following ontological and epistemological assumptions about the issues of reality and truth: (*a*) There is some reality which exists, whatever its nature; and (*b*) Knowledge, defined as the truth, is that which can mirror or represent this reality without distortion. In Held's (1995) terms, the knowing of the reality in question can be direct or mediated, but in either case it need not be influenced by the knower's categories or experience: "Thus, for the realist, nothing—no theory, for instance—necessarily intervenes between the knower and the known" (p. 4, italics omitted). Even on those occasions when theory is involved, it "does not automatically alter or distort the real / independent reality it purports to explain" (pp. 4–5, italics omitted). For a realist, the only true knowledge of reality is that which occurs when the human observer is in some sense eliminated. Consequently, depending on whether one's realism is naive or sophisticated—two positions which will be explored in the review to follow—the process of knowing can be described as "revealing" or "approximating" the truth, respectively.

It could be argued (e.g., Bernstein, 1983) that weaker and stronger forms of *relativism* represent the opposite pole of a contrast to realism or foundationalism. Some relativists don't deny that a reality of some kind might exist but argue that human beings simply can never access it apart from a conceptual scheme (Honderich, 1995, p. 757). The knower's categories, concepts, theories, or experience always act as an intermediary between knower and known, resulting in interpretations of reality that contain some degree of distortion or bias. Therefore, truth is an impossibility because reality can never be apprehended directly or purely by a human being.

A stronger version of relativism "eschews the very idea of an uninterpreted reality that is as it is independently of us or of some scheme of understanding" (Honderich, 1995, p. 757). Because "reality," individual constructions of it, and the social / historical context are all intertwined, it is meaningless to propose that some reality could exist independently of human categories and the social world. There are an indefinite number of potential accounts of reality, and each of these accounts both help to constitute the nature of "reality" and reflect a particular historical and social context. Therefore, "truth" can never be defined apart from that context and its associated standards and values.

While these more "radical" forms of relativism are often associated with postmodern philosophy, many postmodern thinkers object to this description of their position. Like Bernstein (1983), they are interested in moving "beyond objectivism and relativism" or beyond the "Either / Or" which is the heritage of foundationalism. For example, Tomlinson (1989) contends that "the post-modernist is not advancing . . . a 'relativist theory of truth.' Rather, he is drawing out a consequence of the realist's own position. Relativism *is* incoherent but this incoherence belongs to realism not to its opponents" (p. 52). Rorty (1989a) summarizes the postmodernist position regarding relativism when he wryly observes: "For someone who thinks that there is no God there will be no such thing as blasphemy. For there will be no higher standpoint to which we are responsible and against whose precepts we might offend" (p. 50). Therefore, positions associated with postmodern thought are often called "anti-realist," "anti-foundationalist," or "anti-representationalist." *Anti-realism* is the term which will be used here and, along with "postmodern," will be further clarified in the review which follows.

A more detailed analysis of these contrasts will now be undertaken by exploring four different philosophical positions that stake out different views of the possibility of truth and fall at different points along the continuum of realism *vs.* anti-realism. Because of the importance of comparing developments in the philosophy of science with one another and with postmodern philosophy, the realism pole of the contrast will include only forms of common sense and scientific realism.

It should be emphasized, however, that scientific realism or objectivism, which assumes the existence of an external, physical reality that can be known only through objective, empirical methods, is only one variant of realism. One might propose that reality is basically subjective and internal in nature, and this kind of subjectivism is also a form of ontological realism. Further, if it is assumed that the nonobjective means by which one accesses this reality produces undistorted, unbiased knowledge, then this subjective approach would also qualify as a form of epistemological realism. Therefore, philosophical and theoretical positions (subjectivism; transpersonalism) which make different ontological and epistemological assumptions than objectivism will be addressed in chapter 4.

Scientific Realism

The thinking of laypersons is often described in relation to "naive" or "commonsense" realism, which is seen as a precursor to scientific realism. For the ordinary person, commonsense realism corresponds fairly well with the account of philosophical realism in the prior section: There is an external reality which exists independently of human beings, and it can be directly captured through careful observation. What is experienced through the senses, therefore, can be said to be "true." When I see a chair, I know that objects called chairs *really* exist in the external world, and that I just correctly identified one through my own sense perceptions.

While laypersons do not frequently come into disagreement with one another when the object at hand is a chair, naive realism encounters difficulties when different observers, presumably all possessing intact perceptual systems, look at the same object or phenomenon and produce differing descriptions or observations. John and Jane both observe Tom's behavior, and the first characterizes his mood as "depressed" while the second says he is just "tired." Which description is "true?"

Science, which attempts to eliminate the possible biases, errors, or personal preferences of the ordinary person, represents a more refined version of realism. Scientific realism agrees with both assumptions of naive realism: A "mind-independent" external reality exists (Honderich, 1995, p. 746), and proper observation can provide direct access to this reality producing "true" statements about it. However, proper observa-

tion requires following the dictates of scientific method, which can eliminate subjective factors and produce neutral observations that constitute
"objective facts."

The above account of science is also called "naive inductivism" by
Chalmers (1982), because it is based on inductive reasoning (p. 2). Singular observations ("Mars moves in an ellipse around the sun"), if reli-
ably obtained under a variety of conditions and if self-consistent, can
be generalized into a universal law ("All planets move in ellipses
around the sun").

Chalmers points out that induction does not give a full picture of
science since scientists also want to predict and explain phenomena (p.
4). Scientists organize observations and established laws into general
theories and then use deductive reasoning to generate new predictions
which can test the theory. If the predictions correspond to observed
facts, then the theory is confirmed; if the facts deviate from the predictions, the theory is disconfirmed. Scientific progress is assumed and consists of the refinement of knowledge by reality itself, with proven, true
theories displacing disproven, false ones.

The only philosophical position which appears to be completely
congruent with this realist view of knowledge is the aptly named "correspondence theory of truth" (p. 151). According to this position, the
only true propositions are those which correspond to the facts of the
world (Honderich, 1995, p. 166). More broadly, this view would define
the central philosophical task as one of attempting to establish epistemological foundations which will ensure that human knowledge accurately "represents" or "mirrors" nature (Rorty, 1979).

Sophisticated Realism.

The philosopher of science Karl Popper has developed an influential
theory of science which differs significantly from that of scientific realism. H. I. Brown (1977) suggests that Popper's view can be thought of
as "transitional" between older and newer philosophies of science (p.
67), and this transitional status will later point to the conclusion that his
position represents a kind of "sophisticated realism."

Popper (1968, 1976) writes that, around 1920, he became interested
in two philosophical problems which he only later realized were fundamentally related. The first of these is the *problem of induction*. As previously argued, science can be defined in terms of an inductive method,
where generalizations are established by repeated observations. For
example, consider the inductive process that would allow one to move

from the specific, repeated observation, "Every swan I have seen, or that anyone else has seen, has been white," to the generalization, "All swans are white." Following Hume, Popper (1968) asserts that there is no logical reason for us to conclude that those things we have seen allow us to draw conclusions about those things which we have not seen (p. 42). All we really know is that every swan we have seen is white; we don't know for certain that every swan in past, present, or future history has been, is, or will be white.

Popper takes this reasoning further, concluding that induction cannot be the basis for science, and that another principle inherent in the above example might replace it. While no number of observations of swans could allow us to confirm that all swans are white, only one instance of a nonwhite swan would allow us to disconfirm the generalization. Therefore, since a universal statement can be falsified by a single instance, could science actually be based on a principle which involves disconfirmation or falsification?

Popper's (1968) second interest was in reflecting on the *problem of demarcation:* What distinguishes scientific theories from those associated with either pseudoscience or metaphysics? He recognized that it is not convincing to answer the question "What is science?" by responding that it relies on an empirical method, moving from observation to prediction (pp. 33–34). Astrology can superficially fit that description of science, citing masses of observations in support of its predictions, but most scientists, astronomers included, would view it as a pseudoscience.

While astrology provides a good hypothetical example, Popper (1968) was actually more interested in the scientific status of three theories—Marx's theory of history, Freud's psychoanalysis, and Adler's individual psychology—which were all attracting a great deal of popular attention around 1919. He became convinced that there was something about these three theories which differentiated them from genuine scientific theories such as those associated with Newton or Einstein (p. 34).

The difference was not, as prior conceptions of science might contend, that scientific theories are true whereas other theories are not. At the time Popper was working on the demarcation problem, it was not at all clear that Einstein's relativity theory was true. Meanwhile, the three theories in question, like either astrology or primitive myths, were making their own strong claims to truth. Indeed, in reflecting on those of his friends who were attracted to Marx, Freud, or Adler, the commonality across the theories that most struck Popper (1968) was their apparent *explanatory power*. These theories appeared to be able to explain practically everything that happened within the fields to which they referred. The study of any of them seemed to have the effect of an intellectual conversion or revelation, opening your eyes to a new truth hidden from those not yet initiated. Once your eyes were thus opened you saw confirming instances everywhere: the world was full of *verifications* of the theory. Whatever happened always confirmed it. (pp. 34–35)

Popper (1968) actually had come in personal contact with Adler, and on one occasion he described a case which, in Popper's view, did not obviously fit the tenets of individual psychology. Adler had no difficulty in analyzing the case in terms of inferiority feelings, even though he had not seen the child, and when a shocked Popper asked how he could be so sure of his conclusions, Adler replied, "Because of my thousandfold experience" (p. 35). For Popper, the case could just as easily have been interpreted according to Freud's theory, and he was unable to conceive of any human behavior which could not be interpreted within the terms of either theory. It began to occur to him that the seeming strength of these theories, their facility in finding verifications, was actually their great weakness and what differentiated them from scientific theories.

For example, Popper realized how differently Einstein's relativity theory functioned from these three theories. His gravitational theory stated that light would be attracted to heavy bodies, such as the sun. It could then be predicted that light coming from stars close to the sun would create the appearance that the stars were moving away from the sun and from each other. This prediction was not obvious and had to be checked against photographs made during an eclipse of the sun.

The riskiness of this prediction most impressed Popper; it clearly set the conditions under which the theory could be refuted. If observations did not support the theory, then the theory was simply wrong (p. 36). The contrast between Einstein, on the one hand, and Marx, Freud, and Adler, on the other, allowed Popper to formulate a criterion for defining science which would separate it from pseudoscience.

It is easy to find confirmations for any theory, and the scientific approach is unique in that it does not just seek confirmation but rather sets the conditions under which a theory will be modified or given up. That is, a scientific theory is not one which has been proven or confirmed, it is one which can be tested and, therefore, can be disproven or refuted. Thus, *"the criterion of the scientific status of a theory is its falsifiability, or refutability, or testability"* (p. 37).

This conclusion led to the kind of differentiation between science and pseudoscience which Popper had sought. While Einstein's theory of gravitation meets the criterion, astrology and the other three theories do not. Astrology is not a science because it makes its predictions sufficiently vague such that they could fit with any possible observation, rendering the theory nontestable. Freudian and Adlerian theory are similar to astrology in that regard: They are untestable because they, too, can account for any conceivable human behavior. Of possible interest to therapists, Popper (1968) remarks:

> This does not mean that Freud and Adler were not seeing certain things correctly: I personally do not doubt that much of what they say is of considerable importance, and may well play its part one day in a psychological science which is testable. But it does mean that those 'clinical observations' which analysts naively believe confirm their theory cannot do this any more than the daily confirmations which astrologers find in their practice. And as for Freud's epic of the Ego, the Super-ego, and the Id, no substantially stronger claim to scientific status can be made for it than for Homer's collected stories from Olympus. These theories describe some facts, but in the manner of myths. They contain most interesting psychological suggestions, but not in a testable form. (pp. 37–38)

Although Popper saw some Marxist propositions as initially testable—for example, the nature of the "coming social revolution"—he believed that they were subsequently falsified. Unfortunately, Marxists simply "re-interpreted both the theory and the evidence in order to make them agree. In this way they rescued the theory from refutation; . . . and by this stratagem they destroyed its much advertised claim to scientific status" (p. 37).

Combining his interests in the problems of induction and demarcation, Popper's image of science becomes one of "trial and error—of *conjectures and refutations*" (p. 46). Scientists do not just passively record the regularities which nature offers, they anticipate those regularities through offering conjectures about nature in the form of laws and theories. However, the tendency toward "dogmatic thinking," which is inherent in the tendency to posit regularities, is balanced by a "critical attitude," which resolutely attempts to demonstrate the fallacy of the very regularities which have been proposed (p. 49). If this critical effort is unsuccessful—that is, observations do not refute the theory—then the theory can still only be held tentatively; it can never be considered as proven or as true (p. 51).

Therefore, Popper (1968) disabuses us of a central myth of science: Scientific knowledge is not that which has been confirmed; it is knowledge which lends itself to possible disconfirmation. The scientific enterprise has a tentativeness and incompleteness built into its very nature: "As we learn from our mistakes our knowledge grows, even though we may never know—that is, know for certain" (p. vii).

Although science can never lead us to ultimate truth, Popper definitely leaves us with the impression it can at least help us along that path. In the opening lines of his preface quoted above, Popper (1968) assures us that the theme of his essays is that we *can* learn from our mistakes. If scientists are able to learn from their mistakes (reject or revise theory in accord with new observations), then the cherished notion of scientific progress can be retained. Further, combining this perception of science with an acceptance of the correspondence theory of truth (pp. 223–228), it follows that succeeding theories, while never reaching the truth, at least represent closer approximations of it. "The aim is to find theories which, in the light of critical discussion, get nearer to the truth" (Popper, 1970, p. 57). It is in this sense that Popper contends not only that Einstein's theory is preferred over Newton's because of its greater corroboration by the facts (1976, p. 104), but also that it could be characterized as having greater "verisimilitude" (1968, pp. 234–237).

To fully understand Popper's view of science, one must appreciate possible permutations in the relationship of ontology to epistemology. While he proposes a realist ontology (a real world does exists), he combines this position with an epistemology which assumes some degree of uncertainty in our attempts to obtain knowledge—that is, we can only approximate, never capture, this reality. In this important regard, it seems reasonable to characterize Popper's view of science as a form of "sophisticated realism" (Tomlinson, 1989, pp. 48–49).

Old and New Philosophies of Science

The first position outlined above, scientific realism, is compatible in many ways with what has been called "logical positivism" or "logical empiricism." "Positivism" is a term which was applied by Auguste Comte to a "form of strict empiricism" (H. I. Brown, 1977, p. 21). Logical positivism, which developed as a philosophy of science combining empiricism with symbolic logic, states that there are only two methods for attaining knowledge: "empirical research, which is the task of the various sciences, and logical analysis of science, which is the task of philosophy" (p. 21). Like realism, logical positivism insists on the *verifiability* of knowledge claims. Scientific knowledge results when given propositions are studied through an empirical method and their truth or falsity is determined. If there is no empirical or logical method through which a given statement could be proven true or false, then it is simply nonsensical: "Famously, some say infamously, many positivists classed metaphysical, religious, aesthetic, and ethical claims as meaningless" (Honderich, 1995, p. 507).

As we have seen, Popper, as a sophisticated realist, attacks the notions of induction and verifiability which are central to the positivist position and replaces them with the criterion of *falsifiability*. While this approach has the impact of tempering the claims to truth claimed by some positivist philosophers and scientists, two implications of positivism are retained. First, while Popper would not say that metaphysical statements are meaningless or useless, he would say that they are not scientific, since they cannot be falsified. Second, when Popper is speaking as a "strict falsificationist" (H. I. Brown, 1977, p. 67), he is pushed toward the empiricist stance "that the objectivity of science is completely derived from its appeal to observation" (p. 75).

H. I. Brown (1977) contrasts the empirically based philosophy of science described above with a "new" philosophy of science. The key element in this shift involves the relationship between facts ("observation statements") and theories. Whether one supports verifiability or falsifiability as the criterion of scientific knowledge, it is assumed that propositions will be tested against facts, and that the facts will prevail. This agenda would presuppose that propositions and theories, on the one hand, and facts, on the other hand, represent distinct phenomena. If so, the first can be tested against the second in an objective, neutral fashion—assuming that one follows the dictates of scientific method. However, what happens to this agenda if facts and theories, as Popper (1970) himself acknowledges, are not so distinct as has been assumed? What happens if facts are, in Hanson's (1961) phrase, "theory-laden"? Brown writes:

> It is the empirical facts, which are known independently of any theory, that guarantee the objectivity of science. One starting point of the new philosophy of science, however, is an attack on the empiricist theory of perception. In response to the view that

perception provides us with pure facts, it is argued that the knowledge, beliefs, and theories we already hold play a fundamental role in determining what we perceive. (p. 81)

This approach to the philosophy of science, and its implications for the issue of realism-relativism, will now be examined in some detail.

Sophisticated Relativism

Thomas Kuhn's (1970a) *The Structure of Scientific Revolutions* (SSR), originally published in 1962 and later republished with a postscript, is "the most influential book in modern philosophy of science" (Honderich, 1995, p. 451). Kuhn was first trained as a theoretical physicist and then gravitated to an interest in the history of science and describes himself as "a practicing historian of science" (1977, p. 3). Therefore, it is somewhat ironic that Kuhn has played such a pivotal, controversial role in debates in the philosophy of science (Lakatos & Musgrave, 1970) and has had such an enormous impact on other disciplines such as the humanities and social sciences (Gutting, 1980) and psychology (Coleman & Salamon, 1988; O'Donohue, 1993). The present review aims neither to praise nor vilify the account of the history of science which Kuhn offers, and no attempt will be made to generalize his conclusions about scientific progress to other disciplines, including psychology. Further, since the question of relativism is a complex one in relation to Kuhn, the logic of describing his position in those terms will be considered only after a presentation of his views.

While Kuhn (1970b) finds many points of agreement between his own position and that of Popper, there is one striking difference which has enormous implications for the philosophies which they develop. Although both are interested in a non-positivist study of how science is actually practiced, their perceptions of the day-to-day functioning of scientists are completely different. Popper tells us that scientists learn from their mistakes, but Kuhn's examination of scientific history led him to conclude "that much scientific behaviour, including that of the very greatest scientists, persistently violated accepted methodological canons" (1970c, p. 236). That is, the process of falsification championed by Popper, where a theory is revised or discarded based on the facts, is regarded by Kuhn (1970b) as the exception, not the rule, in scientific practice (pp. 5–6). For the most part, scientists presume the utility and accuracy of the theoretical framework or research tradition within which they are working, and facts which contradict it are more likely to be reinterpreted, deemed irrelevant, misperceived, or not seen at all (1970a, p. 24). It is so unusual for scientists to behave as Popper describes them—risking the fate of a theoretical framework on some critical test—that such episodes, and their aftermath, give Kuhn the title for his work. They can be likened to political revolutions where an old order resists and resists forces of change and, at last, is overthrown by a new order.

Implicit in this contrast between the two philosophers is Kuhn's emphasis on the breakdown of the fact-theory distinction, previously outlined by H. I. Brown (1977). Kuhn cites examples from the history of science where certain facts, such as the discovery of a given planet (Uranus), could not be identified until there were changes in the assumptions of the scientific community which would allow for such a possibility (1970a, pp. 115–116). He also focuses on cases where different scientists, working out of different theoretical and methodological frameworks, look at the same phenomena and literally "see" different facts (p. 150). Both the Ptolemaic and Copernican astronomers were practicing science within then accepted norms, and both systems could account for much of the available astronomical data. Yet, one group perceived the earth as quite literally fixed and the other knew just as emphatically that it must move (pp. 149–150).

The creative challenge for Kuhn was to take these observations of how scientists fail to live up to some ideal of scientific objectivity (falsification) and weave them into an account of scientific knowledge which transformed "what had previously seemed aberrant behaviour into an essential part of an explanation for science's success" (1970c, p. 236). He accomplishes this goal through formulating a new theory of scientific knowledge based on the key concepts of the *paradigm, normal science,* and *revolutionary science.*

Some of his concepts, particularly that of the "paradigm," have entered the cultural mainstream, and that is all the more reason for revisiting their specific meanings. Gholson and Barker (1985) suggest that it is important, even within the professional literature, to distinguish "Kuhn's ideas" (what he himself originally said or later clarified) from "Kuhnian ideas" (views associated with his name, but which he would deny) (p. 756). I will attempt to present Kuhn's ideas, and indicate when the discussion shifts to Kuhnian ideas.

Since there is wide agreement, including Kuhn's own assessment, that the concept of the paradigm is the most ambiguous aspect of his theory, it might be helpful to underline its function within the overall development. Masterman (1970), who is well known for her cataloging of different meanings of the paradigm concept, appears to regard Kuhn's concept of normal science as his greatest accomplishment.

> That there is normal science—and that it is exactly as Kuhn says it is—is the outstanding, the crashingly obvious fact which confronts and hits any philosophers of science who set out, in a practical or technological manner, to do any actual scientific research. It is because Kuhn—at last—has noticed this central fact about all real science . . . namely that it is normally a habit-governed, puzzle-solving activity, not a fundamentally upheaving or falsifying activity (not, in other words, a *philosophical* activity), that actual scientists are now, increasingly reading Kuhn instead of Popper. (p. 60)

Thus, for Kuhn, long periods of normal science are punctuated by periods of "crisis," brought on by findings which cannot be explained by normal science. Crises, in turn, can result in periods of revolutionary science, which are then resolved such that a new period of normal science ensues. It is the concept of the paradigm which holds this analysis together, providing an explanation for the nature and function of normal science.

For Kuhn (1970a), a paradigm exists when a given scientific field has reached a certain level of maturity and a consensus has emerged regarding a conceptual and methodological framework, including concrete examples of scientific achievement. In choosing this term

> I mean to suggest that some accepted examples of actual scientific practice—examples which include law, theory, application, and instrumentation together—provide models from which spring particular coherent traditions of scientific research. These are the traditions which the historian describes under such rubrics as 'Ptolemaic astronomy' (or 'Copernican'), 'Aristotelian dynamics' (or 'Newtonian'), 'corpuscular optics' (or 'wave optics'), and so on. (p. 10)

It is through the paradigm, which often is highly specialized, that the student is socialized into the scientific community and learns the nature of scientific inquiry, including the problems to be solved and the methods for doing so.

Masterman (1970), who is sympathetic to Kuhn's analysis but notes his "quasi-poetic style" (p. 61), suggests that his usage of the term in SSR falls into three main categories: *"metaphysical," "socio-logical,"* and *"artefact"* or *"construct"* paradigms (p. 65). Examples of Kuhn's metaphysical usages include "a set of beliefs," "a new way of seeing," or "something which determines a large area of reality" (p. 65). She links the sociological paradigm with statements which liken a recognized scientific achievement to "a set of political institutions" or to "an accepted judicial decision" (p. 65). Finally, the artefact or construct paradigm is defined by those statements which characterize it "as an actual textbook or classic work," "as supplying tools," "as actual instrumentation," "as an analogy," or "as a gestalt-figure" (p. 65). Masterman believes that this last meaning of paradigm is most crucial to Kuhn's theory: Some actual example of scientific practice functions as a concrete "model," "picture," or "analogy" (p. 79) for directing research and for determining what fits and doesn't fit the paradigm.

Kuhn's (1977) "second thoughts" about paradigms (chap. 12), in which he proposes a broad and narrow meaning for the term, seem to take him in a direction similar to that of Masterman. He offers the term "disciplinary matrix" to refer to "most or all of the objects of group commitment described in the book as paradigms, parts of paradigms, or paradigmatic" (p. 297), and this usage would appear to include Masterman's metaphysical and sociological paradigms. "Exemplars" represent the second, more narrow meaning of the term in SSR and refer to "concrete problem solutions, accepted by the group as, in a quite usual sense, paradigmatic" (p. 298). Exemplars would seem to correspond to Masterman's notion of artefact or construct paradigms, and Kuhn devotes the majority of his paper to their explication.

Gutting (1980) offers the interesting perspective that the "alleged vagueness and ambiguity" of the paradigm concept is actually due to the two different roles which it necessarily plays in Kuhn's work (p. 1). Paradigms encompass both actual scientific achievements and what is abstracted from them by the community in the form of various "rules," including scientific laws, experimental methods, and even metaphysical assumptions. When Kuhn uses the term, it may have one or the other of these meanings, depending on the context.

> Thus, the flexibility of 'paradigm' derives from the fact that it refers simultaneously to two aspects of a paradigmatic scientific achievement: first, to a body of *content* implicit in the achievement and second to a *function* of the achievement in the scientific community. (pp. 1–2)

Gutting goes on to liken the content of the paradigm to a "super-theory" or "worldview" (p. 12), notions which no doubt represent "Kuhnian ideas," but the general contrast he offers between content and function helps to clarify Kuhn's concept.

Whatever the precise definition of a paradigm, it includes an agreement about fundamentals and a specification of the nature of research, which allow the activity of normal science to proceed. While it was just the success of the paradigm in explaining phenomena that allowed it to reach its domination of the field, questions always remain—or else there would be no science. It is the task of normal science to address the unanswered questions which can be deduced from the paradigm, and which would both expand the range of its explanations and further articulate the paradigm itself (1970a, pp. 23–24). This activity is described by Kuhn as "mop-up work" (p. 24) and "puzzle-solving" (p. 35).

Kuhn (1970a) goes to some lengths to underline that the function of the paradigm and the activity of normal science are as much to restrict the range of meanings which can emerge, as to reveal the nature of reality. Normal science

> seems an attempt to force nature into the preformed and relatively inflexible box that the paradigm supplies. No part of the aim of normal science is to call forth new sorts of phenomena; indeed, those that will not fit the box are often not seen at all. Nor do scientists normally aim to invent new theories, and they are often intolerant of those invented by others. Instead, normal-scientific research is directed to the articulation of those phenomena and theories that the paradigm already supplies. (p. 24)

Because passages of this kind have been variously interpreted by other philosophers, it is important to clarify what Kuhn is saying. Kuhn believes that he is simply describing how the great bulk of routine, scientific work is conducted. Unlike J. W. N. Watkins (1970) and Popper (1970), Kuhn does not disparage scientists who engage in normal science, nor does he see it as a threat to the integrity of the scientific enterprise. He merely asserts that normal science does exist, assumes it would not exist if it were not integral to the scientific enterprise, and attempts to comprehend what positive contribution it does make. "To explain why an enterprise works is not to approve or disapprove it" (Kuhn, 1970c, p. 237).

Kuhn then proposes that normal science makes two crucial contributions to the development of knowledge. First, the paradigm and normal science *must* restrict the vision of practicing scientists so that they can concentrate on a given aspect of the natural world "in a detail and depth that would otherwise be unimaginable" (1970a, p. 24). In fact, it is this characteristic which allows science to produce cumulative knowledge, and which distinguishes science from "proto-science" (1970c, pp. 244–245).

Second, as indicated below, normal science continues to function as it does only as long as the paradigm remains productive. When the paradigm becomes ineffective in generating new questions or answering existing ones, "scientists begin to behave differently, and the nature of their research problems changes" (1970a, p. 24). Normal science has a "built-in mechanism" (p. 24) that plants the seeds of its own destruction and facilitates the "scientific revolutions" which Popper so values. Moreover, one cannot have a revolution that does not involve the rejection of some framework, and "since the science which I call normal is precisely research within a framework, it can only be the opposite side of a coin the face of which is revolutions" (1970c, p. 242).

Therefore, as normal science proceeds, there are inevitably failures to solve some of the "puzzles" that are posed by the paradigm. Since the scientist does not criticize the fundamentals of the paradigm and assumes that it does hold the answer to its puzzles, such failures tend to be seen as inadequacies of the scientist or method. Further, if the failures persist, they are viewed as *"anomalies,"* not as "falsifications"—that is, they are regarded as unexplained oddities (Chalmers, 1982, p. 92). This resistance of the paradigm to anomalous findings is another of its important characteristics; otherwise, scientists might be distracted into following too many false leads before the productivity of the paradigm in question has been exhausted.

However, in some circumstances, anomalies may provoke a "crisis" among scientists working within a paradigm (Kuhn, 1970a, chapters VII, VIII). Factors which determine this outcome include, for example, whether the anomalies contradict core assumptions of the paradigm, whether they are related to some societal issue or need, and whether they are large in number and/or persist over a lengthy period while resisting the efforts of scientists to resolve them. As the crisis persists, the rules that have governed normal science loosen, and scientists may become more radical in their attempts to resolve the problem (pp. 82–84). If the crisis continues, scientists may experience a period of "pronounced professional insecurity" (pp. 67–68). Kuhn quotes Einstein, prior to the emergence of a new conception of physics, as saying: "It was as if the ground had been pulled out from under one, with no firm foundation to be seen anywhere, upon which one could have built" (p. 83). Scientists may engage in debates over metaphysical or philosophical issues, criticize the fundamentals of the paradigm in which they have been working, or even generate alternative theoretical schemes—actions which signify to Kuhn a move from "normal to extraordinary research" (p. 91). In short, they finally begin behaving more like Popper supposes that scientists should behave. In Kuhn's terms: "Even in the developed sciences, there is an essential role for Sir Karl's methodology. It is the strategy appropriate to those occasions when something goes wrong with normal science, when the discipline encounters crisis" (1970c, p. 247).

Crises can end with the existing paradigm managing to handle the problem which provoked the upheaval, with a decision to put the problem on the shelf for a future generation to handle, or "with the emergence of a new candidate for paradigm and with the ensuing battle over its acceptance" (1970a, p. 84). Kuhn is explicit that a scientific revolution does not occur in the absence of a viable alternative theory which could in time gain acceptance as the new paradigm. Further, the previous period of crisis and extraordinary science may have itself provided such a candidate.

Some of Kuhn's most controversial views are associated with the issue of how scientific resolutions are resolved, and center around his assertion that competing paradigms are "incommensurable" (1970a, p. 4). He likens paradigm conflicts to political revolutions where there is little common ground, where the contending parties tend to talk past each other, and where there is an appeal to "persuasion" as much as "proof" (chapter IX). Moreover, since every paradigm solves some problems and leaves others unsolved, the question of which of these are more important brings up the issue of values and standards.

Kuhn also uses perceptual metaphors to convey the incommensurability of paradigms indicating that "the proponents of competing paradigms practice their trades in different worlds" (1970a, p. 150). He employs notions from Gestalt psychology to describe how scientists internalize paradigms and says that "the transition between competing paradigms cannot be made a step at a time, forced by logic and neutral experience. Like the gestalt switch, it must occur all at once (though not necessarily in an instant) or not at all" (p. 150). He also uses a religious metaphor to describe this same phenomenon: "The transfer of allegiance from paradigm to paradigm is a conversion experience that cannot be forced" (p. 151).

Kuhn points out that many scientists never make the switch to the new paradigm—a hundred years after the death of Copernicus there were still very few Copernicans (1970a, p. 150). For those who do convert, one would think that the most important factor would be the effectiveness of the new paradigm in solving the problems that originally provoked the crisis. Kuhn indicates that such arguments are important but rarely sufficient to account for its acceptance. Sometimes the claims are simply inaccurate: "In fact, Copernicus' theory was not more accurate than Ptolemy's and did not lead directly to any improvement in the calendar" (p. 154). More often, the claims of the new paradigm represent a promise for the future rather than a present accomplishment, since the paradigm has not yet benefited from the work of normal science. In this sense, the scientist who chooses a new paradigm is making a decision based "on faith" (p. 158).

In time, and for reasons that can be quite idiosyncratic, the new paradigm attracts supporters and "if they are competent, they will improve it, explore its possibilities, and show what it would be like to belong to the community guided by it" (p. 159). If the new paradigm is to prevail, a reciprocal relationship occurs between normal science, which leads to more persuasive arguments in the paradigm's favor, and scientists, who can be converted by those arguments and who, in turn, produce further science. Finally, "only a few elderly hold-outs remain. And even they, we cannot say, are wrong" (p. 159).

Hence, science progresses through this interplay of normal science, where the puzzles provided by the paradigm are articulated and solved, and scientific revolutions, where the direction of theory and research are fundamentally recast. In the end, scientific progress depends on the existence of a scientific community that can serve as the ultimate judge of paradigms and their value to the scientific enterprise.

Kuhn observes that the most vehement attacks on his account of scientific knowledge accuse him of advocating "irrationality," "mob rule," and "relativism" (1970c, p. 259). Given some of the rhetoric of SSR, it is understandable why his critics might draw such conclusions. By the same token, both Kuhn (1970c, p. 260) and Gutting (1980, pp. 4–5) point out that the most extreme reactions have come from philosophers, who have perhaps read into the work philosophical claims that he was not intending to make.

In considering Kuhn's responses to these charges, it is helpful to first clarify the interlocking issues of rationalism and relativism. Chalmers (1982) describes the "extreme rationalist" as someone who wants to claim "that there is a single, timeless, universal criterion" which both defines science and allows scientists to choose among rival theories (p. 101). Further, the rationalist is typically a realist who contends that theories which meet the criterion "are true or approximately true or probably true" (p. 102). For example, Popper provides such a criterion (falsification) and seems to apply it according to these rationalist principles.

It follows, then, that a relativist is someone who denies the rationalist/realist agenda: There is no universal criterion, and judgments of competing theories vary with individuals and communities and, therefore, cannot be separated from issues of value. Relativists obviously do not speak of "truth," and "extreme relativists" will become less interested in a distinction between science and nonscience, questioning whether science should be considered superior to other forms of knowledge (Chalmers, 1982, p. 103).

Kuhn's responses to the charges against him include citing passages from SSR which modulate the extreme views that have been attributed to him, clarifying some of his positions, and questioning the very definitions of rationalism and relativism which are given above. This defense will begin with the issue of the presumed existence of a universal criterion.

As with the realist, the rationalist argues for a view of knowledge which only exists when all human influences are eliminated from the equation. A universal criterion of knowledge, which can be applied neutrally, objectively, and consistently by any individual or group, eliminates any variation in the view of what constitutes good theory or good science. This approach thereby removes any "subjective" or "irrational" factors from science.

Given the theme of SSR, Kuhn must reject these rationalist assumptions out of hand. Science cannot be divorced completely from the human observer who conducts it, and "there is no neutral algorithm for theory-choice, no systematic decision procedure which, properly applied, must lead each individual in the group to the same decision" (1970a, p. 200). However, the absence of some universal criterion of rationality does not imply that science is entirely a subjective and irrational enterprise. To say that theory-choice cannot be reduced to matters of proof or rational argument does not mean that proof and rational argument are irrelevant. Bernstein (1983) observes that a "sympathetic reading" of SSR "shows that Kuhn always intended to distinguish forms of rational persuasion and argumentation that take place in scientific communities from those irrational forms of persuasion that he has been accused of endorsing" (p. 53).

In fact, Kuhn is a thoroughgoing rationalist in at least two senses. First, he does provide a universal criterion for demarcating science from nonscience: the existence of normal science and puzzle-solving. Second, he assumes the superiority of science as an approach to knowledge and equates "rationality" with science itself. As suggested by Bernstein (1983), Gutting (1980), and himself (1970c), Kuhn's true intent is to redefine our notions of rationality based on his perceptions of actual scientific practice.

As for the question of relativism, Kuhn writes: "In one sense of the term I may be a relativist; in a more essential one I am not" (1970c, p. 264). Beginning with the latter, if a relativist is someone who believes that no judgments can be made about the comparative merits of competing arguments, then Kuhn is not a relativist. For example, he does not deny that science progresses. He believes that later scientific theories can be distinguished from earlier ones along conventional lines of "accuracy of prediction" (1970a, p. 206), and that the existence of scientific communities guarantees that "both the list of problems solved by science and the precision of individual problem-solutions will grow and grow" (p. 170).

Regarding the issue of subjective factors in paradigm choice, individual scientists may convert to a new paradigm for a variety of idiosyncratic reasons, but, in the end, the paradigm will be judged as better or worse in terms of its effectiveness in facilitating scientific progress (normal science). Similarly, Kuhn (1977) believes that traditional criteria—"accuracy, consistency, scope, simplicity, and fruitfulness" (p. 322)—are relevant to the comparison of competing theories and, with some exceptions, can also be applied to the scientific accomplishments of competing paradigms (pp. 338–339). Likewise, the incommensurability of paradigms is relative, not absolute, and partial "translation" can assist comparison in some instances.

On the other hand, if a relativist is anyone who is not a realist—anyone who denies the possibility of objective truth in the sense of a correspondence with reality—then Kuhn is a relativist. He rejects Popper's criterion of "verisimilitude" and is unwilling to say that a later theory somehow better fits reality, what is "really there," than an earlier one. The notion that the ontology of a theory could somehow be said to match the actual constituents of nature is for Kuhn "illusive in principle" and implausible (1970a, p. 206). Indeed, "comparison of historical theories gives no sense that their ontologies are approaching a limit: in some fundamental ways Einstein's general relativity resembles Aristotle's physics more than Newton's" (1970c, p. 265).

To summarize Kuhn's position, he would suggest that realists might want to consider rethinking their basic notions of rationality, objectivity, and relativism. The scientific community is the ultimate arbiter of disputes among paradigms, and the rational, objective criteria it uses for settling them "function not as rules, which determine choice, but as values, which influence it" (1977, p. 331). It puzzles Kuhn himself "how a value-based enterprise of the sort I have described can develop as a science does, repeatedly producing powerful new techniques for prediction and control" (p. 332).

Yet, it does, and Kuhn would see his argument as simply demonstrating that "existing theories of rationality are not quite right and that we must readjust or change them to explain why science works as it does" (1970c, p. 264). It makes no sense to Kuhn that certain philosophers want to contend that the only "rational," "objective" science would be one which eliminated all vestiges of science as a human endeavor and social institution. Similarly, H. I. Brown argues (1977) that the old epistemology "deems rational only those human acts which could in principle be carried out without the presence of a human being" (p. 148).

This conflict takes us back to Bernstein's notion of the "Either/Or": Either there is an unassailable foundation which guarantees objectivity and rationality or there is relativism, subjectivity, and irrationalism which represent "a danger to science and, indeed, to our civilization" (Popper, 1970, p. 53). Kuhn gently suggests that his view and that of Popper are perhaps themselves separated by a kind of "gestalt switch" (1970b, p. 22). While Popper appears to still be operating in the world of "Either/Or," Kuhn is attempting to define some third alternative between those choices (Bernstein, 1983, pp. 23–24).

In sum, Kuhn rejects the realist assumption of truth as correspondence and attempts to reformulate the realist constructs of rationality, objectivity, and relativism. Although it can be argued that his reformulation is not entirely clear or satisfactory, and "that his rhetoric frequently invites conflicting interpretations" (Bernstein, 1983, p. 23), Kuhn is successful in articulating a position of "sophisticated relativism" which provides a striking contrast to realist thinking.

From the Philosophy of Science to Postmodernism

If Popper represents a transitional figure between logical empiricism and a new philosophy of science, then Paul Feyerabend (1970, 1975, 1978) plays a similar role in the movement from that philosophy to postmodern thought. Because of his reputation as the "enfant terrible" of philosophy of science (Bernstein, 1983, p. 61), who likes to provoke and shock through his writing, it is difficult at times to know just how seriously to take some of the positions that Feyerabend proposes. For example, he suggests that Kuhn's attempt to define science in terms of normal science and puzzle-solving would not exclude "organized crime." He illustrates his point by demonstrating that his term could be substituted for normal science in every statement that Kuhn makes: "Organized crime certainly keeps foundational research to a minimum although there are outstanding individuals, such as Dillinger, who introduce new and revolutionary ideas" (Feyerabend, 1970, p. 200). In any case, a limited comparison of his views with those of Kuhn will define the trajectory which would take the philosophy of science in a post-modern direction.

In brief, Feyerabend pushes the critique of traditional epistemology much further than Kuhn could ever imagine. While Kuhn denies that there is some completely objective method which would allow for rational theory choice, Feyerabend (1975) argues "against method" of any kind. He believes that science and the decisions of scientists are too complex to be directed effectively by any of the "rules" or methodologies proposed by philosophers of science. He states this view with his usual hyperbole claiming that the only principle that does not inhibit the growth of scientific knowledge is "anything goes" (p. 23)—a recommendation which Chalmers (1982) suggests should not be taken too literally.

While Kuhn tries to distance himself from positions of "irrationality," "subjectivism," and "relativism" by cautiously reinterpreting the notions of rationality and objectivity, Feyerabend declares positions that would represent the worst nightmare of an empiricist philosopher attached to the "Either/Or." He advocates an "anarchistic" methodology and science (1975, p. 21) and contends, for example, that the choice between incommensurable theories must be determined on "subjective" grounds (Chalmers, 1982, p. 138). While Kuhn (1970c) can agree with many of Feyerabend's views of the role of reason in science, he believes it is "absurd" and "vaguely obscene" to describe such an argument as a "defence of irrationality in science" (p. 264).

Finally, Kuhn, like most philosophers of science, believes that science is the superior approach to human knowledge, defining "rationality" itself. Feyerabend (1975) points out that this is an assumption, and rails against "rational reconstructionists" who

> take 'basic scientific wisdom' *for granted,* they do not *show* that it is better than the 'basic wisdom' of witches and warlocks.

Nobody has shown that science (of 'the last two centuries') has results that conform to its own 'wisdom' while other fields have no such results. (p. 205)

Feyerabend (1978) unrelentingly argues for a "free society" where science is seen as only one "ideology" among many, and where "all traditions have equal rights and equal access to centres of power" (p. 9, italics omitted). By letting different traditions develop alongside science, such as astrology or forms of tribal medicine, it will become clear if they will remain important only for their supporters or if they will have something to offer to others and to society. He expresses this same idea by urging the creation of a "variety of opinion" (1975, p. 46) through a "proliferation of views" or "pluralism of theories and metaphysical views" (p. 52), both within and outside science—as a counter to "dogmatism" (p. 298).

It is as much the style as the content of Feyerabend's thought which anticipates some postmodern discourses on knowledge. Feyerabend (1975) speaks approvingly of "Dadaism" at several points in *Against Method*, viewing it as a better description of his approach than "anarchism." While the latter reeks of "Puritanical dedication and seriousness," the Dadaist is "utterly unimpressed by any serious enterprise" (p. 21, footnote 12). The Dadaist is not a supporter of any particular program but opposes all programs and especially delights in confusing rationalists "by inventing compelling reasons for unreasonable doctrines" (p. 189). All ideas are considered and no method is "indispensable," and, above all, there is an opposition to "universal standards, universal laws, universal ideas such as 'Truth,' 'Reason,' 'Justice,' 'Love,' and the behaviour they bring along" (p. 189). Feyerabend says that he hopes he is remembered "as a flippant Dadaist and *not* as a serious anarchist" (p. 21, footnote 12).

Bernstein (1983) perceives that Feyerabend is himself still caught in the "Either/Or": "His rhetoric and tropes make it appear as if the choice is between rationalism and a new playful, hedonistic form of irrationalism and relativism" (p. 63). Regardless of the accuracy of Bernstein's interpretation, the juxtaposition of rationality with a playful nonrationality and relativism frequently surfaces in both cultural and philosophical expressions of postmodernism.

Anti-Realism (Postmodernism)

Attempting to characterize "anti-realism," or the "postmodern" context with which it is associated, poses the largest conceptual challenge of this review. Beginning with the latter, Kvale (1992a) suggests that it is important to distinguish among three different meanings of "postmodern": (a) "postmodernity" refers to the present historical period, which is contrasted with the "modern" period that preceded it; (b) "postmodernism" connotes the wildly diverse cultural expressions of this period; and (c) "postmodern thought" is equated to "philosophical reflection on a postmodern age and culture" (p. 2). Unless otherwise noted, any use of the term "postmodern" or its variations in this review is intended to convey the last meaning.

H. Smith (1989) argues that the development of Western thought can be framed in relation to three different world views, loosely associated with historical periods, which provide the context for the emergence of a fourth view in our own time: (a) the "classical" world view, associated with the Greco-Roman period up until the fourth century A.D.; (b) the "Christian" world view, which dominated Europe until the seventeenth century; and (c) the "modern" world view, defined by the rise of modern science during the Enlightenment (p. 4).

The modern world view is closely associated with the kind of scientific realism which was previously outlined: Reality is ordered in accord with laws of nature, this order can be discovered by human reason, and such understanding, coupled with technological advance, will lead to human progress and fulfillment. Postmodern thought, on the other hand, refers to the host of positions in literature, philosophy, the arts, and social sciences which critique these core assumptions of modernity.

There is a necessary vagueness regarding the point at which one can discern a transition from the modern to the postmodern period. Although Kvale (1992b) indicates that the term "postmodernity" was not used until the 1950s and 1960s, and only attracted wide cultural attention in the 1980s, he acknowledges that "postmodern themes" were present in nineteenth-century romanticism and in Nietzsche's turn-of-the-century philosophy (pp. 31–32). Scholars also debate whether the modern and postmodern periods are distinct or overlap, and whether postmodernism represents a fundamental break with modernity or represents its "logical continuation" (Rosenau, 1992, p. 5, footnote 4).

There is even less agreement about the more specific referents for postmodern "thought." Kvale (1992b) indicates that it "does not designate a systematic theory or a comprehensive philosophy, but rather diverse diagnoses and interpretations of the current culture" (p. 32). Rosenau (1992) sees postmodernism as borrowing from a number of, sometimes conflicting, traditions: "It appropriates, transforms, and transcends French structuralism, romanticism, phenomenology, nihilism, populism, existentialism, hermeneutics, Western Marxism, Critical Theory, and anarchism. Although post-modernism shares elements with each, it has important quarrels with every approach" (p. 13).

There is even disagreement over the question of the hyphenation of this term—note Rosenau's usage in the last quote versus my own. Some authors apparently contend that the absence of a hyphen indicates "sympathy" for postmodernism and its presence conveys a "critical posture" toward it (Rosenau, 1992, p. 18). Rosenau denies that she is intending to convey "normative judgment or pejorative innuendo" through her insertion of a hyphen (p. 19), and perhaps I should clarify that its omission from my usage is also not intended as a political statement!

After concluding that there are probably as many different definitions of postmodern thought as there as postmodernists, Rosenau (1992) does distinguish between two broad orientations which she can discern among postmodern thinkers in the social sciences. She sees the *"skeptical"* postmodernist as offering a primarily "pessimistic, negative, gloomy" view of the human condition characterized by "fragmentation, disintegration, malaise, meaninglessness, a vagueness or even absence of moral parameters and societal chaos" (p. 15). Although these thinkers are in the tradition of Continental philosophy, including Heidegger and Nietzsche, they do not typically fall into nihilism but regard the human predicament they outline with a "blasé attitude" (p. 15).

The *"affirmative"* postmodernists share many points of agreement with the skeptics but represent more of an "Anglo–North American" tradition and infuse postmodernism with a more hopeful, optimistic air. One might say that the affirmative postmodernist wants to be able to *act* politically, socially, or ethically despite participating in a critique of modernity which undermines the possibility of action. That is, while postmodern critiques of modernity and postmodern "deconstructive" techniques call into question the holding of any position, the affirmative postmodernists do not

> shy away from affirming an ethic, making normative choices, and striving to build issue-specific political coalitions. Many affirmatives argue that certain value choices are superior to others, a line of reasoning that would incur the disapproval of the skeptical post-modernists (p. 16).

Therefore, a part of the intellectual task of the affirmative postmodernist is to resolve the contradiction between living in a pluralistic, relativistic world and wanting to make nonrelativistic commitments.

These introductory remarks provide some direction for the review of anti-realist or postmodern positions which will now follow. Modeling the approach of Kvale (1992b) and Polkinghorne (1992), I will outline some philosophical "themes" associated with the anti-realist position rather than attempting to identify it with a single philosopher or philosophical approach. Further, because it has some face validity for questions facing psychotherapy, the skeptical-affirmative distinction will be employed. Following a statement of the themes, their implications for the questions of nihilism and relativism—which are associated, respectively, with skeptical and affirmative postmodernism—will be explored.

It seems appropriate to make a final comment about the style and language of some postmodern writers—to normalize potential reactions of those readers who may already feel impatient with the philosophical content of this chapter. Stephen Katz (1995), a sociologist who is interested in postmodern thought, humorously notes some of the linguistic fashions, complexities, and obscurities that are associated with this intellectual and cultural movement. For example, a statement such as "We should listen to the views of people outside of Western society in order to learn about the cultural biases that affect us" might become, in "postmodernspeak," something like: "We should listen to the intertextual multivocalities of postcolonial others outside of Western culture in order to learn about the phallogocentric biases that mediate our identities" (p. 93). I am sympathetic to Katz' point and have attempted, to the extent possible, to provide a clear and direct statement of postmodern themes.

The Centrality of Negation in Postmodern Themes and "Method"

The first, obvious theme of an "anti-realist" position involves the nature of the themes themselves. The philosophical themes of the postmodern literature often take the form of negations, because they are intended to oppose the assumptions which underlie realism. If realism assumes the existence of a "mind-independent" truth, then anti-realism, which assumes that "reality" and language are hopelessly entangled, must deny this possibility. Definition by the negative or the opposite extends as well to the question of "method" in postmodern thought, and this issue will be examined in more detail.

In terms of its wide influence and applicability, "deconstruction" is probably the best candidate for a method associated with postmodern thought. Jacques Derrida introduced this elusive term in the 1960s (Honderich, 1995, p. 180), and its original meaning was restricted to the interpretation of literary and philosophical texts. Specifically, Derrida's

(1976, 1978) approach deconstructs the meaning of a text in two senses. First, he demonstrates that there is no external referent or intrinsic meaning to which the text can refer: All texts are simply collections of language signs which refer in an infinite regress to one another. Therefore, philosophical thought, including metaphysics, can never escape the system of language within which it is expressed and provide the truth about the human condition which it promises. Second, his analyses frequently pit one part of a text against another, emphasizing how that which is "privileged"—for example, reason—is dependent on that which is somehow denigrated or "excluded"—for example, unreason (Parker, Georgaca, Harper, McLaughlin, & Stowell-Smith, 1995, p. 3). This analysis then has the impact of deconstructing the original intent of the text, for example, that reason is superior to unreason, and provides one of many possible alternative readings of it, none of which can be judged as the one true reading.

As for the negations which structure his work, Derrida refuses to characterize his approach in relation to any positive descriptor: "He tells us that deconstruction is neither an analytical nor a critical tool; neither a method, nor an operation, nor an act performed on a text by a subject; that it is, rather, a term that resists both definition and translation" (Honderich, 1995, p. 180). Further, while deconstruction generates alternative interpretations of a text, Derrida provides no guidance for choosing among them. Although Bernstein (1992) agrees with Derrida that deconstruction in some sense represents "a way of taking a position" toward the text (p. 187), he emphasizes that its ultimate impact is, nonetheless, to undermine the grounds for an ethical/political position of *any* kind. It is for these reasons that deconstruction is said to entail a "negative critical capacity" (Rosenau, 1992, p. 118) and that Derrida, who does not himself use the term, can be likened to a skeptical postmodernist. Thus, Hoy (1990) argues: "As opposed to interpreters who purport to enable us to read the text, Derrida would make us unable to read it" (p. 44). Finally, while affirmative postmodernists might utilize deconstruction as a means of critiquing "privileged" texts, "they are, at the same time, wary of it because their views are as vulnerable as anyone else's to being deconstructed" (Rosenau, 1992, p. 118).

Deconstruction has by now been appropriated by many both within and outside philosophy and sometimes is equated with postmodern "tools" or "techniques" (Polkinghorne, 1992, p. 148). Moreover, the "text" which is deconstructed can refer to *any work or existing event* (Karasu, 1996, p. 5), whether psychotherapy, psychiatric diagnosis, or gender. However, even in this broader usage, it often retains its negative function of deconstructing what was presumed to be knowledge and may not put forth a positive statement of what does constitute knowledge.

Knowledge as Non-Foundational and Non-Representational

Although he has sometimes described himself as a "postmodernist bourgeois liberal," D. L. Hall (1994) contends that, overall, Richard Rorty "does not identify himself with the postmodern movement" (p. 51). However, his anti-foundational, anti-representational stance toward knowledge means that his work will appear in any review of postmodernist positions, including this one.

In *Philosophy and the Mirror of Nature,* Rorty (1979) performs a critique of philosophy as a whole which is not dissimilar to that provided for science by Kuhn. For Rorty, as for Derrida and other postmodernist philosophers, language plays a role similar to that of the paradigm in Kuhn's theory. Just as scientific realism assumes that observation can somehow directly reflect the facts of the world without contamination by theory, much of traditional philosophy has assumed that language can serve as a neutral vehicle which, if used appropriately, will describe and "mirror nature." From this perspective, philosophy then becomes the search for that "correct" use of language which will provide the foundation for a realist account of nature, where philosophy and reality become one.

However, following Ludwig Wittgenstein, Rorty argues that language is not a neutral vehicle and that it bears no necessary relationship to that which it purports to describe. For example, to say that a particular color is "red" is merely a rule for the use of the word. This language rule is neither true or false, nor does it correspond with some hypothesized quality or essence of "redness" that exists in reality (Honderich, 1995, p. 914). Therefore, the attempt of traditional philosophy

> to say . . . what *makes* certain sentences true, or certain actions or attitudes good or rational, is, on this view, impossible.
>
> It is the impossible attempt to step outside our skins—the traditions, linguistic and other, within which we do our thinking and self-criticism—and compare ourselves with something absolute. (Rorty, 1987, p. 33)

Rorty (1979) characterizes mainstream philosophers and their historic quest for foundations as "systematic" and contrasts them with "edifying" philosophers who, although perhaps influential, do not establish a "tradition" of thought—and in that sense remain more on the periphery of philosophy (pp. 367–368). He remarks that the latter, including figures such as Goethe, Kierkegaard, William James, and the "later" Wittgenstein and Heidegger, have often been labeled as relativistic or cynical: They would see it as their task to remain skeptical about the claims associated with systematic philosophy (p. 367). Therefore, while systematic philosophers are "constructive and offer arguments," edifying philosophers "are reactive and offer satires, parodies, aphorisms" (p. 369). They also "refuse to present themselves as having found out any objective truth (about, say, what philosophy is)" (p. 370), and are often accused by systematic philosophers of not being philosophers at all.

Although he is consistent in championing the function of the edifying philosopher, Rorty's (1979) argument makes it clear that the two roles are interrelated. That is, edifying philosophers would not exist in the absence of the systematic viewpoints which they critique, and "their work loses its point when the period they were reacting against is over" (p. 369). According to Carr (1992), some of Rorty's work presents the more radical thesis that we should not attempt to preserve the reciprocal relationship between these two forms of philosophizing, and that "Philosophy," meaning systematic philosophy, should be completely abandoned (p. 93). This kind of thinking represents "Rorty's entrance ticket to the halls of deconstruction" (p. 94), and leads Baynes, Bohman, and McCarthy (1987) to place Rorty's work in a section entitled, "The End of Philosophy."

Knowledge and the End of Metanarratives

Jean-François Lyotard's (1984) assessment of the status of knowledge in the modern world, *The Postmodern Condition: A Report on Knowledge,* has itself been instrumental in the wider use of this term to describe our cultural predicament. Like Derrida and Rorty, he emphasizes the limitations of knowledge and the inherent constraints of philosophical inquiry, but does so in a language which has an affinity for certain developments in the world of psychotherapy.

Lyotard (1984), like Feyerabend, critiques the dominance of science as a form of knowledge but frames his argument differently through the introduction of the concept of "narrative knowledge" (p. 18). For Lyotard, all forms of knowledge, including science, are inherently narrative in nature. A narrative is the basic form of "customary knowledge" (p. 19) and essentially tells a story. Such narratives attain their "legitimacy" or validity in the culture in a natural or intrinsic fashion—that is, what is judged "good" or "correct" by the community is transmitted through the narratives. Whether the form of the narrative is a "primitive" myth, a nursery rhyme, or a popular saying or proverb, the existence of this kind of knowledge "makes it possible to distinguish one who knows from one who doesn't (the foreigner, the child)" and defines "the culture of a people" (p. 19).

Like Rorty, Lyotard uses Wittgenstein's (1953) notion of "language games" to develop his understanding of narrative knowledge. Human utterances are governed by rules which define their functions and properties in the same fashion that the rules of chess specify the properties (the moves) of the different pieces. As was implied in the above paragraph, these rules "do not carry within themselves their own legitimation" (Lyotard, 1984, p. 10). As products of a social contract or agreement, they may remain largely implicit; nevertheless, they must be known and observed by the players, or else there is no game.

This background is preparatory to Lyotard's (1984) chronicle of the sleight of hand that science has performed in establishing its own claims to secure knowledge while critiquing any like claims of the narrative tradition. First, traditional or narrative approaches to knowledge are characterized by science as "fables, myths, legends, fit only for women and children" (p. 27). Second, the narrative components of scientific knowledge are ignored, denying that science, too, is a "language game" which is the product of a social contract. Third, and related to point two, science seeks to legitimate itself by an appeal to an unquestioned grand scheme which actually constitutes a "metadiscourse" or "metanarrative" (pp. xxiii–xxiv). Thus, the metanarrative of modern science, as it is transmitted through the popular media, frequently includes a character and plot such as the struggling scientist, often working alone, who resolutely brushes aside societal superstitions and heroically pursues the scientific method to reach objective truth.

Lyotard uses the metanarrative to demarcate modern and postmodern accounts of knowledge. A modern approach to knowledge, whether metaphysical, scientific, economic, or political in nature, is one which attempts to legitimate itself through the appeal to some metanarrative. On the other hand, the postmodern, in Lyotard's well-known phrase, involves "incredulity toward metanarratives" (p. xxiv).

This postmodernist abandonment of metanarratives leads Lyotard to a position of incommensurability which is defined in much more absolute terms than in Kuhn's theory. Different language games, including those associated with scientific knowledge and narrative knowledge, are incommensurable, and the validity of the latter cannot be judged by the criteria of the former. How, then, are judgments about different forms of knowledge to be made? Lyotard cryptically remarks: "All we can do is gaze in wonderment at the diversity of discursive species, just as we do at the diversity of plant or animal species" (p. 26). He is saying here that there are no universal criteria for determining what constitutes knowledge, since such criteria would themselves reflect another illusory metanarrative. Consequently, we arrive at a pluralistic view of knowledge where all discourse, argumentation, and legitimization are "local" in nature: "Any consensus on the rules defining a game and the 'moves' playable within it *must* be local, in other words, agreed on by its present players and subject to eventual cancellation" (p. 66).

Knowledge and the Dissolution of the Autonomous, Coherent Self

What has been described as the "linguistic turn" in philosophy is certainly obvious in the work of Derrida, Rorty, and Lyotard, and the pivotal role of language in postmodern thought has direct implications for the issue of the subject or self. If the self is defined as a stable, autonomous, coherent core of experience, it is not stretching the point to say that a postmodernist or linguistic analysis ultimately leads to the dissolution of this self.

Haber (1994) maintains that the self, for Lyotard, is given or constituted by the "social bond" whose medium is language. Since language does not refer to a "monolithic discourse" but to a heterogeneous collection of games and elements, "there is no reason to believe that . . . we can establish stable self-identities" (p. 9). This means that the self is "essentially fragmented, decentered, protean, and incomplete" (pp. 13–14). Polkinghorne (1992) agrees with this portrayal, citing "fragmentariness" as one of the four themes which he associates with a postmodern epistemology. Whether speaking of knowledge claims as a whole or the specific issues of the self, the postmodernist emphasizes "differences and uniqueness," and any attempt to "totalize" through the imposition of a single, unitary understanding does violence to the diverse and indeterminate nature of that which it would describe or explain (pp. 149–150).

How does one reconcile this viewpoint with the concrete experience of having a stable, coherent self? The notion of a "self" or "subject" can itself be likened to the existence of a metanarrative. Although this self can be experienced individually and psychologically, and definitely is buttressed by social and cultural assumptions, it has no real existence. This is the point that Cushman was making within a different idiom in the last chapter. The "bounded, masterful self," however robust its appearance in the individual or the culture, is actually a fiction.

Of course, most skeptical postmodernists would not lament the dissolution, disappearance, or "death" of the bounded, coherent self (Rosenau, 1992, pp. 42–44). Affirmative postmodernists, however, hold a more complex view of the issue: While they, too, typically applaud the demise of the coherent, autonomous self, they may offer arguments for the emergence of a new self—or rather new "selves." This postmodernist self "will not be same subject who was banished, and s/he will not take on a single form or personality. . . . S/he will be a decentered subject, an 'emergent' subject, unrecognizable by the modernists, empiricists, and positivists" (Rosenau, 1992, p. 57).

Manifestations of this philosophical viewpoint frequently appear in contemporary psychological and psychotherapeutic approaches. The "essential" self is rejected and replaced with a form of identity which is "protean" (Lifton, 1993), "relational" (H. Anderson, 1997), or "narrative" (Freedman & Combs, 1996). The psychologist-cum-popular philosopher Kenneth Gergen (1991) has provided what is perhaps the definitive psychological portrait of this new multiple self:

> In the postmodern world there is no individual essence to which one remains true or committed. One's identity is continuously emergent, re-formed, and redirected as one moves through the sea of ever-changing relationships. In the case of "Who am I?" it is a teeming world of provisional possibilities. (p. 139)

Lyotard's "just society" is a clear example of this affirmative postmodernist redefinition of the self. His society values multiplicity and incommensurability and allows "the invention and expression of new selves, and guards against terroristic moves which would force conformity and belittle inventive and even contradictory forms of expression" (Haber, 1994, pp. 29–30). While this society would be liberating to those groups whose voices previously were silenced or marginalized, Haber asks how it could lead to community in the absence of any consensus—since consensus is defined by Lyotard only in negative (terroristic) terms. She wonders if it is not possible to "have an idea of consensus which at the same time respects multiplicity" (p. 38) but concludes that Lyotard has not provided it. Similarly, Lifton (1993) separates himself from those "who equate multiplicity and fluidity with disappearance of the self, with a complete absence of coherence among its various elements" (pp. 8–9). Proteanism—his characterization of the multiple self—involves "a balancing act between responsive shapeshifting, on the one hand, and efforts to consolidate and cohere, on the other" (p. 9).

Knowledge as Power

While Michel Foucault, like Derrida, never himself relied on the term (Bernstein, 1992, p. 11), his approach to knowledge is frequently utilized in postmodernist critiques of societal practices, including those associated with psychology (Richer, 1992) and mental health (Parker et al., 1995). In the context of this review, Foucault can be seen as extending the implications of the linguistic analysis presented thus far through anchoring it much more firmly in a historical and sociopolitical context.

In his earlier work, Foucault (1973) designates his approach to knowledge as "archaeological" and contrasts it with the "epistemological" (p. xiii). This contrast emphasizes his interest in unearthing the hidden dimensions of the systems of knowledge which he studies. It also signals his lack of interest in the question of the actual truth or falsity of these knowledge systems, although he is intently focused on how they attempt to establish their presumed truth.

In later works, Foucault (1978, 1979) follows Nietzsche's lead and describes his approach to analyzing knowledge as "genealogical." This shift came from the realization that any analysis of human discourse must be grounded in actual, accepted social or cultural "practices," which "possess up to a point their own specific regularities, logic, strategy, self-evidence, and 'reason'" (Foucault, 1987, pp. 102–103). Therefore, his analysis takes the familiar, seemingly "given" practices and objects of individual and cultural experience—for example, aspects of the body and self such as sexuality, social institutions such as prisons and schools, or "scientific norms" such as sanity and insanity—and demonstrates their status as forms of knowledge which are historically, politically, and socially situated (Haber, 1994, p. 79).

Foucault's investigations are frequently guided by those historical moments when events and phenomena which are not necessarily in the nature of things are transformed into that which is obvious, self-evident, and unquestioned. Thus, "it wasn't as a matter of course that mad people came to be regarded as mentally ill; it wasn't self-evident that the only thing to be done with a criminal was to lock him up" (Foucault, 1987, p. 104).

He uses this aspect of his method to contrast his genealogical approach with that of the historian or sociologist who might ask, for example, what social norms govern sexual behavior during a particular historical and cultural period. For Foucault (1987), such a question reveals the social scientist's own assumptions: It is taken for granted that there is a domain called "sexuality" which can be studied, perhaps in relationship to "repression." But Foucault is interested in the prior question of just how a discourse emerged and how a domain of experience became constituted, in concrete historical, social, and political terms, which would only much later be termed "sexuality" (p. 116).

Foucault argues that power is inherent in the process which transforms a domain of human experience into that which can be labeled as above, whether as "sexuality," "sanity," or "delinquency." In so doing, he extends the concept of power from one that depends on a top-down exercise of brute control to the bottom-up, subtle manifestations that are associated with "modern power" (Fraser, 1989, p. 22). Modern power cannot be divorced from language and its categories, whereby cultural definitions of sexuality or sanity become self-evident constituents of the self. In that regard, Foucault employs the metaphor that modern power is *capillary*—"The economic changes of the eighteenth century made it necessary to ensure the circulation of effects of power through progressively finer channels, gaining access to individuals themselves, to their bodies, their gestures and all their daily actions" (Foucault, 1980, pp. 151–152). Through this means, modern power becomes pervasive and omnipotent and, by wearing the mask of knowledge and truth, "normalizes" individual and social experience. Its agents include "social scientists, social workers, psychiatrists, doctors, teachers, and the ordinary citizen who internalizes the categories and values of the power regime" (Haber, 1994, p. 81).

While Foucault is no fan of "deconstructionism" or, for that matter, any simple categorization of his views or approach, it is easy to understand why some of his supporters have applied that interpretation to his work. Rather than restricting deconstruction to the analysis of texts, broadly considered, there is an increasing tendency to apply it to social situations (Richer, 1992; Parker, et al., 1995), and Foucault's focus on power lends itself to sociopolitical analysis of this kind. Richer, writing as a skeptical postmodernist on the development of a deconstructionist psychology, describes it as "a pessimistic activism that expects to find domination and control in the most innocent places, especially in the innocent places. Like the innocent places of the 'reformed' mental health system" (p. 116).

However, like Derrida, Foucault does not give much direction to those who would like to act upon his analyses of the ubiquity of modern power. His notable statement that everything is "dangerous" but not necessarily "bad" (Foucault, 1980) implicitly conveys his disinclination to make moral or ethical judgments. While Foucault's method seems intent on merely describing modern power, Nancy Fraser (1989) sees his rhetoric of "domination" and "subjugation" as implying that we should struggle to free ourselves from its grasp (p. 29). Yet, he does not provide any criteria that would allow one to distinguish "acceptable from unacceptable forms of power" (p. 33).

Bernstein (1992), in reviewing more sympathetic readings of Foucault's intent, characterizes his strength as "a radical questioning and a withholding and suspending of judgment" which itself is an "ethical stance," linking skepticism with freedom (p. 161). For example, Haber (1994) sees Foucault as providing "tools" of analysis for those who are struggling against power, without offering suggestions for *what* should be done. Yet, like Fraser, Bernstein (1992) can point to statements where Foucault is "tempting us with his references to new possibilities of thinking and acting," and these promises can be seen as creating a problem for his position (p. 162). Unless such statements are "empty," it is not possible to talk of new possibilities or changes without broaching the issue of what is *"desirable"* (pp. 162–163), and, in keeping with a skeptical postmodernist outlook, Foucault refuses to take this step.

POSTMODERNIST IMPLICATIONS FOR NIHILISM AND RELATIVISM

Looking back over the realist and anti-realist positions which have been reviewed, the former assumes that *either* there is an unshakable foundation for truth *or* the only option is chaos (relativism) and resulting despair (nihilism). Anti-realist thinkers reject this "Either/Or" position, and the nature, as well as the successes and failures, of their attempts to transcend it will now be further examined.

Skeptical Postmodernism and Nihilism

Before asking how postmodern thinkers respond to the question of nihilism, it is important to consider what this ambiguous, provocative term might connote. Karen Carr (1992) reviews different meanings of nihilism, and three of her definitions are most relevant to the present discussion. *"Alethiological nihilism"* denies that truth exists, while *"epistemological nihilism"* denies that knowledge exists (p. 17). Carr indicates that these forms of nihilism are not synonymous unless one defines knowledge as "justified true belief" (p. 17). For example, if knowledge is defined as beliefs which meet certain criteria of a particular group or community, then it is possible to deny that truth exists while claiming that knowledge does. *"Existential nihilism"* is the more common use of the term and refers to negative feelings such as those of meaninglessness or emptiness which are associated with the judgment "Life has no meaning" (p. 18).

In the context of these interrelated concepts, it is possible to understand in a different manner the "Either/Or" of realist and foundationalist positions. These thinkers do not differentiate between alethiological and epistemological nihilism, since the only real knowledge is true belief. Further, they associate anything less than the possibility of true belief with existential nihilism: The loss of secure foundations must lead to meaninglessness and despair. On the other hand, postmodernists break the connection between either alethiological or epistemological nihilism and its existential consequences. They may deny that either truth or knowledge is possible but, unlike their nineteenth-century predecessors such as Nietzsche, associate this development, not with a crisis in human affairs, but with either a stifled yawn or mild euphoria.

Thus, Rorty (1979, 1991) believes that the preoccupation with finding secure foundations for knowledge has simply been a waste of time and can't imagine why anyone would mourn its loss. It will be replaced with an "ironic" sensibility where individuals do not take themselves too seriously because they are "always aware that the terms in which they describe themselves are subject to change" (Rorty, 1989a, pp. 73–74). Similarly, Lyotard (1984) tells us that "lamenting the 'loss of meaning' in postmodernity" (p. 26) is a misunderstanding and that the abandonment of metanarratives actually represents an opportunity for personal and cultural emancipation. We should welcome the radical pluralism which will replace the impossible quest for foundations because "postmodern knowledge . . . refines our sensitivity to differences and reinforces our ability to tolerate the incommensurable" (p. xxv). Gergen (1994) seems to follow such thinking in declaring that a psychology reformulated on postmodernist principles could "mean not the loss of self but its enrichment" (p. 415). Finally, while Derrida is less sanguine about the consequences of deconstructionism, his approach leaves us with nothing but the "freeplay" of the text: "the endless play of signifiers devoid of decidable meaning which makes of reading itself not interpretation aiming at truth but free, parodying play" (Madison, 1991, p. 123).

The title of the previously cited work by Carr (1992), *The Banalization of Nihilism: Twentieth-Century Responses to Meaninglessness,* gives away her consternation with postmodern responses to nihilism. While she focuses specifically on Rorty, who as an affirmative postmodernist rejects truth but claims the existence of knowledge, her analysis applies even more powerfully to the position of the skeptical postmodernist. Skeptical postmodernists deconstruct any conception of either truth *or* knowledge but, quite consistently with their assumptions, see absolutely no reason to bemoan the loss of something which could never have existed anyway. Yet, Carr sees some problematic consequences of this postmodern tendency to regard nihilism as "in three short words, no big deal" (p. 131).

Carr (1992) believes that something important is lost in denying that existential nihilism poses an intellectual, moral, and emotional struggle for human understanding. For example, Friedrich Nietzsche, within philosophy, and Karl Barth, within theology, regarded nihilism as provoking a profound crisis of meaning in their domains of knowledge, and this crisis, in both instances, served to take each of these thinkers to a deeper understanding of the human condition. While Nietzsche likened nihilism to a "disease" through which we might "perish" (p. 124), he saw it as a necessary stage in development which could lead to a more authentic experience of the world (p. 128). For Barth, our inability to know provokes a painful, existential crisis, but this state is "the precondition of genuine religious faith" (p. 127). Rorty eliminates all need for a struggle by concluding that absolute truth never existed and that there is no loss to regret—but the potential benefit of a clash between the urge for truth and the recognition of its impossibility is eliminated as well.

Carr's point can be made in a more general fashion through a brief comparison of postmodernism and existentialism as philosophical positions. Certainly, the latter has its own definitional problems—for example, although Martin Heidegger is usually regarded as "a founder of Existentialism" (Honderich, 1995, p. 345), he, in fact, rejected this label (D. E. Cooper, 1990). Yet, it is generally understood that this term has no meaning at all if we cannot at least apply it to Heidegger and Sartre (D. E. Cooper, 1990, p. 6), and Carr (1992) would add Karl Jaspers and Albert Camus to this short list (p. 2).

Interestingly, D. E. Cooper (1990) positions existentialism within a larger current of thought, including "American pragmatists, the later Wittgenstein, and contemporary deconstructivists," which may well define the "distinctive direction of twentieth-century philosophy" (p. viii). All of these thinkers, postmodernist and existentialist alike, reject the possibility of foundational, representational knowledge and its associated assumption of an isolated, "internal" self that somehow obtains such knowledge of an "external" world. As will become more apparent in the later discussion of neopragmatism, it is in this sense that Rorty is indebted to the edifying existentialist writers who preceded him (p. viii).

On the other hand, as Carr illustrates, existentialists part company with postmodernists in their emphasis on the centrality of existential nihilism to the human experience. The human condition juxtaposes a being who must seek meaning with a world which is "silent," that is, unable to provide any firm ground for belief, leading to the "absurd" (Camus, 1991) or to "the experience of nothingness" (Novak, 1971). In turn, approaching existential nihilism or nothingness brings one closer to the experience of "terror. . . . a kind of death, an inertness, a paralysis. . . . a desert-like emptiness, a malaise, an illness of the spirit and the stomach" (p. 11). Therefore, as in Yalom's (1980) account of existential therapy, existentialist philosophers assume that living a full human life means confronting the "givens of existence" or "ultimate concerns" of death, freedom, isolation, and meaninglessness (p. 8, italics omitted).

Nonetheless, most existentialists agree with Camus (1991) "that even within the limits of nihilism it is possible to find the means to proceed beyond nihilism" (p. v). As with Barth and Nietzsche, the problem of "existence" offers human beings an opportunity for growth through exercising choice and taking responsibility. Sartre, despite his bleak philosophical pronouncements, often created fictional characters who "discover something to live *for* and something to live *by*" (Yalom, 1980, p. 428). Speaking more generally, D. E. Cooper (1990) maintains that existentialists emphasize the importance of struggling against the Cartesian split between subject and object in the daily conduct of one's life (p. viii), and provide philosophical analyses and ethical guidelines which will help us to move in this direction. Therefore, with their emphasis on acknowledging, confronting, and moving beyond nihilism, existentialists provide a contrast to the views of skeptical postmodernists and offer an alternative which affirmative postmodernists might consider.

A final commentary on the postmodernist stance toward nihilism comes from a tradition completely removed from Western philosophy. It could be argued that the Buddha was "the first deconstructionist" (Zwieg, 1995, p. 145), who anticipated by some 2500 years the postmodern view that the coherent, stable self is an illusion. However, Buddhism assumes that the forces which prevent recognition of this understanding are formidable. It is in the nature of the ego / self to assume and defend its stability and coherence, and this clinging to the experience of separateness can be likened to "a spiritual disease" (Buddhadāsa Bhikkhu, 1994, p. 11). Typically, this disease cannot be cured by a simple exposure to "right thinking"—that is, the intellectual or philosophical view that the self is illusory. Rather, the meditation practices of Buddhism have developed over the millennia because the struggle between that disease and right thinking must be joined on an experiential level. This engagement often entails a wrenching cognitive and emotional battle between forces associated with meaning and meaninglessness. From a Buddhist perspective, the postmodernist attempt to cure the foundationalist assumptions of the human being through a simple adjustment of intellectual categories is itself illusory.

Affirmative Postmodernism and Relativism

From the perspective of the "Either/Or" of foundationalist or realist accounts of knowledge, the postmodernist positions reviewed in this chapter all represent some form of relativism. Derrida and Foucault, as representative skeptical postmodernists, take a stance of extreme relativism: They reject any possibility of truth and provide us with no criteria for choosing among different forms of knowledge, whether defined as interpretations of a text or as power arrangements. Of course, Lyotard and Rorty also reject the possibility of truth and would never posit universal criteria by which knowledge claims could be evaluated. However, as affirmative postmodernists they do assume that knowledge claims can be made—for Lyotard it is in reference to the standards of the "local" community and for Rorty it is in relation to "pragmatic" grounds which include the purposes of a particular group.

From the vantage point of foundationalism or realism, the position of the affirmative postmodernists is no less relativistic, since it defines knowledge in relation to the views of a social group. The postmodernist retorts that this view presupposes that knowledge could be evaluated in relation to some "objective," nonsocial standard which can never exist, and the "relativism" that is being seen here is entirely the creation and the problem of the foundationalist agenda (Lather, 1992, p. 99). One might note that the nature of this debate closely parallels the earlier contrast between scientific realism and Kuhnian, socially mediated science.

Does relativism actually exist or is it simply in the eye of the beholder? While this question might initially appear of interest only to those caught in obscure, academic debates, it does have quite direct implications for what social philosophers call "praxis." Praxis is the Greek word for "action," and was originally used by Aristotle to refer to "doing" something. It later became associated with political philosophy and ideology, particularly that associated with Marxism (Honderich, 1995, p. 713).

The issue of the relationship between relativism and praxis becomes, therefore, a crucial question for those postmodernists who are interested in taking action of any kind. If there are no universals which guide knowledge, how do we decide among alternative interpretations of a text, narrative, or human life when it is important to do so? By the same token, how do postmodernists who are interested in challenging contemporary cultural understandings of gender, sexual identity, race, or class take a stance in a postmodern context where no position is privileged? For example, while a postmodern analysis of power/knowledge structures could support a feminist position, "relativistic assumptions of a free play of meaning . . . are of little use for those struggling to free themselves from normalizing boundaries and categories" (Lather, 1992, p. 100). Accordingly, the possibility of taking a position that includes action is a pivotal issue for affirmative postmodernists, and is inherently relevant to psychotherapists—who, by definition, are involved with both theory and practice.

When postmodern philosophers and psychotherapists are challenged regarding the grounds for their choices and actions, they frequently turn to one of two positions in the literature: *philosophical hermeneutics* and *neopragmatism*.

Philosophical Hermeneutics

Philosophical hermeneutics and postmodernism have both their areas of agreement and disagreement, and these are succinctly conveyed by the title of Hans-Georg Gadamer's (1975) major work, *Truth and Method*. On the one hand, his reference to "method" is actually the opposite of what it seems, for he rejects the very notion of a method (Outhwaite, 1990) and defines an epistemological position which is as anti-foundational in some ways as that of any skeptical postmodernist. On the other hand, the "truth" in his title reveals an ontological position which represents a form of "hermeneutic realism" (Richardson, 1998), suggesting that nonrelativistic meaning can be found despite the absence of an objective method. Understandably, some affirmative postmodernists, who "reject universal truth" but "accept the possibility of specific local, personal, and community forms of truth" (Rosenau, 1992, p. 80), are intrigued by hermeneutic thinking.

Therefore, philosophical hermeneutics will be presented and evaluated in this chapter solely from the vantage point of its success in providing an alternative to postmodernist assumptions. Given the current influence of hermeneutics on many intersubjective, narrative, and dialogical approaches to psychotherapy, this philosophical position will be explored in greater detail when the therapeutic frameworks of Donna Orange, Philip Cushman, and Harlene Anderson are discussed in chapters 4 and 6.

Following Heidegger, it is not Gadamer's intention to replace the methods of knowing of the natural sciences or to create a new methodology for the human or social sciences. Instead, he wants to demonstrate that hermeneutics, defined as interpretative understanding, is basic to all human activity (Baynes, Bohman, & McCarthy, 1987, pp. 319–320). The act of understanding is a universal one, and he reveals its constituents by focusing on the example of how one interprets a text. Equating the interpreter with the "subject" and the text with the "object," Gadamer argues that the interpretation which results is neither subjective nor objective in nature. Like the postmodernists, Gadamer does not believe that a hard-and-fast line can be drawn between subject and object. Both are situated by language and history, and each influences and co-constitutes the other in every moment of their encounter (p. 320).

His view of the subject's contribution to the interpretation is crucial to his account and initially seems quite compatible with postmodern notions. We bring "prejudgments" or "prejudices" to the encounter with the object which will influence what is seen in the text. These prejudgments, in turn, are the manifestation of the language, culture, and history in which we are immersed. Since we can never escape these influences, objectivity in interpretation—that is, capturing the intent of the author or the one true meaning of the text—is out of the question.

However, in Warnke's (1987) view, Gadamer goes beyond postmodern skepticism when he turns the above argument around and contends that "our prejudices are as much thresholds as limits, that they form perspectives from which a gradual development of our knowledge becomes possible" (p. 4). How does Gadamer transform prejudice into the ground for understanding?

Gadamer addresses this question by borrowing the concept of the "hermeneutic circle" from his predecessors such as Friedrich Schleiermacher and Wilhelm Dilthey. There is a unity or internal coherence to the text which represents the "whole," and the prejudgments we bring to it represent a necessary starting point constituting a "part" understanding (Warnke, 1987, p. 83). A back-and-forth movement then ensues between part and whole, where the text's internal consistency guides the interpretation in the direction of an integrated whole. This aspect of Gadamer's approach can be likened to what has been called the "coherence theory of truth" wherein a "statement is true if it 'coheres' with other statements—false if it does not" (Honderich, 1995, p. 140).

The internal coherence which is ascribed to the text could still be overly determined by the historical tradition within which the interpretation has been made, and more is required of us to minimize "misunderstanding." Therefore, Gadamer now shifts the burden to the interpreter who must approach the text with the conviction that it is "true," meaning that it has something to teach us which will alter our own categories and initial understanding—that is, our prejudices (Warnke, 1987, pp. 86–87). The point here is that one does not always adopt the views of the text, since there are texts or objects whose claims may no longer appear plausible, for example, *Mein Kampf*. Nonetheless, it is crucial that we approach the text with an attitude of *"openness"* to its *"possible"* truth, which represents the basic precondition for real understanding (p. 89).

Clearly, Gadamer has not provided us with a formal "method" but has told us what "attitude" to take to the encounter with the text: an attitude which combines a willingness to acknowledge our own prejudices with a receptivity to the truth which the text might reveal (M. Freeman, 1993, pp. 141–142). Furthermore, the process of understanding resulting from this attitude is necessarily open-ended and never reaches finality (Bernstein, 1983, p. 139). The prejudgments and prejudices that influence our interpretations continue to change in interaction with both history and the object of interpretation, which then sets up yet another turn of the hermeneutic circle.

Gadamer compares the optimal encounter between a text, having its own potential truth, and an interpreter, bringing prejudices of one's time and place, to dialogical understanding. "Genuine conversation" recognizes one's own fallibility, the concrete historical situation within which one is immersed, and the possible contribution to further understanding that the other might offer (Warnke, 1987, p. 100). Again, this means that the different participants in a conversation neither cling to nor simply desert their positions. Through a clash of differences, in which each participant challenges and weighs the validity of one's own position and that of the other, a view emerges which represents a transformation of those individual positions—and which holds more truth than that which began the dialogue (p. 101). Thus, genuine conversation and genuine understanding are one and the same. Both reflect an ethical stance, characterized by a deep "respect" for and "devotion" to what the other might offer to our understanding of the world (M. Freeman, 1993, p. 143).

Of course, skeptical postmodernists would find several problems with Gadamer's position. Not only would deconstructionists suggest that Gadamer overestimates the inherent coherence of the text (Warnke, 1987, p. 83), but they also might argue that his characterization of the possible "truth" of the text contradicts his own anti-foundational views.

If the hermeneutic task is not to capture the one true meaning of the text, what is this "truth" of the text which allows for the give-and-take with the interpreter's categories? Bernstein (1983) concurs that it is curious that an author who places "truth" in his title never makes the term "thematic" and only discusses it briefly near the end of the book (p. 152).

Gadamer might respond to these criticisms by arguing that deconstruction cannot occur except in relation to some perceived coherence through which self-contradictions can then become evident (Warnke, 1987, p. 84). Further, while Gadamer's concept of truth remains elusive (Bernstein, 1983, p. 152), he could contend that it does not refer to some essential quality which exists "in" the text, but rather to a potentiality which emerges through the "fusion of horizons" of subject and object (Warnke, 1987, p. 103).

A more telling criticism of Gadamer comes from the tradition known as critical theory, which combines hermeneutics with a modified Marxist emphasis on social and economic factors (Woolfolk, Sass, & Messer, 1988, p. 21). While Jürgen Habermas (1977) sees philosophical hermeneutics as offering a valuable alternative to positivistic accounts of knowledge, he believes that Gadamer's approach underestimates the potential role of ideological factors in distorting understanding. Warnke (1987) illustrates Habermas's point by suggesting that women would not have been well served to approach the given societal texts on gender differences from the perspective of assuming their truth value. Such an approach, which is essential to Gadamer's hermeneutic attitude, would have only delayed the recognition that such texts hide and maintain inequitable power relations (p. 112).

Although Gadamer can handle this critique when the subject is aware of the distortion in the object, that is, the previous example of *Mein Kampf,* Habermas is concerned with just those situations where the ideological impact is insidious and invisible. For such situations, Gadamer's hermeneutic approach must be complemented by what Habermas calls a "reference system" or "critical theory" of society which more explicitly considers issues related to power and economics (Warnke, 1987, p. 116). Such a theory would define the ideal situation for understanding as one of "unconstrained communication": "All parties affected are able to examine disputed claims on an equal basis with equal chances to perform all kinds of speech acts and without fear of force or reprisal" (pp. 129–130). Gadamer sees this proposal as nonsensical because it rests on an ideal. Understanding can take place only in reference to the degree of present knowledge or openness which real people can muster in the concrete situations that face them, not in relation to some hypothesized ideal of absolute knowledge or "constraint-free consensus" (p. 130).

Bernstein (1983) formulates the above disagreement by returning to Gadamer's concept of truth and suggesting that it implicitly refers to the consensus of opinion regarding interpretation within a given community or tradition at a given time. Whether this interpretative tradition is "valid" or not depends in turn on the ability of that community to embody the communicative attitude and characteristics which Habermas wants to *prescribe* and which Gadamer simply *assumes*. Both thinkers realize that either dogmatism or relativism can be escaped only in relation to a community that values "the type of mutuality, sharing, respect, and equality required for a genuine dialogue" (p. 190). Bernstein asks rhetorically, "But what, then, is to be done in a situation in which there is a breakdown of such communities, and where the very conditions of social life have the consequences of furthering such a breakdown?" (p. 226).

Neopragmatism

Polkinghorne (1992) proposes that the three postmodern themes of "foundationlessness, fragmentariness, and constructivism . . . produce a negative epistemology," and he contrasts them with a fourth theme, "neopragmatism," which can provide criteria for judgments and actions (p. 151). It represents a contemporary form of pragmatism which "denies the possibility of universal conceptions of truth or reality" and defines knowledge in relation to a social and practical context (Honderich, 1995, p. 614). Rorty has been the foremost spokesperson for this position within postmodernist circles, and his views and criticisms of them will be briefly discussed.

Rorty falls within the tradition of American pragmatism represented by William James and John Dewey, a viewpoint which can be likened to what is known as "instrumentalism" within the philosophy of science. Instrumentalism, unlike realism, does not assume that scientific theories describe the nature of reality, although they can serve as useful fictions for organizing observations and making predictions (Chalmers, 1982, pp. 146–147). For example, from an instrumentalist perspective, the forces postulated by Newtonian mechanics are not assumed to exist in reality but are regarded as useful devices for making accurate predictions about the movements of bodies in motion.

In Rorty's hands, pragmatism is not restricted to the scientific domain and becomes a general position toward knowledge that can replace the foundational philosophy which he rejects. He believes that any attempt to capture (capital T) Truth, defined as that which actually corresponds with reality, is futile. However, following James, he can define "truth" (knowledge) simply as those beliefs which "each of us . . . finds good to believe" (1989b, p. 11). Further, for a pragmatist, "good" opinion has necessarily attained that status by producing results which consistently meet the purposes of the individual or group in question.

Accordingly, knowledge is inherently linguistic, social, and purposeful in nature, and both the self and what we attribute to the world are open to indefinite reformulations, since human goals can be widely divergent. This embrace of radical pluralism, "ironism," or "perspectivism" in no way means that Rorty accepts relativism as its consequence (Haber, 1994, pp. 43–47). Relativism is a concern only for those who cling to a foundational position, trying to hold their "Cartesian Anxiety" at bay by seeking justification from nonexistent metanarratives.

Rorty (1989a) skillfully refuses to engage in debates which would replicate the very position which he is attacking. He does not offer a conventional argument in defense of his position, based on notions like "objectivity, neutrality, and justification," since this would require pretending that he can step outside of his own linguistic and social position (Haber, 1994, p. 46). Nevertheless, his perspectival position still must face the same question as Lyotard's: How does this position function in a pluralistic society characterized by a variety of social groups, language games, purposes, and subsequent versions of truth?

One of Rorty's (1989b) answers to this question depends on his valuing of science—a strategy which is not entirely surprising, since Rorty is a pragmatist and science clearly works. Of course, it is not that scientists are more "objective" or "logical" than anyone else. It is the social institutions that science has created which are valuable and can serve as "models for the rest of culture" (p. 15). Scientific communities embody practices and values that lead to "unforced agreement": They favor persuasion over force, respect the opinions of colleagues, and show curiosity and openness to new data (p. 15). Because scientific communities appropriately mix "unforced agreement with tolerant disagreement" (p. 17), they demonstrate the "solidarity" which other language communities would do well to emulate.

Rorty (1989a) offers a more direct response to the question of relativism through his description of the "liberal ironist" as the exemplar of anti-foundational, pragmatic knowing. A "liberal" is someone who believes "that cruelty is the worst thing we do" (p. xv), while an "ironist" knows that his or her own most central beliefs are *contingent* and do not refer "to something beyond the reach of time and chance" (p. xv). The concept of the "final vocabulary" further delineates the assumptions of the ironist. These are the words which individuals use "to justify their actions, their beliefs, and their lives," and they are "final" or ultimate in the sense that, when challenged, "their user has no noncircular argumentative recourse" (p. 73).

Therefore, Rorty (1989a) describes the ironist as someone who meets the following three conditions:

> (1) She has radical and continuing doubts about the final vocabulary she currently uses, because she has been impressed by other vocabularies, vocabularies taken as final by people or books she has encountered; (2) she realizes that argument phrased in her present vocabulary can neither underwrite nor dissolve these doubts; (3) insofar as she philosophizes about her situation, she does not think that her vocabulary is closer to reality than others, that it is in touch with a power not herself. (p. 73)

Within this context, Rorty as a "liberal ironist" can offer rational arguments for his own position only up to a point. For example, there is really no answer to the question, "Why not be cruel?" Any answer would be circular, not rational, in nature (1989a, p. xv). A liberal who would try to answer this question would be, in Rorty's view, not an ironist but a metaphysician.

What happens, therefore, when two different individuals or groups have contrary final vocabularies and visions of what is the good? What happens when there is sufficient incommensurability in viewpoints that solidarity does not really exist? Ultimately, the speaker—including Rorty and his philosophical recommendations—can only affirm his or her convictions and hope that the other will come around and be convinced. Rorty (1989a) acknowledges that this is a kind of "ethnocentrism," but argues that there are good and bad forms of ethnocentrism, and the better kind is associated with liberal ironists "who have been brought up to distrust ethnocentrism" (p. 198). If pressed further as to why his is a better form of ethnocentrism, Rorty would reply that the questioner is again attempting to extract some kind of metaphysical grounding for one's final vocabulary—a grounding which cannot exist. No one can escape being ethnocentric, and all we can choose are better or worse forms of ethnocentrism.

Rorty's position is a provocative one and has been critiqued by those representing all points on the philosophical and political spectrum.

Newton-Smith (1989), defending a realist position, finds it odd that Rorty would want painting, music, or poetry to emulate the solidarity of science, and sees this stance as going "well beyond the already extreme scientism of the positivists" (p. 38). Tomlinson (1989), writing as a fellow non-realist, believes that Rorty has not adequately addressed the question of diverse language communities and relativism. More importantly, both he and Bernstein (1992), who is sympathetic in many ways to Rorty, discern a kind of absolutism in his thinking.

While Rorty's position defines truth as relative to the group in question, Tomlinson (1989) argues there are in fact no "alternative truths" because of the difficulty of stepping outside the historically mediated final vocabulary which one's group has come to represent. Therefore, Rorty's position becomes an "absolute relativist" view of knowledge, since "Truth, *for us,* is as absolute as can be" (pp. 53–54). When Rorty attempts to arbitrate disagreements between language communities by appealing to his own final vocabulary of ironic liberalism or "liberal bourgeois democracy" he, too, becomes absolutist. While Rorty's liberal ironist may be ready to accept that the vocabulary of the Western social democratic tradition is the "best" that we have been able to find, Tomlinson argues that it is only one of many forms of rationality or justification, and one that many groups would resist (p. 54).

It is also not clear to Bernstein (1992) how Rorty has evaded the relativist objection, beyond his unwillingness to acknowledge it. Rorty's liberal ironist knows that there are alternative, incommensurable languages for describing reality, and that "there are no rational criteria for adjudicating rival vocabularies" (p. 279). Even if one calls this "contingency" instead of relativism, as Rorty would want, it is still a problem. Further, Bernstein does not see Rorty as practicing what he preaches. The liberal ironist is supposed to remain permanently doubtful about his or her final vocabulary, but Rorty never seriously questions his "commitment to liberal democracy" (p. 280).

A similar charge can be made against Lyotard. Kvale (1992b), who is sympathetic to postmodernism, indicates that Lyotard's critique of legitimizing narratives is paradoxical because his book can be read "as legitimizing a non-necessity of legitimation" (p. 33). Harris (1992), arguing against radical relativism of any kind, makes the same point: "Everything is relative to a multiplicity of language games except what Lyotard has to say about those language games. . . . Surely Lyotard's analysis of knowledge is as much a narrative account as are any that he criticizes" (p. 117). Both Rorty and Lyotard come up against the paradox which occurs when any relativistic position is universalized. A position which says that there is no truth becomes self-contradictory when, implicitly or explicitly, it makes its own claim to truth (Honderich, 1995, p. 757).

The Dialectic of Critique and Affirmation

While both hermeneutics and neopragmatism have much to offer in defining the nature of a non-foundational approach to knowledge, it is apparent from the above review that neither has completely put to rest the issue of relativism. Honi Fern Haber (1994), a philosopher who is interested in the relationship of postmodernism to "oppositional politics," draws confounded ethical and political implications from the work of Lyotard, Rorty, and Foucault. Bernstein's (1992) broader survey of "modernity/postmodernity," while having a less defined political agenda and employing different language, appears to come to a similar conclusion. I will combine their perspectives and state the ethical and political dilemma facing postmodernism as follows.

On the one hand, postmodern accounts of knowledge are radically deconstructive and pluralistic: There is no metanarrative, and the existence of differences in tradition, opinion, language, and justification must be allowed. Indeed, many postmodernists—Lyotard, for example—would see any movement toward consensus or unity as "terroristic." On the other hand, these approaches define knowledge as social, intersubjective, and dialogical in nature: to know is to know with and through others. How, then, can a focus on radical deconstructionism and pluralism be reconciled with the need for affirmation, communication, and dialogue?

Haber's (1994) resolution is to suggest that the postmodern emphasis on deconstruction, difference, and pluralism must coexist with a need for the existence of "structure." She argues that such structure is necessary for language and thought, much less for any "viable political theory" (p. 114). Her term refers to the coherence of self and consensus of opinion that together define a community and may even include, heaven forbid, "grand" narratives (p. 130) which promote a shared identity and political purpose. However, her view of the relation of deconstructionism and pluralism to structure is thoroughly postmodern in that "all structure is temporary and even artificial, and is always open to the possibility of being redescribed" (p. 114).

Bernstein (1992) seems to offer a similar argument although couched in a dialectical tradition. Hegel construes human thought and history in relation to a dialectical process where internal contradictions to a position first manifest and then are transcended, although that resolution itself gives rise to new contradictions which require further resolution (Honderich, 1995, p. 198). Of course, Hegel's belief that some final unity will emerge which could resolve all contradictions represents a metanarrative that is out of temper with "modernity/postmodernity" (Bernstein, 1992, pp. 307–309). Yet, an open-ended dialectic might prove useful in describing the relationship between critique and affirmation, pluralism and structure.

Critique is essential, but Bernstein cites Habermas and Derrida in support of the view that radical critique is inconceivable if it is not motivated by some affirmation, whether acknowledged or not. Without the possibility of affirmation,

> those who engage in a totalizing critique—where critique turns upon and undermines itself—are caught within a "performative contradiction" where they at once seek to practice critique and at the same time undermine the very possibility of critique. They consume "the critical impulse." (Bernstein, 1992, p. 317)

Thus, deconstruction/critique and affirmation require one another, and in a postmodern age where all of us are "participants" and not neutral observers, "our critiques and affirmations are always tentative, fallible, open to further questioning" (p. 319).

SUMMARY

It may not be obvious to the reader what implications for psychotherapy are to be drawn from a review which has considered such a diversity of philosophical positions, and the integration of these two domains will be explored quite concretely over the next two chapters. In time, the philosophical positions which have been outlined will become the building blocks for an understanding and formulation of the operating assumptions of practicing psychotherapists.

For now, this summary will return to the more general question which began the chapter: How does contemporary philosophy define the limits of what scientists and other human beings, including psychotherapists, *can* know? Toward that end, a comparison of four major positions which have been reviewed—scientific realism, sophisticated realism, sophisticated relativism, and anti-realism (postmodernism)—is provided in table 1.

Aside from naive realists of either the lay or scientific variety, the positions within the philosophy of science which were reviewed are all

TABLE 1

Philosophical Positions Regarding Truth

	Scientific Realism	Sophisticated Realism (Popper)	Sophisticated Relativism (Kuhn)	Anti-Realism (Postmodernism)
	Scientific truth is possible	Scientific truth isn't possible but our tested theories can approximate it	Scientific truth isn't possible but *scientific* communities can produce socially mediated knowledge	*Skeptical:* Neither truth nor knowledge is possible *Affirmative:* Truth is not possible but socially mediated knowledge can be produced by any language community
Affirmation Confirmation Scientific Method Fact-Theory Distinction Self-Object Distinction				Critique Disconfirmation Deconstruction "Facts" as constructed "Self" as constructed
	Theories can be proven	Theories can be falsified, and this process can lead to closer approximations to objective realty	Theories are not easily falsified because there is no clear-cut fact-theory distinction; however, they can be compared and evaluated if criteria are agreed upon	Scientific theories have no more truth or knowledge value than any other socially constructed belief system

"fallibilistic" in nature; they assume that "scientific knowledge-claims are invariably vulnerable and may turn out to be false" (Honderich, 1995, p. 267). Accordingly, Orange (1995) proposes a psychoanalytic epistemology wherein "we . . . hold our theories lightly, in a fallibilistic spirit" (p. 52).

However, with their questioning of the very possibility of objective or universal truth, Kuhn and the postmodernists go beyond a fallibilistic stance. Our present knowledge claims do not reflect the truth, and we will never be in a position to assert differently. At best, we will be able to make a claim to provisional knowledge as it meets the standards of a specific community, scientific or otherwise. Hermeneuticists, as well as some affirmative postmodernists, hold that socially mediated knowledge can still represent a form of dialogical "truth," but—just as with Rorty's neopragmatic concept of "contingent" knowledge—this linguistic shift does not solve the problem of relativism. Therefore, these philosophical positions pose a fundamental challenge to what can be known, including what can be known by scientists and psychotherapists, whose presumed status as knowers certainly provides them no privileged position regarding their knowledge claims.

Finally, the last section of this chapter hints that the relationship between realist and anti-realist views of knowledge may be more complex and interdependent than the supporters of either position might like to assume. The realist operates according to assumed beliefs and the non-realist questions all beliefs, but can the one exist without the other? Kuhn's statement that normal science and scientific revolutions are simply two sides of the same coin, and Haber's view that structure and deconstruction must coexist, are not irrelevant to this question. Bernstein answers the question more directly by underlining that affirmation and critique, knowing and not knowing, necessarily exist in a *dialectical* relationship to one another. It will become apparent in the following chapters that this perspective toward knowledge has important consequences for our understanding of the philosophical grounds for psychotherapeutic practice.

Chapter 3

The Revelatory and Restrictive Functions
of Psychotherapeutic Theories

The task of relating the previously described philosophical positions to the presuppositions and practices of psychotherapists is a complex one. This chapter and the next will begin to explore this relationship by first examining the question on the level of theory. Do the philosophical positions have implications for our understanding of the *functions* of theory in psychotherapeutic practice, and do they encompass something of the *range* of theoretical assumptions which are currently available in this field?

Turning first to the question of function, I would argue that Kuhn's approach to the history and philosophy of science has particular relevancy to our understanding of the purposes served by theory in the realm of clinical practice. Because the application of Kuhn's approach to psychology has been so controversial, this issue must be briefly considered before attempting to establish a linkage.

MISAPPLICATIONS OF THE PARADIGM CONCEPT
TO THE HUMAN SCIENCES

Although Kuhn does not devote much attention to the human or social sciences, including psychology, he observes that debates about their scientific status tend to focus on the question of the proper "definition" of science. He believes that this focus may be misplaced because the problems facing such disciplines do not disappear "when a definition is found, but when the groups that now doubt their own status achieve consensus about their past and present accomplishments" (1970a, p. 161). He does underline that such debates "have parallels in the pre-paradigm periods of fields that are today unhesitatingly labeled science" (p. 160).

This characterization of the human sciences as "pre-paradigmatic" or as "proto-sciences" (1970c, p. 244) would seem to follow directly from his identification of science with the attainment of paradigm-guided, puzzle-solving, "normal" science. Disciplines which are marked by continuous "claims, counterclaims, and debates over fundamentals" (1970b, p. 6) and by "incessant criticism and continual striving for a fresh start" (1970c, p. 244) are not good candidates for paradigmatic status. He does acknowledge, however, that some murkiness lingers around the entire account of the development of sciences from their pre-paradigm to their post-paradigm periods. He describes his formulation, as it appears in SSR, as "too schematic," and highlights the following ambiguities: "Each of the schools whose competition characterizes the earlier period is guided by something much like a paradigm; there are circumstances, though I think them rare, under which two paradigms can coexist peacefully in the later period" (1970a, p. ix).

Given Kuhn's assessment of the current status of the human sciences, it is remarkable that psychologists (Coleman & Salamon, 1988; O'Donohue, 1993) and sociologists (Eckberg & Hill, 1980) have shown such enthusiasm for applying his thesis to their fields—and with so little agreement among themselves. For example, Eckberg and Hill report that "Kuhnian" analyses of sociology find this discipline to possess "anywhere from two to eight paradigms, depending on which analyst one chooses to cite" (p. 117). Valentine (1982) cites D. S. Palermo, who suggests that structuralism was psychology's original paradigm, and was succeeded by a behavioral paradigm and then by a linguistic / computer science paradigm (p. 87). Friman, Allen, Kerwin, and Larzelere (1993), employing a citation analysis, do not find support for the thesis that two older paradigms, behaviorism and psychoanalysis, are now being displaced by a cognitive paradigm. Valentine believes that "behaviourism comes as close to the notion of a paradigm as anything could" (p. 87), and, if it is to be displaced, its successor will not likely be a cognitive paradigm but a humanistic / phenomenological one.

At times it appears that the concept of "paradigm" can be stretched indefinitely to meet the purposes of anyone who takes a fancy to it. Thus, the term "paradigm shift" has been applied to a bewilderingly heterogeneous group of phenomena within psychology including the contrast between an older (medical) and newer (social psychological) approach to schizophrenia (Braginsky, Braginsky, & Ring, 1969), the clash between "straight" (ordinary) and "hip" (altered) states of consciousness (Tart, 1975, pp. 209–210), the displacement of a computer model for the brain by a holographic paradigm (Ferguson, 1982), and the movement from an internal, drive model to a relational model within psychoanalysis (Mitchell, 1988). As Gholson and Barker (1985) cautioned earlier, it is clear that when psychologists appropriate Kuhn's thesis and terminology, they typically are postulating "Kuhnian ideas," not necessarily "Kuhn's ideas."

Accordingly, Gutting (1980), Eckberg and Hill (1980), O'Donohue (1993), and Robins and Craik (1994) emphasize that social scientists who persist in offering Kuhnian accounts of the current status of their disciplines are contradicting central tenets of Kuhn's own analysis of the natural sciences. If so, what would motivate them to engage in this futile exercise? Gutting suggests that social scientists, by equating paradigms with "super-theories" such as Freudian psychology or functionalist sociology, are able to reassure themselves that their disciplines are indeed scientific (p. 13). Further, the competition between competing super-theories could be seen as a necessary developmental phase of these disciplines, rather than as an embarrassing lack of progress regarding agreement about fundamentals. However, as Eckberg and Hill observe within sociology, "the discovery of paradigms across the field of sociology has been made possible only by redefining the concept" (p. 130)—because Kuhnian science does not exist *until* consensus has been achieved. Robins and Craik argue that the citation data collected by Friman et al. (1993), which confirmed the continued robustness of three different paradigms or "subdisciplines" of psychology (behaviorism, psychoanalysis, and cognitivism), are most compatible with the conclusion that this field "may be better situated in a much earlier pre- or multiparadigmatic stage" (p. 815). It is not surprising that Gholson and Barker (1985), O'Donohue, and Friman et al. advise psychologists to look elsewhere in the history and philosophy of science than Kuhn for a model of scientific development which would fit their discipline.

KUHN'S HISTORY AND PHILOSOPHY OF
SCIENCE AS PSYCHOLOGY

Based on the above considerations, it would be foolhardy for me to join those who have attempted to reflect on the developmental level of psychology by drawing an analogy to Kuhn's analysis of the natural sciences. Yet, there is another sense in which I want to establish a link between his work and psychology—and he and others might object no less strongly to the "Kuhnian ideas" which I will now propose. Rather than attempting to apply Kuhn's thinking to psychology, I suggest that Kuhn has offered us a kind of psychology of his own.

There can be little disagreement that a crucial aspect of Kuhn's work is sociological or, better, social psychological in nature. When Kuhn (1970b) offers his own comparison of his work to that of Karl Popper, he argues that Popper's "logic of discovery" neglects what he would call the "psychology of research." Popper would like to remove the scientist as a social being from the scientific equation and focus only on those formal and logical elements of science by which scientists learn from their mistakes. Kuhn reaffirms the centrality of the professional community to which the scientist belongs, concluding that no scientific decisions can be made apart from one's socialization into a group. It is exactly Kuhn's emphasis on the sociology and social psychology of science that has led some critics to accuse him of reducing science to "mob rule."

My real interest, however, is not in Kuhn's sociological / social psychological thesis but in a more subtle aspect of his psychological thinking—one which forms something of a subtext to his overall argument. Closer to this theme, he acknowledges in the preface to SSR that he had been exposed to the work of Jean Piaget, to papers on perceptual psychology, especially those of the Gestalt psychologists, and to "B. L. Whorf's speculations about the effect of language on world view" (1970a, p. vi). It is easy to recognize the impact of both perceptual psychology and Whorfian ideas on the metaphors which Kuhn chooses to employ in his writing, particularly those which attempt to capture the struggles of scientists during periods of scientific revolution. He likens the movement from an old to a new paradigm to "a switch in visual gestalt. . . . What were ducks in the scientist's world before the revolution are rabbits afterwards" (1970a, p. 111). Indeed, throughout his argument, Kuhn most frequently employs the metaphor of how scientists "see the world" to describe the experience of operating within a given paradigm.

Kuhn's thinking in this area is perhaps best summarized by his citation and interpretation of a classic experiment from perceptual psychology. Bruner and Postman (1949) were interested in investigating the manner in which perception is influenced by observer variables such as "set or expectancy" (p. 207). Specifically, they wanted to demonstrate what occurs when expectancies are disconfirmed, and they hypothesized that subjects would deal with "incongruity" by warding off the perception of the unexpected as long as possible. This hypothesis was tested by using a tachistoscope to project playing cards for very brief exposures onto a screen and asking subjects to identify what they were seeing. Initially, the exposure times were so brief that subjects could only guess. As the exposure times increased, subjects began to correctly identify the cards, "It's the Ace of Hearts."

While most of the cards were "normal," some of the cards were "anomalous"—that is, the *red* six of spades or the *black* four of hearts. The data obtained are in support of the hypothesis: Normal cards were identified more quickly than anomalous cards, and only 89.7% of the anomalous cards were recognized at maximum exposure compared to 100% of the normal cards (pp. 210–211). The subjects' responses to incongruity, which the researchers placed in four different categories, are perhaps more interesting than the summary data. "Dominance" responses, which occurred for 27 of the 28 subjects, consisted of a "perceptual denial" of the incongruity. Presented with the red six of spades, the subject might report with no hesitation, "the six of hearts." "Compromise" responses seemed an attempt to forcibly integrate two percepts which didn't fit: The red six of spades was seen as "the purple six of spades or hearts" or as "black with red edges" (p. 216). "Disruption" seemed to occur when subjects had exhausted their perceptual repertoire for dealing with the incongruous stimulus: "I don't know what the hell it is now, not even for sure whether it's a playing card" (p. 214). Finally, "recognition" of incongruity occurred when the subject correctly identified the anomalous card.

Through presenting different orderings of the cards, Bruner and Postman were also able to demonstrate that it became easier for subjects to recognize incongruity once they had experience with even one previous anomalous card. "When one has experienced an incongruity often enough, it ceases to violate expectancy and hence ceases to be incongruous" (p. 211). Combining that finding with the subject responses to incongruity presented above, one typical sequence for subjects in the experiment could be described as follows. With increasing exposure times, the tendency to deny incongruity by simply incorporating a novel stimulus into one's usual categories is followed by a transitional period where there is a sense that there is something "wrong" (p. 220). Two different percepts might then be merged and/or uncertainty and confusion might be directly experienced. With increasing familiarity, a correct identification was made, and then other similar incongruous stimuli presented less of a problem. However, over 10% of the anomalous cards were never correctly identified even when exposed for a period roughly 40 times that required to obtain recognition for a normal card.

Kuhn (1970a) then offers the following commentary on this experiment's relevancy to his work as a historian of science:

> Either as a metaphor or because it reflects the nature of the mind, that psychological experiment provides a wonderfully simple and cogent schema for the process of scientific discovery. In science, as in the playing card experiment, novelty emerges only with difficulty, manifested by resistance, against a background provided by expectation. Initially, only the anticipated and usual are experienced even under circumstances where anomaly is later to be observed. Further acquaintance, however, does result in awareness of something wrong or does relate the effect to something that has gone wrong before. That awareness of anomaly opens a period in which conceptual categories are adjusted until the initially anomalous has become the anticipated. At this point the discovery has been completed. (p. 64)

Before attempting to draw out further the psychological implications of Kuhn's statement, it is useful to return briefly to the work of Paul Feyerabend, who has suggested a significant modification of Kuhn's thesis. Feyerabend (1970), following the work of Lakatos (1970), redefines Kuhn's contrast between normal and revolutionary science in the following manner. He equates normal science with the tendency of scientists to cling protectively to their positions and associates revolutionary science with the contrary inclination to allow for a proliferation of viewpoints. However, unlike Kuhn, who regards science as a "succession" of periods of normal science and revolutionary science, Feyerabend, like Lakatos, sees "proliferation and tenacity . . . always copresent" (p. 211, italics omitted). Feyerabend then replaces Kuhn's language of "periods" with that of "components" and contrasts a *normal* component with a *philosophical* component. The former assumes that science will advance most surely if one holds tenaciously to one's own framework and traces out its implications. For the latter, the advance of knowledge depends on a proliferation of viewpoints and a willingness to consider the advantages and claims of each. While the normal component may—and almost always does—dominate in a given period of science, one should not be blinded to the simultaneous existence of its counterpart. "For what we are investigating is not the size of a certain element of science, but its *function* (a single man can revolutionize an epoch)" (p. 213).

This Feyerabend-Lakatos modification of Kuhn is actually quite compatible with statements he makes in an interesting paper which was originally presented while the argument of SSR was still in progress. At a 1959 conference that addressed the relationship of "convergent" and "divergent" thinking to the identification of creative individuals, Kuhn linked this theme with an "essential tension" between "tradition" and "innovation" in science (1977, pp. 225–226). From his perspective, basic research discoveries are likely to come, not from those who solely value divergent thinking (flexibility and open-mindedness), but from those who also value convergent thinking (commitment to a consensus and tradition). He sees it as inevitable that these "two modes of thought" are in conflict (p. 226), and "very often the successful scientist must simultaneously display the characteristics of the traditionalist and of the iconoclast" (p. 227). Kuhn then clarifies this last statement by indicating that it is actually the scientific group or community as a whole that must embody these characteristics simultaneously, while individual scientists may differ in their propensities to be traditional or iconoclastic (pp. 227–228, footnote 2).

What psychological subtext to Kuhn's thinking am I attempting to extract for the reader from these several examples? Returning to his comparison of the playing card experiment to the process of scientific discovery, I would like to treat his summary statement very seriously. I believe that both that experiment and his own historical work may reveal something important about the "nature of the mind." Harvard/Radcliffe undergraduates in an experiment and natural scientists in the field both encode the world through what can be called, respectively, implicit or explicit theories which determine to a great extent what is "seen." These theories are conservative by nature, and the new tends to be seen in light of the old. Change does not result from any simple appeal to the "facts" that are before the undergraduate or the scientist, since the facts that are seen are in part determined by what the theory might allow. Yet, over time novelty does emerge and both implicit and explicit theories must change to accommodate it, and it is the tension between tradition and innovation which defines human thinking about the world.

COMPARISONS TO THE THEORIES OF
GEORGE KELLY AND CARL ROGERS

O'Donohue (1993) views Kuhn as quite unsophisticated regarding the psychological literature and charges that his sporadic use of psychological concepts is "informal" and "pedestrian" (p. 281). I agree that Kuhn's psychological thinking is largely implicit and informal in nature, yet I am struck by its parallels to contemporary developments within many areas of psychology including perceptual/cognitive psychology, social psychology, developmental psychology, personality theory, and psychotherapy.

By juxtaposing Kuhn's approach with selected aspects of the theories of Carl Rogers and George Kelly, the chapter goal of linking philosophical thinking with the functions of psychotherapeutic theories will now be specifically addressed. These particular theories have been chosen because of one formal similarity which crosscuts all three positions. One could argue that Kuhn has formulated a theory about the behavior of scientists, and Rogers and Kelly have proposed theories about the behavior of ordinary persons—while in some sense likening the ordinary person to a scientist constructing a theory about self and other.

Kelly's (1955, 1963) theory of personality and his selected papers (Maher, 1969) converge on the image of the human as a meaning-seeking, theory-building creature. Like scientists, ordinary persons make observations about the world, generate hypotheses from these observations, test out the hypotheses, and gradually build a largely implicit theory about the world which can be described as a system of "personal constructs" (Kelly, 1963). Once in existence, this personal construct system, like the scientist's more formal theory, allows the individual to predict and control the events of the world. This implies that one function of the personal construct system is inherently conservative; we anticipate the future based on what we have encountered in the past. Of course, personal constructs vary in their susceptibility to change, what Kelly calls their "permeability" (p. 79), and, optimally, ordinary persons would function much like Popper's view of the good scientist. That is, like Popper's scientist, ordinary persons would learn from their mistakes and selectively modify their personal constructs based on new information. Unlike the scientist's formal theory, however, Kelly allows for a good deal of inconsistency in personal construct systems through his "fragmentation corollary." The individual's constructs need not be logically derivable from one another: "It is possible that what Willie thinks today may not be inferred directly from what he was thinking yesterday" (p. 83). Nonetheless, the individual's personal construct system should function to allow for enough change so that there is neither stasis nor chaos in one's self-perception and perception of the world.

If the optimally functioning person has a personal construct system which neither becomes too rigid nor bends too much, then it follows that psychological problems may result when this balance is not obtained. For example, assume that an individual dichotomously views the world through a core construct of introversion-extroversion. He sees all of his siblings as extroverted, socially connected, and happy while he sees himself as introverted, socially isolated, and unhappy. If this person had come to Kelly for therapy, Kelly would not have assumed that the problem is necessarily "introversion." Rather, indirectly or directly, he would have attempted to loosen the hold that the *construct* of introversion has had on this client.

In one of his most engaging essays, Kelly (1958a / 1969) maintains that a statement such as "I am an introvert" typically mobilizes the listener to decide on its truth or falsity—that is, the speaker must be either right or wrong in this self-assessment:

> According to this dogmatism, when I say that Professor Lindzey's left shoe is an "introvert," everyone looks at his shoe as if this were something his shoe was responsible for. Or if I say that Professor Cattell's head is "discursive," everyone looks over at him, as if the proposition had popped out of his head instead of out of mine. Don't look at his head! Don't look at that shoe! Look at me; I'm the one who is responsible for the statement. After you figure out what I mean you can look over there to see if you make any sense out of shoes and heads by construing them the way I do. (p. 72)

Kelly observes that it will be exceedingly difficult to change this tendency because it means giving up an "ancient way of thinking and talking to ourselves" (p. 72).

As these statements imply, Kelly was perhaps more explicit about his philosophical presuppositions than any other therapist / scholar writing during the 1950s. He calls his philosophical position "constructive alternativism," and it assumes that "reality is subject to many alternative constructions, some of which may prove to be more fruitful than others" (1961 / 1969, p. 96). Like Kuhn's position regarding the realist approach to truth, Kelly assumes that establishing a correspondence between our constructions and the actual events of the world is "an infinitely long way off" (p. 96). Therefore, for Kelly, neither personal constructs nor scientific theories are simply "true" or "false," and we would be better off attempting to establish the relative value of different ways of construing the world, depending on context and purpose.

Carl Rogers' (1951) work on client-centered therapy includes his first formal statement of a theory of personality and psychotherapy, and it was followed by a more rigorous formulation in volume 3 of *Psychology: A Study of a Science* (Rogers, 1959). He, too, attempts to be explicit about his philosophical assumptions and emphasizes that his starting point is reality as it is experienced by the individual. Rogers contends that it is the person's phenomenal or perceived reality, rather than objective reality, which influences behavior, and he does not believe that we need to address "the difficult question of what 'really' constitutes reality" (1959, p. 223). Of course, the relationship between the individual's inner reality and any outer reality represented by the environment remains "transactional," and perceptions are likely to change if they are consistently invalidated by this interaction.

Rogers posits that there are two major components to the phenomenal field of the person. "Experience" is a holistic concept which refers to the totality of the person's phenomenal field at a moment in time. It includes everything that is "potentially available to awareness" (1959, p. 197), whether these experiences are sensory, physiological, affective, cognitive, or behavioral in nature. Rogers sometimes refers to experience as "organismic" or "organic" to capture something of the quality of a direct, holistic perception of one's inner reality.

"Symbolization" refers to the process of awareness or consciousness through which experience in made known to oneself (1959, p. 198). Generally, the field of experience is more extensive and textured than the portion of it which we accurately symbolize, and many inner events may remain on the periphery of awareness or become only partially symbolized. He alludes to work of the general semanticists to clarify the relationship between our perceptions of experience (symbolization) and experience itself:

> They have pointed out that words and symbols bear to the world of reality the same relationship as a map to the territory which it represents. This relationship also applies to perception and reality. We live by a perceptual "map" which is never reality itself. (1951, p. 485)

As the child grows, a crucial aspect of symbolized experience develops in relation to what is experienced as "I," "me," or "myself"—thus, the "self," the "self-concept," or the "self-structure" emerges (1959, p. 200). Accompanying the emergence of the self is a "need for positive regard" (p. 223): a universal human need, whether inherent or learned, for feeling accepted or prized by others. When important figures are conditional in their responses to the emerging self of the child, that is, some aspects of self are rewarded and others are punished, these "conditions of worth" become internalized and influence the child's own "self-regard" (p. 224). This development sets the stage for "incongruence" between self (symbolized experience) and actual (organismic) experience, since the child may not accurately symbolize those aspects of experience that conflict with the conditions of worth which have been incorporated from the outside world.

Like Kuhn's paradigm and Kelly's personal construct system, the self-structure, once formed, functions in a largely conservative manner in relation to the processing of information. For example, Rogers (1951) describes a woman who was very angry over having been abandoned by her husband, and who interacted with her daughter in a fashion such that she, too, internalized these feelings. In time, the daughter's self-structure included statements of the sort, "I feel nothing but hatred for my father, and I am morally right in feeling this" (p. 528, italics omitted). While her self-structure was congruent with those experiences of her own where the father had disappointed her in some way, it was incongruent with any experience involving positive feelings. She either denied such feelings or symbolized them in a distorted fashion: "I am like my father in several ways, and this is shameful" (p. 528).

Rogers' approach to personality change and psychotherapy follows directly from these theoretical assumptions. If the problem is inaccurate symbolization due to the imposition of conditions of worth from the outside world, then therapy must provide a relationship where those conditions of worth are reversed. If the self-structure can be likened to a personal, implicit theory about oneself, then the client must be encouraged—through the congruence, warmth, and positive regard offered by the therapist—to risk change in this theory by directly contacting organismic experience. For example, the young woman described above might make these statements about her experience following therapy: "I perceive that my mother hates my father and expects me to do the same. . . . I dislike my father in some ways and for some things. . . . And I also like him in some ways and for some things, and both of these experiences are an acceptable part of me" (p. 530, italics omitted).

A THEORY ABOUT HUMAN THEORIES

Thus far, Bruner and Postman's perceptual concept of "set or expectancy," Kuhn's paradigm, Kelly's personal construct system, and Rogers' self-structure have been analogized as sharing certain functional characteristics. One might add to this list other concepts from the psychotherapy and personality literature such as "the assumptive world" (Frank & Frank, 1991) and "lay" or "implicit" theories of personality (Hampson, 1988), as well as social psychological research on "attribution theory" and "social cognition."

According to Fletcher and Fincham (1991), the classic research on attribution identifies the layperson as a kind of "naive scientist," who is interested in discovering the truth by generating accurate theories for perceiving self and others. By contrast, a "less flattering picture of the layperson" emerges from research on social cognition (p. 29). This "cognitive miser" model characterizes the layperson less as a dispassionate scientist and more as someone whose implicit rules produce "endemic bias and error in social judgments"—thereby guaranteeing that support will be found for one's preformed personal assumptions (p. 7). Fincham and Jaspars (1980) suggest a third possibility: the layperson as "naive lawyer." While laypersons do make many errors in judgments of others when operating on an "automatic level," these errors decrease "under conditions that promote a more controlled and in-depth mode of cognition" (Fletcher & Fincham, 1991, p. 29). Fletcher and Fincham conclude that all three models have some applicability to the implicit theories of laypersons and offer hypotheses about the variables that influence whether one concept or another represents the better fit with a given situation.

Rogers and Kelly, as well as Frank and Frank (1991), would no doubt agree that all of us function both as naive scientists interested in truth and as cognitive misers interested primarily in supporting our pet theories. The Franks' comparative approach to psychotherapy begins with the assumptive world of the individual and conceptualizes psychotherapy as the diverse approaches which are available for modifying these implicit theories. Like Kelly and Rogers, these authors contend that assumptive systems emerge because the "need to make sense of events is as fundamental as the need for food or water" (p. 24). Although these belief systems, like scientific theories, function to make the world more predictable and understandable, they tend to assimilate experiences that are validating and resist those that are not (p. 32). Indeed, surprise or uncertainty results when events of the world which are not confirmatory somehow penetrate the system, and the amount of emotional upheaval associated with the disconfirmation depends on the centrality of the belief in question to the person's security (p. 31).

As chapter 1 suggests, psychotherapists make use of their explicit theories much like the laypersons and clients described above employ their implicit theories. Atwood and Stolorow (1993) document how quite personal, subjective elements became integrated into the theories generated by some of the great names of our field. Further, the resulting reified metapsychological constructs function within these theories akin to "character defenses" in the personality (p. 175). Barton (1974) illustrates how the reality of the same client would be successively transformed when seen by a Freudian, a Jungian, and a Rogerian, and his vivid descriptions bring to mind Kuhn's likening of paradigm shifts to "changes of world view" (1970a, chapter X). Although Barton, as well as Frank and Frank (1991), acknowledge the necessity of training therapists within a given theoretical system or systems, they caution that this training often instills a belief system that is quite resistant to change.

In summary, a review of observations from areas as diverse as perceptual psychology, social psychology, personality theory and psychotherapy, and the history of science points to an important commonality which crosscuts these domains of knowledge. Specifically, subjects in experimental studies of object and person perception, laypersons in their everyday lives, clients in psychotherapy, therapists in their offices, and natural scientists in the field all employ theoretical assumptions which decisively impact what they take to be the "reality" of themselves, others, and/or the impersonal world. Further, the commitment and confidence surrounding these assumptions may at times bear little relationship to their validity.

Several interesting implications can be drawn from this heterogeneous set of observations. They suggest that human theories, whether those of laypersons, psychotherapists, or natural scientists, have two interrelated, opposing functions. Theories appear to *reveal* some facet of reality to the person who is looking through the particular lens which the theory provides, and they simultaneously *restrict* the range of alternative views of reality.

A fuller statement of this "theory about human theories" can be found in table 2. The first four generalizations in the table are intended to apply in differing degrees to the work of Kuhn, Rogers, and Kelly. The fifth generalization is more typical of Kelly's thinking, and reflects his insistence that we should not have two different theories—one for subjects, clients, or laypersons and the other for the experts who would

TABLE 2
A Theory About Human Theories

---

1. Our most basic or distinctive characteristic as human beings is our need and ability to impose meaning and understanding on the world.

2. The world is not directly knowable.

3. Our attempts to understand the world represent interpretations or hypotheses about reality rather than statements about the nature of reality itself.

4. Through continued interaction with the world, we develop implicit theories (personal construct systems, self-structures, etc.) or explicit theories which express our understanding of the world. These theories tend to interpret the new in light of the old, and such interpretations serve two functions:

    A. They represent our best understanding of the nature of reality at a given moment—*they appear to illuminate or reveal reality to us.*

    B. They also represent a constraint on alternative ways of understanding reality—*they restrict the range of interpretive possibilities.*

5. This theory about theories is *reflexive*—it applies to itself as well as to other human theories.

---

explain their behavior. On the contrary, the terms of any theory should apply at once to the events or persons it purports to explain, to the person who generated the theory, and to the theory itself. "The way the client is explained can be used to explain the therapist as he or she creates this explanation" (Epting, 1984, p. 28).

A recognition of the shared functions of implicit theories in lay psychology, explicit theories in professional psychology, and paradigms in the natural sciences could also clarify much of the confusion surrounding the application of Kuhn's ideas to areas outside the sciences which he studied. Isn't it possible that many of the sociologists, psychologists, and psychotherapists who find Kuhn's thinking so congenial with their own are in fact simply recognizing that "theories" *function* in their disciplines just as "paradigms" *function* in Kuhn's account? For example, as a psychotherapist who has had a penchant for "trying on for size" a number of theoretical frameworks in our field, my experiences of learning to "see" the world from these differing vantage points can readily be transposed with some of Kuhn's descriptions of scientists experiencing the power of a paradigm shift. It seems undeniable that therapists who embrace a given psychotherapeutic theory and scientists who embrace a given paradigm will directly experience some facet of (what appears to be) reality, while at that very moment becoming blind to (what could be conceived as) its other, possibly incompatible features.

Nonetheless, if this simple recognition is twisted into a statement that theories in psychotherapy and paradigms in natural science are equivalent, then confusion abounds. "Paradigm" is, after all, a technical term which is different in many ways from what may be called a "theory" or even a "super-theory" in psychology and the social sciences. Similarly, it would be ludicrous to argue that the implicit theories of laypersons are "paradigms" in Kuhn's sense, but this does not mean that they might not share some formal characteristics. Therefore, although it is a moot question if any theories outside of the natural sciences conform to Kuhn's definition of a paradigm, I would argue that all theories, whether explicit or implicit in nature, and all paradigms serve some similar functions in the human attempt to understand the world.

Chapter 4

The Range of Philosophical Assumptions
in Psychotherapeutic Theories

R. A. Neimeyer (1995), in agreement with Mahoney (1991) and Howard (1991), proposes a philosophical and theoretical contrast in contemporary psychotherapy which is quite relevant to the formulation of philosophical positions presented in chapter 2, and which bears on the question of their fit with the current *range* of theorizing in psychotherapy. More pointedly, this contrast seems pertinent to a discussion of the range of philosophical assumptions on which contemporary therapeutic theories are built.

Neimeyer suggests that psychology and psychotherapy have traditionally been based on *objectivist* assumptions. Objectivist approaches, whether associated with the traditions of empirical research in academic psychology or with varieties of psychotherapeutic theory and practice, assume that scientific method can lead to the discovery of "objective, verifiable facts" (p. 12). These facts are then integrated into research programs and/or theories which allow for the establishment of general laws of human behavior whose validity is guaranteed "by their correspondence with observable, extratheoretical realities" (p. 12). Thus, the world is knowable, and scientific observations can directly reflect the nature of its constituent parts: They can correspond with the nature of reality itself. In relation to the framework of philosophical positions which was previously developed, objectivism corresponds to "scientific realism" and, therefore, represents one form of the larger category of realism/foundationalism.

121

On the other hand *constructivist* approaches, which Neimeyer links with "the postmodernist project," explicitly reject the assumption of a knowable world, because that world is to a lesser or greater degree "constructed" by the person who perceives it. The objectivist agenda is turned on its head by the simple insertion of an information-processing, language-using, knowledge-seeking human being into the equation. Ulric Neisser (1967), writing near the beginning of the "cognitive revolution" in psychology, nicely captures the essence of this constructivist turn in psychology and alludes to its relationship to philosophy:

> It has been said that beauty is in the eye of the beholder. . . .
> This is not the attitude of a skeptic, only of a psychologist. There certainly is a real world of trees and people and cars and even books, and it has a great deal to do with our experiences of those objects. However, we have no direct, *im*mediate access to the world, nor to any of its properties. The ancient theory of *eidola,* which supposed that faint copies of objects can enter the mind directly, must be rejected. Whatever we know about reality has been *mediated,* not only by the organs of sense but by complex systems which interpret and reinterpret sensory information. (p. 3)

Of course, from the vantage point of the assumptions of later constructivists, even Neisser's assumption of a "real world" of objects would be challenged. The gradations of "anti-realism" reviewed in chapter 2 are paralleled by gradations of constructivism in contemporary psychology and psychotherapy. For example, while Kelly's theory of personality is explicitly built on constructivist assumptions, and Rogers' theory appears to incorporate some of these assumptions as well, Gergen's (1985) version of "social constructionism" should be differentiated from any "constructivist" position which would assume the continued importance of something akin to a "self." Gergen (1991, 1994), like some of his postmodernist comrades in philosophy, wants to recommend the experience of approaching life in the absence of any of the anchors offered by an illusory self.

While the objectivist-constructivist contrast in psychology parallels the broad distinction between realism and anti-realism in philosophy, it remains to be seen if these dimensions can adequately capture the full range of philosophical and theoretical assumptions associated with contemporary psychotherapy practice. The following review has been structured around three issues, framed as questions, which arise when one attempts to apply the objectivist-constructivist contrast to therapeutic theories.

First, does this contrast apply to theories, theorists / therapists, or therapeutic practices? This section of the chapter explores whether a given theoretical orientation—for example, psychoanalysis—necessarily corresponds to a fixed point of objectivism-constructivism. Or do the assumptions associated with a given theory move about this dimension depending on the theorist who is holding it or the therapist who is applying it?

Second, what are the varieties of "constructivism" in contemporary psychotherapy? Although there is good consensus about the nature of objectivism as a philosophical and theoretical position, the defining characteristics of a constructivist approach to psychotherapy are still being debated. This section of the chapter presents and critiques four positions within the field today which can be broadly described in either "constructivist" or "constructionist" terms. The complex relationship that exists between certain of these positions and philosophical hermeneutics is also emphasized.

The final question of the chapter aims to correct an imbalance in the argument up to this point by exploring the relationship of the objectivism-constructivism contrast to two other philosophical / theoretical positions—"subjectivism" and "transpersonalism." The contrast between realism and anti-realism was developed in chapter 2 by pitting forms of objectivism against varieties of postmodernism. The former holds that objective truth is possible, and the latter rejects all truth claims, but these are not the only philosophical positions which are available. Some phenomenological, humanistic, and transpersonal theorists and therapists would like to retain a realist ontology while emphasizing that these truths cannot be reached through objective means. Therefore, representative examples of such thinking are discussed in this section.

DOES THE OBJECTIVIST-CONSTRUCTIVIST CONTRAST APPLY TO THEORIES, THEORISTS / THERAPISTS, OR THERAPEUTIC PRACTICES?

The objectivist-constructivist distinction offers a useful starting point for reflecting on the differences in fundamental assumptions which can characterize our field. Until now, this contrast has been stated in abstract terms and it is important to examine its application to psychotherapy in a more concrete fashion. This section will examine this question through considering its application to psychoanalysis.

When classical psychoanalysis is regarded as a particular theory of human behavior, it seems reasonable to place it squarely in the objectivist camp. R. D. Laing (1969) makes this point in dramatic fashion by comparing Freud to a hero who went on a journey filled with unknown terrors:

> He carried with him his theory as a Medusa's head which turned these terrors to stone. We who follow Freud have the benefit of the knowledge he brought back with him and conveyed to us. He survived. We must see if we now can survive without using a theory that is in some measure an instrument of defence. (p. 24)

Mitchell (1993) also makes a linkage, in a less dramatic style, between the assumptions of realism/objectivism and psychoanalytic theory. Freud did not doubt that psychoanalysis is a branch of science and saw it as no less objective in its methodology than other sciences. He viewed the scientific enterprise as offering a means of producing knowledge which would correspond directly with reality, and thereby represent "truth." Therefore, he and his contemporaries could assume that the theory which they built upon clinical observation provided an accurate, literal "map of the underlying structure of mind" (p. 41). In the context of these assumptions, Mitchell hardly finds it surprising that "the traditional psychoanalytic literature is filled with claims to Truths" (p. 41).

A counter to this view of psychoanalytic theory comes from an unlikely source and alerts us to the importance of considering the variable of a therapist/theorist's individual approach to a theory. After commenting that the only assumption he makes about theory is that it inevitably contains "an unknown (and perhaps . . . an unknowable) amount of error and mistaken inference" (p. 190), Rogers (1959) has this to say about psychoanalysis:

> For Freud, it seems quite clear that his highly creative theories were never more than that. He kept changing, altering, revising, giving new meaning to old terms—always with more respect for the facts he observed than for the theories he had built. But at the hands of insecure disciples (so it seems to me), the gossamer threads became iron chains of dogma from which dynamic psychology is only recently beginning to free itself. (p. 191)

In this quote, Rogers is operating from his own assumption that facts and theories are quite distinct, so he is not moving Freud the entire distance from the objectivist to the constructivist camp. However, he is suggesting, in the philosophical categories of chapter 2, that Freud functioned more as a "sophisticated" than a "naive" realist. More importantly, Rogers underlines the importance of considering the variable of the therapist who is holding a particular theory at a particular time. Some therapists may cling more tightly to the same theory or ascribe to it more truth value than other therapists.

Certainly, some very influential revisions of psychoanalysis appear to be less about changing traditional theory and more about changing the attitude we as therapists should bring to the use of that theory. Sass (1992) describes how revisionists such as Roy Schafer, Donald Spence, and Richard Geha have challenged the classical theory's "realist assumptions, arguing that psychoanalytic interpretations are less discoveries than creations and that memories are more invented than retrieved" (p. 167).

This perspective is well summarized by Spence's (1982) contrast of "historical" and "narrative" truth. Spence does not attempt to recast the structure of psychoanalytic theory but reinterprets the function that it serves for the understanding of client and therapist alike. Interpretations "work," not because they represent an accurate reconstructing and reexperiencing of the past, but because they offer the client a new set of meanings which are actually "constructions" about the client's past and present experience. These constructions are compelling just to the extent that they allow the client to "see" reality in a new way and to understand something which was previously "unknown or misunderstood" (p. 166). To speak in this manner requires us to redefine what is meant by "truth," narrative or otherwise, and Spence turns to literature and the arts for a model of therapeutic understanding. Accordingly, the "aesthetic appeal" of the interpretation is crucial to its acceptance by the client, and factors such as form and context are as important as inner coherence and content (p. 270). Is it surprising that a revisionist such as Geha (1993) takes this argument to its logical conclusion, likening an individual analysis to a work of fiction and suggesting that psychoanalysis should be recognized as a form of literature?

Thus far, we have considered classical psychoanalysis as a theory which is based on realist assumptions. The equation, psychoanalysis=objectivism, is complicated, however, by the possibility that different analysts could take either an objectivist or a constructivist stance toward the interpretations which they offer to clients. Any simple equation is confounded even further by the addition of three other variables.

First, returning to the views of Laing, Mitchell, and Rogers regarding Freud's attitude toward theory, I would contend that different positions could be supported, depending on the particular Freudian statements which one would choose to cite. At times he functioned as a naive realist who had no reservations about the truth value of his observations or the theories which he generated to account for them. At other times he critiqued and revised his theories based either on new or reformulated observations, while no doubt retaining the assumption of sophisticated realism that his theories were steadily moving "closer" to a fit with reality.

Similarly, Spence's (1982) reformulation of the nature of psychoanalytic interpretation is sometimes presented in the voice of an objectivist and sometimes in the voice of a constructivist. His argument is, for that very reason, paradoxical at certain points. On the one hand, he seems to be urging us to adopt an attitude toward interpretation which doubts its correspondence with the "truth." On the other hand, analysts often frame interpretations in "pragmatic statements"—utterances which are not necessarily true but are hoped to be true for the sake of both therapist and client (p. 271). This is a way of speaking which may greatly impact the client's willingness to accept an interpretation as true. Therefore, not only can different analysts employing the same theory differ in their assumptions about its truth value, the same analyst employing the same theory may at different times speak from different points along the continuum of objectivism-constructivism.

Second, although the Spence critique does not fundamentally change the structure of psychoanalytic theory, other developments in psychoanalysis have moved the theory itself toward a constructivist position. This literature is reviewed by Sass (1992), Mitchell (1993), Orange (1995), and Soldz (1996) and is too extensive to be considered in detail here. However, the "intersubjective" perspective was implicitly present in the psychobiographical approach to personality theory offered previously by Atwood and Stolorow (1993), and it will be discussed as an example of psychoanalytic constructivist thinking in the next section. These developments make it important to ask "Which psychoanalysis?" when considering the question whether psychoanalysis is objectivist or constructivist in its philosophical assumptions.

Third, we have considered what the theory "says" regarding the issue of objectivist *vs.* constructivist assumptions, and what the therapist "says" he / she assumes about this theory when applying it. Unfortunately, it is also necessary to consider the issue of what the therapist actually "does"!

It has long been one of the vexing issues of psychotherapy research that therapists' verbalized descriptions of their theoretical / therapeutic approach may not accord with their actual behaviors in the consulting room. Or, at a minimum, their behavior may be less consistent than their verbalized attitudes and descriptions would lead one to believe. The movement toward manualized treatment protocols in psychotherapy research is a direct response to this dilemma and represents an attempt to standardize the behaviors associated with different therapeutic approaches which are being compared in a given study (Kiesler, 1994, pp. 145–146). In a related vein, R. A. Neimeyer (1997) points out that constructivist theories of therapy can be framed so abstractly that it would be difficult to know what specific therapeutic interventions might follow from them. He cites a study by Vasco (1994) in which Portuguese therapists were administered two measures: One assessed adherence to a constructivist epistemology and the other measured preferences regarding a broad range of therapeutic "helping styles." While there was a negative correlation between a constructivist orientation and a directive approach to therapy, this verbalized epistemology did not positively correlate with any specific helping style or intervention. The author concluded that constructivist therapists in this sample were better able to say how they do *not* practice than to state what they actually do in therapy.

In conclusion, this review suggests that the objectivist-constructivist contrast has potential for understanding the range of assumptions on which contemporary theories of personality and psychotherapy can be built. However, its application to a given theory or theoretical school is complex, and it is likely that this complexity holds for areas other than psychoanalysis. For example, the teasing out of the philosophical assumptions of rational-emotive, cognitive, and cognitive-behavioral therapy has not yet been settled—that is, see R. A. Neimeyer (1993), Lyddon (1995), Mahoney (1995a), and Gonçalves (1995). Such debates have led R. A. Neimeyer (1996), who initially championed the objectivist-constructivist contrast, to complain of "a kind of conceptual vertigo" associated with "the blurring of familiar boundaries as proponents of apparently contrasting philosophical and psychological traditions . . . identify themselves as constructive or narrative theorists" (p. 372). If the traditions of cognitive-behavioral modification (Meichenbaum, 1993) and rational-emotive therapy (Ellis, 1993) are seen as constructivist by their proponents, what then can differentiate the objectivist and constructivist positions?

Based on the application of this contrast to psychoanalysis, it is possible to understand why such analyses can produce conceptual ambiguities and to discern the outlines of an approach to moderating their impact. Although it can be useful as an orienting device to apply the objectivist-constructivist contrast to global theories of personality and psychotherapy, such analyses will inevitably produce some inconsistencies and confusion. Ultimately, it is the therapist's assumptions about the theory and the therapist's concrete implementation of those assumptions that determine what is "objectivist" and what is "constructivist." Moreover, it should not be assumed that therapists are "just" objectivists or "just" constructivists, but that their attitudes and behaviors shift around this dimension depending on a number of factors.

WHAT ARE THE VARIETIES OF "CONSTRUCTIVISM" IN CONTEMPORARY PSYCHOTHERAPY?

"Constructivism" shares some of the definitional problems associated with its close cousin in philosophy, postmodernism. Mahoney (1995a), Rosen (1996), Chiari and Nuzzo (1996), and R. A. Neimeyer (1997) all acknowledge that there is no consensus regarding the meaning of this term. As a result, any attempt to impose conceptual order on this literature will be shaped to some extent by the author's own assumptions and goals, and the following classification was particularly influenced by three considerations: (a) It is important to clarify the philosophical assumptions associated with different varieties of constructivism. Therefore, an attempt is made to differentiate four proposed categories of constructivism on theoretical, ontological, and epistemological grounds; (b) In fairness to the objectivist / realist position in psychotherapy, which was subjected to a thoroughgoing critique in chapter 1, a similar critical attitude should be taken to a review of constructivist positions; (c) As with psychoanalysis, it is important to consider that constructivist theorists and therapists, regardless of their stated "positions," may actually shift their thinking around a range of constructivist, or even realist, positions.

One other position in contemporary philosophy and psychotherapy was introduced in chapter 2 and, given its prominent role in the following review, would now benefit from further clarification. While this position clearly contrasts with objectivism, it bears a complex relationship to constructivism. This complexity is due in part to the quite elastic manner in which the term "hermeneutic" is used in contemporary psychology and psychotherapy. In its generic meaning, hermeneutics refers to any approach which restricts objective methods to the study of the physical world and insists on the central role of interpretative dialogue to the understanding of the human world. Not surprisingly, as will become apparent below, many narrative, intersubjective, constructivist, social constructionist, and postmodern therapists characterize their work in hermeneutic terms.

Woolfolk (1998) asserts, however, that the ontological assumptions of such therapies generally run counter to the specific nature of hermeneutics as a philosophical position. Unlike postmodern and social constructionist positions within philosophy and psychology, which he defines primarily in terms of their relativistic or anti-realist epistemology, Woolfolk views philosophical hermeneutics as foremost an ontological position that makes its own truth claims.

> Gadamer attempted to demonstrate the historical situatedness of the human sciences and to show that understanding the actions of human beings involves uncovering truth, but truth that is constrained by a sociocultural horizon, truth that can be identified only from a particular vantage point. (pp. 135–136)

While Woolfolk would restrict hermeneutics to this Gadamerian tradition, the nature of the survey which follows necessarily includes both its generic and specific meanings. In the interest of a more sympathetic reading of the admittedly confused state of the current literature, I would suggest that the reader take the following perspective: If generic and specific meanings of hermeneutics could be considered to correspond, respectively, to the epistemological and ontological assumptions of this philosophical position, then theorists/therapists might choose to emphasize one or both of these elements in articulating their own position.

For example, a narrative therapist, like her affirmative postmodernist colleagues in philosophy, might discern a close relationship between constructivist and hermeneutic epistemologies: Both assume that our interpretations always come from a particular human vantage point. As Woolfolk indicates, the two positions may part company over the issue of ontology—that is, the narrative therapist assumes that therapeutic "truth" is an impossibility. Nonetheless, this therapist, who is battling against the specter of radical relativism, may be quite appreciative of the hermeneutic concepts and methods which allow her to claim that work with the client which is genuinely collaborative can yet generate new "knowledge." In her defense, as the discussion in chapter 2 demonstrates, philosophical hermeneutics has not established beyond reasonable doubt that this approach yields "truth" rather than "knowledge." Logic akin to that of this hypothetical narrative therapist, which emphasizes the epistemological status of hermeneutics, lies behind certain concepts, for example, "hermeneutic constructivism" (Chiari &

Nuzzo, 1996), that are discussed later. By contrast, other therapists who are discussed in the review embrace both components of the hermeneutic position. Orange's (1995) intersubjective theory is built on "perspectival realism," which links a constructivist or perspectivalist epistemology with a realist ontology in true Gadamerian fashion, and Cushman's (1995) therapeutic approach attempts to integrate social constructionist and hermeneutic assumptions.

Personal Constructivism: Constructs as Mediated by Personal Reality

The "theory about human theories" proposed in the last chapter is itself representative of a class of constructivist theories. Being mindful of the need for choosing a term that will later render an intelligible contrast with that of "social constructionism," this class of theories is designated as "personal constructivism." George Kelly represents the earliest and most influential proponent of this approach to theory and therapy.

Each individual has a personal construct system which allows for the imposition of understanding, order, and control on the external world. There is a firm distinction between inner and outer reality implicit in Kelly's statement, and Chiari and Nuzzo (1996) propose the term "epistemological constructivism" for capturing the implications of these assumptions. That is, the question of the existence or nature of an external reality is moot, because any contact with reality is always mediated by the constructs which make up one's personal system. Thus, from their perspective, this form of constructivism is defined in relation to its epistemology (what it says about knowing), not in relation to its ontology (what it might say about being) (p. 173).

Returning to the general semanticist metaphor, if external reality can be likened to a real territory, then the constructs which we employ for describing it are our ways of mapping that territory. However, the map is always different from the territory itself, and it is not even possible to judge whether different maps represent better or worse fits with it. Ultimately, the only judgments which can be made are pragmatic in nature: What is the relative utility of the personal construct systems which we employ as human beings? Those judgments will depend on a number of variables including context and purpose—that is, a construct system which maximizes my happiness in a relationship may not necessarily contribute to my effectiveness on the job.

Personal construct therapy, according to Chiari and Nuzzo (1996), is the "prototype," and in many ways remains in the "the avant-garde," of approaches to change that are based on epistemological-constructivist thinking (p. 173). Change itself defines optimal functioning within the personal construct framework because only continual modification of constructs "results in the maintenance of an adaptation between a knowing system and its environment" (p. 173). Therefore, Kelly (1958b / 1969) repeatedly "invited" clients to reconstrue the events of their lives and saw clients, like the rest of us, as needing "to assume that something can be created that is not already known or is not already there" (p. 229).

It is very difficult to maintain the purity of this kind of constructivist position when writing about it, and one of Kelly's (1958a / 1969) more provocative statements underscores the dilemma:

> This paper, throughout, deals with half-truths only. Nothing that it contains is, or is intended to be, wholly true. The theoretical statements propounded are no more than partially accurate constructions of events which, in turn, are no more than partially perceived. Moreover, what we propose, even in its truer aspects, will eventually be overthrown and displaced by something with more truth in it. Indeed, our theory is frankly designed to contribute effectively to its own eventual overthrow and displacement. (p. 66)

While the intent of Kelly's paper is clearly to reject realism or objectivism of any sort, he constantly recreates its specter through his choice of words. If he were thinking only as a personal or epistemological constructivist, there would be no talk even of "half-truths" because there could be no talk of truth of any kind. When he says "what we propose, even in its truer aspects, will eventually be overthrown and displaced by something with more truth in it," then, implicitly, he has retreated from a purely constructivist position to the position of sophisticated realism. That is, an external reality does exist, and approximations of it can be judged as "closer" or "truer" in nature.

Earlier, it was argued that Kelly's personal construct systems and Kuhn's paradigms have some commonalities in relation to their functions as theories. Since there are also obvious differences between the two concepts, it would be both awkward and misleading to try to call Kuhn a "personal constructivist." Nevertheless, Kuhn can be accurately described as an "epistemological constructivist"—in fact, this term appears to be nearly synonymous with the philosophical stance of "sophisticated relativism" previously used to describe his epistemology.

As a scientist, Kuhn might not deny the existence of a real physical world, but he would insist that we can never know it directly. The paradigms generated by scientific communities represent attempts to map and understand that reality, but they do not literally reveal it. Although decisions can be made regarding the relative scientific usefulness and productivity of different paradigms, Kuhn remains adamant that no judgments can ever be made regarding their relative correspondence with reality (truth value). The fact that he is more successful than that master of epistemological constructivism, George Kelly, in consistently maintaining this stance in his writing may be a reflection of the subject matter which occupied him. It may be easier to maintain one's distance when writing about scientific paradigms than personal construct systems, since the writer and the subject matter cannot be easily distinguished in the latter.

Intersubjectivity: Constructs as Mediated by Intersubjective Reality

Both generic and specific approaches to intersubjectivity are evident in the current literature. Natterson and Friedman's (1995) more generic approach essentially transforms the therapeutic relationship from one involving a single participant (the client) to one where there are two participants (client and therapist). Client and therapist each bring their own subjective view of reality to this encounter, and a new shared, interpersonal reality—which is the vehicle of therapeutic change—is "co-created" by them over time. Like Spence's reformulation of psychoanalysis, Natterson and Friedman's intersubjective approach "does not require that a therapist repudiate Freudian, Kleinian, interpersonal, object relations, or self psychological theories of personality and therapy" (p. xii). By contrast, Atwood, Stolorow, and their colleagues have developed a more specific theory of intersubjectivity which represents "a sweeping methodological and epistemological stance calling for a radical revision of all aspects of psychoanalytic thought" (Atwood & Stolorow, 1993, p. 179).

In their first major theoretical statement of this position, Stolorow and Atwood (1992) address one of the givens of psychoanalysis as "The Myth of the Isolated Mind" (chapter 1). They decry the tendency to treat the mind as an object which is alienated from nature (body), social context, and, most importantly, from the nature of subjectivity itself. Both the alienation from other and from oneself presuppose a mind that can somehow be defined as apart from the world: "Invariably associated with the image of mind is that of an external reality or world upon which the mind-entity is presumed to look out" (p. 11). Therefore, within this myth, the world has an independent, outer existence and it is "heroic" for us to sustain a separate, inner sense of self.

Stolorow and Atwood (1992) reject this image and replace it with one where human experience is always embedded in an intersubjective context—and this assumption defines the ontological and epistemological thrust of their approach. To illustrate their thinking, they turn to the developmental literature and evidence that "the developing organization of the child's experience must be seen as a property of the child-caregiver system of mutual regulation" (p. 23, italics omitted). Child and caregiver engage in a dance of mutual influence where it is crucial that the former's shifting states are intuitively met by appropriate responses from the latter. The child's sense of what is "real" itself emerges in relation to this "validating attunement of the caregiving surround" (Atwood & Stolorow, 1993, p. 188). Over time, the child's intersubjective experiences result in the formation of certain "invariant principles that unconsciously organize the child's subsequent experiences" (Stolorow & Atwood, 1992, p. 24). This process constitutes the personality development of the individual, who then takes these principles into situations as potentialities for the organization of experience. That is, the intersubjective context that the person enters will determine which of the principles will be called upon to organize his or her experience.

This formulation has radical implications for both psychoanalytic theory and practice. Regarding theory, Atwood and Stolorow (1993) follow Merton Gill and George Klein in defining metapsychology as "those propositions that attempt to explain clinical psychoanalytic observations in terms of hypothetical energies, forces, and structures that are presumed actually and objectively to exist" (p. 168). Although they retain theoretical concepts which could be described as "experience-near," Stolorow and Atwood (1992) reject all metapsychological constructs—whether Freudian, self psychological, or interpersonal in nature. For example, they acknowledge the importance of Kohut's "selfobject function" to their own thinking (p. 16) but critique any position which would claim the existence of a "self" as a structure or agency which determines behavior. While it is important to recognize the inherent organizational properties of "self-experience," positing the self as a reified structure or agent—"not unlike the impersonal mental apparatus of Freudian theory"—returns us to the myth of the isolated mind (p. 17).

The theory of intersubjectivity, as was noted earlier by Natterson and Friedman (1995), redefines the clinical situation as one involving two participants whose subjectivities profoundly influence one another. Stolorow, Brandchaft, and Atwood (1987) argue that certain psychotic and borderline states, which would simply be regarded as products of inner, intrapsychic processes from the vantage point of the isolated mind, can be reconceptualized as intersubjective phenomena. Such case histories suggest that the relatedness between analyst and patient can "play a constitutive role in forming and maintaining the particular pathological constellations" that manifest in treatment (Atwood & Stolorow, 1993, p. 179, italics omitted). This perspective would imply that psychopathology can never be diagnosed, much less understood or treated, apart from the intersubjective context in which it appears.

Stolorow and Atwood (1992) acknowledge that the myth of the isolated mind is "a difficult demon to exorcise" and propose that this difficulty may be due to the vulnerability inherent in "an unalienated awareness of the continual embeddedness of human experience in a constitutive intersubjective context" (p. 22). While that is an interesting conjecture, the model which they propose also poses daunting epistemological problems for the practicing psychotherapist. It, like all models of intersubjectivity, opens wide the door to relativism. If the analyst's perceptions of the client's subjectivity cannot be separated from his/her own subjectivity, and if the analyst's perceptions are no truer than those of the analysand, exactly where does this leave us?

Interestingly, Stolorow and Atwood (1992) do not give much space to a consideration of the philosophical implications of their approach. They do characterize the traditional analytic assumption of the isolated mind as resting on an "objectivist epistemology" and contrast it with their own "perspectivalist" epistemology. From their position, it is not assumed that the analyst's subjective reality is truer than that of the patient or that the analyst can ever fully know the patient's own subjective reality. However, they differentiate their position from a "radically relativist position, which denies the existence of a psychic reality that can be known" (p. 123). By contrast, their perspectivalist position "assumes the existence of the patient's psychic reality but claims only to be able to approximate this reality from within the particularized scope of the analyst's own perspective" (p. 123).

These statements raise as many questions as they answer and again accent the difficulty which was previously noted in relation to George Kelly's writing. Stolorow and Atwood must find it problematic to write consistently from an intersubjective stance, which does not assume the existence of independent psychic realities, when describing a situation where one person is attempting to know another person's experience.

Consequently, the writing comes across at points as if the authors are lapsing into personal constructivism, if not into a form of sophisticated realism. However, they do cite Richard Rorty and Donna Orange as compatible perspectivalist thinkers, each of whom has been much more explicit about their philosophical assumptions. Since Rorty has been discussed previously, Orange's position will be considered below as an elaboration of the views associated with Stolorow and Atwood.

Orange (1995), who is trained both as a psychoanalyst and as a philosopher, is interested in developing a framework which is both clinically relevant and philosophically sophisticated. She acknowledges that her philosophical position is influenced by the American pragmatists, especially by the work of C. S. Peirce (pp. 146–147); Gadamer's hermeneutic approach to understanding also assumes a central role in her thinking (pp. 68–74). Although her view excludes "common-sense realisms, correspondence theories of truth, and scientific empiricisms" (p. 62), she does keep "truth" and "realism" in her vocabulary and sees the former as that which gradually emerges in a "community of inquirers" or in a "dialogic community" (p. 61). Thus, she articulates an ontology of "perspectival realism" which would define "reality" as a process of socially mediated understanding.

> Each participant in the inquiry has a perspective that gives access to a part or an aspect of reality. An infinite—or at least an indefinite—number of such perspectives is possible. . . . Since none of us can entirely escape the confines of our personal perspective, our view of truth is necessarily partial, but conversation can increase our access to the whole. (p. 61)

Later, she also describes this position as a kind of "collaborative pragmatism" and as "fallibilistic" in spirit (chapter 10). Pragmatism shifts the question away from what might be the "truth" about a client's behavior and toward its meaning as defined by its "practical bearing" (p. 148). These meanings are explored through a collaborative process between client and therapist, and therapists must live with the recognition that they can always be mistaken. Fallibilism recognizes the limits on our ability to know and "replaces the search for certainty and distortion-correction with a dialogic search for reasonableness or meaning in a community of inquirers" (p. 149).

Orange removes her position from those associated with "cultural and epistemological relativism" (p. 61) through the use of terms like "truth" and "realism": "In such a moderate realism, the real is an emergent, self-correcting process only partly accessible via personal sub-jectivity but increasingly understandable in communitarian dialogue" (p. 62). A contemporary pragmatist like Rorty would likely take little issue with Orange's argument aside from suggesting that the proper ref-erent for her statement above is "knowledge," not "truth." Of course, the older generation of American pragmatists frequently speaks a lan-guage of pragmatic truth, and Rorty (1989b) presents his version of Jamesian truth defined as beliefs which one "finds good to believe" (p. 11). However, when Orange uses a phrase like "the real is an emergent, self-correcting process," she acknowledges her specific debts to Peirce and Gadamer and signals a shift to the possibility of another kind of truth—while partial, this truth is somehow ontologically "real."

Although a philosophical hermeneuticist might contend that Orange has it just right, Chiari and Nuzzo (1996) seem to side with Rorty's view when they argue against any position which combines a perspectivalist epistemology with a realist ontology: "Realist constructivism appears to be a contradiction in terms in light of our understanding of construc-tivism" (p. 178). Although philosophers can debate whether "perspecti-val realism" does or does not represent a contradictory position, it will later become apparent that therapists are simply being human when they think and act at times as constructivists and at times as realists.

Narrative Approaches: Constructs as Mediated by Language, Story, and Dialogue

It has been acknowledged that terms like "constructivism" in psy-chology and "postmodernism" in philosophy have about as many dif-ferent meanings as those who choose to use them, and the same could be said for the next two categories of this review: "narrative" and "social constructionist" approaches to psychotherapy.

As a means of staking out the territory for his edited volume review-ing contemporary narrative and solution-based therapies, Hoyt (1994a) points to "signposts" represented by terms "such as solution-oriented, solution-focused, possibility, narrative, postmodern, cooperative, com-petency-based, constructivist" (p. 2, italics omitted). Whatever their sim-ilarities, practitioners of these different therapies also have their differences, and it is simply a matter of emphasis whether one chooses to focus on the former or the latter. Further, narrative therapists some-times also describe themselves as "hermeneutic" and "social construc-tionist" in orientation. Therefore, does the "narrative" approach which will now be described have sufficient internal coherence to constitute a distinct category? Can it be adequately distinguished from the "social constructionist" category which will follow?

I believe that these questions can be clarified by making a distinction between generic and specific statements of the narrative approach. At the generic level, the narrative approach and the social constructionist approach hold some, although not necessarily all, assumptions in common. However, as the narrative approach becomes translated into more specific therapeutic interventions, these methods may differ markedly both from one another and, as a group, from the social constructionist position.

Hence, like hermeneutics and intersubjectivity, the literature on narrative psychology and psychotherapy is characterized by general and particular formulations and applications. Jerome Bruner's (1986) broad contrast between "paradigmatic" and "narrative" modes of thinking is an oft-cited generic statement of a narrative perspective. The "logico-scientific" or paradigmatic mode of thought employs those very cognitive abilities (categorization, classification, logic) which in combination with scientific method result in the building and testing of scientific theories (p. 12). Through providing a logically consistent, theoretically derived, empirically supported account, the paradigmatic mode hopes to convince the listener of its truth value.

By contrast to the cognitive processes and associated rules which can produce a "well-formed argument," the narrative mode of thinking relies on capacities which can produce "a good story" (p. 11). While arguments attempt to convince one through offering truth, the narrative mode convinces by offering stories which offer "lifelikeness" and "verisimilitude" (p. 11). Bruner sees a place for each of these modalities, but is particularly interested in his essay in understanding the application of narrative understanding to literary texts.

In the hands of other psychologists and psychotherapists, this generic narrative mode has been extended from texts to persons and identified as the defining characteristic of our humanity. Spence's (1982) reconceptualization of psychoanalysis is a case in point. He contends that both client and therapist unavoidably function from within a narrative mode which leads to its own truth, not from a paradigmatic mode leading to historical truth. Howard (1991) concludes that for a number of contemporary narrative psychologists, including himself, "the essence of human thought can be found in the stories that we use to inform and indoctrinate ourselves as to the nature of reality" (p. 193). White and Epston (1990) extend the distinctions made by Bruner, rejecting paradigmatic thinking as a basis for therapy and articulating the broad principles and specific interventions associated with a "storied therapy" (p. 77). Freedman and Combs (1996) offer their reconceptualization of the family therapy field, replacing a "systems" metaphor with metaphors of "narrative" and "social construction" (pp. 1–2).

Thus, human beings are most fundamentally meaning-generating, purpose-seeking beings who organize their experience through stories which include elements such as plot, coherence, and temporality. This conceptualization implies that advocates of a narrative approach embrace, implicitly or explicitly, a larger theme that was explored in the chapter on philosophical positions. It became evident there that one defining aspect of postmodernism is its insistence on the centrality of language to the construction and apprehension of reality. Moreover, it is not quite right to say that language provides a "window" on reality. Just as Stolorow and Atwood (1992) argue that there is really no "outer" and no "inner" to the constituents of experience, so would postmodernists argue that "reality" and "language" are indivisible. Berg and de Shazer (1993) associate this philosophical view with "constructivism" and draw out its implications for psychotherapy as follows:

> This view has led us to believe that we need to study language in order to study anything at all. That is, rather than looking behind and beneath the language that clients and therapists use, we think that the language they use is all that we have to go on. . . . Contrary to the commonsense view, change is seen to happen within language: What we talk about and how we talk about it makes a difference, and it is these differences that can be used to make a difference (to the client). (p. 7)

The generic characteristics of narrative therapy can then be seen as following directly from these assumptions about the primacy of story and language. If human beings are basically storytelling animals, then human problems will be conceptualized as stories which are somehow not serving individuals or groups as well as they might. If story and reality are inextricably interwoven, then psychotherapy becomes the process of assisting clients to consider "an alternative story" (White & Epston, 1990), a "preferred reality" (Freedman & Combs, 1996), a "story revision" (Parry & Doan, 1994), or "solution talk" (Furman & Ahola, 1994). If therapists necessarily function within a narrative mode no less than their clients, then all they can offer is "therapeutic conversation"—not the "truth" (H. Anderson & Goolishian, 1992, p. 29). If therapists and clients are more alike than not, then clients should be treated in a nonauthoritarian, collegial, and collaborative fashion such that genuine dialogue can occur. If it is not possible to find universal causes of human problems, then any solutions which are offered will be specific to the "local" context (p. 33), represented by the parties (client and therapist) doing the negotiating and their respective language, purposes, and values.

The last authors cited above touch on many of these common themes of narrative therapy by suggesting that the "client is the expert," and that therapists should practice a "not-knowing" approach to therapy. The therapist functions as a "conversational artist—an architect of the dialogical process—whose expertise is in the arena of creating a space for and facilitating a dialogical conversation" (p. 27). A dialogue of this kind represents a search for mutual understanding, and it is impeded if the therapist insists on asking questions "that are informed by method and demand specific answers" (p. 28, italics omitted). Only through approaching the client with an attitude of "genuine curiosity" and not-knowing does the therapist allow for the emergence of a conversation where something new can arise and be seen. Too much effort in trying to produce change can stand in the way of this kind of narrative transformation. Simply by opening space for conversation, "new narrative, the 'not-yet-said' stories" will emerge because "change in story and self-narrative is an inherent consequence of dialogue" (p. 29). This process is itself transformational because "we live in and through the narrative identities that we develop in conversation with one another" (p. 28, italics omitted).

As narrative therapists move beyond the generic to the specific, they tend to part company on certain key issues. On the theoretical level, much of the writing associated with "brief" and "solution-oriented" therapies (Hoyt, 1994b) is pragmatic and problem-solving in style in contrast to the heavy philosophical overlay typical of some of the prominent therapists in the narrative movement. Another way of framing this difference is to say that some narrative therapists place the stories which clients present in a larger philosophical, social, and political context. For example, White and Epston (1990) turn to Foucault to ground their analysis of human narrative and thereby decrease the distance between their position and that of social constructionism.

Once the discussion moves from theory to method and technique, differences overwhelm the commonalities among this group of therapists. Gergen (1993), in an introduction to an edited volume surveying language-sensitive therapies, observes that all the therapists in the volume share a goal of attempting to free clients from limiting constructions by opening up new possibilities for apprehending reality. Yet, when he describes the various approaches which these therapists employ to reach this goal the list is a hodgepodge of techniques: "scaling questions, reflecting teams, positive reframing, solution talk, problem redefinition, self-perception questions, exception-oriented questions, goal enactment, externalizing conversation, artistic expressions, and metaphorical explorations" (p. x). Understandably, Efran and Clarfield (1992), while sympathetic to the narrative approach, poke fun at some of its current shibboleths including the use of reflecting teams, Milan-style therapeutic letters, and special questions.

What then are the philosophical assumptions of therapists who approach therapy as has been described above? While this question would be answered somewhat differently by different therapists, it should be apparent that one generalization can be made. Aside from some of the brief-strategic and solution-oriented therapists who acknowledge a specific debt to Milton Erickson (Hoyt, 1994c), therapists whose work is broadly narrative in nature hold implicit or explicit assumptions which are most closely aligned with affirmative postmodernism and hermeneutics. In addition, it can be anticipated that narrative therapists struggle especially with the philosophical problem of relativism.

Spence's (1982) account of narrative *vs.* historical truth is a good starting point for considering these issues. In moving away from the empirical or historical accuracy of interpretation in psychotherapy, he also abandons the correspondence theory of truth. According to Held (1995) and Orange (1995), he replaces it with a "coherence" theory of truth where true ideas are defined as those which constitute a certain aesthetic and coherent whole. Because this notion of truth depends so heavily on the interaction between the client and the therapist, it also includes collaborative and pragmatic elements—but these elements are not developed in depth in Spence's own philosophical thinking.

Spence is aware of the relativistic thrust of his work and, unlike many therapists in the narrative tradition, is ambivalent about it. The narrative understanding that occurs in the analytic situation is characterized by "flexibility" (p. 183) to the point of an "embarrassing elasticity"—an unfolding story of a human life "can embrace almost any piece of information," which, once integrated, becomes "genuine" (p. 187). Therefore, narrative flexibility can pose a serious problem for the analyst, and Spence admits that the criteria for narrative truth (aesthetics or coherence) may at times appear to be "a poor substitute" for the criterion of historical truth (accuracy) (p. 183).

Earlier it was noted that Spence sometimes talks like an objectivist and sometimes like a constructivist, and Woolfolk (1998) makes a similar point. He and Louis Sass have suggested that Spence's position is incoherent because it is not hermeneutic enough—that is, "there are no uninterpreted 'facts' behind human experience" (p. 88), so the distinction between historical and narrative truth does not really hold. However, Woolfolk acknowledges that, depending on Spence's understanding of hermeneutics, this shift could take him even further toward epistemological relativism.

Without doubt, the philosophical and theoretical path taken by many narrative therapists heads straight for radical relativism. They contend that the "real" doesn't exist anywhere because language and reality can never be separated. There is no higher court (an extralinguistic reality) to which we can appeal to determine the truth of the various stories which constitute our experience of the world. How could there be? Thus, beyond the criteria of how a story "fits" with one's behavioral goals and personal preferences, the attempt to establish the truth or validity of narrative or hermeneutic understanding is simply abandoned by many narrative and constructivist therapists (Woolfolk, 1998, pp. 134–135). For example, Freedman and Combs (1996) equate different narratives with different "selves" and indicate that their task is to help clients to discover and develop "various experiences of self and to distinguish which of those selves they prefer in which contexts" (p. 35). Sluzki (1992) observes that "the 'story' that our social world is constructed in or through multiple stories or narratives" is itself one of them (pp. 218–219), and this statement represents the definitive expression of a relativistic stance.

Nonetheless, since narrative therapists are by definition interested in "praxis," in taking action even in the absence of any clear guidelines for doing so, radical relativism poses the same dilemma for them as it does for affirmative postmodernists. On what grounds does one make a commitment to a personal position—whether it is the therapist's commitment to narrative therapy or the client's commitment to a new narrative—when "postmodern consciousness favors a thoroughgoing relativism in expressions of identity" (Gergen & Kaye, 1992, p. 179)? It is not surprising, therefore, that philosophical positions associated with affirmative postmodernists such as Lyotard and Rorty find their way into the defense of the narrative approach. While the possibility of truth is rejected, knowledge claims can be made in reference to the "local" community (Lyotard) or in relation to "pragmatic" considerations (Rorty) which include the purposes of a particular group. Philosophical concepts from the hermeneutic tradition, that is, "the hermeneutic circle" or "dialogical understanding," are also frequently cited in defense of narrative, intersubjective, discursive, and dialogical approaches to therapy.

For example, in the section following their statement about clients' "preferred selves," Freedman and Combs (1996) refer to Bruner and Rorty, and claim that—rather than meaning that "anything goes"—their position requires them to examine even more mindfully their own assumptions. "Not only do we carefully examine the beliefs and values that we choose, but we invite the people who come to see us to examine their beliefs and values as well" (pp. 35–36). Unfortunately, they do not clarify how this argument bears on the question of "moral relativism" which the section purportedly addresses.

Richardson and Fowers (1994) contend that the pragmatist criterion for knowledge—that beliefs and values can be evaluated solely in relation to their consequences or implications for the purposes of a given group—is itself characterized by "a certain amount of conceptual incoherence" (p. 5). In a like manner, the prior review of philosophical positions indicates that a lively debate continues regarding the success of hermeneutic discourse in separating itself from a relativistic position. Whatever one's evaluation of the philosophical status of neopragmatism and hermeneutics, their application to the field of psychotherapy will require more than an obligatory citing of the work of Rorty, Gadamer, or some other philosopher. By example, when narrative or intersubjective therapists employ philosophical terms such as a "dialogic community" or a "community of inquirers" (see the previous discussion of Orange), it is often not clear how these concepts translate to the concrete context of psychotherapy. Do the client and therapist constitute such a community? If so, under what circumstances might a narrative or intersubjective approach result in a dyadic muddle rather than in a dialogical meeting? If it includes other therapists, would they be like-minded? If not, how does the existence of so many distinct communities of inquirers in the field of psychotherapy extricate us from relativism?

In the end, many narrative therapists, like their affirmative postmodern colleagues in philosophy, see "relativism" as a problem created by the objectivist/realist epistemology which they have rejected. Relativism is a concern only for those who cling to a foundational way of thinking; it is dissolved by a narrative approach which views knowledge as inherently linguistic, social, and purposeful in nature. Efran and Clarfield (1992) comment on a book on narrative therapy which Efran and his colleagues had published. It was critiqued by some readers as focusing unduly on how they ran their own therapy sessions and for being too much about the authors and not enough about constructivism as an approach. Efran and Clarfield reply that of course it is about "us":

But constructivism isn't a special method. Part of the virtue of the approach is that it *legitimizes* an unabashed presentation of who we are and where we stand. . . . Constructivists are not prohibited from having and expressing preferences, hopes, and opinions. They are only enjoined from claiming that these belong to someone else, or derive from a privileged access to an outside, objective reality. (p. 205)

Held (1995) argues, however, that many of the opinions and beliefs of narrative therapists represent a contradiction between the realism they have supposedly rejected and the form of constructivism which they theoretically uphold. Berg and de Shazer (1993) would appear to be in accord with this view when they begin an article on language in therapy with the following statement:

The metaphor of therapy as conversation is simultaneously useful and dangerously misleading. The danger lies in what is probably an inevitable shift from *a* to *i*, that is, from "therapy *as* conversation" to "therapy *is* conversation." The vowel shift marks a transformation from metaphor to metaphor disguised as concept. (p. 5)

As if to prove their point, within the next few pages they endorse the poststructuralist view that "language *is* reality" (p. 7).

Such theoretical pronouncements *do* make reality claims, and Held (1995) cites many of them in her extensive review of the narrative literature (pp. 96–101). As Held argues, such statements, to a lesser or greater degree, are inconsistent with the anti-realist epistemological position which the therapist is articulating. A position which rejects realism cannot be stated in a form which presupposes that truth can be discerned or known. An analogous point was previously made by Bernstein (1992) when he accused Rorty of not practicing what he preaches. Although his liberal ironist is supposed to remain permanently doubtful about his / her final vocabulary, Rorty never questions some of his own commitments (p. 280). Similarly, when narrative therapists state their assumptions as if they are self-evident facts, they run into the same paradox which bedevils relativism as a philosophical "position."

As might be expected from their prior statement, Efran and Clarfield (1992) accept some of Held's observations but reinterpret their meaning. Yes, it is necessary for narrative therapists to hold certain beliefs including those about "why people get stuck, and what therapists can do about it" (p. 201). However, they see the beliefs and personal preferences of therapists as entirely consistent with the narrative / constructivist approach as long as these are not presented as "objective truths or realities" (p. 201).

It is a subtheme of this review that therapists have difficulties in exactly this area: It is not easy to find or speak a language which would consistently eliminate "objective truths or realities." Thus, Held (1995) concludes that narrative therapy is characterized by an "oscillation between the antirealism it propounds and the realism it unwittingly expresses" (p. 135), and Stancombe and White (1998) believe that there is a "stubborn paradox in postfoundational psychotherapy" (p. 587). While anti-realist therapists claim that they have given up both authority and epistemic certainty, therapeutic practice necessarily seeks change in clients, and "the pursuit of change is, by its very nature, normative" (p. 587). Therefore, the defining of "what serves as real" remains in the therapist's hands, and "it is through the exercise of this productive power that the potency of narrative approaches lies" (p. 588).

The above-mentioned authors offer proposals which would address these issues and, predictably, their recommendations would take psychotherapy in opposite directions: For Held (1995), it is back to a "modest realism" (p. 250) while for Stancombe and White (1998) it is toward "a, yet to be defined, *post*-therapeutics" (p. 594). My own analysis, to this point, is confined to a clear statement of the problem. Both the paradox and oscillation in the anti-realist position of many narrative therapists reveal the difficulties posed by radical relativism for practicing clinicians. Earlier, it was found that relativism has not been eliminated as a philosophical problem by the sophisticated arguments developed by philosophers such as Lyotard, Gadamer, and Rorty. It is unlikely that more abbreviated accounts offered by psychologists and psychotherapists have been more successful in resolving relativism as a practical problem in the context of therapeutic discourse.

Social Constructionism: Constructs as Mediated by History, Culture, and Power

As an orientation to the topic of social constructionism, it is useful to reflect on the review as it has progressed to this point from the perspective proposed by Chiari and Nuzzo (1996). As was previously indicated, the position which I designated "personal constructivism" is described by these authors as "epistemological constructivism." They then contrast it with a position, modeled primarily on the perspectivalist (epistemological) component of hermeneutics, which crosscuts a variety of contemporary approaches including narrative psychology, "postmodern psychology," and social constructionism—and I would add intersubjectivity to this list. "Hermeneutic constructivism" refers to any position which assumes that "reality" does not exist independently of the observer, such that knowledge constitutes a form of "linguistic action" (p. 174).

Epistemological constructivism assumes that reality is unknowable because of the existence of a construct system that mediates its apprehension, and this construct system has personal and individual characteristics. Hermeneutic constructivism assumes that any separation between an unknowable reality and a personal construct system which attempts to map it is untenable. Because we are social, cultural beings who live our lives in a medium of language, reality and person are hopelessly entangled.

In this context, Gergen's (1985) preference for the term "social constructionism" is understandable. This usage has a history within sociology and social psychology and, unlike "constructivism," underlines that reality is always *socially*, not personally or individually, constructed. Moreover, it will become apparent that much of what we take to be the personal or the individual is but another social construction.

It should now be clear how social constructionism differs from personal constructivism, but how does one distinguish it from the intersubjective and narrative approaches which have preceded it—particularly if Chiari and Nuzzo's concept of hermeneutic constructivism applies to all three? Success in defending any proposed distinction will depend in large measure on how specifically one defines social constructionism, and for that reason my review will be quite specific. I am interested in asking if the social constructionist arguments of two psychologists, Kenneth Gergen and Philip Cushman, can be distinguished from intersubjective and narrative approaches.

Before considering the similarities in their positions and contrasting them with those which have been reviewed to this point, it is useful to anticipate the differences between Gergen and Cushman—which will also become obvious as the discussion proceeds. Gergen (1991) represents the prototypical social constructionist and postmodernist, who apologizes not at all for his anti-realist position—indeed, who proclaims its advantages as a new ground for personal understanding and societal functioning. Cushman speaks with two different voices—that of the social constructionist and that of the philosophical hermeneuticist—and, as Woolfolk (1998) has stressed, some tension exists between the relativistic implications of the former and the ontological commitments of the latter. In the major statement of his outlook, Cushman (1995) appears to minimize the potential conflict between the two positions by compartmentalizing his use of them: He focuses his social constructionist thinking on a theoretical and political critique of psychotherapy as a social institution but embodies more of a Gadamerian sensibility in his own therapeutic work.

When both are speaking as social constructionists, it is useful to liken Gergen and Cushman to skeptical postmodernists who are interested in further deconstructing the assumptions of their intersubjective and narrative colleagues. "Deconstructionism," considered broadly in the sense of a critical tool or technique, has been seen as expressive of a philosophical theme associated with skeptical postmodernism. It was argued that the philosophical themes of the postmodern literature are necessarily stated largely as negations, because they are by definition "anti-realist" in nature. Therefore, a deconstructionist approach serves the negative function of taking apart that which is presumed to be truth or knowledge, and does not necessarily come forth with a positive statement of what would constitute more secure knowledge.

Although neither Gergen nor Cushman would employ this term to describe their overall approach, it is obvious that an important component of their work is deconstructive in intent and impact. Gergen (1985) acknowledges that a social constructionist approach to psychology "begins with radical doubt in the taken-for-granted world—whether in the sciences or in daily life—and in a specialized way acts as a form of social criticism" (p. 267). More recently, he admits that "for many of us, it has been necessary . . . to go through a critical or deconstructive phase" (Misra, 1993, p. 413). Cushman (1995) focuses his social constructionist thinking on psychotherapy, and it is no less critical in intent. He begins his book by alleging that "we take psychotherapy for granted today" (p. 1) and then develops an argument for the necessity of critiquing its most taken-for-granted characteristics. "We do not often question the assumptions of many of its theories, such as the underlying ideology of self-contained individualism or the valuing of 'inner' feelings or the unquestioned assumption that health is produced by experiencing and expressing those feelings" (p. 2).

Therefore, as social constructionists, Gergen and Cushman resolutely remind psychologists and psychotherapists that their research and practice occur within a particular social, historical, and political context. Most generally, the topics that we choose for study, the methods that we employ for understanding, and the explanations that we then offer to others represent cultural products which reflect the dominant arrangements of the society within a particular historical period. According to Foucault (Baynes, Bohman, & McCarthy, 1987), the most important of these dominant arrangements concerns the distribution of power and its embeddedness in the production of knowledge itself. What we take to be as the nature of things—the nature of our sexuality, our mental health, our individual self-knowledge—is actually a manifestation of the "capillary" circulation of power arrangements throughout "the cells and extremities of the social body" (p. 96).

Gergen (1985) cites analyses which deconstruct the taken-for-granted nature of phenomena such as suicide, schizophrenia, altruism, psychological disorder, childhood, domestic violence, and menopause. He points out that the "objective criteria for identifying such 'behaviors,' 'events,' or 'entities' are shown to be either highly circumscribed by culture, history, or social context or altogether nonexistent" (p. 267). Similarly, social constructionism is compatible with feminist and multiculturalist critiques of the alleged "universals" associated with a white, patriarchal, Eurocentric culture (Cushman, 1991) and is allied with the call for a diverse, pluralistic society in which many different groups are accorded equal access and voice (Misra, 1993).

The objective of applying this general critique to the specific area of psychotherapeutic theory and practice will be most quickly met by turning to one particularly controversial question which social constructionists are convinced must be addressed: Does a separate, personal "self" actually exist? While it was assumed during the modern era that the world is composed of "various essences" or "things in themselves," Gergen (1991) sees the postmodern turn in the academy and the culture at large as signaling their "disappearance" (pp. 112–113), and our experience of the "self" is no exception. He traces the impact of a number of postmodernist perspectives, including Rorty's anti-foundationalist thinking and Derrida's deconstructive approach, on the concept of a separate, individual self. Since these critiques undermine any distinction between inner and outer, personal and public, or subjective and objective, Gergen asks: "Why then must we presume that there is an internal world of the self—private and isolated—that thinks, knows, and expresses itself in words?" (p. 103).

Cushman (1990) would see the answer to this question as residing in the assumptions, practices, and purposes of the particular historical period and culture which are under consideration. Within our own time, a variety of economic, political, and cultural influences have culminated in the creation and maintenance of an "empty self." This concept was explored briefly in chapter 1, and for the present purposes it can be sum-marized in terms of the following contradiction. On the one hand, this self is "bounded" and "masterful" (p. 600)—it is separate from the world and capable of taking action in the world, meaning that it is empowered. On the other hand, it "experiences a significant absence of community, tradition and shared meaning," and these absences are experienced subjectively as forms of disempowerment—"as a lack of personal conviction and worth" and "as a chronic, undifferentiated emotional hunger" (p. 600).

For Cushman, the contradictions of this self serve very well the needs of late capitalistic society. The isolated, bounded, autonomous, individualistic self requires little in the way of direct social control. Yet it is easily managed and manipulated by the state through indirect means. Advertising and the promotion of consumerism promise to meet the wishes of the citizenry "to be soothed, organized, and made cohesive" by being filled up (p. 600). Unwittingly, psychotherapy enters this picture as another means of indirect control:

> Psychotherapy is the profession responsible for treating the unfortunate personal effects of the empty self without disrupting the economic arrangements of consumerism. Psychotherapy is permeated by the philosophy of self-contained individualism, exists within the framework of consumerism, speaks the language of self-liberation, and thereby unknowingly reproduces some of the ills it is responsible for healing. (1995, p. 6)

The implications for psychotherapeutic theory and practice of this social constructionist critique are best framed in relation to different levels of analysis, which can be stated in the form of two questions. First, do our existing theories and practices give adequate recognition to the social, political, and historical context in which individuals with "problems" seek psychotherapy? Second, even if our theories did adequately recognize this context, is it possible to practice a psychotherapy which would be truly liberating, that is, one which would change something other than the problems of a bounded, individualistic self?

Do Existing Therapeutic Practices
Sufficiently Acknowledge the Sociopolitical Context?

Both Gergen and Cushman would answer the first question above with an emphatic "No!" Gergen and Kaye (1992) contrast therapeutic approaches in relation to modernist and postmodernist assumptions and use a narrative metaphor to articulate the goals and practices of each. The modernist conception of narrative corresponds to what has been called "realism" or "objectivism" in this review and invests the psychotherapist's narrative with considerable power and authority. "Thus, with few exceptions, therapeutic theories (whether behavioral, systemic, psychodynamic, or experiential/humanist)" allow the well-trained therapist to enter the consulting room "with a well-developed narrative for which there is abundant support within the community of scientific peers" (p. 169). On the other hand, the narrative which the client brings to the encounter is seen by the therapist as something less substantial—a personal story "replete with whimsy, metaphor, wishful thinking, and distorted memories" (p. 169). Therefore, in Gergen and Kaye's provocative account, psychotherapy practiced from a modernist perspective fundamentally entails a process wherein the client's story is gradually *displaced* by the therapist's story. Moreover, they contend that most modernist schools of therapy in the end aim for hegemony: "All other schools of thought, and their associated narratives, should succumb" (p. 171). The authors view such approaches as naive in their philosophical assumptions and as "decontextualized" (p. 172) from culture and history in their therapeutic applications.

Therapeutic approaches associated with a postmodernist perspective, including "narrative therapies," are regarded by the authors as having much to offer compared to the modernist alternative described above. These therapists acknowledge that no narratives, including their own, actually represent reality or the truth. While the therapist's narratives may prove to have utility in certain contexts and for certain purposes, they are not considered superior to those of clients or those of other societal groups. These assumptions lead the postmodernist therapist to approach the therapeutic relationship as a dialogic encounter where client and therapist will together co-create new narratives.

Despite what they view as this more enlightened stance, Gergen and Kaye detect vestiges of the modernist or realist agenda in the thinking of such therapists. Although they do not cite specific therapeutic approaches in this regard, a brief discussion of the work of White and Epston (1990) would perhaps best illustrate their argument.

There is no question that White and Epston attempt to situate their narrative approach within a theoretical framework which acknowledges the social, historical, and political context. Their Foucauldian analysis leads to the concept of the "dominant narrative" (p. 18) as a carrier of societal power/knowledge which subjugates "alternative stories" (p. 27). Clients who present with problems often display the consequences of having taken on a dominant narrative that conflicts with their own "lived experience." Therefore, therapy assists clients in reclaiming their own previously marginalized experience, allowing it to coalesce into a new narrative which better suits their needs, values, and situation.

At one level, such therapies appear to offer liberation in both a personal and political sense, but Gergen and Kaye (1992) critique the modernist assumptions lurking within the concepts of narrative "construction" and "reconstruction." By assuming that the narrative functions either as a "lens" through which the world is seen or as an "internal model" which guides action (p. 176), the therapist offers the client an analysis and a recommendation for change which actually contradicts his/her own constructionist assumptions. At best, the therapist has regressed to the position of personal constructivism with its individualistic assumption that "the final resting place of the narrative construction is within the mind of the single individual" (pp. 178–179). At worst, the therapist has embodied assumptions of "singularity in narrative" (a single way of looking at the world is enough) and "commitment to narrative" (the new narrative is "true") which take us all the way back to naive realism (p. 179, italics omitted).

Cushman (1995) does not specifically discuss intersubjective or narrative therapies in his review of therapeutic approaches, but his extensive treatment of psychoanalytic developments makes it possible to extrapolate his views to the former. He documents how psychoanalytic thinking in this century has moved toward acknowledging the role of the social environment but has done so in such a fashion that the concept of a bounded, individualistic self is largely retained. Because environmental influences and relationships with others are seen as incidental factors, having little impact on the mechanistic internal structures and processes which actually determine behavior, Freudian drive theory can be likened to a "one-person" psychology and psychotherapy. While some variations of object relations theory and self psychology locate personality development within a social milieu and may attend carefully to the manner in which the therapist-client dyad replicates or transforms prior relationships, they represent an attenuated version of a genuinely "two-person psychology" (pp. 337–345). That is, the real drama is still played out within an individual self which is preoccupied with internal object relations and/or issues of self-enhancement in order to fill its emptiness.

Cushman believes that there have been some two-person psychologies which have shown more promise for providing psychotherapy with a truly interactionist conception of the person. He laments that the work of Harry Stack Sullivan (pp. 169–185) was not more directly incorporated into subsequent thinking and lauds the work of more contemporary "radical interpersonalists" such as Edgar Levenson and Merton Gill (p. 347). Cushman comments that the hermeneutic approach which he favors is "easily mixed with forms of interpersonal, constructivist, and intersubjective theory" (p. 301), and it would stand to reason that he sees intersubjectivity as another example of a truly interactionist psychology.

However, a morally situated psychotherapy requires grounding, not in a two-person psychology, but in a three-person psychology. The third element which the latter would add could be characterized, in language used earlier in this review, as "reflexive" or, better, as "deconstructive" in nature. There must be some framework which allows therapists to turn their vision back on themselves and to situate their assumptions and practices in a political, historical, and moral context.

Intersubjectivity is exquisitely attuned to the subtleties of the client-therapist interaction and graphically describes how the therapist's subjectivity influences the client's subjectivity. Further, this approach could claim that the intersubjective field itself represents the needed third component for psychology—for example, see Ogden's (1994) concept of the "analytic third." I assume that Cushman (1995) would object vehemently to this conclusion. In the absence of a language for situating itself in a moral and political context, the subjective and intersubjective components of the dyad are left floating in a kind of neutral ether. In the end, this kind of thinking in psychotherapy and in the larger world reduces the political and moral dimensions of our experience to the dyadic. All human problems are seen as *caused by* (e.g., a relationship with a parent or lover) or *resolved by* (e.g., a relationship with a therapist) the vicissitudes of the dyad.

> If we cannot entertain the realistic possibility that political structures can be the cause of personal, psychological distress, then we cannot notice their impact, we cannot study them, we cannot face their consequences, we cannot mobilize to make structural changes, and we will have few ideas about what changes to make. (p. 337)

Can Psychotherapy Lead to Personal Liberation
and Social Transformation?

What, then, do Gergen and Cushman have to offer in the way of recommendations for a psychotherapy which would take us beyond, respectively, mere narrative reconstruction or utterly decontextualized change of the individual/dyad? Is a therapeutic change which would be truly liberating and transforming possible? Gergen and Kaye (1992), from their social constructionist / postmodernist stance, answer this question with an enthusiastic "Yes." Cushman (1995), from his social constructionist/hermeneutic framework, offers a more qualified, even ambivalent, response which has its affirmative moments.

For Gergen and Kaye (1992), any therapeutic approach that simply replaces the client's existing narrative with a new one does the client a disservice, especially if the client regards the new narrative as a real component of self.

> To be committed to a given story of self, to adopt it as "now true for me," is vastly to limit one's possibilities of relating. To believe that one *is successful* is thus as debilitating in its own way as believing that one *is* a *failure*. (p. 179).

They urge social constructionist therapists to implement on the level of practice what they preach on the level of metatheory: invite clients to consider a multiplicity of ways of understanding the self but discourage them from making a commitment to seeing any one of this multitude as somehow "true."

Gergen and Kaye (1992) acknowledge that they are asking clients to abandon "that cherished possession in Western culture, personal identity" (p. 180). In its place, Gergen (1991) would suggest a "relational self" which is process-oriented, locates the experience of self as much in outer as inner space, and does not reify its constituent social roles and language games into real "things" which exist (pp. 156–160). In describing the psychological attitude which accompanies this shift in thinking, Gergen distances himself somewhat from the qualities of "playfulness" and "ironic drollery" which he associates with an affirmative postmodernist like Rorty (p. 193). He (1994) also wants to draw a firm line between his position and the nihilism which hovers around skeptical postmodernism. Deconstructionism carried to its logical end can result in a posture where neither action nor commitment is possible, and Gergen is interested in promoting more, not less, moral deliberation and social engagement. Therefore, he proposes that an attitude of "serious play" might allow us to enter into the various social forms of the relational self "while at the same time treating the forms as contingent or contextually bounded" (1991, p. 196).

As a statement of goals for human change, Gergen's account is open to questioning from several angles. Gergen and Kaye (1992) offer only a few, fairly general suggestions about how therapists might work toward these goals, and their chapter is clearly intended as a theoretical statement rather than as a set of practical recommendations. Even if their intent is primarily theoretical, however, one can ask if the goals which they state represent practical—that is, achievable—therapeutic objectives.

From the standpoint of human change processes, Gergen and Kaye's (1992) goals for therapy seem to be extraordinarily ambitious. In fact, their argument actually underscores the marked resistance to change which characterizes the modernist or realist view of the world. Narrative and social constructionist therapists, who by definition have accepted an alternative world view which holds that the autonomous self is an illusion, persist, nevertheless, in employing therapeutic formulations and practices which assume and reinforce that a self does exist. Material reviewed in this chapter and the last would point to a similar conclusion: Laypersons and psychotherapists alike are predisposed to generate theoretical accounts which are resistant to change and which equate what is seen with the "real." More specifically, constructivists and constructionists of all persuasions have difficulty in maintaining the consistency of their position and repeatedly lapse into language which is based on a realist epistemology. If therapists who are intellectually committed to the project of an alternative epistemology "can't get it," how realistic is it to assume that clients will?

Moreover, even if clients could undergo the conceptual transformation "beyond narrative" which Gergen and Kaye have in mind, should they? Picture a 50-year-old African-American woman from a small town in the South who identifies herself primarily in terms of her Christian faith and her family values. She has developed panic attacks with agoraphobia, has become housebound, and to date has received only misdiagnoses and ineffective treatment. She comes for help to a social constructionist therapist who espouses the kind of therapeutic goals discussed in this section.

Assuming that this social constructionist therapist practices some form of a narrative approach, I would argue that the fit between the woman's needs and the therapist's orientation raises at least two ethical questions. First, is social constructionist therapy, narrowly defined, the most appropriate approach for this woman? Although social constructionists might challenge the realist assumptions behind either a diagnosis of panic disorder or the research-based, exposure / cognitive behavioral treatment protocol now recommended for it, would they be remiss if this option were not explored with the client?

Second, regarding the issue of therapeutic goals, this scenario brings to mind Sue and Sue's (1990) "critical incidents" in multicultural counseling, wherein a psychotherapist and a client can be working out of completely different "world views." This client only wants to get rid of a painful and inconvenient symptom; she does not want to change her life any more than is necessary, much less question the fundamental assumptions upon which it is built. Asking her to learn to radically relativize her experience of what is "true" would make this therapeutic approach liable to the same criticism of "decontextualization" which Gergen and Kaye (1992) leveled at modernist therapies. The social constructionist's narrative of a self which is relational, multiple, and relative can itself become "an abstract formalization—cut away from particular cultural and historical circumstances" (p. 172).

Richardson and Fowers (1994) broaden the above critique and wonder if Gergen and Kaye (1992) haven't in fact offered us "a new metanarrative, indeed a rather 'singular' one" (p. 6). In an interview with Misra (1993), Gergen anticipates this type of criticism by making a distinction between "metatheoretical" and "theoretical" paradigms (p. 403). The former would include social constructionism as an epistemological position, while the latter would refer to specific psychological or psychotherapeutic theories such as psychoanalysis or behaviorism.

Given a goal of articulating an alternative to realist epistemology, Gergen sees value in generating a "unified position" on the level of metatheory—that is, tracing out the implications of a social constructionist epistemology while rejecting alternative epistemologies. However, he insists that social constructionism "does not demand or require any particular commitment at the level of theory. Unlike its competitors, constructionism is not committed to first principles, propositions about what is *truly true* about human functioning" (p. 403).

I would side with Richardson and Fowers in this debate. Surely, when social constructionism as an epistemology is generalized to the issue of therapeutic goals and informs us how clients should regard the world and themselves, it has itself become a statement of the "truly true": It has become a metanarrative. Further, it is a strange argument which contends that social constructionism allows one to subscribe to any theory whatsoever, if such inclusion requires that one first reject the theory's own epistemological foundations. A radical behaviorism based on social constructionist epistemology would quite simply no longer be radical behaviorism, and the same could be said for a host of other theoretical positions. I salute Gergen's consistent appeal for "pluralism" in our field and in our culture (Misra, 1993). However, anticipating a theme which will be developed in the final chapter, social constructionism will not resolve the contradictions inherent in its own position until it allows for the possibility of *epistemological* pluralism. Within the framework of therapeutic practice, this kind of pluralism would include, most decidedly, respect for the implicit epistemological positions which clients happen to bring to us.

In order to reflect on what conventional psychotherapy does and does not offer, as well as to frame the nature of an alternative, Cushman (1995) imports from philosophical hermeneutics the metaphors of the "clearing" and the "horizon" (pp. 20–23). Like Heidegger and Gadamer, he utilizes these metaphors to dramatize the embeddedness of the human being in the social and cultural world.

Consider that there is such a thing (which there is not) as an undifferentiated, uninterpreted, unmediated perception of the world and liken it to a forest. This forest is so dense and dark, so unorganized and confusing, that you actually see "nothing" when you look at it. Then imagine that you look again and suddenly see a space where you can make out shapes and forms. This clearing in the forest is created by the totality of cultural assumptions and social practices which define what it means to be a human being in this particular time and place. Now look as far around in the clearing as you can, and that represents the horizon. The same assumptions that allow you to carve out a niche of meaning in the form of a clearing also restrict the range of meanings which might arise within it. By definition, you cannot see beyond its horizon.

Cushman then uses this metaphor to convey the intimate relationship between the practice of psychotherapy and its cultural context. In relation to the larger, fundamental dimensions which define humanity within a given place and time, psychotherapists and clients have generally been situated within the same clearing and able to grasp the same horizon. If it is the bounded, masterful, empty self "which shows up" in that clearing, then that is what both therapist and client will experience and work around. If it is the moral and political dimension of human experience which lies beyond the horizon, then neither therapist nor client will fathom its relevancy or importance.

Stretching this metaphor to its limit, such therapists cannot assist clients in extending the horizon, but they may be able to help clients learn to live with more ease within the clearing which the society has allowed. In the popular stereotype, psychotherapists are seen as a bit odd or at least as nonconventional, and certainly there is a mildly subversive attitude which is often implicitly or explicitly expressed in therapy. Concepts like normality, authority, and power may be demystified and challenged, and clients may be encouraged to question a variety of societal givens. Therefore, the following contradiction arises: The client may exit therapy with subjective feelings of greater freedom, but the therapy has also added a few more bars to the cell block (the masterful, empty self).

The hermeneutic alternative which Cushman recommends is intended to provide therapists with some way of extending their own horizon in the hope that they might do the same for their clients. Gadamer (1975) proposes that the horizon can be extended through a process of "fusion of horizons"—that is, two persons whose clearings are constituted by somewhat different cultural assumptions can develop a common language and each can learn to see differently. However, Bernstein (1992) suggests that Gadamer's term "does not do adequate justice to those ruptures that disturb our attempts to reconcile different ethical-political horizons" (p. 10). Bernstein's quote implies that the attempt to extend one's horizon always involves a difficult act of confrontation with self and other, and, when successful, the person who exists afterwards is not quite the same person who entered into the dialogue.

Cushman conveys very well the kind of open-ended self-confrontation which therapists must themselves allow if they are to move toward a perspective that is socially, morally, and politically situated. Although he acknowledges that it "continues to be a difficult task" to embody a hermeneutic perspective, Cushman (1995) still believes that it represents our best hope for approaching the practice of psychotherapy with more integrity (p. 290).

It would be understandable if there were some debate about the adequacy of the governing metaphors in Cushman's analysis for the purposes he wishes them to serve. Flax (1996) is not happy with the singularity of Cushman's use of concepts like the "self" or "the clearing," wherein each historical period of a culture is associated with "one dominant self-configuration and one clearing" (p. 852). She is more Foucauldian in her thinking and is interested in finding "marginalized and silenced discourses *within* any apparent unity and in exploring how the effect of unity is generated and reproduced" (p. 853). Specifically, by focusing only on the dominant discourse within a given era, Cushman's analysis replicates society's silencing of marginalized others who differ regarding color, gender, or sexual orientation.

Cushman (1996) replies to Flax by asking that she allow more than one approach to the goal of increasing political awareness and resistance in this culture. While listening to the voices of marginalized groups is one such approach, it is also important to contribute to the political awareness of the middle class. His argument, including the concept of the "empty self," can then be seen as "about the ways that middle-class whites are distorted, misused, and left unfulfilled in service of a cultural, political, and economic agenda that is often reinforced by aspects of psychotherapy theory and practice" (pp. 886–887). As for the issues of the clearing and the horizon, the former includes many traditions and positions and the latter "does not delineate only one understanding of human being, but rather the totality of possible understandings within a culture" (p. 886).

Within the context of his overall argument, I would interpret Cushman's last remarks above as follows. Depending on vagaries of culture and history, each of us may differ somewhat in the particular clearing we see and the horizon that it provides. However, for the group that is the focus of his argument—"mainstream, middle-class whites" (p. 887)—any differences in horizon would be trivial compared to the political, moral, and historical context which they share. Therefore, the majority of clients who seek therapy within the United States and the majority of therapists who provide it share fundamental assumptions about what it means to be human and to have a "self."

With these clarifications in place, it is now possible to turn again to the key question still before Cushman's alternative approach to practice: Does its adoption allow for the possibility of an actual change of horizon in the client? His direct and indirect responses to this question are surprisingly ambivalent.

Cushman (1995) does stress again and again that adopting a hermeneutic stance has the advantage of allowing the therapist to move away from the use of "interiorizing, hyperindividualistic language" (p. 306). For example, he asserts that "hermeneutics can help lessen the practitioner's contribution to the construction of the empty self, the normalization of consumer activities such as acquisitiveness, competitiveness, and envy, and the medicalization of behavior caused by political structures" (p. 292).

It would seem to follow from such statements that the "nonuse" of this language, coupled with the grounding of the therapy in an explicitly social / moral / historical context, would help clients to somehow shift their horizon, but Cushman does not go that far. Instead, he wonders if a hermeneuticist should attempt to answer the question "How does psychotherapy cure?"—remarking that for Gadamer the "horizon is *always* moving" (p. 318). In the next paragraph, he then states: "In other words, how the horizon shifts is not a mechanical or technological question of how a therapist can cause a horizonal shift; instead, perhaps the horizon moves precisely *because of*—that is, in response to—the new moral terrain that has emerged" (p. 319).

Whatever their merit for hermeneuticists, his responses to the question of whether/how fundamental change occurs in therapy are likely to seem ambiguous to the majority of therapists. Fortunately, Cushman (1995) gives many examples of his own work with clients, and it is possible to see more concretely what this therapist actually does. It is in this context that certain contradictions in his hermeneutic approach become apparent, which in turn may better explain Cushman's own ambivalence about the nature and possibility of transformative change.

He speaks of a client who has been seen in therapy for approximately four years, twice a week (pp. 302–306). The client is a male professional in his mid-thirties who not infrequently slips into excruciatingly painful experiences of feeling that others will not know how he feels, reject him for what he thinks, and ignore his needs. Cushman experienced the client on one particular day as "describing a world to me, the world that he lived in when he was in this particular state of mind" (p. 303). He then vividly conveyed this image to the client, explicitly situating the client's horizon in his early life experience. The client confirmed the accuracy of the image but was incredulous that Cushman would imply that there might be an alternative way of experiencing the world.

This metaphor then frequently reappeared in the course of the therapy as they dialogued about the other worlds which might be available to the client, their comparison to the worlds of his mother and father, the alternative world represented by their therapeutic interaction itself, and the way in which different worlds (for example, gender) are societally constituted. As the client learned that he has some part in summoning the appearance of this world, he experienced feelings of fear, anger, and hope. They wondered what it would be like for the client to experience this hope and aliveness—feelings which were outlawed in the old world—more often: "what it would take to *move back* the horizon so that there would be room for that feeling" (p. 305)? They realized in time that he feels guilty if for even a moment he escapes the old world and "lets the clearing open up, and resides somewhere else" (p. 305). This guilt was in turn related to a fear of losing "the terrain that contained his relationships with those he loved and needed so desperately and the moral frame that explained and justified their particular pattern of relating" (p. 306).

Cushman acknowledges that either psychoanalytic drive theory or object relations theory could explain the client's attachment to an old, pain-producing constellation of relationships. However, by replacing drive energies or internal object relations with "the horizonal metaphor, we can describe the behavior without as much recourse to . . . language that unknowingly contributes to the reproduction of the empty self" (p. 306).

He also admits that his work with the client could be construed in relationship to interpersonal psychotherapy, including his focus on evoking a new world for the client through their dyadic interaction. Thus,

> hermeneutics is in part simply a different, more direct way of talking about what some other theories have also described. But by placing an emphasis on the *moral* constellation of the psychological world, and by situating psychological processes in the social space *between* people, hermeneutics offers a new perspective, one quite relevant to the socially constructed nature of human being. In effect, we are continually asking the question "How are you treating others?" and "How are you treating yourself?" (p. 304)

In a variation on a theme of this chapter, I see the primary contradiction in Cushman's position as one between *theory* and *practice*. On the level of stated theory, he has no doubts about the contribution that hermeneutics can make to the thinking of the therapist. Yet, how does one carry this frame to the consulting room and hold it in such a fashion that the client can actually extend his or her own horizon? Cushman's clinical vignettes suggest that his own success in doing so is ambiguous at best.

The last quote above is a good case in point. After an abstract statement of the contribution of hermeneutics to psychotherapy, he gives examples of concrete questions which are intended to evoke the client's world. From my perspective, these general questions—and other examples like them—cannot be discriminated from a host of therapeutic interventions associated with alternative theories, some of which are based on alternative epistemologies. For that matter, if one distinguishes between Cushman's theoretical framing of his interventions in the case and the interventions themselves, there is little in the latter which is unique to a hermeneutic approach. Indeed, his work is compatible with that of a variety of therapeutic orientations beyond the interpersonal school of psychoanalysis which he acknowledges. Among others, personal construct therapists, narrative therapists, solution-focused therapists, and some cognitive therapists might all employ language similar to his metaphor of "worlds" and be no less insistent that the client come to realize its socially constructed nature.

More importantly, the gap between theory and practice bears directly on the question of the nature of therapeutic change. Although Cushman (1995) notes that his vignettes are meant as illustrations and not as "examples of 'successful' outcomes brought on by a transformative technology" (p. 410, footnote 18), his language in these vignettes does make *some* such claims. For example, I think that he is taking liberties when he describes the above client's changes in relation to the metaphors of "moving back the horizon" or letting "the clearing open up." No doubt, this client was experiencing significant changes in his feelings and world view, but these changes would be better formulated in relation to a concept like Gergen and Kaye's (1992) notion of "narrative reconstruction." That is, Cushman's critique of conventional therapy was based on the assumption that client changes which manifest within it are restricted to moving around in the given clearing, such that the horizon does not fundamentally change. In the absence of more compelling evidence that the client has undergone a transformational process, it does not seem fair to now describe his own therapy case as if such changes in clearing and horizon have occurred. In choosing to employ these terms, he diminishes the very metaphor which is intended to hold his philosophical position.

I believe that Cushman's ambivalence about the issue of change in psychotherapy is foreshadowed by a statement made in his initial presentation of the "empty self" argument:

> In a world sorely lacking in community and tradition, the most effective healing response would be to address those absences through structural societal change by reshaping political relationships and cultural forms and reestablishing the importance of their transmission. Because that avenue is closed for normative psychology, psychologists can only provide guidance and caring within the therapist-patient dyad. (1990, p. 607)

Although the context of Cushman's quote indicates that "normative psychology" refers to therapists who do not explicitly address the sociopolitical context and who offer a cosmetic, "life-change" solution to sufferers, the statement would apply equally to social constructionist and hermeneutic therapists. Until it is radically redefined, therapy of any kind promotes a process of change involving individuals, dyads, and small groups—not larger social and political structures. As applied to the above case, the very *form* of a relatively intense (twice-a-week), fairly long-term (four-year), largely psychodynamic / interpersonal therapy no doubt reinforces certain assumptions of the empty self experience. This form communicates to the client that deep change is dyadic in nature and that it involves a process of intensely personal inner work, and these powerful messages are likely to overwhelm the impact of any discrepant, noninteriorizing language employed by the therapist to reframe the experience.

Therefore, from my perspective, there is an underlying tension in Cushman's work which results from the juxtaposition of theoretical statements which are often overly optimistic in tone with case material which is more textured, complex, and ambiguous in its implications. To his credit, Cushman does provide sufficient case material that one can make a judgment about the relationship of the clinical material to his theoretical overlay. Even more to his credit, at the end of his chapter on hermeneutics, Cushman (1995) agrees that there is a problem here.

He returns to a statement of Rabbi Nachman with which he began the book: "Life is a very narrow bridge between two eternities—do not be afraid" (p. 329). Cushman uses the metaphor to make a connection between our past and future as social communities, and he then indicates that he introduced Gadamer's notions of "the cultural clearing" and "the moveable horizon" as a means of anchoring both sides of the bridge. However, he reminds himself and his readers that even these notions may not be able to hold the bridge aloft because

> life is *just* a bridge—and a narrow one at that. It is shaky, and when there is a storm it swings back and forth too much. In times of trouble we will want the bridge to be more than a bridge; we will try to pretend that it is solid ground. We might even, to assuage our fears, try to build a permanent house on it. . . .
>
> No theory . . . will ultimately be able to transform the bridge into solid ground. No theory can be a permanent house. (p. 330)

I take Cushman's statement to mean, in the language of this review, that he and others can unknowingly slip into holding naive realist assumptions about a hermeneutic approach to psychotherapy, despite its intellectual grounding in a contrary ontology and epistemology. He recaptures the spirit of a truly deconstructionist stance toward theory, turned now against the social constructionist / hermeneutic alternative itself, when he writes:

> So let's not get overexcited about using constructionist and hermeneutic ideas in psychotherapy. These ideas might help us build and maintain our bridge, for a while. But let us remember that the two ends of the bridge, when you get right down to it, are not really anchored to much of anything. (p. 330)

Rappaport and Stewart (1997), in a chapter which reflects critically on the possibility of a "critical psychology," indicate that this endeavor is one which is ultimately ironic in nature. It is ironic because by definition it presupposes a majority view from which it deviates, and "its way of thinking cannot in itself become the dominant way of thinking" (p. 305). Should that occur, then a new sequence of criticism would be set in motion which would take as its object that which previously constituted criticism and which now has become yet another status quo. Thus, while the critical psychologist is driven to propose changes which would right the injustices associated with the dominant viewpoint of the discipline, these changes themselves "could never satisfy critical psychology's own criteria for justice, democratic participation, and social change other than in a very momentary way" (p. 305).

I would argue that the social constructionist positions of Gergen and Cushman represent different responses to the dilemma of practicing a critical psychology. Gergen would like to adopt a posture similar to that of the affirmative postmodernist. On the one hand, he wants to critique the status quo of psychology and psychotherapy, laying bare its tendency to produce a knowledge which seeks "hegemony" and is "decontextualized" and "totalizing" in nature. On the other hand, he would like to see social constructionism break free of its "critical or deconstructive phase" and begin to make "positive moves" (Misra, 1993, p. 413). These moves, at least as they have been translated into the field of psychotherapy, are producing the very outcomes that Rappaport and Stewart would predict. Gergen's proposal that therapeutic goals be defined in terms of some ideal of a multivocal, postmodern human—who has given up personal identity and lives life with "serious play"—could not itself be more ironic. It is a recommendation full of contradictions which inevitably will be charged with the very metanarrative crimes it has criticized: "decontextualization," "totalization," and "hegemony."

Cushman, as has been noted, speaks with several voices, including those of the skeptical postmodernist, the affirmative postmodernist, and . the hermeneuticist. He deconstructs conventional psychotherapy with aplomb, and has no difficulty on the theoretical level extolling the virtues of a hermeneutic alternative. When it is time to move from theory to practice, however, another voice begins to intrude into the conversation he would have with himself and his readers. He knows at some level that a dialectic is at work here, and he is just too honest not to recognize its manifestations in himself. He is aware that he wants to resist much of what is associated with the status quo but realizes the impossibility of single-handedly eliminating individualism, including his own. He admits that he lives in a very Western, individualistic world "and I know there are aspects of it that I enjoy and would not want to lose" (1995, p. 308). He recognizes that, according to his own analysis, the process of awareness and change which he recommends may not be "entirely possible" (p. 310) and, in the end, he suggests that we regard his proposed framework with healthy skepticism. Whatever one's evaluation of that framework, Cushman appears to have learned something important about irony. In the practice of critical psychology, there comes a time for strategic retreat, and it *is* the better part of valor.

HOW DOES THE OBJECTIVIST-CONSTRUCTIVIST CONTRAST RELATE TO SUBJECTIVISM AND TRANSPERSONALISM?

In considering this last question of the chapter, it is important to begin by clarifying terms. Regarding the objectivism-constructivism distinction, "constructivism" will be used in a generic sense, referring to all four varieties which were reviewed in the prior section. "Subjectivism" refers to a philosophical position shared by a number of phenomenological and humanistic theorists and therapists, and "transpersonalism" is a new term for an ancient religious and philosophical position which both shares and goes beyond some of the assumptions of subjectivism.

Within psychology, subjectivism and transpersonalism represent movements which attempt to broaden the debate in this field beyond the alternatives of "objective truth" or "no truth" provided, respectively, by objectivism and constructivism. As was indicated in chapter 2, objectivism is only one variant of the larger category of realism. Realism, as a foundationalist philosophy, makes the ontological assumption that some reality, whatever its nature, exists; epistemologically, it holds that knowledge, defined as truth, can mirror or represent this reality. Since knowledge and truth must be synonymous, nothing should intervene between the nature of reality and our perception or experience of it—that is, the nature of reality can directly impress itself upon our consciousness as human beings if we employ the correct method for apprehending it. While objectivists insist that a scientific method will allow us to grasp external reality directly, subjectivists and transpersonalists also assume their own versions of ultimate reality, and they are just as confident that it can be reached through some alternative, nonobjective means.

A discussion of the full range of contemporary theories and therapies associated with subjectivist and transpersonalist assumptions is beyond the scope of this chapter. Rather, the goal here is to concretize those assumptions by citing a few representative theoretical and philosophical examples, while contrasting them with objectivist and constructivist thinking. Since it is newer to the field and is also characterized by an ontology which may seem elusive to some readers, transpersonalism will receive more attention than subjectivism.

From Subjectivist to Transpersonalist Thought

Rogers' (1959) theory of personality and psychotherapy appears to be based on a combination of objectivist, constructivist, and subjectivist assumptions, but the subjectivist elements dominate the approach to therapy which results. As presented in chapter 3, Rogers grounds his theory in the phenomenal world or subjective experience of the individual. This subjective experience is what the person takes to be the reality of the world, and within this inner world Rogers differentiates "symbolized" experience from "organic" or "organismic" experience. It is the latter which could be said to represent ultimate reality for Rogers, and his therapy is built on the principle that individuals must be brought back into direct contact with it. Further, he proposes a specific method for facilitating this process, and it is the opposite of an objective, detached, "scientific" approach to the client. The therapist must demonstrate qualities of nonpossessive warmth, congruence, and empathy so that the client's conditions of worth are reversed and direct organismic experiencing is restored.

Mitchell (1993) sees comparable subjectivist developments within psychoanalysis as representing a response to the constructivist critique of theory. If psychotherapists necessarily impose their own categories and beliefs on the client through the theories which they employ, then one solution to this problem would entail eliminating theory and simply returning to the client's own experience. Mitchell calls this approach "the phenomenological solution," and it assumes that therapy works when the client is allowed to "discover, express, and capture her own experience" (p. 51). It also assumes the existence of some substrate of inner experience which exists independently of an observer and which can be directly accessed without distortion or contamination by the client. He links these assumptions with realism as follows:

> The phenomenological solution, while decrying objectivism in any form, ironically represents the return of a form of the naive realism of Freud's day. Although the analyst as scientific observer has no privileged vantage point from which to discover the truth, it is assumed that the patient does, and the analyst has the power to know what the patient knows, even if the patient is not aware of it herself. (p. 54)

Therefore, both Rogers and the analysts which Mitchell (1993) describes would assume that there is a "singular, unmediated reality" (p. 54) that can be directly experienced. The immediate discovery and expression of this reality by the client, in turn, defines progress in psychotherapy and, ultimately, optimal psychological functioning. It is not surprising that this ideal level of functioning is currently described in relation to concepts of a "true" (Winnicott, 1960/1965) or "real" (Masterson, 1988) self.

Moving from the issue of the client's self-knowing to the therapist's knowing of the client, Laing's (1969) existential-phenomenological approach echoes Rogers' view that therapists must shift their mode of relating to the other. If we are truly interested in knowing the internal experience of the client, then Laing suggests that we should develop methods of study closer to those of the historian than those of the scientist. Laing's aversion to the canon of "objectivity" in therapeutic method and understanding is most apparent when he writes: "I think it is clear that by 'understanding' I do not mean a purely intellectual process. For understanding one might say love. But no word has been more prostituted" (p. 35).

The assumptions associated with subjectivism can be critiqued from either wing of the objectivist-constructivist split. As Mitchell suggested, many contemporary subjectivist therapies have emerged on the heels of the constructivist critique of objectivism, and they represent an attempt to reestablish the possibility of real "truth" in the therapeutic situation. Therefore, the counterattack which constructivists have mounted against this position has been particularly devastating. From a constructivist perspective, subjectivists are deluded if they think that there is any such thing as a pure, unorganized, uncontaminated substrate of experience which can be accessed by a client and known by a therapist. Citing material from cognitive psychology comparable to that which was reviewed in chapter 3, Mitchell (1993) concludes that consciousness—or unconscious experience, for that matter—"is fragmentary, discontinuous, and much too complex and inaccessible to be captured in a singular, true report" (p. 53). All experience is organized and structured to lesser or greater degrees, including the client's experience, the therapist's experience, and the therapist's experience of the client's experience. While approaching the client from a less objective stance might bring the therapist closer to the client's experience, both client and therapist will always remain a step (or more) removed from the truth they seek.

Up to this point in the discussion, the term "humanistic psychology" has been avoided. I have done so because it includes such a heterogeneous collection of philosophical assumptions, theoretical positions, and therapeutic approaches (Royce & Mos, 1981) that its use would detract from the clarity of the presentation. For example, humanistic psychology is typically described as rejecting the assumptions of both behaviorism and psychoanalysis, and Rogers' approach is usually seen as an exemplar of this orientation. However, as has just been demonstrated, Rogerians and analysts of a certain persuasion share key assumptions and—while it might be awkward to place them both under the humanistic flag—it is reasonable to say that both are phenomenologists or subjectivists.

Having introduced a term like "transpersonalism," however, I now have no choice but to try to locate it within the psychological movement from which it is borrowed. Transpersonal psychology is seen as a further development of humanistic psychology and is sometimes called the "fourth force" in psychology, following those associated with behaviorism, psychoanalysis, and humanism (Maslow, 1968).

When does a particular set of theoretical interests and psychotherapeutic practices attain the status of an identifiable, respected "subfield" within the larger discourse of psychology and psychotherapy? Although transpersonal psychology does not yet have its own division within the American Psychological Association, the *Journal of Transpersonal Psychology* has been published since 1969 and the first introductory text was introduced by Walsh and Vaughan in 1980. These authors tell us that there was a lively debate regarding the question of a name for this approach, and "transpersonal" was chosen "to reflect the reports of people practicing various consciousness disciplines who spoke of experiences of an extension of identity beyond both individuality and personality" (p. 16). To oversimplify, if humanistic psychology represents the study and promotion of actualization of the self, then transpersonal psychology extends this agenda to states of consciousness and being existing beyond the individual self.

Western psychology has been based largely on objectivist assumptions which would regard such interests as nonsensical, and many transpersonal psychologists have turned to nontraditional approaches to psychology, including those associated with both Western and Eastern philosophy and mysticism. Because transpersonal psychology breaks down barriers separating the disciplines of philosophy, religious studies, and psychology, I have chosen to illustrate it through presenting a strand of the work of Martin Heidegger.

Heidegger as Transpersonalist: Calculative vs. Meditative Thinking

Some readers may find it odd that Heidegger is likened to a transpersonal psychologist in these pages, and I would readily acknowledge that his thought is immensely more variegated and complex than the rubric under which it is considered here. Heidegger is usually regarded as an existentialist (chapter 2), but his work is also representative of the tradition of philosophical hermeneutics (Cushman, 1995). In fact, his philosophical position continued to evolve over his lifetime, and D. E. Cooper (1990) describes one aspect of the famous "turn" in his thinking through an anecdote involving another noted existentialist: "When a few years after the war, Sartre visited Heidegger in his mountain retreat, his disillusioned verdict was that Heidegger had gone mystical" (p. 7). While both Heidegger's earlier and later thinking is directed toward resolving the subject-object split in human experience, the nature of his approach to this problem, as will be indicated below, changed quite radically.

Accordingly, Heidegger's later thinking is presented as a form of Western "contemplation" in Hixon's (1978) excellent summary and formulation, having affinities with Taoism and Zen Buddhism (von Eckartsberg & Valle, 1981; M. E. Zimmerman, 1981). If mysticism is not defined in theistic terms but means "being emancipated from egoism and opened up to the mysterious presence of things, then both Heidegger's thinking and Zen are mystical" (M. E. Zimmerman, p. 270). Mystical discourses on the nature of a selfless or nonegoic "reality" typically emphasize the importance of method but discuss it in a paradoxical fashion. Experiencing a reality beyond the self depends on abandoning conventional methods of knowing and finding some alternative method which, from the standpoint of the self, appears to be a nonmethod. Heidegger's (1966) *Discourse on Thinking* represents a specific expression of this more generic mode of argument.

This small book contains an address which was delivered to an audience and an essay in the form of a conversation or dialogue which further develops its themes. In the introduction, John Anderson observes that, compared to his earlier writing, Heidegger in these essays takes a less technical and more poetic approach to exploring the question of ontology or *Being*. In fact, he does not even use the latter term, but it can be assumed that phrases like "a new ground for meaning" are synonymous with it. If the ground for meaning can be likened to his notion of ultimate reality, then Heidegger moves away from an analysis of its characteristics within a philosophical system and toward describing its direct manifestations in immediate human experience (Heidegger, 1966, p. 21).

Heidegger's address provides the terms which help to frame the dialogue which then follows. He tells us that real or deep thinking is always "meditative" or contemplative in nature and contrasts it with surface or "calculative" thinking. The two are interrelated, and under ideal circumstances the latter is grounded in the former. More frequently in the current age, however, we attempt to approach the world only through calculative thinking, because it is this mode which expresses our *will* to understand, organize, and dominate. It accomplishes these ends in part by "re-presenting" the world. Heidegger's term here conveys that calculative thinking simultaneously recreates the world based on past experience and represents the world through the medium of thought—such that our thoughts are taken as equivalent to the world itself. This implies that calculative thinking can make each of us into a foundationalist or realist philosopher whose own self represents the ground of existence: "Under the domination of egoism and self-will, an individual regards himself as the self-grounding vantage point around which everything else is organized as an object for him" (M. E. Zimmerman, 1981, p. 245). Therefore, calculative thinking taken to its extreme—which is something most of us do daily—is actually quite delusional in nature. The world is not based on the individual self, and reality can never be found through the will.

How, then, do we find true grounding, and what is its nature? If calculative thinking is an abstraction untethered to immediate reality, then the way back to "rootedness" is something that is close at hand (Heidegger, 1966, p. 48). Meditative thinking need not be "high-flown," and "it is enough if we dwell on what lies close . . . upon that which concerns us, each one of us, here and now" (p. 47). However, the very simplicity of meditative thinking may be deceiving. In psychological terms, Heidegger is merely asking us to give up all the ways we have of "re-presenting" the world—that is, all representations of the world including those which constitute the "self."

He then develops his ideas further by allowing us to drop in on a conversation among a Scientist, a Scholar, and a Teacher (himself?) which is unfolding on a walk along a path in the country. Metaphorically, the path might be seen as that which will take them to Being (reality), but they will lose their way if they don't first come to a better understanding of "thinking." Better yet, the path and Being can be seen as identical in nature, and this unbroken, authentic apprehension of reality is revealed as the participants move closer to embodying meditative thinking in successive moments of the conversation. Because this way of thinking is foreign to our usual mode, the characters struggle to express their insights and employ language which at times may seem awkward and obscure.

Near the beginning of the conversation, the protagonists realize that calculative thinking, which is defined by willing, cannot be transcended through an act of will. Although it is clear that they must learn to explore a non-willful thinking, it can neither be sought nor grasped. If they could actually experience non-willing, however, "releasement" would be let in. This term is an important one for Heidegger and the original German word was used by early mystics such as Meister Eckhart to mean "letting the world go and giving oneself to God" (p. 54, footnote 4).

The Scientist observes at several points that it is unclear how one can "re-present" this way of thinking, and some of my readers may in frustration be reaching the same conclusion! No, this way of thinking cannot be represented, just as it cannot be willed, since both go counter to meditative thinking. Indeed, the only "method" available for approaching this thinking is "waiting," but it can never involve an "awaiting" (p. 64). There is nothing to do but wait without expectation, since this thinking is not about "doing" but about Being.

This kind of waiting is relevant to the question which was asked in the last section about the possibility of transformative change, defined as a fundamental shift in one's horizon. The horizon itself is constituted through the re-presenting of objects, and waiting releases us from it and into the openness which surrounds us. Hixon (1978) relates the notion of openness to Heidegger's visual metaphor that "the field of vision is something open, but its openness is not due to our looking" (Heidegger, 1966, p. 64), and then comments:

> Openness is not due to any specific point of view but is, rather, the absence of single-perspective perceiving and thinking. And openness, not created by any effort on our part, is always present as primal awareness. Upon this openness we superimpose various worlds . . . that we organize through surface thinking. To representational thinking our world appears to contain objects, but it is revealed to contemplation as the open expanse of primal awareness. Mystics often assert, in their various languages, that there are no objects, that all is one flow, that what we actually perceive are the facets or textures of one harmonious Reality. (Hixon, 1978, p. 9)

The Teacher recognizes that this reality manifests as a kind of "enchanted region" (Heidegger, 1966, p. 65), an image that suggests a particular space which could again be reified into an object by calculative thinking. Therefore, in the continuing dialogue, "region" is replaced with "that-which-regions" or "regioning": "That-which-regions is an abiding expanse which, gathering all, opens itself, so that in it openness is halted and held, letting everything merge in its own resting" (p. 66). Hixon (1978) observes that Heidegger is using the dialogue to demonstrate that we must remain vigilant regarding subtle forms of calculative thinking which can continue to arise even in the presence of meditative thinking.

It should also be emphasized that Heidegger's language parallels "expressions in traditional mystical literatures that describe ecstatic experiences of leaving objects behind . . . as one expands into the Absolute" (Hixon, 1978, p. 10). Thus, the protagonists discover that they can be "exulting" in their waiting for they (their selves) become at once "more waitful and more void" (Heidegger, 1966, p. 82). Experiencing the voidness or emptiness of self and connecting with a larger ground of being is often accompanied by feelings of profound gratitude, and the characters later realize that this kind of thinking is actually a "thanking." They conclude that their walk has been a "moving-into-nearness. . . . She binds together without seam or edge or thread . . . She neighbors; because she works only with nearness" (pp. 89–90).

Heidegger's account concretely illustrates a philosophical position which is transpersonalist in its assumptions and mystical in its approach.

A reality exists, larger than that known by the individual self, and its direct apprehension represents ultimate truth. However, the door to this reality is closed to any method associated with the self or its representations, and one must search for another way in. When the ways of the self are finally exhausted, one suddenly finds oneself inside rather that outside this reality, but the method of entry cannot be completely described or codified. In fact, this very description—with its language of a different reality and a doorway to it and its categories of inside and outside—obscures more than it reveals.

Objectivist and Constructivist Critiques of Transpersonalism

While the general status of transpersonal psychology as a subfield will not be evaluated here, it is safe to say that Heideggerian thinking and other spiritual, mystical, or religious approaches still represent "marginalized" discourses within the fields of psychology and psychotherapy. Jones' (1994) call for establishing a "constructive relationship" between religion and psychology makes the point. This proposal would not be necessary if religion and spirituality were already integrated into mainstream psychology and psychotherapy.

Although such a relationship might be defined in a variety of ways, I am interested in examining objectivist and constructivist responses to the strong form of this proposal. That is, transpersonal psychotherapy has been characterized as approaches which are

> concerned with the psychological processes related to the realization (i.e., making real) of such states as "illumination," "mystical union," "transcendence," "cosmic unity," etc., as well as concerned with the psychological conditions or psychodynamic processes that are directly or indirectly a barrier to such transpersonal realizations. (Sutich, 1973, p. 3)

The reader is now asked to imagine that such a transpersonal therapy has been built on the Heideggerian concepts just presented—and then to picture an objectivist and a constructivist discussing it.

The objectivist, who contends that there is a firm line between religion and science, disapproves of this proposed therapy on principle:

> It is nothing more than the belief system of a therapist masquerading as the truth. First, those alleged "concepts" of Heidegger are so vague and confusing that it's hard to know what

he is talking about. Even if they could be translated into something more concrete, they do not lend themselves to empirical validation of any kind. All a therapist can ever offer in their support is his or her personal, subjective experience. Moreover, I didn't like the way that "calculative thought" was subtly disparaged by Heidegger. These spiritual and humanistic types always sound to me as if they are not just critiquing the dominance of rationality but are giving up on critical thinking of any kind. Now just where would that leave us as a field? I'll tell you. It leaves us unable to make distinctions of any kind so that when the next therapist comes along and says that his / her clients really were abducted by aliens and can be treated with hypnotic regression techniques, well, that "theory" must also be accepted. And it will then be accorded the same status as empirically validated interventions like cognitive-behavioral therapy and interpersonal psychotherapy.

The constructivist, who in this instance is more specifically a social constructionist, replies:

I wouldn't be quite so confident if I were you that science and religion represent fundamentally different kinds of activities. If you think that your beliefs don't impact what you do with clients, well then you are quite mistaken. I suppose that you also believe that "facts" can be completely separated from "theories!" As for Heidegger, it was also hard for me to follow his thinking at various points. But I found it fascinating that he anticipates so much of what postmodernists say about the problem of "representation" and the fiction of a separate self. My problem with his approach, however, is that the "ultimate reality" being talked about is just another narrative created by human beings. The social group creating this narrative may be mystics, accomplished in navigating and cataloging inner experience, but it's still a constructed human narrative, nevertheless. However, it is presented as something true and eternal, untouched by human thought: It is presented as a metanarrative. And that, in a nutshell, is the history of the psychotherapy field, and it has led to no end of philosophical, moral, and ethical problems. It also seems contradictory that an approach which wants to take us beyond the individual self is so exclusively individual and "interior" in its language. Finally, regarding your worries about opening the door to any theory whatsoever, I would be concerned if a therapist were *imposing* some view on clients. But keep in mind that your empirically validated treatments are no "truer" than a theory about alien abduction, although they may in general be more "useful." However, while I don't personally subscribe to it, if *clients* found an alien-abduction narrative to be useful, then I suppose. Hmm. Let me think more about that one.

I have sympathy for some of the issues raised by both of these hypothetical colleagues and will underscore them by reference to a tape recording of a meeting between a contemporary spiritual teacher and a group of psychotherapists. Gangaji grew up in this country and traveled to India to become the student of the spiritual teacher H. W. L. Poonja, who in turn was the student of the Indian Saint Ramana Maharshi. She and her teachers fall within the Hindu tradition of Advaita Vedanta, which asserts the nonduality of reality. Relative knowledge requires a subject and an object, but absolute knowledge or ultimate reality, defined as the "Self," is "not an experience of individuality but a nonpersonal, all-inclusive awareness" (Godman, 1985, p. 9). Following her direct realization of this Truth, Gangaji returned to the United States to teach and has attracted a large following here and abroad.

In the tape (Gangaji, 1994) of her meeting with a group of San Francisco Bay Area therapists, Gangaji acknowledges that she is not a trained psychotherapist, but indicates that she and her teacher are "secret therapists." She begins by suggesting that the goals of psychotherapy and spiritual work are the same and wonders how it could be otherwise. In both instances, the goal is to break the "linchpin" of identification which holds a separate sense of self in place and which blocks the direct experience of reality. Therefore, the most important factor in promoting change in the client is the therapist's "own depth of understanding . . . own depth of presence . . . own release of the linchpin."

None of the therapists dissent from this formulation, and it appears that some of them define the situation as one where Gangaji will function as a kind of clinical supervisor. Gangaji confirms this interpretation by offering an anecdote involving a therapist who came to her during a visit to Germany. The therapist wanted to see Gangaji rather than her regular supervisor "because I knew my supervisor couldn't understand this." The therapist described her work with two particular clients with whom she found herself falling asleep whenever they began to tell their personal "stories." Gangaji laughingly responded, "That's wonderful, that's great." The therapist felt validated by Gangaji's view that one shouldn't "buy into the story . . . it's not real." One of the clients left therapy, while the other began to "get it" that it was time to move on from just telling her story. Other therapists in the group echo that it is difficult to bring real presence to the work with clients who are too attached to their pain, suffering, and personal stories. One therapist adds that she is no longer willing to do therapy in any other fashion, that she brings a nondual approach to her work with every client, and that "if they are not ready for it at all, they can leave."

This example appears to validate some of the concerns of the objectivist and the constructivist alike. From an objectivist stance, no critical thinking was brought to the discussion. What should have been a question, "How is psychotherapy related to spirituality?" was turned into an assumption, "They are not different." No distinctions were made regarding the differing presenting problems, goals, and situations of clients who might seek therapy from these therapists, and on this issue the social constructionist would agree. No distinctions were possible because the participants in the discussion were speaking from the vantage point of a shared metanarrative. They have experienced the truth for themselves and now are predisposed to search for it in others regardless of the "local" context, language, or goals of those who are seeking their assistance.

Of course, there are transpersonal therapists who attend to the issue of context and adapt their approach to the needs of the client (Boorstein, 1986), and who engage in the critical discussion of cases (Waldman, 1992). The above observations are intended to convey that transpersonal psychotherapy is particularly susceptible to philosophical and ethical problems when its realist assumptions are applied uncritically to clinical situations.

SUMMARY AND CONCLUSIONS

This chapter and the last have reviewed the relationship of philosophical thinking to the nature and use of theory in psychotherapy. The previous chapter proposed a perspective toward the general functions that theory serves, and this chapter has investigated a wide range of specific theoretical positions and their associated philosophical assumptions.

Beginning with the latter, the present review has revealed that theories in the field of psychotherapy can be arrayed along a continuum which parallels the philosophical contrast between realism and anti-realism. Theories which are objectivist, subjectivist, and transpersonalist in assumptions represent the realist pole of this continuum, while theories which embrace one or another variety of constructivism cluster at the anti-realist pole.

However, it is not quite accurate to say that "theories" can be arrayed along this dimension. Upon closer examination, it is difficult to place approaches such as psychoanalysis or cognitive therapy at a single point on the continuum because of the heterogeneity of theoretical developments, therapeutic interventions, and therapist assumptions which can be associated with each. Further, it has not been easy at times to find consistency in assumptions, even when a theoretical analysis is restricted to a given therapist who is attempting to speak and practice from a given philosophical position. This tendency has been especially apparent for constructivist therapists, who frequently "regress" to realist assumptions in their theoretical statements and/or therapeutic interventions.

It is at this point in the discussion that the formulation of theoretical functions developed in the previous chapter becomes relevant. Observations from many different areas of study converge on the conclusion that human beings are theory-generating creatures. Whether we approach the world as laypersons or as psychotherapists, we take with us a perceptual/cognitive system which is constitutionally vulnerable to equating our implicit and explicit theories with "reality" or the "truth." Accordingly, alternative perceptions of reality are temporarily or more permanently suspended.

If we are naturally predisposed as human beings to approach the world with an implicit realist agenda, this proclivity will manifest despite our explicit philosophical and theoretical commitments as psychotherapists. From this perspective, it makes sense that constructivists have more difficulty than realists in maintaining consistency in their theoretical assumptions. Psychotherapists who embrace a constructivist epistemology of some type are going counter to the deeply ingrained habits of realism with which humans perceive, approach, and discuss the world. Therefore, at times, constructivists may speak in a fashion which proclaims the truth of their theoretical presuppositions, even if the content of those assumptions denies its possibility. On the other hand, psychotherapists who hold to a realist epistemology in their professional work should find less dissonance between their explicit and implicit philosophical commitments and can more easily maintain a consistent position. Finally, some therapists influenced specifically by philosophical hermeneutics might argue that any perceived inconsistency between their perspectivalist and realist thinking is altogether congruent with their philosophical and theoretical orientation. However, a position of "perspectival realism" does not necessarily exempt hermeneuticists from the *tacit* realist predispositions which plague constructivists, nor does it automatically close the gap between theory and practice which was noted in Cushman's therapy.

In the spirit of acknowledging the contributions of the marginalized discourse of transpersonalism, it is possible to draw implications from both Buddhist and Heideggerian thinking which might deepen our understanding of these observations about psychotherapists. Thurman (1989) underscores that debates among various Buddhist factions were preoccupied for centuries with the very questions which perplex modern and postmodern philosophers. The "Centrist" or "Middle Way" of Buddhism begins with the work of Nagarjuna, an Indian sage, in the second century A.D. and culminates with the thinking of Tsong Khapa, a Tibetan master, in the fifteenth century. Batchelor (Rabten, 1983), in an introduction to a translation of some of the Centrist texts, observes that "their closely reasoned arguments are principally aimed at uprooting the deep-seated tendency of the human mind to ascribe a certain concrete, inherent self-existence to phenomena" (p. 5).

Consider the proposition that human beings are characterized by a real, enduring self which orders the world of experience. The idealist says that such a self exists and allows us to find the truth, and the nihilist says that there is no self and that truth is impossible. The Centrist way "deconstructs" any notion of a real, enduring self but also contends that the nihilist is just as absolutist as the idealist. To say that the self does not exist is to make a truth claim no less than the claim that it does exist. This is so because both absolutism and nihilism represent *concepts* or intellectual constructions of a mind which has not yet discovered "emptiness" or "voidness."

As Heidegger's presentation made clear, it is easier to say what voidness or emptiness is *not* rather than what it *is*, but for my purposes the former is enough. Although Buddhadāsa Bhikkhu (1994) represents a different Buddhist tradition, he succinctly summarizes the negative definition of voidness by saying "Nothing whatsoever should be clung to" (p. 15). This statement applies to voidness or emptiness itself. When voidness is clung to in any way—that is, experienced through the self and presented as a concept or view associated with an intellectual system—then it is no longer true voidness. Thurman (1989) quotes Nagarjuna as also warning us about this possibility: "One who adopts emptiness as a view is thereby pronounced incurable" (p. 153). If one substitutes "postmodernism" or "anti-realism" for "emptiness" in Nagarjuna's statement, the contemporary relevance of his thinking is brought home.

Heidegger's (1966) contrast between calculative and meditative thinking could be employed to make the same point. If openness is equated with meditative thinking or Being in Heidegger's account, then any statement about openness which is made within the form and frame of calculative thinking is by definition false and misleading. In the context of these Buddhist and Heideggerian cautions, it follows that the Zen tradition developed "tests" (koans, stories, interviews with the Master) to differentiate true from false realization and favors forms of expression which are beyond the intellect and directly, concretely, and unmistakably convey the *experience* of emptiness (Watts, 1957).

I am not proposing that contemporary philosophical thinking be based on transpersonal assumptions, or that we should devise "tests" to determine if philosophers and psychotherapists actually understand "true emptiness." Rather, I am hoping to emphasize a point, through stating it within the language of another tradition, that was made earlier by a contemporary Western philosopher. Bernstein (1992) suggests that absolutism (realism) and nihilism (anti-realism) are simply two sides of the same coin, and that they necessarily exist in a dialectical relationship to one another. Given our finiteness, human knowing must be critiqued; but in order for there to be a critique, there must first be some affirmation, something which is known or believed to be known. However, there is a tendency to assert the primacy—or truth—of either affirmation or critique because of the absolutist tendencies of the human knower.

This chapter has illustrated how affirmation and critique manifest within the assumptions associated with contemporary theories of psychotherapy. It has also been demonstrated that the dialectic between these opposing positions toward knowing is ultimately played out by the individual theorist or therapist who holds and applies a given theory and its assumptions. What was a subtheme of this chapter will now become the focus of the argument.

Chapter 5

Philosophical Assumptions
as Lived Modes of Knowing

Eleanor Rosch (1991), who has contributed significantly to the development of cognitive science, reflects on the relationship between theory in this area of psychology and actual or "lived" experience by turning to Wittgenstein (1967). He asks us to picture two philosophically informed parents, one a "convinced realist" and the other a "convinced idealist," each of whom attempts to teach their children accordingly. The former aims to convey to her children that a real, external world exists and the latter strives no less intently to impress upon his children its fundamental nonexistence. However, the idealist will necessarily teach his children words like "chair," so that they can function and act in the physical and interpersonal world—for example, so that they can "fetch a chair" (p. 74e). Wittgenstein asks: "Then where will be the difference between . . . the idealist-educated children . . . and the realist ones? Won't the difference only be one of battle cry?" (p. 74e). Rosch comments that, from Wittgenstein's perspective, contemporary theories of cognitive science would represent no more than "entertainment" for the psychologists who produce them. They are not to be taken seriously because they are too far removed from the way that humans actually live.

It is interesting to compare Wittgenstein's remarks with those made more recently by two dedicated radical constructivists. Efran and Fauber

(1995) believe that their perspective has "perturbed" others because it undermines the world view which grounds daily living for most people. "The sophisticated epistemologist may regard objectivism as naive and antiquated, but everyone else still relies on it to get through breakfast" (p. 276). Wittgenstein would say, I believe, that Efran and Fauber have it right—if only they would include the sophisticated epistemologist in the group who rely on objectivism to get through breakfast!

TOWARD THE INTEGRATION OF PHILOSOPHY AND LIVED EXPERIENCE

What are the possible advantages of regarding philosophical assumptions as "lived experience" rather than solely as conceptually stated "positions?" If human knowing is characterized by a pull between affirmation and critique, then this dynamic ultimately is played out in the experience of the individual therapist who has made certain philosophical and theoretical commitments within a particular community of knowers. Exploring philosophical assumptions as lived experience might provide tools for understanding how the therapist actually functions moment-to-moment in the interaction with the client, whether or not this functioning conforms with the stated theoretical or philosophical position. Accordingly, this kind of study would take away the burden of consistency which is imposed on the therapist simply by holding a "position." If we did not assume that psychotherapists are or should be more consistent in the living out of their assumptions than other human beings (Mischel, 1968), we might discover something new about the practice of psychotherapy.

Therefore, the next question concerns how one might define an approach which would investigate philosophical assumptions as lived experience. Unfortunately, the existing empirical literature is not very helpful in clarifying this question. Some studies (e.g., Lyddon, 1989; G. J. Neimeyer & Morton, 1997) examine the relationship between clients' "epistemic styles" or "personal epistemologies" and their preferences for particular therapeutic approaches. Other research focuses more explicitly on the philosophical commitments of different types of therapists. Following the lead of Royce (1964), who proposed rationalism, empiricism, and metaphorism as exemplars of styles of knowing, Schacht and Black (1985) investigated the epistemological commitments of behavior *vs.* psychoanalytic therapists. DiGiuseppe and Linscott (1993), building on Mahoney's (1988a) contrast between "rationalist" and "constructivist" approaches to cognitive therapy, developed a questionnaire which might differentiate the assumptions of rational-emotive therapists from those of other cognitive-behavioral therapists.

The design of this research likens epistemological styles to dimensions of individual difference, akin to personality factors, and does not fit well with the present exploration—which anticipates some inconsistency in the philosophical assumptions held by therapists. However, not all of the results of these studies supported the experimental hypotheses and, therefore, are of more interest. In the Schacht and Black (1985) study, 86% of the psychoanalysts, as predicted, endorsed metaphorism as their dominant position, but the behavior therapists' responses were equally distributed among metaphorism, rationalism, and empiricism. DiGiuseppe and Linscott (1993) found that rational-emotive therapists endorsed more rationalist beliefs than "general" cognitive-behavioral therapists but also demonstrated as much endorsement of constructivist attitudes as this group. These results do not support the "hypothesis that the rationalist *vs.* constructivist philosophies are bipolar opposites which serve to distinguish between cognitive behavioral therapists" (p. 127). R. A. Neimeyer (1993) reaches a similar conclusion, proposing that this distinction might better be used to characterize differences "within" rather than "between" different approaches to therapy (p. 160, italics omitted).

The above studies were not designed to investigate whether therapist differences in stated epistemology translated into differences in how therapists actually conduct therapy, and DiGiuseppe and Linscott (1993) indicate that this question is a matter for further research. In the meantime, some aspects of therapists' lived experience could be clarified by appropriate conceptual analysis. For example, if many behavior therapists and rational-emotive therapists endorse more than one philosophical position, then it would be helpful to develop a mode of inquiry which would allow us to better understand the nature of this intra-therapist variability.

Although their general purpose is different, Hoshmand and Polkinghorne (1992) point the way to such an analysis. They argue that it is naive to assume that therapist behavior corresponds in some one-to-one fashion with a formal body of knowledge (theory, training, and research). Rather, more experienced therapists often have learned to modify this knowledge in a manner that is appropriate to the concrete situation. Moreover, practice offers the therapist the opportunity to develop new knowledge and to test out the pragmatic utility of both old and new knowledge claims such that this field "requires a well-articulated *epistemology of practicing knowledge*" (p. 59).

While Hoshmand and Polkinghorne are speaking specifically of psychotherapists, Schön (1983) draws some similar conclusions for skilled professionals as a group. He emphasizes the relationship of theory to practice by describing how professionals learn by processes of trial and error and "reflection-in-practice." The latter refers to the manner in which an experienced professional can simultaneously apply and critique a particular intervention, modifying it as necessary to fit the situation at hand but also holding in mind alternative approaches should a fit not prove possible.

Protter (1988), following Schön's lead, frames the relationship between theory and practice in psychoanalysis in terms of an "action theory." His "epistemic model" holds that there are three different, although interrelated, *ways of knowing* in psychoanalytic practice: (a) existential or experiential knowing which focuses on the subjective experience of the client and includes notions such as empathy, phenomenological understanding, and so forth; (b) contextual or interpersonal knowing which refers to the knowing of self and other within an intersubjectively constructed, dyadic relationship; and (c) textual or narrative knowing "which encompasses knowing the other in such a way as to confer a sense of meaningful, coherent order" (p. 507). Protter clarifies that "coherent" could also mean "accurate," "truthful," or "based on reality": It refers to the "hanging together" of what we know, whether reached by scientific, aesthetic, or other means (p. 507).

Protter (1988) believes that psychoanalytic work, broadly considered, employs these three modes, although a given school may emphasize one to the relative exclusion of the others. However, he contends that in the "fullest" psychoanalytic encounter, the analyst's work is "punctuated by vicissitudes of going in and out of these different modes," and the modes themselves interrelate in a kind of "circular interplay" (p. 519). That is, one mode both supplements and to some extent "deconstructs" (points out the limitations of) that which has preceded it. For example, the therapist's interpretation may be needed to supplement the client's own subjective experience at times, but the client's experience may also lead the analyst to completely modify or reject a given interpretation.

Protter's model, although grounded exclusively in psychoanalytic thinking, includes many of the necessary elements of a lived approach to philosophical assumptions. Of course, a more comprehensive framework would encompass the full range of theoretical and philosophical positions that have been reviewed here, and the categories could be adjusted accordingly. In addition, I would like to modify somewhat his central concept to emphasize other facets of the lived experience of the therapist. While it is apparent from Protter's writing that it is not what he intends, "ways of knowing" or like terms such as "epistemic styles" or "personal epistemologies" might be interpreted to mean that the therapist's assumptions about reality and its knowability exist solely on the cognitive plane.

Although their focus is the larger issue of the development of personal epistemologies in women, Belenky, Clinchy, Goldberger, and Tarule (1986) do not restrict these "ways of knowing" to the cognitive domain but include other dimensions such as "voice" and separation-connectedness in relationship. Mahoney (1996), in reflecting on their contribution, agrees that "our styles of knowing and our constructions of reality are not things we 'have' in the sense of possessions, but processes we live. We do not just 'think' them; we eat and breathe them" (pp. 133–134).

Hoshmand and Polkinghorne's (1992) notion of "practicing knowledge," as well as Woolfolk's (1998) similar concept of "practical knowledge," suggest another elaboration of "ways of knowing." Psychotherapy, as an endeavor that attempts to ameliorate the real problems of clients and as a practice that occurs within the medium of human interaction, depends upon—but can never be fully encompassed by—formal theory, method, and technique. Psychotherapists also rely heavily on "tacit" and "background" knowledge, including everyday, commonsense understanding, which "can never be made entirely explicit" (Woolfolk, pp. 111–112). For example, whatever our level of scientific or philosophical sophistication, we also function as naive realists, carrying with us an irreducible element of taken-for-granted understanding of the world—for example, we generally regard a "table" as a real, solid object rather than as an assemblage of space and atoms (p. 110). This material converges with that reviewed in chapter 3 on the functional linkage between lay and professional theories of human behavior and suggests that psychotherapists' ways of knowing must include commonsensical, realist elements.

Developing a concept which directly conveys that the therapist's assumptions about the world are not restricted to that which is explicitly, formally, or cognitively known would be in keeping with the example from Wittgenstein which began this chapter. Therefore, as a means of emphasizing that philosophical assumptions are embodied in human experience, I propose the term *"lived* modes of knowing." It will be defined by relating different components of the above discussion of ways of knowing to aspects of the concept of "ego states" as it has been developed in the clinical literature. This concept is generally credited to Paul Federn (1952), a psychoanalyst, and was then modified by Eric Berne (1961) and John G. Watkins (1978). Berne's transactional analysis approach conceives of ego states as "coherent systems of thought and feeling manifested by corresponding patterns of behavior" (1972, p. 11), and he popularized the division of such ego states into the categories of parent, child, and adult. Although Watkins also develops a general theory of personality, his interests include hypnotherapy and the exploration of dissociative states, and his modification of the ego state concept is particularly relevant to the description of these phenomena.

I would like to borrow selectively from Berne's and Watkins' clinical use of the ego state concept without importing the metapsychology in which it is embedded. For the purpose of formulating a practical concept which would encompass what it means for the therapist to live out different philosophical positions, it seems important to include the following elements: (a) A *lived mode of knowing* refers to the organization of experience which is associated with holding a given philosophical position. Experience coheres or "hangs together" when one is operating within the given mode, but there may be a radical change in experience if one shifts to a philosophical position characterized by a different mode of knowing (J. G. Watkins, 1978, pp. 194–195); (b) The ontological or epistemological stance expressed by a lived mode of knowing may correspond to naive or commonsense realism rather than to that of a more formal philosophical or theoretical position (Woolfolk, 1998); (c) The therapist's experience within a lived mode of knowing may include cognitive, affective, and behavioral (interpersonal) components (Berne, 1972); (d) Lived modes of knowing may function at different levels of awareness, and the therapist may also be selectively aware of the different components of a given mode (J. G. Watkins, 1978, pp. 204–205). For example, a therapist committed to an anti-realist epistemology may at times behave in a realist fashion without consciously acknowledging this discrepancy; (e) In accord with the functions of theory outlined in chapter 3, lived modes of knowing function both to reveal and restrict what the therapist sees in the world; (f) Finally, following Protter (1988), while lived modes of knowing can be separated for purposes of explication, they are not completely independent and often function in a dialectical relationship to one another, wherein a given mode both supplements and partially deconstructs that which has preceded it.

This concept of lived modes of knowing is intended to be descriptive and "experience-near" rather than explanatory in nature. No assumptions are made about specific metapsychological constructs including those proposed by Freud, Federn, Berne, or Watkins. Rather than referring to a psychodynamic structure of some kind, the referent for this concept is closer to that of the "organizing schemes" that therapists bring to their practice (Hoshmand & Polkinghorne, 1992, p. 60)—if it can be assumed that such schemes derive in part from implicit and explicit philosophical positions, exist at varying levels of awareness, and include cognitive, affective, and interpersonal components.

A FRAMEWORK FOR LIVED MODES OF KNOWING

A categorization of lived modes of knowing, based on the philosophical and theoretical positions which have been reviewed in previous chapters, will now be introduced. Before turning to that framework, it is useful to first clarify its status in the overall argument. Indeed, just as clinically oriented readers were asked to show forbearance with some of the philosophical content of prior chapters, the same may now need to be asked of readers who are either more empirically minded or philosophically inclined. A critic could argue that the likening of philosophical positions to "ego states" has not been adequately justified to this point, whether one evaluates "justification" primarily on empirical, theoretical, or philosophical grounds. Instead, a clinically based "action" concept has now been introduced into the argument, and its justification is similar to that given for other concepts generated from case material. Does it provide an integrative focus for one's present clinical observations? Does it have useful implications for one's future clinical judgments and interventions?

Articulating this justification somewhat more formally, the framework of lived modes of knowing is intended as a "heuristic" device in the development and presentation of this argument. Philosophically, heuristic means "conducive to understanding, explanation, or discovery" and particularly refers to investigations "conducted by trial and error" (Honderich, 1995, p. 354) whose validity has not yet been completely established. Most clinical concepts rest on heuristic grounds, and the value of the one proposed here will be measured by its success in allowing the reader to discover, understand, or "see," especially through the more concrete examples given in the next chapter, these lived modes of knowing in one's own and others' clinical work.

Of course, the proposed framework also has its disadvantages. There is an arbitrary element to any taxonomy or classification system,

TABLE 3

Lived Modes of Knowing in the Therapist's Experience

Therapist Mode of Knowing:	REALIST	REPRESENTA-TIONAL	PERSPECTIVAL
Related Philosophical Position:	Realism	Sophisticated Realism	Sophisticated Relativism
Function of Theory:	REVELATORY		
Outcome for Theory User:	PRODUCES CONFIRMATION		
Nature of Implicit or Explicit Theory Use:	*Metaphorical:* directly reveals reality	*Hypothetical:* extends a model	*Constructive Alternativist:* chooses among alternative perspectives in relation to internal (coherence) or external (empirical; pragmatic) criteria
Status of Therapist Perceptions and/or Interpretations:	Reveal truth *in* client, therapist, or situation	Are testable hypotheses which, if supported, can approximate the truth	Are constructs which can represent knowledge, not truth
Therapist's Own Experience:	Meaning; belief; confidence; affective connection with client		
Expected Client Response:	Meaning; belief; coherence; hope; faith in therapist		
Identity of Therapist:	Scientific Healer; Knower; Shaman; Wise Woman/Man; Role Model	Scientist-Practitioner	Scientist-Practitioner

TABLE 3 *(continued)*

DIALOGICAL	CRITICAL	NIHILISTIC
Affirmative Postmodernism	Skeptical Postmodernism	Skeptical Postmodernism
		RESTRICTIVE
		EXPERIENCES DIS-CONFIRMATION
Collaborative: generates a new dialogical perspective in relation to ethical, political, aesthetic, or pragmatic factors	*(Limited) Deconstructive:* critiques existing perspectives	*(Unlimited) Deconstructive:* negates any possibility of a perspective
Interpretation is rejected, but dialogical narratives can represent knowledge, not truth	Interpretations and narratives reveal therapist's socially mediated knowledge, not truth	Neither truth nor knowledge is possible, so interpretation is moot
		Meaninglessness; anxiety; despair; uncertainty; ironic detachment
		Meaninglessness; lack of faith in therapist; lost hope
Accomplished Rhetorician or Conversationalist; Agent of Empowerment	Social Critic; Agent of Empowerment	No therapist role / identity is possible

and, depending on one's goals and assumptions, a compelling argument could be made for a different set of categories than that which is proposed here. There also can be an artificial quality to aspects of an analysis of this kind, where the fit between a proposed category and the therapist's experience may at times seem forced. Further, as Protter (1988) emphasized with his own formulation, the lines of difference between some of the categories are exaggerated for the purpose of exposition. Despite these limitations, I believe that the inclusion of this framework will serve the heuristic goal of assisting clinicians in recognizing how their work with clients is impacted, both formally and informally, by philosophical assumptions.

An overview of hypothesized lived modes of knowing and their differences is presented in table 3. Both this table and the individual discussions of each way of knowing in the next chapter are intended to provide a descriptive account of the therapist's experience within and across the different modes. Since the table offers some direction and structure to that account, I will begin with a preliminary clarification of some of its entries.

In this discussion, "ways" or "modes" of knowing, "approaches" to knowing, and "stances" toward knowing will be used interchangeably with the primary term, "lived modes of knowing." Although these terms emphasize the epistemological assumptions which therapists bring to therapy practice, it will become apparent that the framework, like the prior reviews on which it was built, also includes ontological assumptions. Finally, the modes will be capitalized, not as an honorific gesture, but to indicate that generic terms are being used in a quite specific fashion which will become clearer as the discussion unfolds.

Beginning with the entries on the left side of the table, the first entry proposes a summary term for each mode of knowing and the second entry links it with a dominant philosophical position, and detailed justifications for these choices will be provided in the next chapter. The next two entries are intended to convey that the Realist and Nihilistic modes of knowing represent the poles of a continuum. The Realist mode is associated with the revelatory function of theory while the Nihilistic mode focuses exclusively on its restrictive function. Operating from the Realist mode will seem to *produce* confirmation of one's theory or experience of the client, while functioning within a Nihilistic mode will lead the therapist to *experience* disconfirmation of that same theory or experience.

The next two entries focus on the therapist's use of theory and interpretation and are intended to outline in a more specific fashion the ontological and epistemological assumptions which are associated with each mode of knowing. The wording of the first entry indicates that the therapist's approach to the client is always characterized by some implicit or explicit theoretical stance or set of philosophical assumptions, whether or not the therapist is aware of it. This point, as well as the ontological and epistemological status of the therapist's perceptions and / or interpretations, will be covered in much greater detail in the individual discussions of the different modes.

The entries "Therapist's Own Experience" and "Expected Client Response" are intended to capture something of the affective and interpersonal components of functioning, again, from within ways of knowing which are polar opposites. However, in this instance, it is not assumed that the modes of knowing are arrayed as a continuum. Although one will likely experience the world as meaningful from a Realist mode and as meaningless from a Nihilistic mode, the other modes of knowing are also associated with the experience of meaning. The last entry attempts to characterize the identity for the therapist that emerges if therapeutic practice is defined solely in relation to a given mode of knowing, and this issue will be considered in more detail in the final chapter, which addresses the moral implications of this framework.

Chapter 6

Lived Modes of Knowing
in the Therapist's Experience

Using table 3 as a compass, each of the six modes of knowing will now be reviewed separately with the goal of providing the reader with a set of referents for identifying what it means for a therapist to *live* a given ontological and epistemological position. These descriptions encompass commonsensical, philosophical, theoretical, methodological, and phenomenological dimensions of therapist functioning and, where possible, are illustrated with case or other therapeutic examples. Inevitably, there is some redundancy with materials reviewed in previous chapters as philosophical and theoretical assumptions are translated to the context of applied understanding and therapeutic method. If this presentation is successful, readers will leave it with referents which are sufficiently detailed and concrete as to allow them to recognize or "see" lived modes of knowing in their own or others' work as therapists.

Before turning to this review, two of its key assumptions will be acknowledged and clarified. First, as was the case for the objectivist-constructivist contrast presented in chapter 4, this framework is intended to apply primarily to the therapist's behavior and experience rather than to global theories of personality and psychotherapy. Therefore, it is not assumed that a given theoretical orientation necessarily can be reduced to a single mode of knowing. Even those theoretical positions which emphasize one mode of knowing—for example, classical psychoanalysis (objectivist or Realist knowing) and cognitive therapy (Representational knowing)—may depend on other modes as well. In addition, some orientations are theoretically grounded in the interaction of two or more modes of knowing—for example, social constructionist therapies which alternate between Dialogical and Critical knowing. Other theoretical orientations relate even more complexly to this framework—for example, some hermeneutically influenced therapists might adopt the epistemology, but not the ontology, of Dialogical knowing. However, despite an explicit attempt to ground their collaborative knowing in a nonobjective, hermeneutic realism, such therapists would find it impossible at times to avoid "living out" this position as a form of commonsensical (objective Realist) knowing. Indeed, congruent with the dialectical perspective that has been developed to this point in the argument, it is assumed that the interrelationship of different modes of knowing in the therapist's experience becomes thematic when the question turns from theory to practice.

Second, the Realist mode of knowing is meant to encompass a quite large and heterogeneous collection of ontological and epistemological positions, including commonsense or naive realism, scientific realism, subjective realism, and transpersonal realism. In defense of this approach, an analogy can be made to Jerome Frank's (1973) work on comparative psychotherapy, which was cited in chapter 1. He proposes that it might be clarifying to bracket the question of the unique "contents" of different therapeutic theories and methods, and instead look for common factors which crosscut them. While this strategy necessarily glosses over important differences, it has the potential for revealing something which applies to all psychotherapy as practiced.

Similarly, the approach which has been taken here emphasizes that therapists who are holding, in the moment, quite different assumptions—including those associated with common sense, objectivism, subjectivism, or transpersonalism—may yet have something in common. When therapists assume that their perceptions can provide an untainted, veridical account of "reality," they are functioning from a Realist mode of knowing. This is not to say that one could not mount an argument regarding differences in the evidential base of common sense *vs.* "mysticism" *vs.* objectivism. Rather, this comparative approach suggests, as does Frank, that the theoretical frameworks of therapists who rely heavily on Realist knowing tend to function as "myths" whose truth value is not easily shaken. This formulation then allows for these variants of realism to be contrasted with alternative epistemological positions.

THE REALIST MODE OF KNOWING

Staking out the territory of the Realist mode will be accomplished in part by contrasting it with its close neighbor, the Representational mode. This contrast will depend in turn on an understanding of the difference between thinking which can be described in terms of "metaphor" rather than "model."

The Metaphorical Nature of Realist Knowing

Textbooks (e.g., C. S. Hall & Lindzey, 1978) tell us that the theories which underlie an understanding of personality and psychotherapeutic change have neither the formal characteristics nor the empirical support of comparable theories in the natural sciences. Therefore, some psychologists and psychotherapists have attempted to recognize the current level of theory-building of these disciplines by describing their own efforts as "models" of human behavior (Price, 1978).

The prior review of the philosophy of science suggests that the above view considerably oversimplifies the problems facing the knowledge claims made by the natural sciences themselves—that is, it can be argued that they, too, can offer only "models" of the nature of the world. Nonetheless, the proposed term does capture one key element of the theoretical rationales which are most commonly generated in the field of psychotherapy. Some phenomenon is not understood, and an analogy is made: Light is shed on the unknown by attempting to bring it into some relationship with the known. When Freud says that we might think of the client's hysterical symptoms as if they were "strangulated emotions" or that we might conceptualize libido as if it were a quantum of energy which can be dammed and then diverted into side channels, he is making analogies.

The problem with concluding that our theories of psychotherapy function primarily as models, however, is the way that we often apply and "live" them. Ideally, a model is a hypothesized, tentative representation of reality that is incomplete and that retains its "as if" quality. But what happens when we are working with a client from the standpoint of a given model, whether that model is psychoanalytic drive theory, Jungian theory, control mastery theory, or cognitive theory? Oftentimes, there is no "as if" quality to the experience whatsoever. Suddenly, the process of working within a model becomes more like "seeing" or "experiencing" with conviction. We see the client's behavior or experience as a literal manifestation of repressed sexuality, the collective unconscious, unconscious tests, or faulty cognitions. When concepts like libido are reified into existence, instantly the world becomes populated with the terms of our theories, and this process is more akin to the use of metaphor than the use of a model.

Like a model, a metaphor makes an analogy but does so in a more literal, concrete, and compelling fashion. Metaphors such as "All the world's a stage" or "Love is war" immediately and concretely fix our attention on some similarity between two domains which might previously have been regarded as quite distinct. Lakoff and Johnson (1980) insist that metaphor pervades all human discourse, and Olds (1992) contends that "metaphor characterizes science as well as the humanities, and provides a nexus for approaching issues of truth" (p. 24). Yet, what is most crucial to the present argument is the manner in which metaphor transforms human thinking and experience.

Price (1978) illustrates the transformative power of metaphor in the context of examining theories of abnormal behavior. Although a given scientist may propose a model for accounting for some phenomenon, Price argues that "metaphor . . . more adequately describes the scientist's thought processes" (p. 14). He then concretizes his approach by demonstrating how a model of abnormal behavior ("Let us think of abnormal behavior *as if* it were like an illness") can become transformed into a metaphor ("Abnormal behavior *is* an illness").

Following Schön's (1963) characterization of metaphorical thinking as a process of "displacement of concepts," Price (1978) describes four interrelated phases by which a metaphor like that of mental illness is born. *"Transposition"* involves transferring a concept from one domain ("People who act strangely") to another domain ("are similar to people who have physical illness"). *"Interpretation"* consists of drawing out more specific applications of the general analogy. A specific phenomenon associated with the old category ("Visions") is reinterpreted within the new category ("are symptoms of illness"). Since not every concept of the old category will fit into the new category, *"correction"* refers to the back-and-forth process where the connections are refined ("Not all unconventional beliefs are symptoms or signs of illness"). *"Spelling out the metaphor"* entails examining further areas of similarity and difference between the two domains and then drawing implications from the areas of similarity ("Since people who have visions are sick, they should be treated in hospitals") (pp. 15–16).

Price (1978) emphasizes that once these phases have been completed, the metaphor is in place: Abnormal behavior *is* illness. Although metaphor shares some characteristics with a model—for example, it is based on analogy—it serves other, intriguing functions in relation to human cognition and perception. As a process of thinking: (a) Metaphor *transforms* the original concept which was applied to the new situation, thereby creating a "new" concept. For example, not only is abnormal behavior seen in a different fashion when regarded as a symptom of illness, the concept of illness is itself transformed, because mental illness and physical illness are not quite the same; (b) Metaphor *"fixes our view of the situation in question.* Once our view of the metaphor is established, further inquiry into the meaning of the events in question tends to stop"; and (c) Metaphor *"makes the new construction seem very real to us. . . .* Once the metaphor of mental illness is established, we do not doubt its reality." Price summarizes these effects of metaphor on thinking in terms of its *"perceptual"* impact: We simply "see" the world differently once it is in place (pp. 17–18).

To say that the Realist mode and metaphorical thinking are synonymous would bring this material on metaphor directly to the issue of psychotherapeutic practice. While metaphor has been discussed in the context of developing an explicit theoretical stance (the illness view of abnormality), commonsensical metaphorical thinking is pervasive and can influence perception regardless of the therapist's position regarding the importance of theory. Even a therapist who rejects all theory and attempts to remain as "experience-near" as possible will at times, by virtue of being human, have perceptions of the client which are metaphorical in nature. In fact, the view that therapeutic progress consists of the movement of the client ever closer to some substrate of uninterpreted experience which represents the "true self"—and which the therapist can also recognize and directly contact—is itself metaphorical in nature.

However, it is important to differentiate one specific meaning and use of metaphor from the more generic thrust of this discussion. The intentional use of "therapeutic metaphors" (e.g., J. C. Mills & Crowley, 1986) covers a great many different kinds of therapeutic interventions and associated theoretical and philosophical assumptions. Depending on those assumptions, such therapeutic interventions could be associated with several modes of knowing. Only if the therapist "believes" the metaphor which is presented to the client or "sees" the metaphor as manifested in the client's behavior would one say that the therapist is, in that moment, operating from a Realist mode of knowing.

The Phenomenology of Realist Knowing:
Objective *vs.* Subjective Approaches

What, then, is the phenomenology of a therapist who is experiencing a client from within a broadly metaphorical or Realist mode? Given that this mode of knowing can occur whether one views therapy as art, science, or spiritual discipline, and regardless of one's stated philosophical or theoretical commitments, it is impossible to characterize all of its differing, concrete manifestations. However, I can give a hint of the range of those manifestations by contrasting Realist knowing within objective *vs.* subjective approaches to therapeutic understanding, and can then attempt a description which might apply to both.

The objective approach to psychotherapy begins with Freud (1912/1958), who modeled his relationship with the client on that of the investigative scientist or, better, "the surgeon, who puts aside all his feelings, even his human sympathy" (p. 115). The therapist should be a keen observer who maintains neutrality, such that the material which arises within the client is uncontaminated by the therapist's influence. In listening to the client, the therapist should maintain an attitude of "evenly suspended attention" and not attempt to relate the client's material to any consciously held preconceptions. However, the therapist understands the unconscious in a way which the client does not and offers interpretations from that understanding which will help the client replace unconscious battles between instinct and defense with rational choice. Freud graphically conveys how the analyst's unconscious "tunes in" and receives direct communications from the client's unconscious: "He must turn his own unconscious like a receptive organ towards the transmitting unconscious of the patient. He must adjust himself to the patient as a telephone receiver is adjusted to the transmitting microphone" (pp. 115–116). Mitchell (1993) summarizes very well these premises of classical psychoanalysis and their relationship to Realist knowing with the following observation: "The analyst has privileged access into the patient's experience; the analyst knows what is real and what is not" (p. 17).

By assuming that the unconscious really exists and that the client's free associations represent derivatives of this unconscious, the analyst can reconstruct its original form and do so with supreme confidence. Spence (1987), in a work entitled *The Freudian Metaphor*, cites the following example of analytic reasoning to make the point:

> A young man talks in his hour of his anger and disgust at his older sister's toilet habits. She leaves the door slightly ajar so he can accidentally see her ugly naked breasts. He can even hear the different toilet noises and they are disgusting. . . . Despite the loud conscious anger and disgust it is quite easy to hear in the background the young man's sexual interest in his sister's

bodily activities. His unconscious fantasies of taking the different parts of her in his mouth make him feel disgust and nausea.
He is not angry at her for being ugly; quite the contrary, he is
angry at her for being exciting. (Greenson, 1967, pp. 365–366)

Spence then comments on the conviction conveyed by this analyst's
Realist knowing:

The patient's sexual fantasies about his sister are the clear and
certain cause of his reaction; there seems no possibility for error
or for the contribution of other factors. There is no discussion
of the possibility that what Greenson "hears in the background" may not be "heard" by other readers. (p. 24)

Today, many therapists are no longer so confident that the rational
understanding which Freud sought is entirely possible, or that the kind
of objective relationship through which he pursued it is quite feasible.
Empathy may be valued as much or more than a rational understanding
of the client, and it is seen as occurring within a relationship that inherently includes subjective and intersubjective components (Kahn, 1991).
Tansey and Burke (1989) contend that the therapist's empathy is always
based on identificatory processes, and they make the unconventional
suggestion that it actually represents an interpersonal response to the
"projective identifications" of the client. Natterson and Friedman
(1995) suggest that the concept of empathy, especially as it has developed within self psychology, itself "tends to objectify or reify" the experience which occurs whenever the client and therapist have "a rich and
productive intersubjective engagement" (p. 127).

To illustrate, Natterson, the senior author above, speaks of a 30-
year-old, single, female client who was seeing him in analysis. She presented a dream which included, in his view, themes of sexual
transference, hurt/humiliation, and rejection which seemed to place him
in "an unpleasant light" (p. 81). The client's father was to arrive the day
she brought the dream to analysis, and she often experienced feelings of
hurt and resentment in that relationship because of his greater investment
in her brother. Although the analyst was aware of these themes, he chose
to interpret the dream in a different fashion. He pointed out the paradox
between her negative feelings toward him in his transference role and
her growing willingness to be open with him (e.g., remembering and
bringing the dream), thereby allowing more intimacy in the relationship.
The client accepted the interpretation as an accurate perception of her

feelings and, in the subsequent session, shared more of her distress about her father which led the analyst to experience "acute empathic pain" (p. 82). He indicated that he was "experiencing her feelings, albeit in an attenuated form" (p. 82), and this comment brought forth more tears and revelations regarding the father's emotionally withholding relationship with her.

Natterson then suggests that this interpretation, like all interpretations, expresses an aspect of the therapist's own emotional life. The specific interpretation which he offered arose while he was listening to the dream:

> Although she pictured me in the dream as hurting her feelings in several ways, I was deeply impressed by the paradox: I felt quite close to and respectful of her, and I assumed that she was feeling the same toward me. This experience constituted the gist of my interpretation. It is clear that my subjectivity was crucial for the interpretation (p. 83).

He goes on to link his subjective response to her with his wish "to be an effective parent who could help her find her own voice and her own self and in that way continue to develop my own identity" (p. 84).

Although it is not assumed that either Freud's or Natterson's entire work as a therapist can be reduced to a single mode of knowing, the specific examples of objective *vs.* subjective understanding given above can be combined to produce a more general picture of the Realist mode. Functioning within this mode involves an act of reaching out to the client with our own consciousness and sharing something which we perceive as "true." Some understanding which is within us is seen or experienced as if it also describes, applies to, or exists within the client. This process may have a quality of joining, meeting, sharing, merging, giving, or even imposing. It is an act of discovering, recreating, and validating our own meanings through finding and experiencing them within the client's experience. This discovery is often quite compelling to us, and it may be communicated to the client in a compelling fashion as well. If the client accepts what we offer, whether it is an interpretation or simply our empathic understanding, there may be a heightened state of increased contact and mutuality in the relationship, as well as a sense of increased meaningfulness, well-being, and confidence within ourselves.

Therefore, therapists generally assume the accuracy of their interpretations and empathic responses when operating within the Realist mode and expect the client to respond in kind. Should the client share the therapist's perceptions, however, there is no independent means by which accuracy or truth might be evaluated. The success of an interpretation can also represent a measure of the therapist's influence and the client's quest for new meanings (Frank & Frank, 1991). Similarly, "given the intuitive conviction that often accompanies empathic experiences," the question of the validity of empathy as a form of understanding is often overlooked, nor is such validity easily established (Eagle & Wolitzky, 1997, p. 233). Bracketing the issue of truth, therapeutic progress might often be served by shared understandings which both therapist and client *believe* to be true (Frank & Frank, 1991). However, there are exceptions to this generalization, and the prior example of a client and therapist sharing a UFO etiology of symptomatology could represent a case in point.

As will become apparent, the Realist mode and the metaphorical thinking which is associated with it are ubiquitous experiences which can intrude into any human discourse. At key therapeutic moments, all therapists will at times present their understandings to the client in the form of Realist knowing.

THE REPRESENTATIONAL MODE OF KNOWING

The above discussion has laid the groundwork for an understanding of Representational knowing and also has introduced the rationale for the term which was chosen to describe this mode. An attempt is made to understand a phenomenon by drawing an analogy from another domain, and the latter is intended to provide a model, picture, or "representation" of the former.

Representational Knowing and
Scientific Models of Psychotherapy

Pribram (1990), discussing the growth of knowledge in the area of neuropsychology, contends that "analogical reasoning" is crucial to scientific discovery (p. 79). In his view, this process usually begins with metaphor, and he documents how analogies drawn from telecommunications, control systems engineering, computer science, and holography have influenced the understanding of the nervous system during this century.

> Often the analogical thinking is implicit. Sometimes it is explicit, as when the brain is compared to a telephone switchboard or to

the central processing unit of a computer. In either case, the analogy provides a step in the understanding of how the human brain functions. (p. 81)

Therefore, scientific investigation often begins with a rough analogy or metaphor which, according to Price (1978), serves the following functions. It helps us to "select" certain events as relevant to an investigation and allows us to discard others; it provides us with a "mode of representation" of that which we would like to understand better; and it provides a way of "organizing" the observations that we make (pp. 12–13, italics omitted).

However, Pribram (1990) believes that metaphor alone can provide only a kind of "existential understanding" (p. 80), and that science depends on refining the metaphor into a model. This transformation includes attitudinal, cognitive, and methodological components. Attitudinally, the analogy that has been made must be treated as a tentative representation of reality, not as reality itself. Cognitively, investigators must continue to bring critical thinking to the original metaphor, trimming it "into more and more precise shape, primarily through reasoning by analogy back and forth between the two things being compared" (pp. 97–98). Methodologically, there is an insistence on the ground rules of science, namely, empirical work which is open to the scrutiny of one's peers. Through critical reasoning based on maintaining an "as if" attitude and empirical testing, the original analogy is eventually refined into a "precise scientific model" (p. 98).

The comments by Price and Pribram characterize very well what I have called the "Representational" mode of knowing, and this description can also be linked with concepts from the philosophy of science. Like Popper's philosophy, this approach to knowing assumes that scientists can learn from their mistakes: A given model will be revised in light of disconfirming evidence. Or, as Pribram indicates in his account of neuropsychology, one model can be displaced by another through testing in the scientific community. For example, the view of the brain as a telephone-like system gave way over time to a computer analogy, and, in some circles, that model has now given way to a holographic analogy. Although it should never be assumed in Representational thinking that a model is equivalent to reality, this mode of knowing does share the ontological and epistemological assumptions of Popper's sophisticated realism. It is assumed that successive models, refined through testing against the "facts" of the world, represent closer and closer approximations to the nature of reality.

Therefore, a therapist operating within a Representational mode can be described as having made—at least for the moment—an implicit or explicit theoretical commitment of some kind. Like Kuhn's scientist who is practicing "normal science" or Feyerabend's scientist who is emphasizing the "normal component," this therapist assumes that understanding is most likely to result if he or she defines a particular theoretical or therapeutic approach, sticks with it, and traces out its implications. This attitude toward theory and therapy is the opposite of what Feyerabend would call the "philosophical component." Yes, many different perspectives about the nature of personality and psychotherapy are out there, but progress in understanding is more likely to result if I tend my own garden and not worry about what you are growing in yours. We'll then see who produces the most interesting varieties.

The Representational mode of knowing can be found in countless examples of theory development and application in contemporary psychotherapy. For that matter, one way of accounting for the proliferation of psychotherapeutic approaches in the field today is to underscore the dominance of Realist and Representational modes of knowing. If it is assumed that one's approach either is essentially true or is the most likely candidate to approximate the truth, then, given the immense variety of ways in which human truth can be defined, proliferation is inevitable.

For example, within the area of short-term dynamic psychotherapy alone, Crits-Christoph and Barber (1991) bring together ten different models, including those associated with James Mann, Lester Luborsky, and Jeffrey Binder and Hans Strupp. At the end of this edited volume, they comment: "The multitude of brief dynamic psychotherapies puts a burden on practitioners and researchers about how to distinguish between them, which form to choose, and for what purposes" (Barber & Crits-Christoph, 1991, p. 323).

Of course, not all of the models in this collection have been subjected to close empirical scrutiny, and one might ask if all should be considered as examples of the Representational mode of knowing. Although the discussion to this point has placed Representational knowing squarely within a scientific approach to understanding, keep in mind that "science" is defined quite generically within the field of psychotherapy. Freud considered himself to be a scientist because his clinical observations represented the "data" against which his theories could be tested. As the literature on the relationship between research and practice reveals, the great majority of practicing therapists do not actively engage in empirical work as conventionally defined, nor are they particularly interested in the empirical work produced by others. However, this does not mean that they might not regard themselves as broadly "scientific" in their approach to clinical practice.

For example, Baker (1991), in his articulation of a self psychological approach to "shorter-term psychotherapy" in the above volume, comments:

> There have been scores of excellent case studies on self psychology, and self psychologists are generally agreed that this theory has yielded superior results. We have found that we are able to help most patients more effectively and that we can treat patients previously considered unreachable. However, there are no experimental outcome studies, and all descriptions of the therapeutic process are merely anecdotal. (p. 317)

Baker does suggest that the self psychological approach has received indirect empirical support from studies that correlate good outcome with a positive therapeutic alliance. Further, he admits that any theory will clarify some aspects of the client's life while obscuring others, and that clients certainly can be helped with entirely different techniques than his own. Yet, speaking of self psychology, he still can conclude: "I have found this perspective useful—I think more useful than alternate approaches" (p. 319). Acknowledging a multitude of plausible perspectives within the field while contending, nonetheless, that one's own approach is superior—based on nothing more than clinical observation— is altogether typical of Representational knowing in psychotherapy.

The Phenomenology of Representational Knowing: Beck's Cognitive Therapy

Representational knowing has been defined in relation to philosophical commitments and general attitudes toward theory, and I would now like to illustrate some of its phenomenological characteristics in the context of therapeutic application. Aaron Beck's approach to cognitive therapy provides what is perhaps the quintessential example of the Representational mode in actual work with a client.

Beck, Rush, Shaw, and Emery's (1979) cognitive approach to depression is based on the commonsense view that there is an intrinsic relationship between thoughts (cognitions), emotions, and behaviors. While a problem such as depression may have cognitive, emotional, biological, and behavioral components, it is assumed, in most instances, that the first component is primary. If changes can be made in the manner in which the client cognitively structures the world, then comparable changes can occur in the other components of experience.

This therapy assumes, therefore, that each of us has developed his or her own theory which is itself a kind of "model" or "representation" of the world. Individuals who have difficulties and develop depressive symptoms are basing their interpretations of the world on models which are not working very well. The inadequacies of these models can be described in relation to underlying dysfunctional assumptions, beliefs, or schemas ("If I am not perfect in all I do, I'm a failure"), which in turn produce negative "automatic thoughts" ("I will fail at that test, I just know it") (pp. 3–4). Since clients with such schemas and automatic thoughts are not necessarily failures in all that they do, how do they maintain their models in the face of contradictory facts? Beck and his colleagues suggest that depressed clients are characterized by "systematic errors" in thinking which allow them to maintain their existing models of the world. For example, their thinking may be "absolutistic" or "dichotomous" in nature, so that all events are interpreted either as success or failure (p. 14).

In the language of this chapter, the assumptions of cognitive theory can be summarized as follows. Clients have problems because they treat their views of self and the world as metaphors (the truth) rather than as models (tentative representations which may require correction), and cognitive therapy helps them to restore the latter perspective. Therefore, the cognitive approach to therapy explicitly states goals and employs methods which are synonymous with Representational knowing.

Cognitive therapy techniques "are designed to identify, reality-test, and correct" (p. 4) distorted thinking and the schemas which underlie it. This goal is accomplished through the method of "collaborative empiricism" (p. 6) in which the therapist both structures the session and actively engages the client in a cooperative process. The client is taught to function as a kind of scientist who takes a hypothetical stance toward his / her own thoughts and assumptions, continually asking "What is the evidence?" The authors stress that the therapist should take an inductive approach to this teaching, asking questions which open up the client's "closed logic" and modeling how the client can challenge that logic (p. 29). Freeman, Pretzer, Fleming, and Simon (1990) illustrate how "guided discovery" or the asking of a sequence of simple questions can assist the client in recognizing the nature of the problem and steps to its resolution. For example, the following questions might be used by a therapist to help a social phobic recognize and challenge automatic thoughts:

"So you were standing there at the party wanting to join in but feeling really awkward. Do you remember what was going through your head?" "One thought you mentioned was, 'If I open my mouth, I'll make a fool of myself.' Do you have any evidence as to how often you'd say foolish things if you spoke up more often at parties?" "Suppose you did say something foolish, how would you expect the others to react?" "If you said something foolish and the others laughed, you'd feel embarrassed, but what would be the lasting consequences?" (p. 9)

When cognitive therapy is successful, clients have modified their underlying assumptions and automatic thoughts such that their models again represent a better fit with (or approximation to) reality, and, consequently, problematic symptoms have diminished. In this sense, an implicit goal of cognitive therapy is for clients themselves to internalize the therapist's own ontological and epistemological assumptions of sophisticated realism.

The Relationship of Representational Knowing to Realist Knowing

It has been implied to this point in the discussion that the Representational mode can stand alone as a lived, philosophical position. Since a theme of this chapter is the dialectical relationship existing among the different modes of knowing, it is important to correct that perception. The Representational mode cannot stand alone because, ultimately, the distinction between metaphor and model cannot be sustained by the human observer. To argue otherwise would mean siding with Popper over Kuhn, denying the ubiquity of normal science, and concluding that scientists always are capable of learning from their mistakes.

Recasting Kuhn's argument in the present terms, scientists working within a given paradigm act very much as if they are looking at the world from the vantage point of a metaphor, rather than a model. If they maintained the "as if" nature of a model, their perceptions would not become so wedded to a particular vision of how the world is put together, and they would not remain so blind to evidence which would disconfirm that vision. In the language of chapter 3, any theoretical system simultaneously reveals what we take to be as reality and blocks the perception of other possibilities.

From this perspective, making a commitment to a given psychological theory or therapeutic approach necessarily involves elements of

Realist knowing, which will then provide the ground against which Representational knowing appears as figure. Thus, a practitioner of Beck's cognitive therapy might bring Representational knowing to a research question (How can we improve the effectiveness of cognitive interventions?) or to a clinical question (How do I implement interventions with this particular individual or presenting problem?). Yet, I assume that it would be unusual for a cognitive therapist to question the core constructs of the theory, and, therefore, assumptions will at times be communicated to the client as if they are "true." For example, note the metaphorical (Realist) knowing conveyed to the client in the following exchange, which is intended to help clients do their homework:

> Patient: Sometimes I feel so bad that I can't get up the energy to write down these thoughts and answer them.
>
> Therapist: When this happens, do you feel like you are being invaded by a foreign force?
>
> P: That's exactly how I feel.
>
> T: In a certain sense, you *are* being invaded by these internal forces. Are there any benefits to passively giving in to this force?
>
> P: No. But I can't do anything about it. Most people do give in to these internal forces.
>
> T: A few fortunate people are able to fight them and win. Consequently, they are all the stronger for it.
>
> P: How can I do that?
>
> T: You have to see these inner forces as an invading army. The first thing invaders do is try to capture the radio station so they can control communications. To counteract this, you have to give yourself loud, direct, simple orders. The best orders are those telling your muscles what to do.
>
> P: Like, "Muscles get up, go to the desk and start writing?"
>
> T: Right . . . (Beck et al., 1979, pp. 278–279)

Of course, Beck and his colleagues are too accomplished as clinicians to contend that cognitive therapy involves only Representational knowing. They make it clear that to be a good cognitive therapist, one must first be a good therapist and bring to the interaction with the client "warmth, accurate empathy, and genuineness" (1979, p. 45). If I could expand their point to include the metaphorical thinking of the above excerpt, then it could be argued that nonspecific therapist qualities and

Realist knowing are "necessary but not sufficient to produce an optimum therapeutic effect" (p. 45). That is, explicit and sustained practice in Representational knowing defines what is unique to cognitive therapy and must be added to the mix of factors characterizing traditional psychotherapy for the client to achieve maximal improvement.

THE PERSPECTIVAL MODE OF KNOWING

A host of philosophers, theorists, and psychotherapists use the term "perspectival," and not all of them would subscribe to the particular meanings which I will associate with this mode of knowing. After his review of the importance of metaphor in theories of abnormality, Price (1978) suggests that "perspective" best captures the perceptual aspect of functioning within a given theory: "Concepts and their application to new situations have a Gestalt character. When we view a relatively ambiguous set of events, our view of those events . . . is structured by that concept" (p. 18). Therefore, he believes that it is more appropriate to speak of perspectives rather than theories or models in characterizing the frameworks through which abnormal behavior is described, assessed, and treated. Stepping into one or another of these frameworks, one simply will no longer view the same behavior in the same fashion.

The Philosophy of Perspectival Knowing

Perspectival knowing is based, therefore, on constructivist assumptions which explicitly acknowledge the metaphorical basis of human thinking and theorizing. The human observer intervenes between observation and fact, bringing along an active perceptual / cognitive system which influences what is seen as a "fact." This way of talking should bring to mind specific positions which were reviewed in chapter 4. In terms of a psychological theory, Perspectival knowing is best defined in relation to the "personal constructivism" of George Kelly. In relation to a philosophical position, it corresponds with what Chiari and Nuzzo (1996) describe as "epistemological constructivism" and with what I have described as Kuhn's "sophisticated relativism."

Perspectival knowing bears some resemblance to Representational knowing, but there is one very important difference. Representational knowing posits that each of us generates a model of the world, that this model can then be tested against the world for fit, and that the better the fit the more accurate the model. Perspectival knowing assumes that each of us generates a construct system for imposing order on the world. Since the facts of the world and the constructs through which we construe them cannot be entirely separated, it is not possible to say that one construct system more "accurately" represents the world than another. All we can really say is that there are a number of different construct systems or perspectives through which one might look at the world.

This position pushes Perspectival knowing toward the radical relativist stance which holds that no judgments can be made regarding the relative value of different construct systems, perspectives, or theories. Advocates of Perspectival knowing, including Kuhn, respond to this charge by developing a more sophisticated relativistic position. While we can never say which perspective or construct system represents the better fit with reality, we can compare or judge differing perspectives in relation to specified criteria, assuming that there can be agreement regarding the nature of those criteria.

Kuhn's thinking can easily be illustrated within the psychotherapy domain, especially if contrasting perspectives are compared at the level of practice rather than theory. While advocates of different theoretical positions (e.g., behaviorism and psychoanalysis) might have trouble agreeing on the criteria by which their theories would be compared, a client who is seeing either a behavior therapist or a psychoanalyst brings a pragmatic urgency to the question. The client wants to improve, change, get better, and both the behaviorist and the psychoanalyst, in their own ways, must deal with this issue. The behaviorist would address it by directly changing the symptom, and the psychoanalyst would address it by facilitating change in the presumed sources of the symptom. While there may still be disagreement over criteria for comparison (How should outcome in psychotherapy be defined?), both the behaviorist and analyst can mount their own arguments, which must contain some pragmatic content. The behaviorist might argue that her treatment was more effective and time-efficient regarding the symptom in question, and the analyst might argue that his treatment was more thoroughgoing and meaningful from the standpoint of the person considered as a whole. Lazarus (1971) could add his view that this distinction between behavior change (of a symptom) and insight (into an underlying conflict) is a false one, and that there are more productive conceptualizations of therapeutic change. These arguments could then be weighed by both the community of psychotherapists and the consuming public regarding their persuasiveness.

The Relationship of Perspectival Knowing
to Eclecticism / Integrationism

Perspectival knowing can manifest either as a general orientation to the field or as a specific approach to practice. Regarding the former, it can be argued that Perspectival knowing, as well as the Dialogical mode that will follow, represent forms of psychotherapeutic *pluralism*. For differing reasons, both would endorse "the doctrine that any substantial question admits of a variety of plausible but mutually conflicting responses" (Rescher, 1995, p. 79). If the eclectic and integrationist movement can also be framed in broadly pluralistic terms, does this mean that it depends on Perspectival and Dialogical knowing?

The answer to this question is complex because there is little agreement in the literature regarding the meaning of pluralism in eclectic or integrationist thinking. Rescher's account, which distinguishes between a generic position of "pluralism" and different, specific "reactions" to pluralism, holds promise for clarifying this literature and its relationship to the modes of knowing at hand. For example, consider the debate between Lazarus and Messer (1991), as well as the views of Omer and Strenger (1992).

In the above paper, Lazarus sees the proliferation of therapeutic theories, including those associated with eclecticism / integrationism, as producing confusion and chaos. He attributes this state of affairs to the preoccupation of psychotherapists with theory, and his approach of technical eclecticism promises to minimize "intellectual fluff" (p. 155) and concentrate on the "facts" (p. 146). In Rescher's (1995) terms, Lazarus recognizes that the field is pluralistic, but his reaction to it—as regards the role of theory—comes close to "scepticism" (p. 80). To the ancient skeptics, the obvious contradictions among different philosophical and theological viewpoints showed "the futility and inappropriateness of the whole process of theorizing about first principles" (p. 82). Although Lazarus is not "atheoretical," he strips away the theoretical overlay of any alternative position and incorporates into his practice only those "observations" and "techniques" which would improve outcome (Lazarus & Messer, pp. 145–147).

Omer and Strenger (1992) also acknowledge that the "pluralist revolution," which has swept away the assumptions of a single true theory and method, can leave therapists feeling directionless. Yet, a diversity of theoretical positions is inevitable because "meanings are not objectively *there* to be found, but are *constructions* of therapists' and clients' minds" (p. 253), and it is crucial for us to acknowledge the worth of alternative approaches. In fact, they find value in all of the approaches to psychotherapy that are extant, and provide a "pluralistic metamodel" (p. 254), based on narrative thought, that would integrate them. Rescher (1995) would characterize their response to pluralism as "syncretism"— "all the alternatives should be accepted . . . they must, somehow, be conjoined and juxtaposed" (p. 80).

Messer (Lazarus & Messer, 1991) frames theoretical proliferation as "creative diversity" rather than as "chaos" and, for reasons similar to Omer and Strenger, argues that it is unavoidable: "I am espousing a postpositivist or postmodernist conception that questions whether there is certain or objective truth or reality, and that challenges the notion that there is only one correct method for arriving at it" (p. 155). However, unlike the above authors, he articulates a position of "assimilative integration" (p. 153) wherein a therapist holds to a dominant orientation but is open to a gradual incorporation of theory and method from other perspectives. This position best fits Rescher's (1995) category of "perspectival rationalism or contextualism": It asserts a rational basis for selecting one's own position while acknowledging that "this basis may differ perspectivally from group to group, era to era, and school to school" (p. 80).

These three responses do not exhaust the pluralistic alternatives within the eclectic and integrationist movement but provide sufficient background to draw conclusions about its relationship to Perspectival and Dialogical knowing. While these modes of knowing are generically pluralistic in nature, not all pluralists—for example, Lazarus—specifically employ them. Lazarus' further statements suggest that we should locate his thinking within entirely different modes of knowing. He hopes that "some truths are not entirely colored by subjective inference" and complains that Messer's position "undermines the view that some theories are open to verification and disproof whereas others defy measurement" (p. 154). Thus, he grounds his form of pluralism in Representational knowing (scientific theories are falsifiable), and he may even shift at times to a position of scientific Realism (scientific theories can be verified).

By contrast, Messer, as well as Omer and Strenger, make statements that are compatible with Perspectival (and Dialogical) knowing. However, in line with a theme of the chapter, it is not assumed that their orientations could be reduced to a single mode of knowing. For example, Messer (1992) associates his approach to integration with "a way of knowing that acknowledges metaphoric, interpretive, and narrative modes of truth-seeking as legitimate, along with traditional empiricism" (p. 151). Similarly, Omer and Strenger (1992) underscore "one of the paradoxes of modern psychotherapeutic thinking" (p. 259). While their Perspectival or Dialogical knowing holds that no theory is uniquely true, effective practice still requires Realist knowing—that is, therapists must maintain "belief in" whatever metanarrative defines their orientation (p. 259).

The Phenomenology of Perspectival Knowing: Personal Construct Therapy

Perspectival knowing, as a specific approach to practice, is perhaps best embodied by George Kelly's personal construct therapy, but it will be supplemented by the work of other therapists who practice at least in part from the stance of "personal constructivism." One of the important goals of this discussion is to distinguish Kelly's approach from cognitive therapy and its associated mode of Representational knowing, with which it is sometimes confused (R. A. Neimeyer, 1993).

Kelly (1958b / 1969) is quite explicit that his approach to psychotherapy represents an alternative to the positions of "dogmatism—the belief that one has the word of truth right from the horse's mouth—and modern realism—the belief that one has the word of truth right from nature's mouth" (p. 226). Instead, his approach will be based on "constructive alternativism," a philosophical position which assumes that human beings can only offer interpretations or constructions of a reality that can never be directly grasped. Consequently, reality is subject to countless interpretations: "Whatever exists can be reconstrued. This is to say that none of today's constructions . . . is perfect and, as the history of human thought repeatedly suggests, none is final" (p. 227, italics omitted). However, to say that events can be endlessly reconstrued is not to say that it makes no difference *how* they are construed (relativism). Clients come to therapy because the personal construct systems that they have generated are not producing the outcomes they wish, and "some reconstructions may open fresh channels for a rich and productive life. Others may offer one no alternative save suicide" (p. 228).

Kelly then defines the therapy situation as a kind of cooperative, scientific inquiry in which the client's personal construct system will be articulated, examined, and modified. He likens the consulting room to "a protected laboratory where hypotheses can be formulated, test-tube sized experiments can be performed, field trials planned, and outcomes evaluated" (p. 229). In this experiment, it is crucial that neither client nor therapist is "the boss," and that a partnership is formed in which the client is encouraged to test out new ways of construing the world.

Thus far, it might appear that cognitive therapy and personal construct therapy are quite similar. In the first instance, the client is seen as generating a model for representing the world, and in the second he/she is described as having a personal construct system for interpreting the world. Both Beck and Kelly invoke the metaphor of personal science to characterize the process of modifying the client's model or construct system, respectively. However, the goals of therapy and the therapist's assumptions about facilitating those changes differ in accord with the dominant mode of knowing associated with the two approaches.

The cognitive therapist defines change in relation to the replacement of "distorted" or "irrational" thinking with "realistic" or "rational" thinking that represents a better fit with reality. The therapist can guide the client in this process because it is assumed that there is some consensual definition reached by therapist and client regarding the "reality" against which "rational" perceptions will be tested.

The goal of change and any possible client-therapist agreement regarding its definition and implementation would be made considerably more complex if, like Kelly (1958b/1969), one concludes the following:

> No matter how close I came to the man or woman who sought my help, I always saw him through my own peculiar spectacles, and never did he perceive what I was frantically signaling to him, except through his. From this moment I ceased . . . being a realist. (p. 225)

How can one define specific goals for change, particularly goals which rest on an implicit definition of reality, when the therapist's mode of knowing rejects this possibility?

It appears that personal construct therapists try to step around this issue by defining goals for change which are more global than discrete. Of course, Kelly (1958b/1969) did develop techniques for working with specific construct dimensions of the client and lists eight of them (p. 231). For example, the client and therapist might decide that the client should reverse his position on an important construct dimension. If that dimension is "strong-weak," and the client usually perceives himself as weak, he might try attempting to perceive himself as strong (Epting, 1984, p. 16). Or, the therapist and client "can select another construct from the client's ready repertory and apply it to matters at hand" (Kelly, 1958b/1969, p. 231). Regarding the above client, he might begin to look at some issue from the standpoint of being "adequate" versus "inadequate" rather than in terms of strong-weak. (Epting, 1984, p. 17).

However, Epting (1984) acknowledges that the above interventions are rather superficial, and he approvingly cites Kelly's view that psychotherapy ultimately is "an enlivening and awakening kind of experience" (p. 6). It is not so much a first order change in a discrete construct dimension which is sought and valued by this therapy as a second order change which leaves the client feeling that change itself is both inherent in life and possible to endure. If our construct systems transform us into creatures who are conservative by nature, always tending to see the new in light of the old, then personal construct therapy aims for a shift in this philosophical position. It encourages us to take a leap into a different way of construing the world in the absence of any guarantee that we will benefit from it or even be able to completely understand or justify it. It is not surprising that Kelly frequently spoke of the curiosity, creativity, and courage it takes to live a full human life. Kelly did not want to just lift people off one set of hooks (constructs) and hang them "on other more comfortable, more socially acceptable, hooks" (1958a/1969, p. 70)—he wanted to demonstrate that it was possible to take a different attitude toward the hooks themselves.

It was amusing to Kelly that comments such as those above led some to label him as an "existentialist" just as others had tried to pigeonhole his approach as "cognitive" theory, "emotional" theory, "dialectical materialism," "learning" theory, and "dynamic" theory. He adds: "I have, of course, [also] been called a Zen Buddhist" (1965/1969, pp. 216–217). Personal construct psychotherapy has been the object of such varying interpretations because, in the end, it cannot be reduced to a set of techniques and its definition of change is actually quite ambiguous and open-ended. For example, while Kelly emphasized the importance of behavior as a measure of a change in the client's way of construing the world, "behavior is not the answer, it is the question" (p. 219).

If it is the values of open-endedness of outcome, creative living, courage to change, tolerance of ambiguity, and continuing self-examination which define personal construct therapy, how can clients move in this direction if therapists do not themselves embody these characteristics? These personal qualities are descriptive of Perspectival knowing in general, and the difficulty therapists may experience in actualizing them is emphasized by Mahoney's (1988b) statement: "The psychological demands of constructive metatheory are unsurpassed by those of any other contemporary perspective" (p. 312, italics omitted). More recently, he (1995b) clarifies this statement by emphasizing that constructivist practice requires operating in the absence of a theoretical framework which clearly specifies problem and solution, continuing to challenge one's own perceptions and biases, and confronting both the client's and one's own existential issues.

The Relationship of Perspectival Knowing to Realist and Representational Knowing

In closing this section on Perspectival knowing, it is important to again emphasize that it, or any other mode of knowing, cannot exist completely independently. It was pointed out in chapter 4 that Kelly could not always maintain his Perspectival mode of knowing even when writing about it on the theoretical level. Epting (1984) appears to have the same difficulty. On the one hand, he contends that current knowledge always represents a construction which is tentative and incomplete. On the other hand, he believes that "over the 'long haul' we will know what things are really like. At some point in the far distant future it will eventually be clear which conception of the world we should accept; which conception is veridical" (p. 24). Whether referring to present or future, this last statement comes from a Realist mode of knowing.

Further, I believe that Kelly himself acknowledges the dialectical relationship between Realist and Perspectival knowing when he comments: "Understand, I am not yet ready to say that dogmatism has no place whatsoever in psychotherapy, especially when weighed against certain grimmer alternatives. It may even prove valuable to all of us as a firm position from which to rebel" (1958b/1969, pp. 225–226). The dialectic of Realist/Representational and Perspectival modes of knowing is all the more apparent when one moves from theory to practice.

Although personal construct therapists do not want to limit outcome to the modification of individual construct dimensions and certainly do not want to define change as correspondence with "reality," many moments of therapeutic interaction are necessarily colored by such assumptions. When clients are encouraged to try seeing themselves as "strong" rather than as "weak," or as "adequate" rather than as "strong," it is implicit that the success of these reconstruals will be evaluated at least in part in reference to the outcomes they produce in the social world. Or, more explicitly, when Kelly suggests that constructs can be tested "for their predictive validity" (1958b/1969, p. 231), the goal is to test the construct based on the constraints which "reality" provides.

Hermans, Kempen and van Loon (1992) agree with the view that personal constructs represent "hypotheses" to be pragmatically or empirically tested by the events of the world, and cite Kelly in support of this Representational approach to knowing. For example, Kelly (1963) writes: "Constructs are used for predictions of things to come, and the world keeps rolling along and revealing those predictions to be either correct or misleading. This fact provides the basis for revision of constructs and, eventually, of whole construction systems" (p. 14).

By contrast, Chiari and Nuzzo (1996) define optimal outcome in Kelly's system in relation to a continuous process of "reconstruction of experience" which allows for an ongoing adaptation between a "knowing system and its environment," without loss of "organizational coherence" (p. 173). Moreover, like Epting, they argue that Kelly "used internal consistency, not correspondence with reality, as a criterion of validity" for construct systems (p. 180, footnote 6).

I believe that these conflicting interpretations of Kelly can be reconciled if one distinguishes between an abstract, idealized goal of therapy and the concrete, lived process of doing therapy. While the goal of therapy can be defined, hypothetically, solely in relation to Perspectival knowing, the process of therapy must also employ Realist and Representational knowing in many moments of therapeutic interaction. I offer the following example of Kelly's own work with a client in support of this point.

The client was a 28-year-old unmarried veteran who, despite his superior intelligence, was not succeeding either in college or at work. In this case, Kelly (1958b/1969) helped the client to "tighten" an important construct dimension by bringing it to the verbal, conscious level, labeling it as "white" vs. "black" moods, and then further refining it into "rational hope versus irrational despair" (p. 238). It is apparent that at key moments in the interaction the client is experiencing himself from a Realist mode of knowing—for example, the metaphor of white vs. black moods was quite literally experienced by the client as the "two halves of me" (p. 243). The client required support and empathic understanding of the process of metaphorical knowing through which he was discovering something important about himself. If Kelly could not have entered into the client's mode himself, empathically and cognitively, there would have been no movement.

On the other hand, Kelly balanced Realist knowing with Representational or Perspectival knowing (it's not completely clear which he was modeling for the client in this excerpt), when he responded to one of the client's childhood memories as follows:

> The fact that it is a story that seems to fit a mood is probably more important than whether the details actually happened in

all the ways that you remember this afternoon. (pause) So the story might be *emotionally* true without necessarily being altogether *historically* true. (p. 256)

Kelly indicates at several points in his commentary that he was struggling to balance the client's needs for structure and change in these interviews. The client was characterized by an overly brittle, intellectualized construct system, but chaotic feelings were beginning to seep through the holes in this system. He indicates that no "responsible therapist" would want to lead this client too far from "firm structure" or let him flounder much longer in the chaos which the present structure was beginning to engender (p. 237). Using Feyerabend's contrast as a metaphor for the therapeutic process, this client required a balancing of the "normal" and "philosophical" components of knowing, and Kelly responded appropriately to those needs.

THE DIALOGICAL MODE OF KNOWING

This mode might also have been characterized as narrative, intersubjective, or hermeneutic knowing, but these terms have many connotations which may or may not be intended here. Therefore, the somewhat more neutral term, "Dialogical," was chosen to simplify the task of definition in this specific context.

The Philosophy of Dialogical Knowing: Contrasts with Other Modes

I will begin by differentiating Dialogical knowing from the Perspectival mode which has preceded it and from the Critical mode which will follow it. First, Perspectival knowing has developed primarily within the context of science or has at least maintained an ongoing, collegial relationship with science. While Kuhn is sometimes cited as a postmodernist philosopher, this is not a designation he would appreciate or accept. He is a historian and philosopher of science who simply has provided an account of how scientists actually practice their craft. He sees science as our surest way to knowledge, and no part of his work is intended to imply that some other approach to knowledge would be as satisfactory, much less more satisfactory. Similarly, while Kelly and other personal constructivist therapists might criticize the scientistic tendencies of academic psychology, they see clinical practice as offering an opportunity for therapists to develop their own meaningful and valid methods of scientific inquiry.

On the other hand, Dialogical knowing is associated with a variety of postmodern philosophical and psychological positions which, at best, reduce science to an approach to knowledge which is no more valid than many alternative approaches. Further, within postmodernist thought, the Dialogical position is associated with an affirmative stance toward knowing while the Critical mode will be linked with a skeptical position. This differentiation will allow for a more precise delineation of components of knowing such that a "postmodern" therapist, for example, could be said to alternate between Dialogical and Critical modes of knowing in interacting with a client.

Second, following a distinction made in the last chapter, Perspectival knowing is associated with the philosophical position of "epistemological constructivism" and the psychological position of "personal constructivism." These positions draw a hard and fast line between an unknowable, external reality and the internal, personal systems of meanings which are generated in response to it.

By contrast, the Dialogical and Critical modes of knowing are characterized by a "hermeneutic constructivism" (Chiari & Nuzzo, 1996) which assumes that "reality" does not exist independently of the observer: Knowledge of reality and the language categories which order it are completely intertwined. Accordingly, the Perspectival assumption of different "views" of reality varying with individual meaning systems is rejected in favor of a notion of reality which is inherently interpersonal and linguistic in nature.

Dialogical knowing as a lived philosophical position is then further articulated, understood, and applied in the context of interaction with the individuals, couples/families, and groups which have been the traditional focus of psychotherapy. As will become apparent in the later discussion of Critical knowing, this unit of study and the interventions associated with it can then be critiqued on sociopolitical grounds. One variant of Critical knowing would take as its unit of analysis the larger institutional, historical, and cultural factors which shape the practice of psychotherapy itself and, from this vantage point, the focus of Dialogical knowing appears to be too narrow.

Therefore, to say that reality is inherently Dialogical in nature indicates that knowledge is always: (a) interpersonally or socially constructed, whether or not one is in immediate contact with other persons; (b) linguistically structured, since dialogue depends on language; (c) pluralistic, since there is an inconceivably large number of social and linguistic groups which represent quite different dialogical realities; and (d) relativistic, but only if one compares this form of knowledge to some fictional standard of "truth" defined as that which actually corresponds with or approximates "reality."

The last point above reiterates the postmodernist response to the charge that this position leads to relativism. As has been discussed at some length, Rorty and his interpreters in the field of psychotherapy reject the "Either / Or" of foundationalist approaches to knowledge: Either there is a firm foundation which will deliver us to the truth, or there is radical relativism where "anything goes." Instead, dialogical "knowledge" is defined in relation to the needs and values of a given language or social community, and these decisions can be based on political, economic, aesthetic, pragmatic, or other "local" considerations. It is the capacity to make a commitment to the knowledge associated with one's language community, while acknowledging the absence of absolute standards of truth or justification, which defines affirmative postmodernism.

The Phenomenology of Dialogical Knowing: The Therapist as *Rhetorician*

This general characterization of Dialogical knowing will now be translated to the context of psychotherapeutic practice, and two rather different approaches to the therapist-client relationship will be explored. I would suggest that therapists can approach Dialogical knowing through defining their expertise either in *rhetorical* or *conversational* terms.

There are some commonalities which crosscut these contrasting definitions of the therapist role. In either case, it is assumed that the problems which clients bring to therapists are reflections of the language that they use and the social contexts that support those meanings. In addition, therapists possess no special knowledge which would allow them to be the expert interpreter and solver of these problems, and a more egalitarian, collaborative relationship must be established between therapist and client. What therapists can offer, however, is their expertise in the use of language and an understanding of the role of dialogue in both constituting and transforming human problems.

An approach which emphasizes the role of the therapist as rhetorician is associated with a more active role for the therapist, and, intentionally or unintentionally, the therapist's communications to the client will at times have a quite persuasive impact (Frank & Frank, 1991). This approach to Dialogical knowing is seen most clearly in certain varieties of solution-based and narrative therapies.

For example, Berg and de Shazer (1993) distinguish between "problem talk" and "solution talk." In the former, clients present the "facts" of their situation, and therapists traditionally have either taken those facts at face value, defining them as the problem, or have tried to "get to the bottom" of those facts, defining some underlying issue related to them as the problem. However, Berg and de Shazer's "poststructural view" leads them to question if it is not language itself which is creating the *appearance* of problems. They have learned over the years from their clients that "solutions involve a very different kind of thinking and talking, a kind of talking and thinking that is outside of the 'facts,' outside of the problem" (p. 9).

Moreover, Berg and de Shazer have found that certain kinds of questions can serve as therapeutic interventions for promoting "solution talk." Examples include "miracle questions" (which help define the client's goals and indicate hypothetical solutions), "exceptions-finding questions" (which focus on those times and experiences when "the problem" is not dominant), and "scaling questions" (which are intended to "measure" the client's view or perceptions) (p. 9). All of these interventions are intended to evoke clients' own perceptions, and perhaps their own problem solutions as well (language as the problem), to elicit information about important persons in clients' lives (the social context of language) and "to motivate and encourage" (the persuasive element) (p. 10).

The authors illustrate their thinking, including the use of scaling questions, with the following case example. An 8-year-old girl had been molested by a stranger in a shopping mall, and during the fourth session of therapy the therapist drew an arrow between 1 and 10 on the blackboard. If 10 represents when therapy would end, the child was asked to indicate, by putting an x on this line, how far they had come to this point. She made a mark that corresponded to about "7," and was then asked how they might get her the rest of the way to 10. After several minutes the client announced that she had an idea, and somberly said: "We will burn the clothes I was wearing when it happened." The therapist replied, "That's a wonderful idea," and soon afterwards "the child and her parents had a ritual burning and then went out to dinner in a fancy restaurant to mark the end of therapy" (p. 23).

J. L. Zimmerman and Dickerson's (1994) narrative approach to eating problems more explicitly places Dialogical knowing in a context of empowering clients against that which has been oppressive. They describe how anorexia nervosa is itself a narrative construction which is anchored in societal definitions of power and gender, and, as such, it should not be conceptualized solely as an individual problem or a "personal preference." From this perspective, most traditional therapy seems "to play into anorexia's hands" (p. 296) because it assumes that this problem is due to individual or family defects. (In terms of the distinctions of this chapter, and as will become clearer in time, Zimmerman and Dickerson to this point are largely speaking from a Critical mode of knowing.)

In their framing of therapeutic goals, these authors acknowledge a specific debt to White and Epston (1990) and Gilligan (1982): Clients will be helped to find a more productive, alternative narrative for their experience corresponding to the discovery of "voice." Like solution-focused therapists, Zimmerman and Dickerson then offer direction to the dialogue with the client through questions and interventions that are intended to challenge the dominant narrative and bring to light an alternative story.

In this case example, the client is a 15-year-old girl who has a three year "career" of anorexia and four hospitalizations. She and her mother sought out Jeffrey Zimmerman because they found the hospital professionals "too oppressive" (p. 301). In these excerpts from the first interview, the therapist initially asked if it was all right to use the term "anorexia" in their discussion and then began implicitly to "externalize the problem" by treating anorexia as a metaphor for that which embodies the client's difficulties.

> Therapist: . . . I'm interested in other ways anorexia affects you. What effect does it have on your attitude to yourself? Does it affect the way you feel about yourself?
>
> Jackie: Mostly in how I look. All of the time I think how bad I look.
>
> Therapist: What should I call this?—a state of constant negative self-evaluation?
>
> Jackie: I do feel awful. For a while, I just didn't feel good enough to want to to do anything. I didn't think I could do the things I used to.
>
> Therapist: So anorexia stole certain activities from you. Like what?

The client responds that she used to be play softball and enjoyed it, but the doctors have told her that she can no longer play because of her low weight. The therapist links the doctor's control of her with her own self-evaluation, proposing that both are due to the influence of "anorexia," and then asks:

> Therapist: Who has made you feel worse about how you look—the doctors or the anorexia?
>
> Jackie: Not sure. Both have.
>
> Therapist: Who has been more restrictive—the doctors or the anorexia? That's what I hear from others. Anorexia's worst trick is that it gets others to control your life. (*Jackie looks sad.*) . . . Are you tired of this? I know anorexia is difficult to resist; but I wondered how you were feeling about it? (pp. 303–304)

The client was seen every other week for six months, and the "sessions uncovered an alternative history for Jackie, one in which she had a strong voice and was considered the rebellious one (although at puberty this was strongly discouraged by her father and extended family). Jackie would prefer to have that voice resurrected" (p. 305). She watched tapes of the "Anti-Anorexia League," which was developed by David Epston (p. 297) and includes letters he has exchanged with clients and videotapes of sessions. It is an attempt to provide social support for women who are rejecting anorexia and creating an alternative narrative about themselves. Jackie concluded from these tapes that "anorexia's purpose was to isolate and control her" (p. 305). The client showed great improvement during the course of therapy: She began to eat more, socialized more, was elected to student government, confronted her father's abusiveness, and had avoided further hospitalizations at follow-up.

The Phenomenology of Dialogical Knowing: The Therapist as *Conversationalist*

Harlene Anderson's (1997) conversational therapy selectively borrows from both postmodern (social constructionist) and hermeneutic thinking and explicitly rejects the role of therapist as rhetorician, which to her means functioning as a "narrative editor." If a therapist helps the client to undermine a dominant problem or narrative and to find new solutions or an alternative narrative, this is "narrative editing—revising, correcting, or polishing" (p. 96). From the standpoint of her understanding of Dialogical knowing, this approach represents a "slippery slope" because it can resurrect the notion that the therapist has knowledge which the client does not.

> It assumes that a therapist can read a client like a text. It makes a therapist an archaeological narrativist who believes there is *a* story, with an imagined significance, that needs to be uncovered or retold. It risks being guided by the notion that there are universal human stories and that there are no new ones to hear. It risks translating the language and metaphor of a client's first-person narrative into professional, technical language and its assumed beliefs about human nature. (p. 96)

As was previously noted, she and her colleague (H. Anderson & Goolishian, 1992) define therapy exclusively as a "collaborative conversation" which the therapist must approach from a stance of "not-knowing." Since this approach is framed in hermeneutic terms, she acknowledges that the therapist brings knowledge and biases, "preunderstandings," to the dialogue with the client. But these should be carried "without prejudice, for instance, without a preconceived plan about how a client should approach a problem's resolution" (H. Anderson, 1997, p. 97). Therefore, a therapist is a "conversational partner," rather than "a describer, an explainer, or an interpreter of actions" (p. 97).

In light of Gadamer's notion of dialogue as a "circular interactive system," H. Anderson (1997) characterizes the therapeutic contribution to a genuine conversation as follows: "A therapist does not control the conversation, for instance, by setting its agenda or moving it in a particular direction of content or outcome; nor is a therapist responsible for the direction of change" (p. 97). Rather, it is assumed that "newness" in "meanings, realities, and narratives" will be co-created by client and therapist as a natural consequence of genuine dialogue (H. Anderson, 1993, p. 325). This means that problems are "not solved but dissolved," and the novel meanings which emerge cultivate "a new sense of agency and freedom for the client" (p. 325).

It should be apparent from her formulation that this approach to Dialogical knowing, like Perspectival knowing, places a tremendous burden on the therapist. While therapists should not allow their prejudgments to direct the conversation, this does not mean that "anything goes" or that therapists are passive or rely solely on nondirective listening or empathic understanding (H. Anderson, 1993, p. 325). The therapist must somehow come up with "conversational questions" that do not lead, pre-judge, or contaminate the dialogue but that open up a space for the client's story and for the possibility of change (p. 325). Therefore, although the therapist is "not directive," she remains "active" and "influential," since client and therapist are always influencing one another (H. Anderson, 1997, p. 98).

Given these conflicting demands on the therapist, it is little wonder that H. Anderson (1997) characterizes the shift to this way of knowing as encompassing a fundamental philosophical change in one's *"way of being"* (p. 94). This more personal stance includes being present in the moment to what is occurring within oneself and with the client, so that whatever one says and does is unique to this particular situation. There-fore, the collaborative therapist must demonstrate enormous flexibility, tolerance of uncertainty, and humility, while risking the possibility of allowing change in oneself. Not only will therapists' thoughts, behav-iors, and feelings about clients change, but "our ethics of practice, deeply held morals, and cherished values will surface, be exposed to challenge, and also change" (p. 100). Referring to Schön's (1983) frame-work for professional development, Anderson contextualizes the thera-pist's responsibility to self-change in relation to a continuing postmodernist gesture toward "reflection and reflections about reflec-tions in action" (1997, p. 102). Further, she also contends that therapists must risk making "public" some of their moments of uncertainty and questioning (pp. 102–104).

In sum, this approach to Dialogical knowing requires that the ther-apist live out moment-by-moment the postmodernist notion that there is not a single, unitary, individual self but a multiplicity of different selves which are anchored by different social and linguistic narratives. By embodying this experience and attitude in the consulting room, a dia-logue can be created through which clients learn to:

> tell their first-person narratives so that they may transform their self-identities to ones that permit them to develop understand-ings of their lives and its events . . . allow multiple possibilities for ways of being in and acting in the world at any given time and in any given circumstance . . . gain an access to and express or execute agency or a sense of self-agency. (H. Anderson, 1997, p. 234, italics omitted)

It is difficult to provide an apt case illustration of the conversational approach to Dialogical knowing because it is not easily captured by a brief piece of therapeutic interaction. Further, H. Anderson (1997) admits that when she works as a consultant in a conference setting, the participants often have quite different perceptions of what she has done, with some contending simply that "Not a lot happened" (p. 56) or that "I don't see anything postmodern" (p. 265). Whatever the difficulty in conveying to others a holistic impression of this therapy, its component parts are more easily specified, and the "not-knowing" approach will be illustrated with the following case.

H. Anderson (1997) relates the story of a competent, although frustrated, psychiatrist who consulted with Harry Goolishian about a Norwegian client, Lars. This client believed that he had an incurable disease and was infecting others to the point of killing them. In his current therapy with the psychiatrist, the client spoke sporadically about his marital problems and inability to work, but remained focused on the disease. When Goolishian saw the client as a consultant, he asked: "How long have you *had* this disease?" (p. 138). Since all of the other physicians and mental health professionals had tried to talk him out of the notion that he had a disease, the client was quite surprised. He disclosed that he once had sex with a prostitute when at sea years ago and afterwards realized he could have been infected. When he went to the local clinic, the nurse told him that they did not "treat sexual perversions," and said that he "needed confession and God, not medicine" (p. 138). When he returned home, he remained afraid that he was infecting others, but "No one believed me," and physicians referred him for psychiatric evaluation (p. 138).

Anderson indicates that the not-knowing position "precluded the stance that Lars's story was delusional. Lars said he was sick. Thus, Harry wanted to learn more about his sickness" (p. 138). Therefore, Goolishian employed "not-knowing questions" since he did not want "to challenge Lars's reality or story, or to talk or manipulate him out of his delusion" (p. 138). The psychiatrist took this advice and six months later, after he had given up on proving that the fears were groundless, felt that the sessions with the client were going better. Two years later, Anderson received a letter from the psychiatrist spurred by his decision to tell the client of Goolishian's death. Lars said he was most impressed that Goolishian had "believed me," but indicated that another of his remarks was also very important. When Goolishian observed, in reference to the client's struggles, "As a man you did what a man had to do," the client said that this statement "just made the difference. I see him every so often in front of me saying that" (p. 140).

The Relationship of Dialogical Knowing
to Other Modes of Knowing

What, then, is the relationship between the Dialogical mode of knowing and the modes discussed in previous sections? This question will first be addressed in relation to the rhetorical approach, and it is important to make a distinction between the mode of knowing employed by the therapist in critiquing the "problem" or "dominant narrative," and the mode of knowing which therapist and client share in generating a "solution" or "alternative narrative." The examples which were given indicate that a disparity often exists between these two components: While Dialogical knowing may be practiced in the first step of understanding, Realist knowing dominates its second step.

For example, Berg and de Shazer (1993) critique the existence in "reality" of the problems which clients bring to them, but use that term when they begin to speak of solutions: "As client and therapist talk more and more about the solution they want to construct together, they come to believe in the truth or reality of what they are talking about. This is the way language works, naturally" (p. 9).

This contrast is clearly manifested in Zimmerman's narrative approach to the client who had struggled with anorexia (J. L. Zimmerman & Dickerson, 1994). He "deconstructs" the dominant narrative of anorexia and its associated social and linguistic context, but the client was then encouraged to treat the alternative narrative of a "strong voice" as quite real. In fact, his approach to the dominant narrative was not just Dialogical in nature, because he transformed anorexia into a metaphorical concept which also had real existence. Then, the client could be encouraged to reject "anorexia," an actually existing thing outside her, and begin to discover her own voice, an actually existing thing inside her. She was further persuaded to reject the old truth and hold onto a new one through integrating her personal experience with the social and linguistic community of other women who are engaged in a similar battle against oppression. Therefore, this treatment process involved elements of Realist knowing ("anorexia" and "voice" are real things), Perspectival knowing (there is a separation between inner and outer, and a new narrative provides a new narrative perspective on the world), and Dialogical knowing (both old and new narratives are enmeshed in language and social context).

The point here is that such examples contradict the assumptions of the very philosophical position on which the Dialogical mode is presumably based—that is, affirmative postmodernism does not claim that the dominant narrative is "false," and that a multitude of alternative narratives are "true" in some substantial or absolute sense. Rather, a multiplicity of different narratives or self-identities exist, each of which is "contingent" on a given social/linguistic context and set of purposes, and none of which is true in the realist interpretation of that term. One might say that H. Anderson's (1997) critique of rhetorical approaches to Dialogical knowing is based on this recognition, and that she then attempts to define and embody a purely Dialogical approach to the therapy situation. Does she succeed?

This question should be addressed in relation to both the moment-by-moment experience of the therapist and the outcome for the client. That is, can the therapist embody a strictly Dialogical mode of knowing in interacting with the client? And, does the client take away from the therapy that which is intended: the capacity to approach life through Dialogical knowing?

Beginning with the outcome for the client, it is difficult to ascertain from the clinical and consultation vignettes which H. Anderson (1993, 1997) provides whether this therapy does typically represent "a transformative event" (1997, p. 234) for clients. Certainly, it is not possible to differentiate the outcome of the case of Lars from the rhetorical approaches which she critiques. Goolishian's questions were not intended to challenge the reality which the seaman brought to him, and—while the client's marriage and work situations later improved and the question of whether he was infected or not was no longer an issue (p. 139)—it is not clear that the client actually moved from Realist to Dialogical knowing.

From the examples which she gives, a better case could be made for the transformative impact of the conversational approach on the professionals who consult with Harlene Anderson (1997, pp. 47–57; pp. 235–242). Similarly, Tom Anderson (1993) has given up his own practice and now only consults with other therapists, and this arrangement "increases my flexibility in many respects, for example, to give up a theoretical idea or a practical mode when the time is ready" (p. 311). Is it possible that working with professionals provides more immediate and definitive feedback about whether or not others can move in the direction of Dialogical knowing? Harlene Anderson's view that psychotherapy should allow clients to transform the self is similar to Gergen and Kaye's (1992) proposal that clients should give up their personal identities, and both approaches represent remarkably ambitious goals for psychotherapy.

So, can therapists themselves actualize the exacting goal that they set for their clients and consistently embody Dialogical knowing in their work? While Anderson's description of this mode of knowing is wonderfully clear and deep on both the theoretical and experiential levels, it is inconsistent with the argument that Dialogical knowing can stand alone as an approach to psychotherapy.

H. Anderson (1997) acknowledges that the philosophical stance which she recommends is necessarily "metaphorical" in nature (p. 94), and we have seen that metaphor unavoidably involves components of Realist knowing. In addition, Anderson's own argument would appear to call for a dialectical conception of the therapist's experience. Her insistence on the importance of "not-knowing" and continuous "reflection" implicitly conveys that therapists enact tendencies toward "knowing" and "non-reflection" in actual practice. Although a therapist might be completely present in a given moment to the experience of not-knowing, there remains a human tendency, in the next moment, to reify that *experience* of intersubjective, Dialogical knowing into some *structure* of individual, Realist knowing. Indeed, it is the continual process of discovering and letting go of these subtle reified structures which, in all likelihood, leads Anderson to associate the therapist's experience of Dialogical knowing with creativity, growth, and renewal.

H. Anderson (1997) comes close to recognizing the dialectical nature of her position when she acknowledges that her presentation of a postmodern therapy runs the risk of "encouraging another taken-for-granted therapy metaphor, promoting certain thoughts and actions and prohibiting others" (p. 264). She realizes that others may interpret her "belief" that genuine dialogue naturally produces change as a statement about reality or the truth.

> I do not believe and do not mean to imply that this is the truth; it is simply a current description and explanation of my experience. I use the language tools available to me at this moment to describe and explain my experience. My experiences and my ideas about them will change in the future, as they have in the past. (p. 264)

The contradiction in Anderson's position is more fundamental and far-reaching than she acknowledges. Like Rorty, she defines knowledge as contingent on a social or language group and rejects any notion of absolute truth. But, as Tomlinson (1989) argued in chapter 2, there are in fact no "alternative truths" because of the difficulty of stepping outside of the historically mediated final vocabulary which one's metaphor and group have come to represent. Whether applied to her clients or herself, Anderson's philosophical position, therapy *is* conversation, becomes an "absolute relativist" view of knowledge—"*either* alternative traditions can be understood in our terms *or* they cannot be understood" at all (Tomlinson, pp. 53–54). Consequently, one can find a supporter of the conversational view of therapy Lynn Hoffman making a statement such as the following:

> I personally believe that all models of therapy that posit causes for pathology, whether of a structural nature (poor boundaries, lack of individuation) or of a process nature (growth impairments, developmental lags) should be thrown out. In fact, it might not be such a bad idea to decide that psychology is a flawed field and replace it with a new emphasis on human communication. (Hoffman-Hennessy & Davis, 1993, p. 362)

Thus, as in Cushman's hermeneutic therapy, a gap inevitably exists between theory and practice in H. Anderson's conversational therapy. This gap can be acknowledged and clarified, but not eradicated, by an alternative set of "language tools" which would draw a line between Dialogical knowing as an idealized, philosophical position and as a lived, human experience. The latter is necessarily defined in dialectical terms, with the concrete experience of Dialogical knowing existing in opposition to the very beliefs and metaphors through which Anderson attempts to characterize it. Or, in Heideggerian terms, a new vocabulary would constantly need to be invented to express Dialogical knowing (meditative thinking), because Realist knowing (calculative thinking) can claim any aspect of experience as its own.

THE CRITICAL MODE OF KNOWING

Given the very generic term used to describe this mode of knowing, it is all the more important to define its referents in this context. While it is associated with the approach which Fox and Prilleltensky (1997) describe as "critical psychology," it is not synonymous with their usage.

The Relationship of Critical Knowing to "Critical Psychology"

Fox and Prilleltensky define *"mainstream psychology"* as the psychological approach which is most often taught and practiced, and which is "portrayed as a science" that can "uncover the truth about human behavior" (p. 4). They then contrast this psychology with a variety of critical approaches which would expose its moral, political, and social underpinnings (p. 4). From their perspective, mainstream psychology appears as a set of practices for producing knowledge which unintentionally support the societal status quo, and critical psychology uncovers this bias while proposing practices and knowledge which would promote the value of social justice.

Of course, a "mainstream psychologist" might object that it is hardly fair for this relatively new approach to claim ownership of a "critical" stance toward human problems, since it is in the very nature of science to provide just that. What differentiates science from other approaches to knowing is a methodology which insists that knowledge will be rationally based on empirical investigation, and new data or a new interpretation of old data could well serve the purpose of social justice. For example, Wallach and Wallach (1983) critique the questionable assumptions that have led academic and clinical psychology to valorize individualism or "selfishness," and Kitzinger (1997) documents how a "lesbian- and gay-affirmative" psychology critiques mainstream views of homosexuality.

Expanding on the latter example, lesbian-gay psychology began to emerge in the 1970s as a challenge to the cultural assumptions that homosexuality is somehow abnormal or pathological and should be rejected on moral and ethical grounds as a viable way of life. These assumptions have been critiqued by psychologists using conventional scientific tools, which have revealed that pathology is not any more characteristic of homosexuals than heterosexuals as a group, and that it represents "a normal variant of sexual behavior" (p. 206). These data have been applied in turn to social and legal questions such as those surrounding adoption, child custody, and visitation rights. If critical psychology, as Fox and Prilleltensky argue, is characterized by a challenging of accepted theories and practices and a promoting of more justice in the world, then wouldn't lesbian-gay psychology, as well as other critical approaches within psychological science, constitute "critical psychology?"

Kitzinger (1997) argues that the question is not whether an approach like lesbian-gay psychology is "critical" in its methods and impact, but, rather, is it "critical enough?" She contends that this approach uncritically accepts key assumptions of the mainstream psychology which it would critique, namely: (a) the assumption of positivist science that "facts" are uncovered or revealed by its methods; and (b) the assumption of individualism which pervades both research and application.

Kitzinger's critique of lesbian-gay psychology and her proposed alternative to it will be considered at a later point in this section. For now, her approach to mainstream psychology will be used to develop a defining characteristic of Critical *knowing*. Critiques of psychological assumptions and practices can derive from Representational and Perspectival modes of knowing, which are broadly associated with scientific method, but the Critical mode of knowing is associated with a critique of scientific knowing, itself. As for the issue of individualism, its critique is not unique to Critical psychology and can be linked with a number of perspectives including those associated with scientific knowing.

What is the relationship of Critical knowing to the "critical psychology" defined by Fox and Prilleltensky (1977)? Their volume includes critical approaches associated with a wide range of alternative philosophical positions, and the Critical mode of knowing will be defined more narrowly. For example, Prilleltensky (1997) has recently provided a useful classification of different approaches to psychology—based on their moral implications—which he summarizes as "traditional," "empowering," "postmodern," and "emancipatory communitarian" in nature (p. 525). Each of his three critical alternatives to traditional psychology represents a particular philosophical position (or positions), but I will associate the Critical mode of knowing specifically with skeptical postmodernism.

That is, Prilleltensky (1997) acknowledges that the emancipatory communitarian approach, with its emphasis on fundamental change in social institutions, "represents an aspirational paradigm more than one that is currently practiced" (p. 519). Indeed, when applied to clinical training and practice (McWhirter, 1998), it appears to overlap significantly with his "empowering" approach. Further, empowering approaches, which might include feminist therapy, gay-lesbian psychology, multicultural psychology, and community psychology, can be seen as having affinities with affirmative postmodernism. Prilleltensky acknowledges that affirmative postmodernists "embrace a political agenda similar to empowerment" (p. 528), which includes promoting "human diversity and self-determination of individuals and of marginalized groups" (p. 525, table 2). By contrast, skeptical postmodernists "are characterized by a doubting stance that ultimately leads to political inaction" (p. 528).

Again, given the purpose of teasing out the philosophical components of knowing in psychotherapy practice, I am going to draw the distinctions somewhat differently from Prilleltensky. While the Critical mode of knowing is associated with a skeptical stance and a deconstructionist method, the skepticism and deconstructionism are practiced *within limits*—otherwise this approach could progress to the position which will be described in the last section as the Nihilistic mode of knowing. The Critical mode takes as its object of deconstruction either societal practices or the practices of psychologists and psychotherapists, themselves. In this regard, it represents the counterpoint to the Dialogical mode and its assumption of affirmative postmodernism. Thus, the Critical mode is associated with critique and the Dialogical mode with affirmation, and a "social constructionist" therapist, for example, could be characterized as alternating between these two modes of knowing.

The Phenomenology of Critical Knowing: The Dialectic of Affirmation *vs.* Critique

The dialectical relationship between the Critical mode and other modes of knowing can be illustrated by returning to the example of lesbian-gay psychology. Kitzinger's (1997) analysis clearly exemplifies the characteristics of Critical knowing that have been stated to this point. She deconstructs lesbian-gay psychology as it is practiced but does not take her analysis so far as to result in the impossibility of an empowering approach to gay-lesbian psychotherapy. How does she balance the two?

Kitzinger points out that lesbian-gay psychology is based on an epistemology which assumes that science progresses and moves toward "ever more adequate approximations to truths about the world" (p. 208). Through this Representational mode of knowing, gay-lesbian psychology replaces an error-ridden science—which equates homosexuality and pathology—with a more "scientific" science, which disputes this linkage. Therefore, rather than representing a "radical" critique of heterosexist assumptions about homosexuality, lesbian-gay psychology serves the "counter-productive" function of reinforcing the role of social science in this debate. She cites Szasz (1970) as advancing a thesis closer to that of a truly critical psychology: Social science inevitably reflects social norms and, in the instance of homosexuality, has served to label as "sick" those who deviate from those norms. Therefore, "calling for 'better science,' or arguing about the validity of tests used, or the appropriateness of control groups, serves only to conceal the power interests at stake, and to reinforce the power of an oppressive discipline" (Kitzinger, 1997, p. 209).

From this perspective, the mainstream literature on gays and lesbians, like the mainstream literature on people of color or women, should not be read to find out what factual or scientific errors have been made in describing these groups. On the contrary, critical psychologists read these texts to understand how such groups are converted into "Other" by social science, how this act basically involves power, and how "rhetorical ploys" function to present this view of "Other" as somehow factual (Kitzinger, 1997, p. 210). In a nutshell, the aim of Critical knowing is to deconstruct that which is taken to be scientific knowledge.

Kitzinger (1997) then critiques the individualistic assumptions of lesbian-gay psychology and underscores their centrality by focusing on the concept of "homophobia." This term, defined as the "irrational persistent fear or dread of homosexuals" or homosexuality (MacDonald, 1976), began to appear in the psychological literature in the late 1960s and entered popular usage in the 1970s. In time, it caught on as a way of characterizing the unenlightened and even pathological views of individuals who oppress homosexual persons. However, not only does this term validate that science, now gay-lesbian science, can label individuals as pathological, "it also depoliticizes lesbian and gay oppression by suggesting that it comes from the personal inadequacy of particular individuals suffering from a diagnosable phobia" (Kitzinger, 1997, p. 211). Advocates of critical knowing are justifiably suspicious of explanations which replace political analyses with personal ones, since this has been the tendency of most mainstream psychology.

The assumptions of Representational knowing and individualism are then carried to the practice of gay-lesbian therapy. It is assumed that many gays and lesbians suffer from "internalized homophobia," and, according to Kitzinger (1997), it is recommended that they seek out gay and lesbian therapists who will assist them in overcoming this problem. Accepting one's identity as a gay or lesbian is seen as a developmental process, which includes recognizing one's own internalized homophobia and moving beyond it to embrace one's "real sexual orientation" (p. 211). Moreover, the concept of internalized homophobia can also be used as a way of explaining how gays and lesbians oppress themselves. Consequently, the focus is shifted away from social institutions and power relations which create oppression and toward the individuals who are the victims of oppression. Kitzinger comments:

> If psychologists' aim is to reduce the "psychological distress" and "internalized homophobia" which results from anti-lesbian and anti-gay discrimination, do they risk losing sight of the need to change society and stop these forms of discrimination altogether? If their aim is to decrease "stress" and to increase the "ego strength" of the victim, do they risk forgetting that it is the

perpetrator, not the victim, who is the real problem? . . . Lesbian and gay psychology, like mainstream psychology, retains a clear focus on *individual* health and pathology and the role of social institutions and structures are only peripheral to this preoccupation. (p. 213)

Up to this point, Kitzinger (1997) has performed a deconstructive analysis of gay-lesbian psychology and psychotherapy from the perspective of "social constructionism and radical feminism" (p. 213), and it has been stated exclusively within the idiom of Critical knowing. She then shifts her tone and acknowledges that both lesbian-gay psychology and critical psychology are committed to fighting oppression and creating a more just world. Since the two approaches take such different paths to a similar goal, she asks if lesbian-gay psychology is "not critical enough" or if critical psychology is "too critical?" (p. 213).

Understandably, Kitzinger concludes that there is value in each of these stances toward criticism. Since she has previously emphasized the problems associated with scientific psychology and individualism, she then examines their benefits—while acknowledging the costs that can accompany a critical psychology. The scientific approach of lesbian and gay psychology has been effective in changing how homosexuality is presented in the academic and popular literature, in helping to establish gay and lesbian legal and civil rights, and in legitimizing a rhetoric which is relevant to social change. She acknowledges that critical psychologists may be less effective in communicating their aims regarding social change when their rhetoric is undercut by the admission that no perspective, including their own, is objectively based. "It is hard to argue for the moral or political superiority of a refusal to attest to the mental health of a lesbian mother in a custody case on the grounds that the concept of 'mental health' is a socially constructed one" (Kitzinger, 1997, pp. 214–215). In other words, maintaining "a high epistemological ground," which insists that critical psychologists never utter a realist statement, leaves them with little to say which is intelligible or influential in the real world of people and politics (p. 215).

Similarly, whatever the ultimate sources of oppression, Kitzinger (1997) emphasizes that it does cause "*individual* suffering," and it is individual gays and lesbians who seek out psychotherapeutic assistance for a variety of personal problems, some of which would occur even if they did not live in a heterosexist world (p. 215). Kitzinger agrees with L. S. Brown (1992) that it is not justifiable for critical psychologists, regardless of their views about social and political change, to have nothing to offer to a suffering individual other than "waiting for the revolution." While Kitzinger is not convinced by arguments that link individual psychotherapy with social and political change, she believes, nonetheless, that psychotherapeutic work is just as essential as critical psychology. Although she does not use the term, her concluding statement proposes a dialectical relationship between critique (Critical knowing) and affirmation (the other modes of knowing):

> It may well be the case that the radical critique of individualism advanced by critical psychologists depends upon the continued existence of therapists who are willing to deal with human suffering on an individual basis, leaving critical psychologists with a clear conscience and free to concentrate on fomenting political revolution. (p. 215)

The Relationship of Critical Knowing to Psychotherapeutic Practice

The reader may wonder why so much time has been spent on the views of an academic psychologist in a chapter which is focused on the phenomenology of psychotherapists' modes of knowing. For Critical knowing, the phenomenology of an academic psychologist and a psychotherapist are largely interchangeable, because this mode is not specifically associated with the "doing" of psychotherapy. While Critical knowing can provide a theoretical framework which guides psychotherapy, a psychotherapist is more than a social critic, and it is not easy to turn social criticism into effective therapeutic interventions.

For example, Kitzinger (1997) observes that many feminist therapists engage in a "desperate search . . . for therapies which will somehow tackle 'individual' problems without being 'individualistic'" (p. 215). Similarly, we have seen how social constructionists like Gergen and Cushman struggle to implement their Critical knowing in the context of psychotherapy. Ultimately, Cushman acknowledges that his hermeneutic approach to psychotherapy, based on Dialogical knowing, falls short of the goals for social change set by his Critical knowing. Gergen critiques "social constructionist" approaches to psychotherapy which are based on Dialogical knowing and asserts that psychotherapeutic goals should be defined strictly in relation to the social transformation associated with Critical knowing. These goals are stated quite abstractly, however, and it is not clear how they might be realistically implemented or achieved.

Given the dilemma of translating an abstract political position into lived experience, a more productive approach to Critical knowing frames it as a supplement to and critique of other modes of knowing. Returning to the anorexic girl who was seen by Zimmerman (J. L. Zimmerman & Dickerson, 1994), Critical knowing complements his Dialogical approach to psychotherapy. Through Critical knowing, he deconstructs anorexia as individual pathology and reformulates it in terms of practices related to power and gender. He then shifts to a Dialogical mode of knowing to carry this understanding to his actual work with the client.

Critical knowing can also serve as a critique of Zimmerman's approach, which I hope was demonstrated in the analysis of his work in the last section. Critical knowing allows us to separate the rhetoric of his narrative or Dialogical approach from the reality of his interventions with the client. It is not the case that he helps the client to create a new narrative space which embodies the ontology and epistemology of Dialogical knowing. Rather, he assists the client in replacing one Realist conception of the world ("I have anorexia") with another ("I have found my voice and now practice anti-anorexia"). This kind of critical awareness could help therapists, especially those who contend that they are offering a radical approach to individual and social change, to become more honest and realistic about the level of "transformation" which they are able to provide. As Kitzinger argues, it is unlikely that fundamental social change will ever be produced by psychotherapy, and it is more likely that psychotherapy—even in its "radical" varieties—will continue to reproduce some of the very philosophical assumptions and political arrangements which it purports to modify or eliminate.

What happens if Critical knowing is removed from its dialectical relationship with other modes of knowing and is asked to stand alone as a basis for psychotherapy? As has been implied above, it will stand as an abstract statement of social change or transformation which cannot be translated into concrete work with a client, apart from the use of other, more affirmative, modes of knowing. In fact, there is no such thing as a "social constructionist" therapy based only on Critical knowing. This point is underscored by the previously reviewed collection, *Therapy as Social Construction* (McNamee & Gersen, 1992), which contains Gergen and Kaye's (1992) recommendation that therapy goals be framed within the transformational language of Critical knowing. Most of the actual therapy work which is cited in this collection is Dialogical in nature, and, as Gergen and Kaye argue, it is not completely true to its own epistemology but incorporates Realist elements of knowing. They mistakenly conclude, however, that the constraints on change inherent in the therapeutic situation can be transcended by a critically correct, abstract statement of therapeutic goals. As was previously indicated, their statement can then be critiqued as a metanarrative which makes its own implicit Realist (truth) claims.

THE NIHILISTIC MODE OF KNOWING

It might seem to the reader that a "Nihilistic" mode of knowing represents a contradiction in terms, and the clarification of this usage will begin with a reintroduction of distinctions offered by Carr (1992) in chapter 2. She distinguishes between "alethiological nihilism" (truth does not exist) and "epistemological nihilism" (knowledge does not exist) (p. 17). "Existential nihilism" then refers to the psychological response to these philosophical positions: One possible response to the realization that neither knowledge nor truth is possible is a sense of meaninglessness which can result in despair.

I will put aside for a moment the issue of existential nihilism and concentrate on outlining the philosophical position which may presage it. Skeptical postmodernism has been associated with the position that neither truth nor knowledge exists, while affirmative postmodernism has been presented as saving the possibility of "contingent" knowledge. However, as has been apparent throughout the discussion of either philosophical or psychotherapeutic approaches to postmodernism, an abiding tension exists between these two positions and their possible implications.

From the vantage point of skeptical postmodernism, affirmative postmodernism—if taken too far—runs the risk of repeating the mistakes of the traditional epistemology it critiques by making its own implicit realist claims. From the perspective of affirmative postmodernism, the deconstructionism of skeptical postmodernism—if taken too far—runs the risk of becoming "totalizing," turning on itself and undermining any possibility of social meaning or political action. Accordingly, a social constructionist such as Gergen alternates between the Dialogical and Critical modes of knowing associated with these different positions, and a radical feminist such as Kitzinger acknowledges the necessary interplay between the Representational knowing of gay-lesbian psychology and her own Critical knowing.

Nihilistic Knowing as Unlimited Deconstructionism and "Self-Reflexive Doubt"

In this context, Nihilistic knowing will be associated with a philosophical position which takes skeptical postmodernism to its logical conclusion. Deconstructionism, defined broadly as a "negative critical capacity" (Rosenau, 1992, p. 118), brings into question any affirmative statement, certainly any affirmative statement that reeks of generalization. Alternative interpretations are always possible, and there is no way to decide among these alternatives. Within this mode, it might be said that any understanding is necessarily a misunderstanding. If one applies that last statement to itself, then the paralysis which can result from this position becomes obvious. Finally, in order to avoid self-contradiction, one would say nothing.

Richer (1992) illustrates this approach to knowing with his "introduction to deconstructionist psychology." He seconds Foucault's (1980) conviction that everything is "dangerous" and then points out how this skeptical rule of thumb can also be applied to Foucault's own work and influence. He indicates that it "maddened" Foucault that his approach to knowledge was not exempt from the power dynamics which are embedded in all knowledge production: "Fringe academic movements have always been integral to the maintenance of liberal, and therefore nonrevolutionary attitudes in the young. . . . Foucault would be the instrument of normalization for those wilder graduate students" (p. 112).

Richer (1992) then articulates a "vigilant" deconstructionism (p. 116) which "aims more to destruct than to construct" and which, following Foucault, results in a "scattering" or "decentering" of knowledge claims such that no viewpoint is privileged (p. 115). From this perspective, the many humanistic, psychodynamic, and hermeneutic trends in psychology today, which attempt to avoid the problems associated with objectivism, can be revealed as simply more subtle means of social control. "Psychology—all of it—is a branch of the police; psychodynamic and humanistic psychologies are the secret police" (p. 118).

This is exactly the kind of rampant deconstructionism which is seen as a threat by many traditional psychologists, critical psychologists, feminists, and affirmative postmodernists. M. B. Smith (1994), an advocate of a reformulated, humane science of psychology, sees it as leading to "radical relativism" and leaving us "bereft of anchors to stabilize a view of self and world" (p. 408). Parker (1997), speaking as a critical psychologist, argues that deconstructionism of this kind not only relativizes the claims of traditional psychology, but also undermines "the truth claims of the critics, potentially sabotaging moral and political critiques of the discipline. For who is to say that the critics have a more ethical view of psychology?" (p. 295). Feminist theorists worry that this approach, which rejects all universal, cross-cultural categories of human experience, would deconstruct the very category—gender—on which a feminist analysis is built (Di Stefano, 1990). Gergen's (1994) defense of an affirmative postmodernism is based on his conclusion that the postmodern literature is turning away from a "nihilistic posture," associated with uncontained deconstructionism, and toward "more promising possibilities" (p. 413).

What these critics have in common is their fear of the "vertigo of self-reflexive doubt" (Gergen, 1991, p. 134) which characterizes Nihilistic knowing. Doubt is first directed against that which has pretended to be truth or knowledge, and which is in actuality just another social construction. However, "once this doubt is unleashed, one confronts the awful irony that all one's doubts are also subject to doubt. After all, these doubts are themselves constructions of the world from a certain vantage point" (p. 134). It is as if one can never quite count on what will be under foot when a step is taken, because what appeared as solid ground in one moment is revealed in the next as nothing more than one's own construction of solidity.

The Phenomenology of Nihilistic Knowing: An Example from Postmodern Fiction

What is the phenomenological experience of those who embrace a Nihilistic position of chronic, self-reflexive doubt? It was acknowledged in chapter 2 that skeptical postmodernists, for the most part, do not admit to the possibility of existential nihilism. Yes, there is no solid ground beneath one's feet, but this realization results in meaninglessness and despair only for those who mistakenly cling to foundationalist or absolutist expectations. Postmodern consciousness manifests as an invitation to play with all the meanings which are possible, and to do so with an attitude of ironic detachment—since there is little point in investing deeply when, in the end, one story is no better than any other (Gergen, 1991). The advice is to step lightly and leave no trace of a commitment.

The notion that there is an intrinsic relationship between absolutism and nihilism as philosophical positions received considerable support in chapter 2, but it is questionable whether a stance of ironic detachment can eliminate the problem of existential nihilism. Given the human tendency to reify concepts, we have seen how difficult it is even for committed postmodernists to rid themselves of all vestiges of Realist knowing. For example, Spretnak (1991) contends that the postmodernist battle cry of "No more worldviews!" itself represents a meaning-giving stance toward the world which "is based on an intensely held set of presuppositions about life" (p. 235). Further, a purely intellectual stance is no doubt easier to maintain within academic debates than in the consulting room, and it can be assumed that the majority of psychotherapists who are caught in "self-reflexive doubt" are quite likely to *feel* something.

So, the question becomes, what would it be like to practice psychotherapy from a stance of total uncertainty? I am not speaking here of a therapist who has only a pang of self-doubt. Neither am I referring to a therapist who has some philosophical or theoretical framework for uncertainty—whether existential therapy, Gestalt therapy, dialogical / conversational therapy, or Zen—which somehow produces "right action" or "presence." I am talking about a therapist who—for a moment or a more extended period—doesn't know up from down, who is caught in the deepest state of confusion and meaninglessness about the understanding of self, other, and the world.

Novelists are sometimes more adept than psychotherapists in conveying the essence of a psychological phenomenon, and I will turn to John Barth (1969) to give more texture to the description of Nihilistic knowing. The protagonist in *The End of the Road* is one Jacob Horner, a 28-year-old graduate student in English literature at Johns Hopkins, who has just passed his orals but is blocked about writing his thesis. Jacob gets up one morning, packs his bag, and heads to the train station with $30 in his pocket and no earthly idea where he should go or what he should do. Thinking that he should keep a little cash in reserve, he asks the ticket agent where he might go from Baltimore for, say, $20. He is given several destinations in Ohio, and Jacob tells the agent he will decide later. He sits down on a bench, and something unusual happens to him:

> And it was there that I simply ran out of motives, as a car runs out of gas. There was no reason to go to Cincinnati, Ohio. There was no reason to go to Crestline, Ohio. Or Dayton, Ohio; or Lima, Ohio. There was no reason, either, to go back to the apartment hotel, or for that matter to go anywhere. There was no reason to do anything. My eyes, as Winckelmann

said inaccurately of the eyes of the Greek statues, were sight-less, gazing on eternity, fixed on ultimacy, and when that is the case there is no reason to do anything—even to change the focus of one's eyes. Which is perhaps why the statues stand still. It is the malady *cosmopsis,* the cosmic view, that afflicted me. When one has it, one is frozen like the bullfrog when the hunter's light strikes him full in the eyes, only with cosmopsis there is no hunger, and no quick hand to terminate the moment—there's only the light. (p. 74)

Jacob sits on the bench all that night and might have been there indefinitely if someone hadn't come along and asked how long he had been there. Jacob is embarrassed and struggles to say anything at all, but the stranger is persistent and invites Jacob for coffee to discuss his "case." Jacob objects that there is no case to discuss and replies that he had only been sitting on the bench for a few minutes. The stranger indicates that he saw Jacob sitting there in the same position the previous night when he arrived from New York, and then observes: "You *were* paralyzed, weren't you?" (p. 76).

Jacob has had the good fortune to meet "the Doctor," a physician who happens to specialize in the treatment of immobility and paralysis, of both the physical and mental variety. The Doctor combines medicine with what might be called a form of therapy, and has his own institute, the Remobilization Farm, where he invites Jacob to begin rehabilitation. Jacob at first hesitates and then complies—because he certainly has nothing better to do. After staying there for a period of time, he is sent back to Baltimore by the Doctor to see if the paralysis will return. He is given a wealth of parting advice by the Doctor and is cautioned, above all, against becoming stuck between alternatives, or he will again become lost.

> You're not that strong. If the alternatives are side by side, choose the one on the left; if they're consecutive in time, choose the earlier. If neither of these applies, choose the alternative whose name begins with the earlier letter of the alphabet. These are the principles of Sinistrality, Antecedence, and Alphabetical Priority—there are others, and they're arbitrary, but useful. Good-by. (p. 85)

Barth again demonstrates the importance of irony to postmodern accounts of living in the world. The comedic elements of this excerpt are contradicted by the underlying seriousness of its existential themes. Yet, as the novel unfolds, Jacob's seemingly detached stance toward the world turns out to offer little protection from the emotional travails that relationship will hold for him.

The experience of admitting Nihilistic knowing into the therapy room will be conveyed in part by juxtaposing it with metaphorical or Realist knowing. In contrast to the latter, where there is an embracing of our own experience and an active reaching out to the client's experience, Nihilistic knowing involves a more passive, resistant stance toward self and other. While Realist knowing results in a general sense of confirmation of our understanding, Nihilistic knowing is associated with its opposite: This mode depends on our letting in anomalous, disconfirming experience. We resist this experience, to varying degrees at different times, because it is contrary to the operating strategy of our cognitive/perceptual system—which is to reduce disorder, impose meaning, and avoid emotional pain. If Realist knowing can be likened to a positive ego state, then, for most of us, most of the time, Nihilistic knowing represents the threat of an "ego alien" state.

The experience of disconfirmation can arise from the client's responses, our own responses, or, more likely, from their interaction. Of course, the therapist can also experience "disconfirmation" in relation to other modes of knowing, whether it is connected with recognizing a wrong interpretation from the Representational mode, with realizing the lack of fit of a framework from the Perspectival mode, or with practicing "not-knowing" from the Dialogical mode. What differentiates disconfirmation associated with the Nihilistic mode of knowing from these other varieties is the depth of our doubt and the strength of our emotional reactions. We may experience disorientation, confusion, anxiety, sadness, meaninglessness, and, above all, profound uncertainty. It isn't just that this or that interpretation or intervention has failed. Rather, it is a sense that all interpretations and interventions are ineffective, and that all theoretical frameworks are useless. Even if, for a moment, we can muster some confidence in our theories and methods, we may still doubt whether our skills are sufficient to the task of implementation. We may experience deeply that we have neither the knowledge nor the presence to be of assistance to another human being and may be aware of the very arrogance behind our wish to help. We may question everything, including the nature of psychotherapy as a social institution and as an existential encounter.

Similarly, Kuhn (1970a) cites the experience of Wolfgang Pauli, writing to a friend before Heisenberg's paper led to a new quantum theory: "At the moment physics is again terribly confused. In any case, it is too difficult for me, and I wish I had been a movie comedian or something of the sort and had never heard of physics" (p. 84). Have you ever heard a therapist, whether trainee or supervisor, say something like this at the end of a hard day? Have you ever thought it or said it yourself after one too many difficulties or disappointments with clients? Five months later, Pauli writes: "Heisenberg's type of mechanics has again given me hope and joy in life. To be sure it does not supply the solution to the riddle, but I believe it is again possible to march forward" (p. 84). The discrepancy between his two statements illustrates the subjective contrast between the revelatory and restrictive, the confirmatory and disconfirmatory, functions of theory use, whether in natural science or psychotherapy.

Nihilistic Knowing and Other Modes of Knowing

There should be no need to address in detail the question of whether this mode of knowing can "stand alone" as an approach to psychotherapy. It is impossible to practice therapy from this stance alone, and therapists whose moments of Nihilistic knowing extend into a full-blown crisis of meaning or faith are in danger of the kind of "impairment" that interferes significantly with providing effective therapy. In any case, it is not likely that therapists who doubt this profoundly would stay in the field for long, unless their doubt is balanced by more affirmative approaches to knowing.

Novak (1971) provides a context for the above conclusion by distinguishing between the "experience of nothingness," which corresponds to Nihilistic knowing, and nihilism as an "ideological interpretation" or philosophical position that is "imposed" on this experience (p. 13). A therapist who is having a protracted crisis of meaning has in all likelihood moved from a more direct experience of nothingness to an implicit or explicit conceptual understanding which, paradoxically, imbues nihilism with something substantial or "real."

Although Nihilistic knowing may be untenable when it is extended into a "position" for life or therapy, it, too, manifests in relationship to other modes of knowing and has an important part to play in the dialectics of psychotherapy practice. Given the human tendency to convert theoretical and philosophical assumptions into world views grounded in reality, coupled with the immense societal pressure for psychotherapy to reveal "the truth," psychotherapists are prone to becoming overconfident about their therapeutic frameworks. This holds whether we are explicitly operating from a Realist mode which asserts that we can know absolutely or from a Dialogical mode which admonishes us to practice not-knowing. Nihilistic knowing, experienced as a counterpoint rather than as a position, can represent a corrective to such theoretical and therapeutic overconfidence.

Chapter 7

Implications for Practice:
Toward a Morally Situated Psychotherapy

Six modes of knowing have now been defined in philosophical, theoretical, and experiential terms, and the thrust of this formulation has
been largely descriptive in nature. The primary goal has been one of providing readers with a sufficiently detailed account of functioning within
different lived epistemologies so that it might be possible to recognize
their presence and impact on the therapist's own experience.

The challenge of this final chapter is to further articulate the
assumptions that have colored this analysis while formulating their
implications in such a fashion that the focus explicitly shifts from
description to "prescription." Specifically, what recommendations are
implied by this account for the question of a philosophically sound psychotherapeutic practice?

This question immediately makes central a feature of therapeutic
practice which until now has assumed a secondary role in the argument.
Successful psychotherapy, whether defined as art, science, spiritual practice, postmodern conversation, or hermeneutic inquiry, necessarily conveys a sense of coherence—a moral vision, if you will—to the client. This
aspect of the therapeutic exchange itself represents a moral dilemma for
the therapist, however, since there is no secure theoretical or philosophical ground on which therapists might build their visions of human reality and its transformation. Therefore, any discussion of "philosophical

guidelines" for psychotherapy practice must locate the therapist's implicit and explicit assumptions about knowledge within this larger context.

As an orienting device to the moral implications of psychotherapeutic knowing, the chapter will begin with a clinical example. It underlines the problems that arise when psychotherapy is practiced from a single approach to knowing, particularly when the practitioner remains unaware of the characteristics and consequences associated with the Realist mode.

THE RISKS OF CERTITUDE: MPD AND SATANIC RITUAL ABUSE

If affirmation and critique, conviction and uncertainty, represent poles of an epistemological continuum which frame contemporary psychotherapeutic practice, then the risks of therapeutic certitude are brought home by recent attempts to link satanic ritual abuse with Dissociative Identity Disorder (American Psychiatric Association, 1994)— better known as multiple personality disorder (MPD). A *Frontline* segment (Bikel & Dretzin, 1995) offers dramatic accounts of the harrowing experiences of two women who received treatment for such abuse, and Dunn (1992), Ofshe and Watters (1994), and Spanos (1996) provide reviews of the relevant clinical and empirical literature.

Spanos (1996) indicates that MPD began to be associated with repressed memories of child abuse in the 1970s, and more specific memories of satanic abuse began to emerge during the 1980s. Just as the popular book *Sybil* (Schreiber, 1973) and its later adaptation as a television movie had a significant impact on shaping the expectations of clients and therapists regarding the nature of MPD, he suggests that *Michelle Remembers* (M. Smith & Pazder, 1980) did much the same for the linkage between MPD and satanic cult abuse.

By 1991, a survey study conducted by Bottoms, Shaver, and Goodman indicated that thousands of clients had recovered memories of satanic abuse in therapy, although the number of therapists seeing such clients was quite skewed. While 70% of the therapists surveyed had never seen this phenomenon, the great majority of the cases were reported by only 2% of the sample. These 16 therapists had each treated at least 100 cases of ritual abuse, and one of the respondents reported treating approximately 2,000 clients of this kind.

Although only a small number of American mental health professionals have been involved in the treatment of satanic abuse, they do not necessarily constitute a fringe group in terms of professional credentials or credibility. One of the treatment facilities featured by both the *Frontline* segment and Ofshe and Watters' first-person account is the former Dissociative Disorders Program of the prestigious Rush-Presbyterian-St. Luke's Medical Center in Chicago. Its then director, Dr. Bennett Braun, has served as president of the International Society for the Study of Dissociation, has been regarded as one of the foremost experts in the area of MPD, and has lent credence to the association of MPD with satanic abuse through lectures and publications.

Spanos, as well as Ofshe and Watters, agree with a number of critics who see the symptoms of satanic ritual abuse as an iatrogenic disorder. The *Frontline* segment indicates that the FBI has found no evidence whatsoever for the kind of widespread cult activity and abuse reported by clients and therapists, and Bromley (1991) contends that there has not yet been one verified casualty of this alleged network. What, then, do the memories and experiences of these clients represent?

Ofshe and Watters (1994) cite Braun himself as admitting that it is the rare client who comes for treatment with intact satanic abuse memories, and that he is more confident that the abuse is real if the therapist has to "pull it out of them" (p. 246). Typically, the intensive treatment of such clients relies heavily on a combination of hypnotherapy, psychotropic medications, and group therapy, and the latter may include the participation of other MPD clients who have acknowledged their own satanic abuse. Spanos (1996) devotes a separate chapter to a critique of the assumption that hypnosis can directly reveal the inner reality of the client, including true or undistorted memories, and emphasizes that both hypnotherapeutic and group interventions are very effective means of communicating the therapist's implicit assumptions and expectations to the client. If the therapist is convinced of the reality of satanic abuse and believes that the lack of evidence in support of extensive cult activity and abuse is simply another manifestation of the power of an international conspiracy and cover-up, then a vulnerable client is ripe to produce what the therapist expects to find.

Several different sources provide striking examples of clients who were treated for satanic abuse and later recanted their stories. For example, Mary S. and Patty B. chronicle their experiences on the *Frontline* video (Bikel & Dretzin, 1995), and, in some instances, hospital records, staff interviews, and session recordings corroborate their accounts of the events that transpired. What comes across most powerfully in this video is the confidence—one might say arrogance—with which their therapists pursued a controversial treatment plan for a questionable condition.

After receiving a diagnosis of MPD, Patty was hospitalized at Rush-Presbyterian-St. Luke's Medical Center in 1986, where she would stay for the next three years. Her sons (ages 4 and 5) were also later hospitalized, spending, respectively, 32 and 39 months in inpatient care—hospitalizations which were terminated only after their parents obtained a court order. The boys were seen as having incipient MPD, and medical records reveal that they were given "stickers" for revealing "yucky" memories of abuse. Patty describes one episode where her son told what it was like to see and smell the intestines "pop out" of a human abdomen after he had allegedly ripped it open with a knife. At the time, Patty told Dr. Braun that she knew the exact scene from a *Star Wars* movie where her son had seen similar material. However, after showing that scene from the movie, the *Frontline* video cuts to Dr. Braun reporting this "evidence" of satanic abuse to his colleagues at a conference. He implies that such evidence is incontrovertible by stating that, as a physician, he knows what it is like to open an abdomen, and the child's report is too accurate to represent something other than a first-hand report.

Following a prior assessment by Dr. Roberta Sachs, Mary was also hospitalized at Rush-Presbyterian-St. Luke's Medical Center for MPD in 1990. Within a few days, she was told that abuse victims across the country had identified her as a fifth generation cult member, and as "cult royalty." She was placed on a locked ward so that other cult members could not harm her, and she was eagerly questioned by Drs. Sachs and Braun. The therapists began to see her as both a victim and perpetrator of abuse within the cult, and they wanted to learn more of its innerworkings. Mary later said that she came to accept these views of her history and condition,

> because they were the experts. They said, "We've been studying this for fifteen years. We've done research. This phenomenon is happening all over the world. . . . We've written books, we give lectures . . . other doctors come to our hospital and are trained by us because we are the experts." (Bikel & Dretzin, 1995)

After a consultation with a cult expert who suggested that she was still programmed in a fashion that could cause danger to the professional staff, Mary was transferred to Spring Shadows Glen Hospital in Houston to continue treatment, now with Dr. Judith Peterson. The staff became convinced that she was a danger to her husband and son, who came to share this view, and Mary's estrangement from her family continued at the time of the *Frontline* report. She was eventually reported for abuse of her son, Ryan, who was also hospitalized at the Texas facility and later diagnosed as MPD as well.

All told, Mary's insurance companies paid over $2 million for her psychiatric care, and the expenses for Patty and her family were near $3 million. Nonetheless, at the end of this extensive treatment, the condition of both of the primary clients had worsened. Each made a decision to halt the treatment, and after going off their heavy medications and seeking nonregressive, supportive therapy, the MPD and the memories of ritual abuse simply "stopped." Lawsuits were pending against the therapists at the time of the *Frontline* report, and all declined to be interviewed. In November, 1997, the suit of Patricia Burgus (Patty B.) was settled for $10.6 million, and the Illinois Department of Professional Regulation subsequently issued a complaint against Dr. Braun, alleging that his techniques "almost destroyed the lives of Burgus and her family" ("Psychiatrist Faces," 1998).

While Spanos (1996) questions whether MPD exists at all as a clinical entity apart from the sociocognitive factors which he sees as creating and maintaining it, that debate goes beyond my purpose here. Whether or not "genuine" or uncontaminated cases of MPD exist, the material reviewed above suggests that therapists' commitment to a belief system led, in this instance, both to the overdiagnosis of MPD and to the creation of a fictional syndrome of satanic ritual abuse. In a press release for the *Frontline* segment (WGBH Educational Foundation, 1995), its producers, Ofra Bikel and Rachel Dretzin, focus the issue in a similar fashion. They indicate that the most "shocking" aspect of the story is not that some patients reported satanic abuse but that they came to *believe* in this abuse while being treated at a very prestigious medical facility. "In the final analysis, it is a story about the power of belief—belief in a conspiracy, belief in the infallibility of medical experts, belief in a diagnosis, and ultimately for both these women, belief in one's self."

THE NECESSITY AND DANGER
OF THERAPEUTIC CONVICTION

Most laypersons and professionals would view the behavior of therapists who treat satanic ritual abuse as an aberration, but I believe it is more useful to see it as an exaggeration of the vulnerabilities shared by all of us who practice in this field. For example, Gold (1995) comments on papers submitted by therapists participating in a symposium on "failure" cases in psychotherapy. He highlights how all of the papers "convey an initial sense of certainty" about the therapist's assessment of the case, including the client's needs, the client's ability to use the therapeutic approach which is offered, and the essential correctness of that approach (p. 168). This confidence is particularly striking in comparison to the therapists' later realization that something significant had been missed in the case. Gold then accounts for this discrepancy by suggesting that "knowledge of our limitations," especially the recognition that "our cherished theories, techniques, and ideologies" simply do not apply well to a given situation, "is too painful for us at times, prompting denial and a flight into a kind of overly optimistic grandiosity and confidence" (p. 168).

Similarly, I assume that the majority of therapists who treat satanic abuse survivors are well-meaning in their intentions and are simply following the dictates of clinical or scientific evidence, as they understand it. Although the issue of therapist ethics will be discussed further in the next section, the immediate lesson to be taken from this example does not concern the individual standards or decision-making of a few therapists. Rather, this episode of therapy practice gone wrong invites a reflection on the larger issue of the role of *belief* in psychotherapy practice.

If the reader has been convinced by even a portion of the argument of the preceding chapters, then it should be apparent that the convictions of the therapist are inseparable from the practice of psychotherapy. Scientific method attempts to separate unsubstantiated belief from empirically supported conclusion, but the former reenters the house of objectivity through the back door of "normal science." Postmodernist, hermeneutic, and constructionist therapists lambaste scientist-practitioners for their failure to acknowledge the inherently uncertain, dialogical nature of human knowing, but cannot eliminate unexamined commonsense realism from their own theoretical arguments and therapeutic practices.

Without doubt, the impact on clients can be devastating when therapists convert a hypothesis or model of satanic abuse into a metaphor and see evidence of its literal existence wherever they look. Yet, the cognitive and experiential process through which this transformation occurs is one that has been shown to be ubiquitous in human functioning. Theoretical and philosophical frameworks, whether implicit or explicit in nature, function both to reveal and restrict our meanings about the world. Through these functions, one set of meanings is experienced as equivalent to reality itself, while alternative meanings are simultaneously excluded. Asking professional psychotherapists to eliminate Realist knowing of this kind from their work would be like asking nonprofessionals to approach the world in the absence of any metaphorical thinking. It would be impossible. Moreover, while this mode of knowing does, in some circumstances, represent a threat to the well-being of the client, therapeutic progress also depends on its very existence.

The philosopher of science Michael Polanyi (1964, 1967) develops a perspective toward scientific knowing which can deepen our understanding of the indispensability of therapeutic conviction to both client and therapist. He proposes the term "tacit knowing" to account for the obvious conclusion that *"we can know more than we can tell"* (1967, p. 4). For example, while we can recognize someone's face out of a thousand, perhaps out of a million, other faces, in all likelihood we cannot put into words how we accomplish this feat. Tacit knowing of this kind depends on our attending *from* one thing (the "proximal" term) *to* another thing (the "distal" term) (p. 10). The proximal term represents that which we know but cannot fully specify, and it is the "appearance" of the distal term which expresses or signifies that knowing (p. 11). Thus, in the previous example, we attend from the features of the face to a recognition of the face itself.

Polanyi (1967) extends the reach of tacit knowing to the use of theory by a scientist and does so by linking it with the notions of "indwelling" and "interiorization." Theory takes on a potency for seeing and acting in the world (the distal term) just to the extent that the scientist "dwells" in it (the proximal term):

> To rely on a theory for understanding nature is to interiorize it. For we are attending from the theory to things seen in its light, and are aware of the theory, while thus using it, in terms of the spectacle that it serves to explain. This is why mathematical theory can be learned only by practicing its application: its true knowledge lies in our ability to use it. (p. 17)

Polanyi's thinking can be paraphrased as follows: To use a theory, it is necessary to suspend disbelief and enter into the theory, thereby experiencing the world from within its terms and frame. In a very real sense, to truly understand a theory and, certainly, to apply a theory, one must "believe" the theory, at least at the moment of its understanding and application. In the absence of what Polanyi describes as the interiorization of theory and what Kuhn characterizes as the "gestalt" nature of paradigms, there would be no foundation on which scientific progress could be built.

If belief is this central to the development of the natural sciences, then how pivotal it must be to a situation where one person comes to another for help, oftentimes in a state of confusion and desperation. In the complex exchange which follows, it is no doubt crucial that therapists teach clients to interiorize some implicit or explicit theoretical rationale and philosophical framework, just as they themselves have interiorized it. This process represents one way by which the client gains a new set of meanings—meanings which are not restricted to the intellectual domain. Although it may be important to develop a new cognitive frame for ordering experience, the client also learns how to see and feel and behave within the terms of the theoretical rationale, philosophical framework, and set of methods that are offered and modeled by the therapist (Barton, 1974).

From this perspective, it is not surprising that Jerome Frank's comparative approach to psychotherapy (Frank, 1973; Frank & Frank, 1991) identifies the creation of meaning and the restoration of hope as powerful common factors which are associated with successful outcome. Yet, the paradoxical role of the therapist's convictions in this change process is an explicit theme of Frank's argument. He finds it implausible that all of the theoretical rationales and methods which are associated with positive change in therapy are somehow "true," and describes the former as having features of "myths." Similarly, Karasu (1996) suggests that therapeutic theories function as "belief systems" or "compelling metaphors" (pp. 15–16) which offer therapists "the foundation for personal conviction as well as professional allegiance" (p. 26). In turn, therapists' belief in their rationales, philosophical assumptions, and methods—whether justified or not—inspires the client's "confidence in the therapist, a major source of the effectiveness of all psychotherapy" (Frank & Frank, p. xiv).

Having emphasized the necessity of therapeutic conviction, defined as Realist knowing, let us turn again to its difficulties and dangers. While the treatment of satanic ritual abuse demonstrates the wages of misplaced conviction, the obviousness of this example misrepresents the ease of coming to some consensus regarding the nature of "acceptable" belief in this field. As indicated in chapter 1, the same client presenting at the doorsteps of different therapists could, and probably would, be confronted with radically different approaches to his or her situation. Within the current therapy marketplace, the same client problem might be approached from literally hundreds of different theoretical rationales and therapeutic methods.

How does one go about choosing among these rationales and methods? Therapists who come from more traditional training programs might recoil when they see clients treated with past-life regression, rebirthing, or varieties of spiritual healing. They may see these approaches as reflecting either religious dogma or New Age mumbo jumbo. Yet, some of these traditionally trained therapists might expand their own repertoires to include bioenergetics, meditation, EMDR, or hypnotherapy, while their more conservative colleagues would reject those methods as well. Within analytic circles, a conservative analyst might be someone who subscribes to drive theory and to certain variations of object relations theory, but who rejects newer developments such as self psychology and intersubjectivity. However, some behavioral and cognitive-behavioral therapists might see this "conservative" analytic position as no less fanciful than those associated with "New Age" therapists.

The question finally becomes: How did any of us go about adopting our theoretical and therapeutic approach and on what grounds do we justify its application to clients? Although not all therapists would explicitly use the term, we typically address this question by citing "evidence" of some kind—whether it is framed in terms of subjective "fit," clinical experience, successful cases, wisdom, a theoretical rationale, or empirical outcome. While those who could turn to the latter would argue that their approaches stand on the firmest ground, material reviewed in chapter 1 indicates that outcome research on psychotherapy offers little validation of the theoretical rationales that therapists employ. Further, it would be implausible to argue that the clinical decisions associated with day-to-day practice can be based solely on the existing empirical literature (Shoham & Rohrbaugh, 1996). Therefore, Barton (1974) can persuasively argue that therapists are often drawn to theories and methods for reasons that are intensely personal:

> Our ease of understanding or not understanding the theories, our liking and disliking of them, our response to the specialized worlds they open up, is not based on a neutral objectivity or logic. As specialized worlds with special emphases and specific values, they appeal to us as ways to live, and we respond intuitively, and quite properly, in terms of our sense of whether they would be helpful in describing, unifying, or making sense of our own lives. (p. 243)

It seems obvious that the expectations which clients bring to therapy deviate significantly from the status of therapeutic knowledge as it has been characterized above, and throughout this book. Mary S. was predisposed to accept the hypothesis of satanic abuse because she saw her therapists as "experts" who had reliable knowledge based on relevant research and training. Although their expectations might not always be stated so explicitly or specifically as Mary's, I assume that all clients come to therapy with the view that therapists have some knowledge or understanding which could be of help to them. What we have to offer, however, is less "objective" or otherwise universal in nature, and more idiosyncratic, than most clients would assume. For example, imagine the reactions of clients if the following information were routinely added to the consent forms which clients usually sign before beginning therapy:

> The particular approach to psychotherapy which I follow was chosen for a variety of reasons, including its fit with my own subjective beliefs about the world, my personality style, and my own personal values. It represents only one of dozens—if not hundreds—of approaches that could be taken and, frankly, there is no evidence that my approach is more effective across the board than these other approaches. In fact, for a few specific problems, there may be more "formal" evidence that other approaches are more effective than my own. However, the approach which I follow has been beneficial in my own life and has been of help to many of the clients I have seen—and colleagues who share my orientation would say the same. While my goal is certainly not one of imposing this approach on you, if therapy is successful you will probably leave having adopted some of my values and beliefs. You just need to trust me that this would be in your best interest!

Even if a consent form of this kind were written with a more serious intent, how many clients would stay around to pay our fees if we honestly revealed the status of our knowledge as therapists?

ETHICS, MORALITY, AND REFLEXIVITY IN THERAPY PRACTICE

If I have been successful in the framing of the issue of therapeutic conviction, then the dilemma it creates should be seen as extending well beyond the boundaries of "ethics" as defined by professional organizations. Nothing could better underscore this point than the problem of applying ethical standards to the egregious misapplication of therapeutic certainty which began this chapter. Will therapists who subscribe to the theory of satanic ritual abuse be seen as guilty of unethical practice if their treatment approaches go awry? While the complaint against Dr. Braun has not been resolved at this writing, one could predict that most therapists who have employed this framework will be neither charged nor found guilty of ethics violations.

Using the revised ethical principles for psychologists (American Psychological Association, 1992) as a model, it is not clear that therapists who base case formulation and treatment on satanic abuse have directly violated any of its standards. Depending on the information provided by a client and the decision-making of a review board, such a therapist might be seen as violating one component of the principle of Competence: "In those areas in which recognized professional standards do not yet exist, psychologists exercise careful judgment and take appropriate precautions to protect the welfare of those with whom they work" (p. 1599). I assume, however, that the accused therapist would attempt to mount an argument that there are emerging standards within the group of professional therapists who treat satanic abuse, and that he/she followed them in good faith. Further, the therapist could contend that it would be an ethical oversight to fail to take seriously the memories of satanic abuse which these patients have brought to treatment. Certainly, the therapist's belief in a questionable theoretical rationale would not itself be seen as an ethical violation—since this would confront the profession with the difficult question of distinguishing founded from unfounded belief in the practice of psychotherapy. For example, what is the likelihood that an ethics complaint about satanic abuse therapy would lead to sanctions if the patient showed evidence of "improvement" during the period of treatment?

Fox and Prilleltensky (1997) agree that current professional standards are limited in scope and introduce the chapter on ethics in their volume as follows:

> To the naive observer, professional ethics should be about a discipline's moral implications, about the harmful and beneficial effects of theories and practices on individuals and societies. But this is a naive view indeed. Organizations of professionals such as doctors and lawyers devise codes of ethics that protect the professional as least as much as they protect the public. (p. 51, italics omitted)

This outcome is accomplished by restricting ethical problems to the "aberrant behavior" of a few misguided therapists and ignoring the larger philosophical, moral, and political dilemmas associated with psychotherapy practice as a social institution. However, there are at least two current developments within the literature that attempt to reintroduce a moral dimension into psychotherapy. While they draw somewhat different implications for practice, both take traditional accounts of psychotherapy to task for their stance of value-neutrality.

The first trend is represented by the political arguments associated with feminist therapists, critical psychologists, and postmodernists and has been extensively reviewed in previous chapters. For example, Cushman (1993) and Prilleltensky (1989) not only believe that traditional psychotherapy is value-laden, but also contend that it assists in the maintenance of the societal status quo. Feminist therapists draw out the implications of such analyses by explicitly injecting a moral perspective into the practice of psychotherapy, and they have attempted to define guidelines for its implementation through drafting a Feminist Therapy Code of Ethics (Feminist Therapy Institute, 1995). These standards address the moral omissions of existing professional ethics codes and commit feminist therapists to assumptions and values associated with the elimination of oppression, the analysis of power, and the promotion of social change.

Doherty's (1995) proposal that psychotherapy should promote "moral responsibility" is representative of a second development in the field today. His analysis is influenced by social scientific writings on the culture of individualism, including the work *Habits of the Heart* (Bellah, Madsen, Sullivan, Swidler, & Tipton, 1985), which charges that psychotherapy as practiced in America today promotes "expressive individualism." They argue that psychotherapists covertly and overtly encourage clients to associate good mental health with the emotional expression of their own desires and needs, to the neglect of what might constitute familial, collective, or community needs.

Doherty (1995) begins his account with a telling example of the above tendency: the testimony of mental health professionals in the child custody case involving Woody Allen and Mia Farrow. He points out that none of these expert witnesses was willing to make evaluative judgments of Allen's behavior—which involved having an affair with his lover's daughter. Their comments ranged from "[Allen] may have made an error in judgment" to the suggestion that this arrangement might simply reflect "the postmodern family." The judge finally became exasperated, criticized the homogenized language of the testimony, and added, "We're not at the point of sleeping with our children's sisters" (p. 4).

The implications which Doherty draws for therapy practice are concrete and practical, and they are not guided by a specific theoretical or philosophical stance, unlike the first trend reviewed above. He explores how therapists might promote moral responsibility in clients, including commitment, truthfulness, and community, and emphasizes the importance of demonstrating our own moral qualities of caring, courage, and prudence. He distances himself from authoritarian approaches to these issues, acknowledges the ambiguities and difficulties in adding this dimension to the therapeutic exchange, and encourages therapists to form consultation groups where case material might be discussed from a specifically moral framework.

These two perspectives reinforce the notion that the implications of the present analysis should be developed within the broader context of morality rather than in reference to traditional conceptions of professional ethics. With the goal of further defining this relationship, the discussion will now turn to a third approach.

While therapist morality is not an explicit feature of Hoshmand's (1994) work, it is intrinsic to her argument for a "reflective professional psychology." She provides a philosophically sophisticated analysis of clinical practice which emphasizes that the knowing of therapists, like that of human beings in general, has its fundamental limitations. She then develops recommendations for sound practice that build on a concept that was introduced earlier in relation to the work of George Kelly.

For Kelly, a "reflexive" theory is one which not only accounts for the experience and behavior of others but also explains how and why the theorist generated this theory (Oliver & Landfield, 1962). Reflexivity has since been acknowledged as an issue confronting all of the social sciences (Woolgar, 1991), and Hoshmand (1994) agrees that human beings necessarily function both as "the knowing subject and objects to be known" (p. 6). Accordingly, psychology "must develop self-referenced knowledge and account for the contributions of the human observer in generating that knowledge" (p. 6). For Hoshmand, reflexivity "involves reflecting on our accustomed ways of thought" and represents "one of the mature human abilities sometimes referred to as 'metacognition'" (p. 6).

As was indicated in chapter 5, Hoshmand and Polkinghorne (1992), like Schön (1983), are particularly interested in the manner in which "reflection-in-action" or reflexivity functions within the "applied epistemology" of professional practice. Given that clinical practice relies so heavily on what has been variously described as Realist, tacit, commonsensical, or metaphorical knowing, reflexivity assumes the status of a moral obligation of the practitioner. Personal beliefs and values influence the theories and methods that we choose (Barton, 1974; Hoshmand, 1994), and, as Polanyi (1967) suggests for interiorized moral teachings, these professional frameworks "function as the proximal term of a tacit moral knowledge, as applied to practice" (p. 17). In the absence of a reflexive gesture, what hope do we have for balancing the safety and danger which our convictions can contribute to the therapeutic situation?

COMPONENTS OF A MORALLY SITUATED (REFLEXIVE) EPISTEMOLOGY

All three of these perspectives make an important contribution to a dialogue about the moral responsibilities of the therapist. Nevertheless, it is the development of a concept of reflexivity which holds the most promise for clarifying and concretizing the implications of the philosophical framework which has been proposed here. Like that framework, reflexivity involves a study of the general question of knowing in psychotherapy. Further, it is not identified with a specific philosophical or theoretical stance (unlike feminism or critical psychology), nor does it promote a particular moral position (unlike Doherty's valuing of community over individualism).

Therefore, the remainder of this chapter will focus on the assumptions and implications of a morally situated approach to psychotherapy, defined as a reflexive epistemology. Two direct moral implications of the preceding philosophical analyses of psychotherapy are first made more explicit—namely, that psychotherapeutic practice should be *dialectical* in nature and *epistemologically pluralistic*. Then the difficulty that therapists may face in implementing these guidelines is explored in relation to three contrasts which are vital to therapeutic practice: "conceptual thought" *vs.* "direct experience," "knowing" *vs.* "being," and "normal" *vs.* "philosophical" components of understanding.

Before turning to this discussion, two comments about its structure are in order. First, given the preceding two chapters, the reader may wonder why it is necessary to develop a rather elaborate argument, based largely on the relevant philosophical and psychological literature, in support of the concepts of dialectics and epistemological pluralism. Wasn't the notion of modes of knowing introduced in chapter 5 to convey that therapists can "live" different epistemological positions, moving fluidly from one to the other, unbeknownst to themselves? Didn't the resulting analyses of these modes of knowing in chapter 6 establish that therapists are often dialectical and pluralistic in their actual therapeutic work, whether they can acknowledge it or not?

While both of these questions could be answered in the affirmative, it remains important to anchor dialectics and pluralism more securely to an intellectual framework. As was indicated at the beginning of this chapter, the argument has moved now from description to prescription. Rather than arguing that psychotherapeutic practice typically incorporates dialectical and pluralistic elements in a haphazard and informal fashion, I am now contending that therapists *should* become *more* dialectical and pluralistic in their work—and do so with *awareness*. This argument demands justification, and the obstacles that would prevent therapists from moving in the recommended direction also require careful exploration.

Second, as the discussion unfolds, the reader will find some overlap among the different proposed components of a reflexive epistemology. My defense for the style of argument which will be offered is to make an analogy to the concept of "construct validity" (Groth-Marnat, 1990, pp. 18–19): There is no single criterion which would define a "reflexive" or "morally situated" psychotherapy. Therefore, a number of conceptually related dimensions will be introduced whose network of interrelationships together defines this construct.

Dialectical Understanding

A dialectical interpretation of philosophical and psychotherapeutic thinking has emerged as a theme of the previous chapters, and the importance of this stance toward knowing has been recognized by a variety of academicians and clinicians. Within academic psychology, Riegel (1979) demonstrates the usefulness of dialectics to an understanding of human development, while Buss (1979, chapter 1) makes a convincing argument that only this approach could halt psychology's back-and-forth movement between self (individual) and object (social) frameworks for explaining behavior. In the more limited arena of personality theory and psychotherapy, Rychlak (1977), Kaminstein (1987), Protter (1988, 1996), Hanna (1994), Hoffman (1994), Hoshmand (1994), and Hanna and Shank (1995) point to the advantages of dialectical thinking in clarifying, and perhaps resolving, some of the longstanding theoretical and philosophical disputes of these fields.

Philosophical Assumptions of a Dialectical Approach
Before turning again to its concrete applications to psychotherapy, the philosophical assumptions of a dialectical approach will be briefly

reviewed. Rychlak (1976), Reese (1982), and Buss (1979, chapter 6) trace the term *dialectic* back to ancient times, and agree that it has come to have multiple meanings and interpretations over its long history. It derives from a Greek word for "conversation," and this meaning is found in contemporary usages that equate it with "dialogue or debate" (Reese, 1982, p. 423). Mueller (1953) summarizes and simplifies some of its other current meanings by defining dialectic as

> a unity of opposites. . . . In a dialectical relation each of the opposed "poles" is incomplete without its own "other," and degenerates if it is abstractly isolated. Since there are many "sets" of opposites, one may also speak of "dialectics" in the plural. (p. 17)

Thus, a dialectic is in place when two tendencies, categories, properties, or qualities cannot exist or be defined except in relationship to one another. For example, just as "dark" has meaning only in reference to "light," the review of philosophical positions in chapter 2 suggests that "critique" has no meaning or existence in the absence of "affirmation." Dialectical understanding results when a human observer is able to comprehend this relationship—that is, to appreciate that not just one or another disparate tendency exists, but that the two are intrinsically related and together constitute a larger whole.

Buss (1979, chapter 6), following Sidney Hook, introduces more complexity into this picture by endorsing a distinction between dialectic as an ontological position and as a method. Dialectic defined as an *ontology* assumes that the oppositions which we see are inherent in nature, and that change cannot occur apart from a process involving contradiction, conflict, negation, and struggle (p. 75). On the other hand, dialectic as a *method* simply assumes that opposition and its associated characteristics of struggle and conflict will become manifest when certain methods or techniques are employed. Generally, a dialectical method stresses the importance of "dialogue" between and among opposing positions, which serves the "critical" function of questioning and testing contradictory ideas (p. 76). By applying this method, "truth" can be "increasingly approximated through a clash of opinions, and conflict is resolved at higher levels of analysis" (p. 76).

Buss points out that one can be a methodological dialectician without committing to a dialectical ontology, and vice versa. The former position would not claim that reality is inherently dialectical in nature, but only that dialectical thinking can help us to understand and perhaps resolve certain contradictions as they *appear* to exist when we try to comprehend the world. Further, one can see the Hegelian influence on any position which proposes that "truth" can be achieved or approximated by a dialectical method, and this assumption was challenged by Bernstein (1992) in chapter 2. Within the modern/postmodern context, it would be naive to assume that any method could provide a final synthesis of the contradictions which pervade personal and social existence. In Hoffman's (1994) terms, dialectic connotes "tension, not resolution" (p. 195, footnote 1).

Like Protter's (1988) approach on which it is modeled, my analysis of lived modes of knowing is most compatible with the assumptions of a methodological dialectic. Each mode of knowing at once supplements and critiques or deconstructs the other modes, such that a "circular interplay" of epistemological positions results. I agree with Protter that an awareness of the interplay among multiple approaches to knowing would lead to the "fullest" or most complete account of what might transpire in the psychotherapy situation, especially when compared to that which results from functioning within any single mode of knowing.

Yet, following Bernstein (1992), I would hesitate to equate this fuller account with some definitive version of the "truth." The dialectic produced by my six categories is not equivalent to that associated with Protter's three categories, and other outcomes might result either from adding further categories or from proposing an entirely different scheme. Similarly, I would be reluctant to ascribe ontological significance to the dialectic which arises from these or other modes of knowing—unless the referent is restricted to "human" nature. Given the conservative tendencies of the cognitive and meaning systems through which human beings interpret the world, one could make a strong argument that conflict and struggle are intrinsic to fundamental change in individuals and society. However, it would require the kind of leap that postmodernists regard as nonsensical to attribute these characteristics to "nature" itself—that is, to the world as it exists apart from human observation or participation.

The final assumption of this dialectical approach to psychotherapy concerns the "more complete" account of the therapy situation which it promises to provide. While it is not possible to equate it with the "truth," dialectical understanding can be explicitly linked with a reflexive, moral stance toward knowing. Hoshmand (1994) indicates that dialectical thinking is related to "moral, epistemological, and metaphysical reasoning" (p. 149), and it appears to represent the cornerstone on which her reflexive approach to professional practice is built.

More precisely, Hoshmand conceives dialectics as including a metacognitive component, a form of reflection on thinking, which enables practitioners to observe and evaluate their own assumptions and frameworks. As a relational approach to knowledge, it attempts to find value in alternative frameworks, even those which would seem to contradict one's own, thereby developing a "tolerance for diverse orientations to knowledge" (p. 150).

The Dialectics of Psychotherapeutic Practice

Given the rough-and-tumble of psychotherapy practice, what does it mean to hold the therapist's philosophical framework to a "moral" standard associated with reflexive or dialectical understanding? No doubt, it is impossible to provide a completely satisfactory, that is, sufficiently concrete and pragmatic, answer to this complex question. However, the lived modes of knowing which were introduced in chapter 5 and explicated in chapter 6 can be utilized to define the contours of a dialectically based, morally informed psychotherapy.

Turning again to table 3, the six modes of knowing are arrayed along a continuum which can be variously characterized as "confirmation-disconfirmation," "revelation-restriction," "conviction-uncertainty," or "affirmation-critique." A dialectical approach to psychotherapy finds value in these opposing poles of human knowing, as well as in each of the six points along the continuum constituting the different individual modes of knowing. It sees the willingness and capacity to move between these poles and across these modes as providing a set of checks and balances that can test and moderate the therapist's own preferred way(s) of knowing. Finally, it emphasizes the importance of the negative claims of Nihilistic knowing, which can serve as a counterpoint to the positive claims of the other modes of knowing.

Illustrating this approach with the clinical example which began this chapter, it would be something of an understatement to say that the treatment of satanic ritual abuse has been marked by an overreliance on Realist knowing. When Braun presented the child's report of seeing an opened abdomen to his colleagues at a conference, he framed it as "evidence" for the reality of satanic abuse. Given that there was an alternative explanation for this report given by the child's mother, it would have been impossible for Braun to make that claim—if only he could have shifted from Realist to Representational knowing.

For that matter, one could argue that the creation of an entire treatment culture for satanic abuse might have been thwarted if the clinicians leading the way had been able to seriously entertain Representational knowing. This approach would have dictated that satanic abuse be regarded as a hypothesis, not as a proven fact. Ideally, it would have brought the critical thinking and research methodology of the scientist-practitioner model to an evaluation of this hypothesis. Given the dearth of nonclinical evidence supporting the "existence" of satanic abuse, coupled with professional disagreement regarding the epidemiology and diagnosis of MPD (Dunn, 1992), the frequent use of these diagnoses by a small group of therapists would have been the first target of Representational knowing.

If it were so simple as the above paragraph suggests to establish an empirical ground for psychotherapy and to eliminate unsubstantiated inference from its practice, then this would have been a much shorter and less complex book. Braun and other therapists who have treated satanic abuse might claim that they *were* practicing Representational knowing to the best of their ability. To make the point with a comparable example from academic psychology, consider the work of Herrnstein and Murray (1994) reported in *The Bell Curve*.

Their review of 156 studies conducted between 1918 and 1990 comparing white and black IQ indicates a mean difference of 1.08 standard deviations—or approximately 16 IQ points (p. 276). Herrnstein and Murray suggest that this difference is largely immutable due to a combination of early environmental and genetic factors, and they go on to argue that social programs like Headstart are both ineffective and ill-conceived. Indeed, they contend that the one intervention which has consistently been associated with a significant increase in cognitive ability is "adoption at birth from a bad family environment to a good one" (p. 389, italics omitted). Therefore, regarding their own social policy recommendations, these authors ask: "If adoption is one of the only affordable and successful ways known to improve the life chances of disadvantaged children appreciably, why has it been so ignored in congressional debate and presidential proposals?" (p. 416). Whatever the opinion of their critics, there is little doubt that Herrnstein and Murray regard their data as an example of the best that the Representational or scientific mode of knowing has to offer.

While the Representational mode often provides useful evidence against which Realist knowing can be evaluated, the metaphorical component of normal science means that such evidence can contain its own systematic biases and distortions. Thus, Representational knowing can degenerate into Realist knowing—which becomes all the more dangerous when it appears to bear the sanction of science. L. S. Brown (1997) writes:

Neither Arthur Jensen nor the late Richard Herrnstein were ever considered by mainstream psychology to have violated psychology's ethics by the questions they asked in their research, even though the goal of those questions was to document the alleged intellectual inferiority of African Americans. . . . This research . . . has introduced the aura and respectability of science into racist discourse. (p. 55)

Although Braun's therapeutic application of a supposedly scientific concept of satanic abuse or Herrnstein and Murray's allegedly empirical support for their conclusions about IQ may or may not constitute violations of the current ethics code, they represent moral failures of the first magnitude. These misrepresentations of knowledge could adversely impact untold numbers of individuals, and directly result from a neglect of the alternative epistemologies which would challenge the status of such "evidence."

Therefore, therapists who continue to diagnose and treat the syndrome of satanic abuse, confounding their Realist knowing with Representational knowing, are in great need of the correctives which other modes of knowing could provide. Perspectival knowing could lead them to the recognition that the notion of "satanic abuse" is itself a construct, not a "fact." This approach to knowing would encourage client and therapist alike to ask if this construct is "useful" in working with the problem at hand, or if alternative conceptualizations of the client's symptoms and experience could be more beneficial. It would also emphasize the importance of a specification of the criteria used by both the client and the therapist in choosing one of these conceptualizations over another.

An encounter with Dialogical knowing would represent a more fundamental challenge to the construct of "satanic abuse." By undermining the distinction between subject and object and focusing on the intersubjective context, Dialogical knowing would point out the impossibility of finding evidence for this construct exclusively "within" the client. Instead, it would be assumed that the "symptoms" of satanic abuse were being co-created through the interaction of the client and the therapist.

The Critical mode of knowing would place this dialogical analysis in a historical, social, political, and moral context, emphasizing the personal motives and societal needs served by the therapist's adoption of a construct of satanic abuse. In an eloquent critique of the objectivist assumptions of academic psychology, Liam Hudson (1972) argues "that a psychology which is both relevant and dispassionate becomes possible only when the psychologist and his preoccupations are included as part of what psychologists seek to explain" (p. 161). Could Braun have developed his treatment approach for satanic abuse and could Jensen and Herrnstein have embarked on their research if they had taken this simple guideline to heart?

It is unlikely that a therapist committed to the treatment of satanic abuse would be open to considering all of these alternative epistemologies or, for that matter, any of them. Nihilistic knowing represents an essential component of a dialectical approach to psychotherapy because it provides therapists with one final opportunity for balancing the excesses associated with therapeutic conviction. Experiencing "nothingness" does not depend on the formal knowing or understanding of alternative epistemologies. It requires only an acknowledgment of one's own humanness and the "irrepressible tendency to ask questions" (Novak, 1971, p. 134) which is a part of that condition.

The following self-dialogue of a therapist illustrates how Nihilistic knowing might manifest in this specific context:

> Many of my patients are just not getting better. Today, when that family member looked me in the eye and asked if I am really sure about all of this, some doubt took hold of me. How can I be sure that my views of the world are correct when I am, after all, a fallible human being no different from anyone else? I feel a great deal of responsibility to my clients, and pressure from them and myself to be "right" about my approach to diagnosis and treatment. But what if I am completely wrong about satanic abuse? The consequences are unthinkable. However, it is even more unthinkable that I could be mistaken and continue with this approach. I believe that it is time to reconsider the issue, no matter what the consequences—including how my colleagues might react.

Until now, the dialectic between affirmation and critique has been examined through a clinical example where the former desperately requires balancing by the latter. Yet, the dialectic which exists between the poles of a dimension necessarily moves in both directions, and it is just as important that affirmation functions to constrain critique. This theme was developed in the previous chapter, and the detailed analyses which were presented there will be summarized as follows.

All of the modes of knowing, including those which explicitly reject the possibility of objective knowledge, implicitly rely on Realist assumptions in certain theoretical and therapeutic contexts. When a narrative therapist who advocates Dialogical knowing proclaims that "psychotherapy *is* conversation," then a reality claim has been made. Such claims function to provide a structure for the therapeutic situation in the same way that like assumptions frame psychoanalytic or cognitive therapies. This general definition of the therapy situation is then operationalized through specific interventions with the client—for example, the client with an eating disorder was encouraged to "externalize the problem" by regarding anorexia as something real which exists outside of her. Therefore, therapists who practice Representational, Perspectival, Dialogical, and Critical ways of knowing, like all therapists, develop their own convictions, and these convictions are essential to the creation of new meaning and hope in the client. Further, not only do postmodernist, hermeneutic, and constructionist therapists who profess to embrace indeterminancy in knowing develop their own beliefs or convictions, but they also can cling to these beliefs no less tenaciously than their Realist colleagues.

To illustrate, the hypothetical example of a fiftyish, African-American woman suffering from panic attacks and agoraphobia was given in chapter 4. Assume that this woman has again sought therapy and happens upon a therapist who practices a form of postmodern "conversational" therapy. This practitioner is particularly influenced by the views of Tom Anderson (1993), who hesitates to even call himself a "therapist." He contends that "therapy is not a technique" and that therapists "are not experts" (p. 305). Therapy is simply a conversation between two parties, and Anderson's role should be one of remaining sensitive to the client's responses to his comments and questions. These interventions should be unusual enough to be "stimulating" but not so unusual or different as to cause the client discomfort (p. 320). Although Anderson sees the therapist as responsible for making contributions which might facilitate change, he does not believe "that a therapist has an ethical responsibility to be outcome oriented" (p. 320).

The therapist follows these guidelines, assuming that change will occur if a "genuine dialogue" is established with the client. After several weeks of therapy, however, the client is still very symptomatic, is housebound, and feels disappointed with what is happening in the sessions. She expects the therapist to function more as an expert, providing methods which will relieve her focal symptoms, and considers leaving therapy.

This therapist rejects the Representational assumptions behind a diagnosis of panic disorder and the research-based treatment protocol which is recommended for its alleviation. However, if this alternative approach is dismissed out of hand and the same Dialogical approach and goals are recommended for all clients and problems—based on the therapist's philosophical presuppositions—is this so different from the therapist who is convinced of the efficacy of the psychotherapeutic treatment of satanic abuse? In either case, the client's needs and goals have been made secondary to the therapist's beliefs, and this gap between client need and therapist belief has moral implications.

Kitzinger's (1997) perspective on gay-lesbian issues, which was introduced in the last chapter, can be utilized to formulate an alternative response to the kind of epistemological and moral dilemma described above. Academic psychologists like herself favor an analysis of gay-lesbian issues which is based on feminism and critical psychology, and many therapists share the view that "gay-lesbian psychology" is too individualistic in its assumptions about social change. However, a therapist who insists on remaining true to this political stance in her conceptualization and treatment of client problems would be of little help when a client actually walks through the door. Although the mode of Critical knowing would hold that gay-lesbian identity is itself a construction, it might be more useful for this therapist to shift to a Realist stance and encourage a client to begin to discover and value his / her "true" identity. While Critical knowing would reject objective methods of studying human beings, an effective therapist might judiciously employ Representational knowing, perhaps informally referring to findings that gay and lesbian individuals are as well-adjusted and happy as their heterosexual counterparts. Nevertheless, this therapist might also feel a strong commitment to continuing to evaluate her practice and interventions from a Critical perspective, worrying that she will become too comfortable with the individualistic assumptions which therapy work demands.

My analysis differs from Kitzinger's (1997) in that she contrasts "critical psychologists" with "therapists" and envisions a dialectic of critique and affirmation which occurs *between* these differing groups (p. 215). Given the implications which I want to draw for psychotherapy practice, I place the dialectic *within* the therapist, who must then move among different modes of knowing both to respond to the client's specific therapeutic needs and to protect the client's general welfare.

In summary, a psychotherapy which recognizes the epistemological and moral dilemmas of our field emerges from the tension generated by conflicting modes of human knowing. For therapists, this entails living out a dialectic that shifts continuously, characterized by a "circular interplay" of its constituent parts. At one moment, the dialectic might manifest as a pull between a therapist's belief in widespread satanic abuse and the empirical evidence that contradicts its existence. In another moment, the assumption that empirical evidence is completely "objective" might itself be challenged by an awareness of its embeddedness in a social and political context. In a third moment, the conclusion that these social and political factors invalidate all research on diagnosis and treatment might be juxtaposed with the recognition that one's work with a given client is not progressing, and that a research-based protocol might better serve this client's immediate needs.

Epistemological Pluralism

Is it possible to find a philosophical position within the fields of psychology and psychotherapy which is compatible with this kind of dialectical understanding? Given some of the clinical examples of dialectical thinking which have been offered above, and given that a form of psychotherapeutic "pluralism" is most likely to be linked with such examples, this section must begin with a clarification. A dialectical psychotherapy, which finds value in opposing modes of knowing, is not synonymous with an eclectic or integrationist approach to practice. The former involves the larger issue of epistemology, while the latter commonly refers to the more specific question of therapeutic theory and method. Although therapists who become more pluralistic in their view of epistemology might also become more eclectic or integrationist in their approach to practice, it is not assumed that this outcome inevitably will or should result (Hanna, 1994; Safran & Messer, 1997).

Thus, a dialectical approach to knowing requires therapists to become more aware of their own assumptions and limitations through an openness to rival epistemologies. The latter are not necessarily associated with alternative theories and methods and may simply suggest taking a different stance toward one's existing theory and method. Spence's (1982) contrast of historical (Realist) and narrative (Dialogical) approaches to psychoanalytic interpretation represents a case in point. Assuming that an alternative epistemology is associated with specific theories and methods, it would depend on the therapist whether the exploration of the position extended as far as "trying on" or even adopting something new. For example, instead of making a premature commitment to a position of either technical eclecticism or theoretical integrationism, Safran and Messer (1997) believe that it is more productive if a "dialogue" among theoretical and philosophical positions "leads over time to a degree of assimilation of ideas and techniques from one theory or therapy into another" (p. 147). Of course, in some clinical situations, the acknowledgment of the limitations of one's own approach might ethically obligate the therapist to inform the client of an alternative treatment approach(es) and to offer a referral if it is not within the therapist's existing repertoire.

With that clarification in place, it is now reasonable to ask if precedents for a pluralistic epistemology can be found in the literature. Fortunately, a number of proposals for some variation of a methodological or epistemological pluralism do exist, although much of this work is focused on the question of expanding the range of acceptable conceptual systems and research methods within academic psychology.

It was previously noted that, since the 1960s, Sigmund Koch has been urging the field of psychology to adopt a pluralistic perspective toward its subject matter. He contends that "psychology is not a single or coherent discipline" and would be better conceived as a grouping of "psychological studies" marked by a diversity of assumptions and methods (1985, pp. 92–93). Some of these areas would lend themselves to study by modes of inquiry associated with the biological and natural sciences, while other areas would require a sensibility and mode of approach more typical of the humanities. Interestingly, he includes among the latter not only the "softer" areas of the field such as social psychology, psychopathology, and personality, but traditionally "harder" areas like perception, cognition, and learning (p. 94).

Koch (1985) explicitly links this more pluralistic stance toward the field with *morality* and does so by underlining the consequences of its opposite. The tendency to equate a true understanding of human behavior and experience with that dictated by a given framework, model, or theory, while dismissing alternative frameworks and understandings,

> raises a grave moral issue reflective of a widespread moral bankruptcy within psychology. In the psychological studies, the attribution to any paradigm of a preemptive finality has the force of telling human beings precisely what they are, of fixing their essence, defining their ultimate worth, potential, meaning; of cauterizing away that quality of ambiguity, mystery, search, that makes progress through a biography an adventure. (p. 93)

He hopes that a willingness to acknowledge the alternative methods and understandings associated with these different "psychologies" would signal an era of "more flexibility in the capacity of inquirers to enrich their vision by trying on the spectacles of their neighbors" (1993, p. 902).

Polkinghorne (1983, 1984, 1988) echoes this theme by critiquing the dominance of objectivist methods within psychology and calls for the addition of hermeneutic and narrative approaches to knowing. He (1983) explicitly refers to his position as a form of "methodological" (p. 9) or "epistemological" pluralism (p. 251) and implicitly conveys its dialectical nature as follows:

> The very acceptance of a possible alternative places one's own assumptions in question. One's point of view is transformed from *the* way of knowing into *one* way of knowing—a context— when alternatives are admitted. Out of the syncretic interaction of various positions, a fuller understanding arises. (p. 251)

Borgen (1984) reviews papers by Polkinghorne (1984) and Howard (1984) which present a pluralistic approach to methodology, and he then proposes that the field is moving toward "epistemological eclecticism" (p. 459). Howard (1991) develops his position further by citing Cook's concept of a "postpositivist critical multiplism" and proposing "a form of Jamesian pluralism" based on "multiple, independent epistemological perspectives (or different frames of reference). . . . Our best ground for belief . . . lies in the areas of agreement achieved from studies proceeding from independent, epistemological perspectives" (p. 188, footnote 2). He contends, for example, that this approach holds promise for reconciling some of the differences which separate objectivist and constructivist views of knowing. While it is assumed that there is a constructive element to all human knowing, this does not mean that all knowledge is "coequal" or that science represents nothing more than a social consensus reached by a particular group of individuals. Therefore, through a clash of epistemological positions representing a range of objectivist and constructivist assumptions, a fuller account of knowledge will emerge.

To this point, it would appear that epistemological pluralism represents an alternative to the Either-Or thinking which has dominated debates in academic psychology and clinical practice. Supporters of science and the scientist-practitioner model typically argue: Either psychology and psychotherapy are based on methods of knowing associated with science, or these fields will have no legitimacy. Postmodernist and constructionist critics of science typically argue in response: Either the assumptions of objectivism and empiricism are banished from psychology and psychotherapy, or these fields will never provide a legitimate (and moral) understanding of the human condition.

A theoretical example of a dialectical, pluralistic approach to academic research is given by Polkinghorne (1983), and his imagery is particularly helpful in conveying what it would mean to move beyond the Either-Or of competing epistemological positions in the practice of psychotherapy:

> A single topic—anxiety, for example—might be approached with the hermeneutic, the systemic, the phenomenological, and the statistically linked measurement systems of inquiry. . . . Each of these systems of inquiry is able to detect and describe some aspects of anxiety, but each of them also misses parts of the full experience. It is as if one is looking at a drop of water through a microscope. As the focus of the microscope is varied, different aspects of the contents of the drop of water can be seen. One can also stain the drop of water so that still other aspects, previously hidden, show up, but when this [is] done, some aspects, previously seen, will no longer be seen. (p. 252)

Not surprisingly, Peterson and Peterson (1997) include "methodological multiplicity" (p. 222) of this kind in their discussion of the "ways of knowing" that are essential to the education of practitioners.

COGNITIVE, EMOTIONAL, AND EXPERIENTIAL BARRIERS TO DIALECTICAL, PLURALISTIC PRACTICE

Unfortunately, both the research and applied areas of psychology and psychotherapy are characterized by formidable obstacles to an epistemological approach based on dialectics and pluralism. Koch (1985) admits that his "psychological studies" would encompass a vast and "disorderly spectrum of human activity and experience" (p. 93), requiring diverse, even contrary, methods of study. Consequently, "the psychological studies . . . will be seen as immensely challenging, immensely difficult, and perhaps in some ranges entirely refractory areas of inquiry" (p. 95). Of course, Koch is implying that the real challenge here is for the psychologist or psychotherapist who attempts to remain open and flexible in the face of this bewildering array. Safran and Messer (1997), reflecting on trends in the clinical area, bring focus to this issue by simply stating: "Calls for methodological pluralism . . . come up against strong emotional barriers" (p. 146). The tendency of clinicians to disregard research findings which are inconsistent with their theoretical orientations and/or personal identities represents a case in point (Cohen et al., 1986).

The problem of fully embracing and operationalizing a pluralistic perspective can even extend to its advocates. For example, Howard (1993a) suggests that various research methodologies are crucial to the "practicing knowledge" which Hoshmand and Polkinghorne (1992) associate with psychotherapy. He argues that a "softer" measure like self-report has actually been demonstrated to be more accurate than "objective" measures of behavior, and, certainly, has greater relevance to the needs of practicing psychotherapists. While Pion, Cordray, and Anderson (1993) agree that self-report, autobiography, and clinical case studies can be descriptively useful, they object to the implication that these methods are "*more* useful" than traditional research methods for purposes such as evaluating treatment effectiveness (p. 245). Howard (1993b) acknowledges that more than one critic thought that he was claiming the superiority of the nontraditional methods and then apologizes for a shift in the tone of his paper, which he attributes to his decision to follow certain editorial recommendations.

Without questioning Howard's explanation of the apparent imbalance in his paper, I believe that this example can also be seen as representative of a general trend in both the research and clinical areas of the field. It appears that researchers, theorists, and therapists simply have a great deal of difficulty in speaking with equal facility and proficiency from opposing epistemological positions, even when they are inclined to do so. For example, assume that my goal is to establish that psychotherapy research should include both objective and narrative methods of study. In order to create a level playing field, I attack the philosophy of science on which objective methods are built, and I then make the argument that narrative methods are better suited to the development of a "human" science. Like Howard's paper above, the thrust of my argument is no longer pluralistic: It now recommends that one approach be replaced with another.

Given the view of theory which has been developed throughout this book, it is hardly surprising that researchers and psychotherapists would struggle in their attempts to move toward a more dialectical, pluralistic stance. If the basic function of implicit and explicit theories is to "reveal" some aspect of reality while bracketing alternative interpretations, then dialectics and pluralism go counter to a very robust human inclination. It follows that an urgent psychological dilemma would be created when this human tendency to cling to a given framework is juxtaposed with a directive to become more *consciously* dialectical and pluralistic in one's thinking.

An exploration of this tangled issue will occupy the remainder of the chapter, and my intention here is to define the parameters of the

dilemma, not to offer a resolution. Toward that end, dialectical and pluralistic understanding will be examined in relationship to three contrasts
which are integral to the practice of psychotherapy. It will become
apparent that these contrasts relate to the possibility of a reflexive epistemology, and to one another, in a complex, interdependent fashion. For
example, not only do the following contrasts further define the nature
of a dialectical, pluralistic approach to psychotherapy, each contrast is
itself framed in dialectical terms.

The Dialectic of Conceptual Thought and Direct Experience

Borgen (1984) unintentionally points the way to the first contrast
which will be considered when he observes that epistemological eclecticism "requires some suspension of logic as the philosopher uses it. The
therapist who can alternate between behavioral and psychoanalytic
technique does not linger over the logical inconsistencies in Watson's
and Freud's basic premises" (p. 459). I would argue, however, that the
"logic" which Borgen ascribes to philosophers is also the usual mode of
cognitive functioning of theorists and therapists, and that it represents a
major stumbling block to a pluralistic epistemology.

The problem will be illustrated by returning to the example of the
woman suffering from panic disorder and agoraphobia. Picture that the
case will now be conceptualized and treated by two different therapists:
one is the conversational therapist mentioned in a previous section and
the other is a cognitive therapist. The former embraces a Dialogical
approach to psychotherapy, and the latter works primarily from a stance
of Representational knowing. The first holds to the postmodernist position that objective methods of study not only are built on an illusory
epistemological premise but also are inappropriate to the understanding
of human experience. The second supports the scientist-practitioner
model of practice and believes that for certain clinical problems, such as
the anxiety disorders, research should guide clinical interventions. In
fact, to ignore what is known about the treatment of panic disorder
would be irresponsible and not serve the welfare of the client.

As in the previous example, imagine that the client seeing the conversational therapist becomes upset with the therapeutic approach and
asks for more structure, direction, and symptom relief. Now imagine
that the same client or a similar client goes to the cognitive therapist,
and after a few sessions complains that this approach is *too* structured,
directive, and regimented. The client complains that her feelings and
experience are not being respected or acknowledged, and that she does

not feel heard. Consider that this client's complaints exceed the usual strategies for establishing rapport and attending to relationship factors associated with cognitive therapy (Persons, Gross, Etkin, & Madan, 1996) and seem to demand a different case conceptualization and therapeutic approach—at least at this point in the treatment.

Keep in mind that the issue here is not whether the therapists shift to an alternative treatment approach, but whether they can question their own epistemological assumptions and seriously entertain the value of alternative assumptions. Each of these therapists will have difficulty learning from the client and understanding the alternative mode of knowing which the client's behavior demands if they remain within the "logic" of their respective positions.

Slife (1987) indicates that logical or conceptual thought is usually described as "demonstrative reasoning." The conclusions that one draws must be consistent with the premises which have been stated, and Aristotle's "law of contradiction" holds: "X cannot be 'A' and 'not-A' in the same space and time; and similarly, 'bachelors' cannot be 'married males' in the usual sense of these terms" (p. 202). In therapeutic practice, this logic links theory, method, and philosophical presuppositions (belief) and converges on the therapist identity which summarizes these different elements (see the last entry of table 3). How can a therapist who has rejected the scientist-practitioner identity see the possible relevance of outcome research to this case? How can a therapist who identifies as a scientist-practitioner acknowledge the value of a mode of knowing which undermines therapeutic knowledge and expertise?

Hanna (1994) believes that a dialectical approach, grounded in "direct experience," offers a way out of the Either-Or thinking which constrains contemporary practice. In accord with the present argument, he contends that different metaphysical assumptions are embedded in the multitudinous theories and methods which characterize the field today. If so, then it is unavoidable that psychology and psychotherapy will be marked by endless debates concerning whose theories and methods rest on better conceptual and moral grounds—since this is the history of philosophy. He doubts the usefulness of many of these debates and admiringly cites Tjeltveit (1989), who observes that "the practice of psychotherapy has always proven to be richer than the theories developed to explain and guide it" (p. 1).

Yet, how can psychotherapists step outside of the metaphysical and theoretical concepts which block both dialogue and flexibility? Following William James and Edmund Husserl, Hanna proposes that therapists can attempt to come back to an experience of the world which is more direct and immediate than that which is seen through theory and concepts. This examination will reveal that many oppositions—such as the one pitting an identity of the therapist as peer and conversationalist against an identity of expert and objective knower—are dialectical in nature. Like metaphysical concepts such as freedom-determinism, embracing one pole of the dichotomy means that the value of the opposite, complementary pole will be lost. If therapists can extricate themselves from their conceptual categories and remain open to the subjective and intersubjective experience of the session, they will probably find themselves valuing, if not enacting, the roles of both peer and expert at appropriate moments.

Therefore, an *experiential* approach to pluralism is one which attempts to circumvent the logic or conceptual thought which would make opposing theoretical and epistemological positions seemingly incompatible. It does so by retaining a focus which is experiential, pragmatic, and idiographic (Allport, 1937). It brackets the general question of the therapist's theory, method, philosophy, and identity, asking what specific approach to knowing is needed by this client in this moment. In this sense, it orients psychotherapeutic practice to the "local" knowledge community (Peterson & Peterson, 1997), represented by the expectations and needs of specific clients and the cultural, familial, or social groups with whom they identify. Although clients, like therapists, can be mistaken about what they "really" need in therapy, and while their stated needs may change over time, it is assumed that some match between client expectation and therapist response must occur before therapy can proceed.

This attempt to ground a dialectical, pluralistic approach in the therapist's direct experience requires two qualifications. First, Hanna assumes that a substrate of "pure" experience exists which is prior to categorization or conceptualization. This assumption—that such a substrate exists and that it can be accessed without distortion by phenomenological investigation—was previously challenged in chapter 4 in relation to subjectivist knowing. Therefore, is it possible to state the contrast between conceptual thought and direct experience in relative rather than absolute terms?

Greenberg and Pascual-Leone (1995) distinguish between "explanation" and "direct experience" (p. 170). The former depends on "consciously mediated conceptualization" while the latter relies heavily on our "bodily felt sense" and represents "automatic, immediate experiencing" (p. 170). However, direct experience "is not simply 'in' us, fully formed; rather, we need to put words to our feelings to bring them to full awareness" (p. 171). Therefore, these authors propose that both conceptual thought and direct experience depend on some level of symbolization, although the mode of this processing (conceptual *vs.* experiential) differs. For example, a theoretical position which asserts that knowledge is inherently uncertain is "more conceptual" in nature, and the therapist's affective and bodily experience of uncertainty and doubt while sitting with a client is "more direct" in nature. While this distinction is relative, it refers to different levels and kinds of symbolization which could be easily identified by most therapists.

Second, while direct experience has been proposed here as a corrective to conceptual thought, the relationship between the two is actually more complex. Just as one can become stuck in conceptual thought, one can become stuck in experience—and the goal of a pluralistic epistemology is to not become stuck in one's own patterns, whether these are more cognitive or more affective/bodily in nature. Indeed, as Greenberg and Pascual-Leone persuasively argue, the relationship between conceptual thought and direct experience is itself dialectical: Experience grounds conception and conception articulates experience. In the present context, this means that the movement toward reflexivity or a pluralistic epistemology depends on an ongoing relationship between conceptual understanding (an awareness of one's own and alternative epistemologies) and direct experience (an awareness of one's own and the client's experience in the moment), with each acting as a corrective to the other.

To illustrate the operation of this dialectic, it was suggested earlier that the Realist assumptions of the therapist who treats satanic abuse could be quite resistant to change on the conceptual level and might first be challenged by his/her direct experience of Nihilistic knowing. However, the therapist will be of little help to the client if he/she remains on the experiential plane of doubt and uncertainty, and this direct experience must function to open up the therapist to the consideration of an alternative epistemology and, perhaps, to an alternative theory and method. This new position and its therapeutic implementation must then be tested again in relationship to the direct experience of the therapist and client, and so the dialectic continues.

The Dialectic of Knowing and Being

Rychlak (1977) contrasts demonstrative reasoning (conceptual thought) with dialectical reasoning and then places these different modalities in a larger historical and philosophical context. He concludes that demonstrative reasoning, as represented by science, has become dominant during the modern era in the West. Dialectical reasoning, in addition to its presence in the work of Hegel and Marx, "is employed in certain religious formulations . . . as well as in the more humanistic psychologies and philosophies of our time—sometimes without being named as such" (p. 72). In addition, he emphasizes that the demonstrative-dialectical contrast also appears historically in the thought of India and the Far East, and that Hinduism and Buddhism place specific emphasis on the honing of dialectical thinking—just as modern science has sharpened the skills associated with its counterpart. He even proposes that the "logic" of Buddhist enlightenment "is our familiar brand of dialectical reasoning" (p. 81).

Rychlak's remarks point to a now familiar philosophical distinction and suggest that his contrast could be integrated with that which was offered in the last section. While conceptual, logical, or demonstrative thought defines a form of *knowing,* direct experience and dialectical reasoning represent aspects of *being.*

Of course, this contrast represents something of an oversimplification because not all modes of knowing are strictly "conceptual" or "logical." For example, H. Anderson's (1997) form of Dialogical knowing, that is, "not-knowing," actually represents a new "way of being" (p. 94). Similarly, Mahoney (1996), following Blythe Clinchy, stresses the importance of "connected knowing" to psychotherapy practice: A form of "respectful . . . inquiry" that plays a primarily "empathic, exploratory, and affirming" role in the relationship with the client (p. 134). At the other pole of the contrast, it is not clear how the "reasoning" associated with dialectics corresponds with "being" nor how it might differ from ordinary conceptual thought.

Despite its inherent limitations, a variation of the contrast between knowing and being will be discussed below in the interest of a deeper understanding of the barriers to a pluralistic, dialectical epistemology. More pointedly, by exploring dialectics within the specific philosophical and psychological context of "nondualism," it will become apparent how certain modes of being contrast with ordinary thought and, thereby, pose an immense challenge to the human mind. In addition, this analysis has the advantage of positioning the relationship of ontology to epistemology, as it manifests in psychotherapy practice, within a dialectical framework.

Stated as a question, the following exploration asks: To what extent does the theorist or therapist approach a given philosophical or theoretical position from the standpoint of *meditative* as opposed to *calculative* thinking? If meditative thinking is viewed as an openness to "presence" or "being," how much openness does the theorist or therapist bring to the articulation and application of philosophical and theoretical assumptions? The contrast of calculative and meditative thinking has obviously been borrowed from Heidegger (see chapter 4), and its meaning and implications in the present context will be clarified as follows.

In turning to Heidegger, one could emphasize the existential, the hermeneutic, or the experiential component of his philosophical approach to nondualism. Given that the prior discussion has prepared the ground for a deeper understanding of his experiential (transpersonal; mystical) work, it will remain the focus here. However, the analysis of Heideggerian "Being" into its constituent parts represents something of a contradiction in terms, and existential and hermeneutic qualities of nondualism will also become evident.

Although Heidegger's (1966) concept of "meditative" thinking was previously linked with the Buddhist notion of emptiness, it is important to emphasize that his term does not refer to some sort of meditation or formal awareness training. Heidegger's concept is defined more broadly, and it would be a mistake to claim that the *Discourse on Thinking* offers a specific "practice" which might be cultivated. Therefore, while Epstein (1984, 1995a, 1995b) suggests that therapists might develop their capacity for openness through meditation practice, this is not the only approach which might move one closer to the kind of thinking that Heidegger explores. For example, Hanna (1994) also makes an analogy between openness and a form of "mindfulness," but he does not suggest that therapists should begin sitting in meditation. Rather, he believes that therapists will move toward "wisdom" if they are "willing to learn from a client" and are "willing to be changed by the experience of therapy itself" (p. 133).

Finally, while Heidegger's construct of meditative thinking cannot be tied to a particular spiritual practice, it constitutes an ontological category which bears a strong resemblance both to the work of the Jewish theologian and existentialist Martin Buber (1958) and to certain Buddhist views. On the one hand, surface or calculative thinking is defined most clearly in regard to two related human tendencies. As an attempt to impose understanding on the world, calculative thinking reflects the function of the *will* and the personal agendas, needs, and expectations associated with it. Further, this understanding is expressed as an attempt to *represent* the world through thought. "Calculative thinking is not merely a euphemism for the approach of empirical science but characterizes any thinking process that plans to dominate and manipulate situations" (Hixon, 1978, p. 4). In Buber's terms, calculative thinking is the relationship of the "I" to the "It."

On the other hand, deep or meditative thinking is neither willful nor representational in nature and deviates so markedly from what we usually consider to be thinking that it might better be called "contemplation" (Hixon, 1978). Heidegger uses the metaphor of "waiting" to characterize this new kind of thinking but cautions us that this cannot be an "awaiting"—which implies that we know in advance what we will find, involving us again in both will and representation. No, this kind of waiting has no object—it leaves "open what we are waiting for"—which then takes us to openness: "Openness itself would be that for which we could do nothing but wait" (1966, p. 68). For Buber, this realm of being in the world and relating to the other is that of the "I" to the "Thou."

Epstein (1988, 1995a, 1995b) offers a similar, but more psychologically based, account of the goal of Buddhist practice. Beginning with Freud's association of meditation practices with a regressive, merged, "oceanic" state, Buddhism has not been differentiated from other forms of "Eastern philosophy" and has been regarded as something altogether exotic, incomprehensible, and "mystical." However, this view fails to recognize the quite sophisticated psychological dimension of Buddhist thinking and practice which has developed over the centuries—a psychology which in many ways parallels recent trends in both psychodynamic theory (Suler, 1993) and cognitive science (Varela, Thompson, & Rosch, 1993).

For example, following Freud, Buddhist realization is still often equated with "egolessness"—the "mystical retreat from the complexities of mental and emotional experience" which would occur in the absence of the ego (Epstein, 1995a, p. 3). Epstein (1988) offers an alternative formulation based on current psychodynamic thinking and begins by distinguishing between the functional and representational aspects of the ego. The former refers to regulative functions that maintain "psychic equilibrium" and facilitate "adaptation and growth." The latter involves "the process by which a picture of the self and the world is built up out of multiple mental images, constructs, or other 'representations'" (p. 63).

> One crucial development of the representational ego is the sense of a substantial, continuing self which is equated with the "I," and which is given agency: It is described as a self-representation *as agent* because it sees itself as the *one* capable of activity. . . . It is an idea, an abstraction, contained within the ego, that embodies the ego's sense of itself as solid and real. It is not, however, to be confused with the entire ego. (p. 64)

From this perspective, the goal of Buddhism is not egolessness or a "going beyond the ego." On the contrary, Buddhist meditation practices actually employ certain ego functions to reflect on the ego itself, including the tendency toward conscious or unconscious identification with an "I" capable of agency.

Therefore, Epstein (1995a) argues that Buddhism is remarkably contemporary in its goals and practices. Like much of recent self and object relations psychology, it is exquisitely attuned to working with the problem of human narcissism, although it views this problem in universal rather than individual terms. The movement toward disidentifying with what we take to be "I," "me," or "mine" constitutes "not clinging" and, in the view of Buddhadāsa Bhikkhu (1994), opens us to some level of the experience of "emptiness." However, this "emptiness" is not what it may sound like to the Western ear. It does not refer to the kind of negative experiences which Epstein (1989) calls "pathological emptiness": meaninglessness, inner longing, despair. Rather, it involves "suspending judgment" about the question of the existence or nonexistence of the self "while still maintaining contact with the stuff of experience" (Epstein, 1995a, p. 100). Interestingly, the Buddhist teacher who can embody this understanding may appear to Westerners as having "a highly developed sense of self" (p. 72). That is, the spontaneity, presence, and authenticity which some contemporary psychoanalysts have associated with the development of the "true self" may, paradoxically, be "achievable most directly through the appreciation of what the Buddhists would call emptiness of self" (p. 72).

John Anderson's (Heidegger, 1966) introduction to the *Discourse on Thinking* acknowledges that Heidegger's descriptions are "cryptic" at various points, and one could say the same for Buber's (1958) *I and Thou* and most Buddhist writings. It is easy enough to define a "nondualistic" approach as one which has severed the distinction between observer and observed through undermining the tendency to identify with self-representations. It is quite another matter to describe the view of reality which then emerges, since the structure of many languages, including English, assumes this distinction. Therefore, Heidegger, Buber, and the Buddhists all attempt to transform language in ways that ask: How would the world look in the absence of an identification with what is assumed to be "I" or "me?"

An important feature of this reformulated approach to language concerns the adequacy of the dimensions and oppositions which are frequently employed in describing the world. For example, Heidegger's (1966) characterization of meditative thinking as "waiting" may suggest to the reader that he believes that one's approach to the world should be "passive" rather than "active." However, he clarifies that this kind of thinking is "beyond the distinction between activity and passivity" (p. 61).

The same nondualistic view could be applied to many other dimensions, including some of those employed in this analysis—for example, consider the relationship of Heidegger's categories to the contrast between conceptual thought and direct experience. Calculative thinking, which attempts to operate on and organize the world through the activity of the mind, appears to be inherently conceptual. However, meditative thinking can include calculative thinking: "The botanist who is developing new strains of wheat need not renounce his scientific calculations when he awakens to deep thinking and contemplates the pervasive radiance of Being" (Hixon, 1978, p. 4). Or, in Buddhist terms, "conceptual thought does not disappear as a result of meditative insight. Only the belief in the ego's solidity is lost" (Epstein, 1995a, p. 99). Therefore, deep or meditative thinking is neither conceptual—in the calculative sense—nor is it nonconceptual.

As for the other pole of the contrast, meditative thinking appears to share some of the attributes of direct experience: Both might be described as "immediate," "present," "direct," "grounded," and "spontaneous." Yet, it would be problematic to argue that meditative thinking is just "experiential" in nature. As Welwood (1996) indicates, experience is accessed through the phenomenological reflection of a "subject" who is observing an internal "object" of some kind—a sensation, an emotion, a felt sense—however subtle or fleeting. Therefore, experience necessarily refers to something that "someone has." But in meditative thinking, the identification with a subject is lessened or perhaps altogether eliminated, and the awareness which results can be distinguished from any specific experiences which it may illuminate. Thus, meditative thinking might be said to be neither experiential nor nonexperiential in nature.

Similarly, the nondualistic approach has implications for the existence of the very dimension which has been proposed in this section. One must be careful in speaking of therapist "openness," "presence," or "being" just as the Middle Way school of Buddhism advised caution around the question of the "self" in chapter 4. These Buddhist scholars argued that it is a mistake to assert either that the self does or does not exist, since "*any* assertion about the self was bound to be distorted because it was in the nature of conceptual consciousness to substantialize that which was trying to be understood" (Epstein, 1995a, pp. 70–71). Statements such as the previous quote from Hixon alluding to "the pervasive radiance of Being" are misleading if they imply to the reader that presence or being is a "thing" with actual existence. On the other hand, to link presence, being, openness, or other such qualities with emptiness "does not mean that they do not exist *at all,* but that they have no *inherent* existence" (Epstein, 1989, p. 66).

From these comments, it would appear that nondualism holds promise for a different understanding of the dialectical approach which has been featured so prominently in this work. If a dialectical psychotherapy acknowledges and utilizes multiple, even conflicting, epistemological perspectives, what kind of thinking allows this process to occur? What *is* "dialectical reasoning"?

If dialectic is defined as a sequential process where the mind alternates between the poles of a contrast, while maintaining a dim awareness that the poles are somehow related, then perhaps it is not so far removed from calculative thinking. Such reasoning might be goal-directed and would allow us to conclude that epistemological position *A* does not apply in a given situation, and, therefore, that we should move to position *B*. Although a dialectical approach to psychotherapy no doubt includes this kind of thinking, it could encompass something more—and philosophical dialectics promises *much* more. Presumably, dialectical reasoning is imbued with a potential for the direct apprehension of the "unity of opposites" (Mueller, 1953, p. 17), allowing us to experience alternatives *A* and *B* as interrelated aspects of a larger whole. Hanna and Ottens (1995) seem to have this expanded meaning in mind when, following D. A. Kramer, they indicate that "dialectical thinking is an aspect of wisdom and, as such, recognizes and incorporates cognition, affect, context, and multiple levels of communication" (p. 197). Hoshmand (1994) makes a similar point within a developmental framework, suggesting that dialectical understanding signals not just a new way of thinking and acting, but also a new "way of personal being associated with a reflexive consciousness" (p. 149).

Slife (1987) sees existing empirical research on "metacognition" as inadequate and contradictory because it is does not provide explanatory constructs that are truly "meta" or "beyond" cognition. A nondualistic perspective would offer support to Slife's position and suggest that some components of "dialectical reasoning" and "metacognition" refer to an entirely new human capacity. This potentiality is neither cognitive nor noncognitive in nature and must be rediscovered in each concrete situation in which it manifests. Further, nondualism would hold that these moments of discovery can be initiated only through the non-willing and not-knowing which Heidegger calls "waiting." The human response to this facet of the existential condition is similar to that which was associated earlier with Nihilistic knowing. Heidegger's Scientist asks, "But then, what in the world am I to do?" After hearing from the Teacher that there is nothing to do but wait, the Scientist admits: "I hardly know anymore who and where I am" (Heidegger, 1966, p. 62). Therefore, from this existential stance, dialectical thinking requires confronting the narcissistic assumption that the human mind can adequately "represent" the world through its existing categories (absolutism), but it also entails moving through the meaninglessness and possible despair which result when this assumption is exposed as illusory (nihilism). In turn, nondualism would equate the purest form of dialectical thinking with those moments when the mind is operating "between" categories but can, nevertheless, see the world clearly, without confusion or distortion.

How does meditative thinking, defined in these nondualistic and dialectical terms, translate to the context of psychotherapeutic practice? Most simply, it refers to the theorist's or therapist's recognition, in the moment, of the givens of the human condition. Whether we approach the world as laypersons or as psychotherapists, we take with us a perceptual/cognitive system which is constitutionally vulnerable to confusing our views of reality with reality itself. Yet, our views are not reality, and they provide no more than a hint of its possibilities. For example, in the face of the vastness of the known physical universe, what constitutes a valid human response other than acknowledging one's *"openness to the mystery"* (Heidegger, 1966, p. 55)? Stephen Batchelor (1990) offers a graceful reflection on the significance of mystery to nondualistic awareness:

> A calculative attitude can serve us in our dealings with the practical concerns of the the everyday, but can only mislead us if we apply its methods to unravel the deeper riddles of life. Calculation can solve our problems but is helpless in penetrating our mysteries. . . .
>
> But the mysterious lies at the heart of our lives, not at the periphery. And its presence is only felt to the extent that a meditative attitude still lives within us. Unlike a problem, a mystery can never be solved. A mystery can only be penetrated. A problem once solved ceases to be a problem; but the penetration of a mystery does not make it any less mysterious. The more intimate one is with a mystery, the greater shines the aura of its secret. The intensification of a mystery leads not to frustration (as does the increasing of a problem) but to release. (p. 40)

The nondualist would ask of us: How concretely and immediately can we experience the contradiction between our need to believe and the finiteness of our beliefs in the moment of embracing and applying a philosophical or theoretical position? Can we allow this experience without turning the contradiction itself into another concept which will again push us toward absolutism or nihilism? Can we follow Rilke's advice and *live* the contradiction?

As an illustration of the proposed contrast, consider again the work of Gergen and Cushman. The social constructionist and hermeneutic approaches associated, respectively, with these psychologists and their related critiques of mainstream psychology and psychotherapy have much in common. When they draw out the implications of their positions for psychotherapeutic practice, there is also a significant similarity in their thinking—up to a point. Eventually, however, they part company. While Gergen continues to praise the virtues of a postmodernist conception of therapeutic change, Cushman retreats and asks if transformative change is entirely possible, and if his hermeneutic therapy can actually provide a bridge to it.

Could one say that Gergen's thinking about social constructionism has remained more "calculative" in nature, while Cushman has gradually become more "meditative" in his experience of a hermeneutic therapy? Hixon (1978) suggests that calculative thinking, when severed from meditative thinking, becomes "an abstraction" (p. 5). While it appears that Gergen has remained wedded to an abstract ideal of therapeutic change, Cushman's like conception has been tempered by a recognition of his own human limitations, including his ambivalence about uprooting all traces of individualism in himself. Further, as a practicing clinician, Cushman has had the opportunity to test his views about change against the reality provided by clients and therapeutic interaction.

As for Gergen, he might also be on his way to a more meditative approach to social constructionism. In a conversation with Michael Hoyt (1996), he reflects on the possibility of moving beyond language and narrative to "relatedness itself." Gergen acknowledges that he has resisted clarifying this notion for fear that any construct would specify "this as opposed to that" (p. 365)—a statement which hints at nondualism. He does borrow the concept of the *"relational sublime"* from the Romanticists, however, and invites us to imagine that

> we might develop a sense of ourselves as fully immersed in relatedness—with all humanity, all that is given—and that we might

conceive of this awesome sensibility of pure relatedness (itself born of relationship) as approaching what we might mean by the domain of the spiritual. (p. 365)

In Heideggerian terms, does this "relational sublime" signify true openness or is it an abstract concept about openness? If it exemplifies the former, then its impact should manifest in time in the very manner in which Gergen holds his constructionist position.

I hope that it is clear from these comments about Gergen and Cushman that presence, being, or openness in one's approach to theory and practice is always a matter of degree. More importantly, paralleling an earlier critique of Harlene Anderson's (1997) approach to Dialogical knowing (see chapter 6), calculative thinking and meditative thinking exist in a dialectical relationship to one another. The openness revealed in a moment of meditative thinking can become linked, in the following moment, with a concept which carries the weight of human purpose and will—as the calculative mind claims it as its own. This agenda then creates another opportunity for meditative thinking to arise and locate experience within a larger ground, and this larger ground can then be reclaimed by calculative thinking, and so on.

For my purposes, these illustrations of the calculative-meditative contrast need not be entirely convincing, nor is it necessary to accept the more general claim that meditative thinking, or the nondual awareness associated with it, is altogether "pure," "true," or attainable. Indeed, it is essential that my presentation of meditative thinking recognize and sustain the dialectical relationship between knowing and being. Ogden (1994) observes: "Dialectic is a process in which opposing elements each create, preserve, and negate the other; each stands in a dynamic, ever-changing relationship to the other. Dialectical movement tends toward integrations that are never achieved" (p. 14). Although the thrust of this section has been to challenge the assumptions of certain forms of knowing from the standpoint of being, knowing must continue to test the very "integration" which nonduality and meditative thinking put forth. Otherwise, this integration may degenerate into an understanding, "psychotherapy *is* nondualism," which brings with it the same moral and philosophical problems as were seen in relation to Gangaji's "psychotherapy" (see chapter 4).

An exchange involving representatives of Western and Eastern approaches to "mind science" represents a healthy expression of the dialectic which I have in mind. Howard Gardner (Eck, Gardner, Goleman, & Thurman, 1991) remarks that cognitive scientists like himself assume that it is impossible to ever "see the world fresh" and that all of us are victims of our own "theories, concepts, and stereotypes" (p. 109). He admits that the Buddhist view that one "could get clear, wipe out, at least temporarily, these ideas and notions and look at the world emptily" (p. 109) poses a fundamental challenge to this belief system. These two conflicting ontologies, Buddhist and cognitive, must be allowed to coexist, with neither reducing the one to the other, thereby constituting a dialectic where each is "perpetually in the process of being created and negated, perpetually in the process of being decentered from static self-evidence" (Ogden, 1994, p. 14).

Therefore, as with the opposition proposed in the previous section, the distinction between calculative thinking and meditative thinking can be stated in relative rather than absolute terms without undermining its potential usefulness. This relative contrast still holds promise for providing therapists with a specific reference axis for assessing their moment-by-moment relationship to both knowing and being. Like realism, calculative thinking represents an essential and unavoidable aspect of psychotherapeutic practice. Yet, if such thinking is not balanced by the therapist's willingness to remain open to that which goes beyond its bounds, how could a morally situated psychotherapy be possible?

The Dialectic of Normal and Philosophical Components of Knowing

Despite the earlier warning about the form of the argument which would be offered, the reader, by this point, may have some complaints about the overlap in concepts which defines my recommended approach to epistemology. A morally situated psychotherapy is reflexive, dialectical, and pluralistic, and balances conceptual thought with direct experience and knowing with being—but each of these characteristics is in part defined by the others. Although the final section of this chapter is no exception to this strategy, it describes a contrast which offers an integrative focus for many of the previously described elements—while emphasizing, once again, the difficulty of embodying the moral implications of this analysis in actual psychotherapeutic practice.

Feyerabend's (1970) modification of Kuhn's concepts of normal and revolutionary science was introduced in chapter 3. Unlike Kuhn, he and Lakatos argue that these forms of science are not confined to distinct historical periods but exist co-presently in every period. Therefore, he substitutes a language of "components" for periods of science and replaces Kuhn's concept of revolutionary science with that of the "philosophical" component.

The normal component assumes that science is most likely to advance if scientists hold tenaciously to their own frameworks and trace out their implications and applications. Feyerabend (1975) asserts that this component resists change because

> skepticism is at a minimum; it is directed against the view of the opposition and against minor ramifications of one's own basic ideas, never against the basic ideas themselves. Attacking the basic ideas evokes taboo reactions which are no weaker than the taboo reactions in so-called primitive societies. (p. 298)

Anything which does not fit the existing framework "is either viewed as something quite horrifying or, more frequently, it is simply declared to be non-existent" (p. 298, italics omitted).

On the other hand, the philosophical component represents the antithesis of the necessary "dogmatism" of the normal component. It assumes a "pluralistic methodology" (p. 47), wherein science advances through a proliferation of viewpoints and a clash of opposing claims. Rather than discarding anomalies, the philosophical component recognizes them and tolerates the contradiction and confusion which they can produce. Therefore, it relies on the counterintuitive strategy of making "the weaker case the stronger" (p. 30, italics omitted)—that is, realizing and strengthening that which is marginalized and discrepant while undermining that which is believed. This strategy derives in turn from a vision of knowledge where no perspective is ever omitted and where "nothing is ever settled" (p. 30).

Obviously, Feyerabend's contrast and the Kuhnian concepts on which it is based were proposed as tools for understanding the development of the physical sciences. However, the argument of chapter 3 establishes that the range of application of this contrast extends well beyond the boundaries of science. These concepts point to general functions which are shared by all implicit and explicit "theories," whether those of scientists, philosophers, laypersons, or psychotherapists.

From this larger perspective, Feyerabend's distinction between normal and philosophical components can be utilized to summarize a host of functional contrasts which have been proposed for defining the process of psychotherapeutic knowing. On the one hand, the normal component of knowing is loosely associated with various forms of therapeutic *affirmation* or *conviction:* "the revelatory function of theory";

"confirmation"; "metaphor"; "belief"; and "realism." On the other hand, the philosophical component is similarly related to therapeutic *critique* or *uncertainty* expressed as: "the restrictive function of theory"; "disconfirmation"; "deconstructionism"; "doubt"; "pluralism"; and, in the extreme, "nihilism." Further, these contrasts and the normal-philosophical distinction which encompasses them exist in a dialectical relationship to one another.

The normal component is in ascendancy when we are operating in the world and in therapy from a stance of unexamined certainty. We take for granted the utility of the fundamental categories through which we are interpreting the world and attempt to extend their range of application. We may not be fully aware of the nature of these categories— that is, they may function more as an implicit ground than as an explicit theory. However, they allow us to "see" the client and his/her experience from a particular vantage point. This ground or theory is not just known by us, it is "lived out" and is conveyed to the client through our gestures and silences, as well as through our words. Its existence allows us to offer a coherence to the client's experience which otherwise would be missing, but it also restricts the range of meanings which the client will be encouraged to consider.

The philosophical component arises when we recognize that some assumption, belief, or ground to our experience has been or could be disconfirmed through the practice of psychotherapy. There is a tendency to defend ourselves from this possibility, but a number of factors may make the anomalies undeniable or increase our sensitivity and openness to them. Once admitted into awareness, disconfirmation leads to a variety of cognitive and emotional responses which may include, in varying intensities, uncertainty, skepticism, doubt, pessimism, disappointment, helplessness, anger, or anxiety. Provided that these reactions do not push us back into the normal component, they represent a further opening of the door to the philosophical component, wherein new alternatives can be considered in the absence of certainty or commitment. If we settle on one of these possibilities as something which can constitute a new ground for our own experience and for our work with the client, then the normal component has again reasserted itself and another cycle of the dialectic has begun.

The framework of normal and philosophical components has the advantage of reemphasizing the continuous, "circular" nature of the dialectics of knowing. Each of the six modes of knowing can represent, depending on the attitude of conviction or uncertainty with which we hold it, either pole of the contrast. For example, even nihilism, when taken to be a self-evident fact of the world, can assume the position of the normal component. The philosophical component would then become defined, paradoxically, in relationship to belief—a possibility whose existence would plunge a nihilist into real uncertainty! Similarly, the dialectical relationship between components of knowing and being which was proposed in the last two sections can also be framed in these terms. Just as direct experience and nondualism can function as the philosophical component, deconstructing the assumptions of human knowing, they also can become convictions which in turn must be challenged by the assumptions of cognitive science.

This description of the interrelationship of normal and philosophical components also has its limitations. They have been defined more distinctly and sequentially than would occur when one is actually *living* the dialectic. Further, it leaves significant questions unanswered. Namely, what does it mean to say that the dialectic between these two components is circular or continuous? How continuous? So continuous that one's head is literally spinning while sitting in the room with the client? If so, how is it possible to practice psychotherapy?

In its weaker form, the dialectic between normal and philosophical knowing *is* continuous. In this meaning, philosophical knowing represents less a rejection or undermining of normal knowing and more a complement to it. For example, in Protter's description of the interrelationship of different ways of knowing in psychoanalysis, he indicates that an analyst, whose theory emphasizes a given way of knowing, still might shift to other modes—as the theory allows and the therapeutic situation requires. Or in my analysis of the relationship of lived modes of knowing in chapter 6, it was shown that therapists frequently move from mode to mode, often without effort or awareness. The cognitive therapist might move between Representational and Realist knowing and the narrative therapist between Dialogical and Realist knowing, even though their verbalized theoretical and philosophical assumptions would discount these possibilities.

The stronger form of the dialectic between normal and philosophical knowing is explicit in Feyerabend's usage and has been the emphasis of this section: It refers to those situations where there is a significant disjunction between the two approaches. Unlike the above examples, the appearance of the philosophical component represents a fundamental threat to the therapist, whether in theoretical, philosophical, or experiential terms. The two components of knowing are seen as contradictory, and the greater one's awareness of the contradiction, the more likely one will experience uncertainty and its consequences. Accordingly, this form of the dialectic suggests a more telling question: How continuously can therapists experience discontinuity of this magnitude? Or, framing the question in moral terms: *What is the optimal relationship between conviction and uncertainty in the practice of psychotherapy?*

Everything that has been written to this point would suggest that it is human nature for the normal component—that is, unexamined, unshakable belief—to dominate the experience of knowing the world. If this were not the case, then the Enlightenment, which promised to replace superstitious belief and myth with reason and science, would have represented a less dramatic shift in the Western history of ideas. But in science, too, "the normal component is large and well entrenched" and "almost always outweighs its philosophical part" (Feyerabend, 1970, p. 213).

I believe that a morally situated psychotherapy depends on our holding higher standards than those which characterize either lay or scientific knowing. Neither a human science nor a humane psychotherapy can be built on an approach which allows the unchallenged dominance of the normal component. When the object of our psychological study or our psychotherapeutic intervention is another person, then the "anomaly" which the normal component ignores is human experience, human life, itself. When disconfirmations are not seen or are brushed aside, then one can be sure that developments like the "treatment" of satanic abuse and the "science" of racial differences in IQ will take root. And, if the normal component is doing its job, an even more chilling realization follows. We will never know when we have done harm to the persons that we study or treat, and, therefore, we will be unable to take responsibility for our actions.

In stressing that the normal component cannot be allowed to dominate the practice of psychotherapy, am I proposing that the philosophical component should rule in its stead? Of course, that is exactly the position which has been put forward by a host of critics whose views have been reviewed here. Within the philosophy of science, Feyerabend (1975) recommends anarchism or, better, Dadaism, as the ideal which science might emulate. Knowledge, from this view, becomes "an ever increasing *ocean of mutually incompatible (and perhaps even incommensurable) alternatives*" (p. 30), where fairy tales stand alongside scientific theories in making their claims to truth. From philosophy proper, a postmodernist such as Lyotard (1984) emerges with a view of knowledge which is no less pluralistic. We must let untold numbers of knowledge-forms bloom, and rejoice at our good fortune to witness this spectacle. Within academic psychology, Polkinghorne (1983) develops a more circumspect position than the above philosophers but does state that researchers, given the reflexive task of the human sciences, should permanently remain in a "state of crisis" in the Kuhnian sense (p. 9). Finally, psychotherapy is enjoined to promote, through its process and goals, "not-knowing" (H. Anderson, 1997), the dissolution of "personal identity" (Gergen & Kaye, 1992), and the construction of multiple "preferred realities" (Freedman & Combs, 1996).

All of this would be enough to give Kuhn, and the scientists he studied, apoplexy. Scientific revolutions, during which multiple realities prevail, are limited to specific periods, because neither science as an institution nor individual scientists could possibly endure a steady diet of uncertainty. In fact, such periods are marked by scientists' "willingness to try anything," "expression of explicit discontent," and a reluctant "recourse to philosophy," in which the fundamentals of the fields are once again questioned and debated—developments which generally are avoided at all cost (Kuhn, 1970a, p. 91).

It is difficult to dismiss Kuhn's observations when they accord so well with the thrust of the present argument. It has been shown over and over again—in contexts ranging from philosophical thought to cognitive science to psychotherapy—that critique, uncertainty, and the philosophical component cannot exist apart from a context of affirmation, conviction, and the normal component. With the possible exception of the Buddhists, no argument which has been reviewed here convinces me that human beings can in actuality circumvent this dialectic, somehow learning to float with ease in Feyerabend's "ocean of mutually incompatible . . . alternatives." The Buddhist view has the advantage of offering some living exemplars of the transformed human capacity which postmodernists, to this point, have only described in abstract, theoretical terms. However, formulating a moral guideline for psychotherapy based on the possibility of Buddhist realization would seem to represent, shall we say, an overly stringent standard of practice.

Therefore, I am going to turn to an unlikely source for a metaphor which expresses the optimal relationship between conviction and uncertainty in the practice of psychotherapy. Like Popper's consummate "critical" or "rational" scientist, *psychotherapists should be capable of learning from their mistakes*. I hope that it is apparent by now that learning from one's mistakes—in any fundamental sense—is no mean feat. For Kuhn, it is such a rare event that it may occur once, or not at all, in a scientist's lifetime. To learn from one's mistakes, it is first necessary to *see* them, and our cognitive/perceptual systems conspire mightily against this possibility. Moreover, this task of recognition becomes even more problematic for psychotherapists, whose mistakes also include errors of omission. In choosing a given approach to a client, alternative frameworks for change—including those from both within and outside psychotherapy—are excluded or ignored, and the moral consequences of such choices must be examined.

In Kuhn's eyes, Popper's scientist appears as a fictional character who only comes to life during periods of "extraordinary" science. In addition, even the "great scientists" did not fully meet Popper's rational standards; for example, based on his religious beliefs, Sir Isaac Newton "would have found the very idea of . . . falsification an impiety" (Newton-Smith, 1989, p. 35). Unlike Kuhn's "real" scientists or Popper's possibly "idealized" ones, psychotherapists—who want to learn from their mistakes—must strive to practice the "unnatural" act of balancing normal and philosophical components of knowing in their ordinary, everyday lives. This dialectic requires an acknowledgment that, whatever our philosophical opinion on the matter, as human beings we *will* tend to approach the world in terms of some theory, belief system, or metanarrative—which contributes structure, meaning, and coherence both to our experience and to that of the client. Equally, it depends on a cultivation of our sensitivity to potential experiences of disconfirmation, a willingness to have our most basic beliefs and assumptions examined and challenged, and a capacity for tolerating the negative emotions which this process can engender. Psychotherapists who embrace this dialectic will find themselves defining their practice neither as normal science, which is morally irresponsible, nor as a permanently foundationless flux, which is humanly unbearable.

Assuming that the best attempts of the natural sciences have not produced the balance between conviction and uncertainty which I propose, could this still be asking too much of psychotherapists? I have no doubt that it will seem, at times, that too much is being asked. Ultimately, nothing can protect the therapist from the incessant demands of this dialectic. It is not resolvable by a philosophical, theoretical, or therapeutic position of any kind. Yes, an awareness of dialectics, a willingness to move to direct experience, a capacity for being, an appreciation of pluralism and philosophical knowing, all these can help to balance the excesses of the normal component. Yet each of these guidelines can itself become an expression of that same tendency, acting as an impediment to discovering the alternative conviction which is truly needed in a given moment of therapeutic interaction. Therefore, age and experience are of limited help, because these different moments require the therapist not just to *understand* the dialectic, but to *live it out,* allowing the fresh response which the situation demands. Each time, this pull toward doubt and uncertainty can be experienced as an affront to what we *know,* to what we think we *should* know, and even to whom we think we *are.*

When psychotherapy is successful, perhaps particularly when it is successful, we must continue to balance our work within the normal component with the skepticism of the philosophical component. It is important to remember that shamans and faith healers have their share of therapeutic successes, and that positive outcome does not necessarily validate our assumptions, rationales, or methods. The search for philosophical, theoretical, and therapeutic understanding begins, rather then ends, with a successful intervention.

It might be assumed that this dialectic would pose particular difficulties for more inexperienced clinicians and for clinical trainees who, understandably, are still attempting to master the normal component—that is, theory and method. Indeed, these epistemological guidelines have paradoxical implications for the question of training. On the one hand, as Frank and Frank (1991) indicate, trainees must be schooled in the normal component to increase their sense of competence and confidence, which in turn is correlated with the client's confidence in the therapist and successful outcome. On the other hand, if trainees are not exposed to philosophical knowing, then another generation of therapists will enter the field who are imbalanced in the direction of therapeutic conviction. Proposals that training should encourage fluency "in more than one therapy language and mode of practice" (Safran & Messer, 1997, p. 148) and include "a broad and diverse presentation of epistemologies" (Peterson & Peterson, 1997, p. 225) are in the interest of preventing this outcome.

The conflict in these agendas implies that it would be useful to take the same dialectical and idiographic approach to training which has been recommended for the practice of psychotherapy. A dialectical approach to training would focus on increasing awareness of the relationship of conviction to uncertainty in the trainees' experiences with clients, their general responses to training, and their specific work with supervisors. Such awareness would depend, in turn, on the supervisors' abilities to hold and track this dimension in their own experience. Further, an idiographic approach would recognize that trainees' needs differ depending on their current relationship to the dialectic. For example, some trainees may be overly preoccupied with philosophical knowing (personal or professional doubt) and may require considerable support for their efforts to establish a more secure professional identity, while others require balancing in the opposite direction.

In closing, I urge my colleagues in the field to aim for a psychotherapy which meets the needs of clients—and ourselves—for meaning and coherence without compromising our responsibilities as reflexive practitioners and moral agents. Current standards of practice cannot prevent therapists from lapsing into views and employing methods which are illusory, self-deceiving, and self-serving. Remaining cognizant of our dual nature—a strong need to believe and a complementary need to question ourselves radically—may be our best hope for retaining our humanity and integrity as psychotherapists.

References

Allport, G. W. (1937). *Personality: A psychological interpretation.* New York: Holt, Rinehart, and Winston.

American Psychiatric Association. (1994). *Diagnostic and statistical manual of mental disorders* (4th ed.). Washington, DC: Author.

American Psychological Association. (1992). Ethical principles of psychologists and code of conduct. *American Psychologist, 47,* 1597–1611.

Anderson, H. (1993). On a roller coaster: A collaborative language systems approach to therapy. In S. Friedman (Ed.), *The new language of change: Constructive collaboration in psychotherapy* (pp. 323–344). New York: Guilford.

Anderson, H. (1997). *Conversation, language, and possibilities: A postmodern approach to therapy.* New York: Basic Books.

Anderson, H., & Goolishian, H. (1992). The client is the expert: A not-knowing approach to therapy. In S. McNamee & K. J. Gergen (Eds.), *Therapy as social construction* (pp. 25–39). Thousand Oaks, CA: Sage.

Anderson, T. (1993). See and hear, and be seen and heard. In S. Friedman (Ed.), *The new language of change: Constructive collaboration in psychotherapy* (pp. 303–322). New York: Guilford.

Arnkoff, D. B., & Glass, C. R. (1992). Cognitive therapy and psychotherapy integration. In D. K. Freedheim (Ed.), *History of psychotherapy: A century of change* (pp. 657–694). Washington, DC: American Psychological Association.

Atwood, G. E., & Stolorow, R. D. (1993). *Faces in a cloud: Intersubjectivity in personality theory.* Northvale, NJ: Jason Aronson.

Baker, H. S. (1991). Shorter-term psychotherapy: A self psychological approach. In P. Crits-Christoph & J. P. Barber (Eds.), *Handbook of short-term dynamic psychotherapy* (pp. 287–322). New York: Basic Books.

293

Barber, J. P., & Crits-Christoph, P. (1991). Comparison of the brief dynamic therapies. In P. Crits-Christoph & J. P. Barber (Eds.), *Handbook of short-term dynamic psychotherapy* (pp. 323–355). New York: Basic Books.

Barlow, D. H. (1988). *Anxiety and its disorders: The nature and treatment of anxiety and panic.* New York: Guilford.

Barlow, D. H. (1996) Health care policy, psychotherapy research, and the future of psychotherapy. *American Psychologist, 51,* 1050–1058.

Barth, J. (1969). *The end of the road.* New York: Bantam Books.

Barton, A. (1974). *Three worlds of therapy: An existential-phenomenological study of the therapies of Freud, Jung, and Rogers.* Palo Alto, CA: Mayfield.

Batchelor, S. (1990). *The faith to doubt: Glimpses of Buddhist uncertainty.* Berkeley, CA: Parallax Press.

Baynes, K., Bohman, J., & McCarthy, T. (Eds.). (1987). *After philosophy: End or transformation?* Cambridge, MA: MIT Press.

Beck, A. T., Rush, A. J., Shaw, B. F., & Emery, G. (1979). *Cognitive therapy of depression.* New York: Guilford.

Belenky, M. F., Clinchy, B. M., Goldberger, N. R., & Tarule, J. M. (1986). *Women's ways of knowing: The development of self, voice, and mind.* New York: Basic Books.

Bellah, R. N., Madsen, R., Sullivan, W. M., Swidler, A., & Tipton, S. M. (1985). *Habits of the heart: Individualism and commitment in American life.* Berkeley, CA: University of California Press.

Berg, I. K., & de Shazer, S. (1993). Making numbers talk: Language in therapy. In S. Friedman (Ed.), *The new language of change: Constructive collaboration in psychotherapy* (pp. 5–24). New York: Guilford.

Bergin, A. E., & Garfield, S. L. (Eds.). (1994a). *Handbook of psychotherapy and behavior change* (4th ed.). New York: Wiley.

Bergin, A. E., & Garfield, S. L. (1994b). Overview, trends, and future issues. In A. E. Bergin & S. L. Garfield (Eds.), *Handbook of psychotherapy and behavior change* (4th ed., pp. 821–830). New York: Wiley.

Berne, E. (1961). *Transactional analysis in psychotherapy: A systematic individual and social psychiatry.* New York: Grove Press.

Berne, E. (1972). *What do you say after you say hello? The psychology of human destiny.* New York: Grove Press.

Bernstein, R. J. (1983). *Beyond objectivism and relativism: Science, hermeneutics, and praxis.* Philadelphia: University of Pennsylvania Press.

Bernstein, R. J. (1992). *The new constellation: The ethical-political horizons of modernity/postmodernity.* Cambridge, MA: MIT Press.

Beutler, L. E. (1995). The germ theory myth and the myth of outcome homogeneity. *Psychotherapy, 32,* 489–494.

Beutler, L. E., & Clarkin, J. F. (1990). *Systematic treatment selection: Toward targeted therapeutic interventions.* New York: Brunner/Mazel.

Beutler, L. E., & Consoli, A. J. (1992). Systematic eclectic psychotherapy. In J. C. Norcross & M. R. Goldfried (Eds.), *Handbook of psychotherapy integration* (pp. 264–299). New York: Basic Books.

Beutler, L. E., Williams, R. E., Wakefield, P. J., & Entwistle, S. R. (1995). Bridging scientist and practitioner perspectives in clinical psychology. *American Psychologist, 50,* 984–994.

Bhikkhu, B. (1994). *Heartwood of the Bodhi tree: The Buddha's teaching on voidness.* Boston: Wisdom Publications.

Bikel, O., & Dretzin, R. (Producers). (1995, October 24). The search for Satan. *Frontline.* (Videocassette Recording No. FROL402). Alexandria, VA: PBS Video.

Boorstein, S. (1986). Transpersonal context, interpretation, and psychotherapeutic technique. *Journal of Transpersonal Psychology, 18,* 123–130.

Borgen, F. H. (1984). Are there necessary linkages between research practices and the philosophy of science? *Journal of Counseling Psychology, 31,* 457–460.

Bottoms, B. L., Shaver, P. R., & Goodman, G. S. (1991, August). *Profile of ritual and religion related abuse allegations reported to clinical psychologists in the United States.* Paper presented at the annual meeting of the American Psychological Association, San Francisco.

Boyers, R., & Orrill, R. (Eds.). (1971). *R. D. Laing and anti-psychiatry.* New York: Perennial Library.

Braginsky, B. M., & Braginsky, D. D. (1974). *Mainstream psychology: A critique.* New York: Holt, Rinehart, and Winston.

Braginsky, B. M., Braginsky, D. D., & Ring, K. (1969). *Methods of madness: The mental hospital as a last resort.* New York: Holt, Rinehart, and Winston.

Bromberg, W. (1975). *From shaman to psychotherapist: A history of the treatment of mental illness.* Chicago: H. Regnery.

Bromley, D. G. (1991). Satanism: The new cult scare. In J. T. Richardson, J. Best, & D. G. Bromley (Eds.), *The Satanism scare: Social institutions and social change* (pp. 49–72). New York: Aldine.

Brown, H. I. (1977). *Perception, theory, and commitment: The new philosophy of science.* Chicago: University of Chicago Press.

Brown, L. S. (1992). While waiting for the revolution: The case for a lesbian feminist psychotherapy. *Feminism & Psychology, 2,* 239–253.

Brown, L. S. (1997). Ethics in psychology: *Cui Bono?* In D. Fox & I. Prilleltensky (Eds.), *Critical psychology: An introduction* (pp. 51–67). Thousand Oaks, CA: Sage.

Brown, P. (Ed.). (1973). *Radical psychology.* New York: Harper Colophon Books.

Bruner, J. (1986). *Actual minds, possible worlds.* Cambridge, MA: Harvard University Press.

Bruner, J. S., & Postman, L. (1949). On the perception of incongruity: A paradigm. *Journal of Personality, 18,* 206–223.

Buber, M. (1958). *I and Thou.* New York: Charles Scribner.

Buss, A. R. (1979). *A dialectical psychology.* New York: Irvington.

Camus, A. (1991). *The myth of sisyphus and other essays.* New York: Vintage International.

Carr, K. L. (1992). *The banalization of nihilism: Twentieth-century responses to meaninglessness*. Albany, NY: State University of New York Press.

Chalmers, A. F. (1982). *What is this thing called science? An assessment of the nature and status of science and its methods* (2nd ed.). Indianapolis, IN: Hackett.

Chambless, D. L. (1996). In defense of dissemination of empirically supported psychological interventions. *Clinical Psychology: Science and Practice, 3,* 230–235.

Chesler, P. (1972). *Women and madness*. Garden City, NY: Doubleday.

Chiari, G., & Nuzzo, M. L. (1996). Psychological constructivisms: A metatheoretical differentiation. *Journal of Constructivist Psychology, 9,* 163–184.

Cohen, L. H., Sargent, M. M., & Sechrest, L. B. (1986). Use of psychotherapy research by professional psychologists. *American Psychologist, 41,* 198–206.

Coleman, S. R., & Salamon, R. (1988). Kuhn's *Structure of scientific revolutions* in the psychological journal literature, 1969–1983: A descriptive study. *Journal of Mind and Behavior, 9,* 415–445.

Common Ground (1996, Summer, 88). (Available from the publisher, 305 San Anselmo Avenue, Suite 313, San Anselmo, CA 94960).

Cooper, D. (Ed.). (1969). *To free a generation: The dialectics of liberation*. New York: Collier Books.

Cooper, D. (1971). *Psychiatry and anti-psychiatry*. New York: Ballantine Books.

Cooper, D. E. (1990). *Existentialism: A reconstruction*. Oxford, UK: Blackwell.

Crits-Christoph, P. (1996). The dissemination of efficacious psychological treatments. *Clinical Psychology: Science and Practice, 3,* 260–263.

Crits-Christoph, P., & Barber, J. P. (Eds.). (1991). *Handbook of short-term dynamic psychotherapy*. New York: Basic Books.

Cushman, P. (1990). Why the self is empty: Toward a historically situated psychology. *American Psychologist, 45,* 599–611.

Cushman, P. (1991). Ideology obscured: Political uses of the self in Daniel Stern's infant. *American Psychologist, 46,* 206–219.

Cushman, P. (1992). Psychotherapy to 1992: A historically situated interpretation. In D. K. Freedheim (Ed.), *History of psychotherapy: A century of change* (pp. 21–64). Washington, DC: American Psychological Association.

Cushman, P. (1993). Psychotherapy as moral discourse. *Journal of Theoretical and Philosophical Psychology, 13,* 103–113.

Cushman, P. (1995). *Constructing the self, constructing America: A cultural history of psychotherapy*. New York: Addison-Wesley.

Cushman, P. (1996). Locating dialogue: A reply to Flax. *Psychoanalytic Dialogues, 6,* 883–894.

Derrida, J. (1976). *Of grammatology*. Baltimore: Johns Hopkins University Press.

Derrida, J. (1978). *Writing and difference*. Chicago: University of Chicago Press.

DeRubeis, R. J., & Crits-Christoph, P. (1998). Empirically supported individual and group psychological treatments for adult mental disorders. *Journal of Consulting and Clinical Psychology, 66,* 37–52.

DiGiuseppe, R., & Linscott, J. (1993). Philosophical differences among cognitive behavioral therapists: Rationalism, constructivism, or both? *Journal of Cognitive Psychotherapy: An International Quarterly, 7,* 117–130.

Di Stefano, C. (1990). Dilemmas of difference: Feminism, modernity, and postmodernism. In L. J. Nicholson (Ed.), *Feminism/postmodernism* (pp. 63–82). New York: Routledge and Kegan Paul.

Doherty, W. J. (1995). *Soul searching: Why psychotherapy must promote moral responsibility.* New York: Basic Books.

Dunn, G. E. (1992). Multiple personality disorder: A new challenge for psychology. *Professional Psychology: Research and Practice, 23,* 18–23.

Eagle, M., & Wolitzky, D. L. (1997). Empathy: A psychoanalytic perspective. In A. C. Bohart & L. S. Greenberg (Eds.), *Empathy reconsidered: New directions in psychotherapy* (pp. 217–244). Washington, DC: American Psychological Association.

Eck, D. L., Gardner, H. E., Goleman, D., & Thurman, R. A. F. (1991). Dialogue: Buddhism, psychology, and the cognitive sciences. In D. Goleman & R. A. F. Thurman (Eds.), *MindScience: An East-West dialogue* (pp. 103–114). Boston: Wisdom Publications.

Eckberg, D. L., & Hill, L. (1980). The paradigm concept and sociology: A critical review. In G. Gutting (Ed.), *Paradigms and revolutions: Appraisals and applications of Thomas Kuhn's philosophy of science* (pp. 117–136). Notre Dame, IN: University of Notre Dame Press.

Efran, J. S., & Clarfield, L. E. (1992). Constructionist therapy: Sense and nonsense. In S. McNamee & K. J. Gergen (Eds.), *Therapy as social construction* (pp. 200–217). Thousand Oaks, CA: Sage.

Efran, J. S., & Fauber, R. L. (1995). Radical constructivism: Questions and answers. In R. A. Neimeyer & M. J. Mahoney (Eds.), *Constructivism in psychotherapy* (pp. 275–304). Washington, DC: American Psychological Association.

Ehrenwald, J. (1966). *Psychotherapy: Myth and method, an integrative approach.* New York: Grune and Stratton.

Ehrenwald, J. (Ed.). (1976a). *The history of psychotherapy: From healing magic to encounter.* New York: Jason Aronson.

Ehrenwald, J. (1976b). Introduction. In J. Ehrenwald (Ed.), *The history of psychotherapy: From healing magic to encounter* (pp. 17–21). New York: Jason Aronson.

Ehrenwald, J. (1976c). Epilogue: The therapeutic triad and the power of insight. In J. Ehrenwald (Ed.), *The history of psychotherapy: From healing magic to encounter* (pp. 569–576). New York: Jason Aronson.

Elkin, I., Shea, M. T., Watkins, J. T., Imber, S. D., Sotsky, S. M., Collins, J. F., Glass, D. R., Pilkonis, P. A., Leber, W. R., Docherty, J. P., Fiester, S. J., & Parloff, M. B. (1989). NIMH Treatment of Depression Collaborative Research Program: General effectiveness of treatments. *Archives of General Psychiatry, 46,* 971–982.

Ellis, A. (1993). Reflections on rational-emotive therapy. *Journal of Consulting and Clinical Psychology, 61,* 199–201.

Emmelkamp, P. M. G., Bouman, T. K., & Scholing, A. (1995). *Anxiety disorders: A practitioner's guide*. Chichester, England: Wiley.

Epstein, M. D. (1984). On the neglect of evenly suspended attention. *Journal of Transpersonal Psychology, 16*, 193–205.

Epstein, M. (1988). The deconstruction of the self: Ego and "egolessness" in Buddhist insight meditation. *Journal of Transpersonal Psychology, 20*, 61–69.

Epstein, M. (1989). Forms of emptiness: Psychodynamic, meditative, and clinical perspectives. *Journal of Transpersonal Psychology, 21*, 61–71.

Epstein, M. (1995a). *Thoughts without a thinker: Psychotherapy from a Buddhist perspective*. New York: Basic Books.

Epstein, M. (1995b). Thoughts without a thinker: Buddhism and psychoanalysis. *Psychoanalytic Review, 82*, 391–406.

Epting, F. R. (1984). *Personal construct counseling and psychotherapy*. New York: Wiley.

Erwin, E. (1997). *Philosophy and psychotherapy: Razing the troubles of the brain*. London: Sage.

Eysenck, H. J. (1952). The effects of psychotherapy: An evaluation. *Journal of Consulting Psychology, 16*, 319–324.

Federn, P. (1952). *Ego psychology and the psychoses*. New York: Basic Books.

Feminist Therapy Institute. (1995). Feminist Therapy Code of Ethics. In E. J. Rave & C. C. Larsen (Eds.), *Ethical decision making in therapy: Feminist perspectives* (pp. 38–41). New York: Guilford.

Ferguson, M. (1982). Karl Pribram's changing reality. In K. Wilber (Ed.), *The holographic paradigm and other paradoxes: Exploring the leading edge of science* (pp. 15–26). Boulder, CO: Shambhala.

Feyerabend, P. K. (1970). Consolations for the specialist. In I. Lakatos & A. Musgrave (Eds.), *Criticism and the growth of knowledge* (pp. 197–230). Cambridge: Cambridge University Press.

Feyerabend, P. (1975). *Against method: Outline of an anarchistic theory of knowledge*. London: NLB.

Feyerabend, P. (1978). *Science in a free society*. London: NLB.

Fincham, F., & Jaspars, J. M. (1980). Attribution of responsibility: From man the scientist to man as lawyer. In L. Berkowitz (Ed.), *Advances in experimental social psychology*. (Vol. 13, pp. 81–138). New York: Academic Press.

Flax, J. (1996). Review of *Constructing the self, constructing America: A cultural history of psychotherapy*. *Psychoanalytic Dialogues, 6*, 847–857.

Fletcher, G. J. O., & Fincham, F. D. (1991). *Cognition in close relationships*. Hillsdale, NJ: Lawrence Erlbaum.

Foucault, M. (1973). *The order of things: An archaeology of the human sciences*. New York: Vintage Books.

Foucault, M. (1978). *The history of sexuality*. New York: Pantheon Books.

Foucault, M. (1979). *Discipline and punish: The birth of the prison*. New York: Vintage Books.

Foucault, M. (1980). *Power/knowledge: Selected interviews and other writings, 1972–1977*. New York: Pantheon Books.

Foucault, M. (1987). Questions of method: An interview with Michel Foucault. In K. Baynes, J. Bohman, & T. McCarthy (Eds.), *After philosophy: End or transformation?* (pp. 100–117). Cambridge, MA: MIT Press.

Fox, D., & Prilleltensky, I. (Eds.). (1997). *Critical psychology: An introduction*. Thousand Oaks, CA: Sage.

Frank, J. D. (1961). *Persuasion and healing: A comparative study of psychotherapy*. Baltimore: Johns Hopkins University Press.

Frank, J. D. (1973). *Persuasion and healing: A comparative study of psychotherapy* (Rev. ed.). Baltimore: Johns Hopkins University Press.

Frank, J. D., & Frank, J. B. (1991). *Persuasion and healing: A comparative study of psychotherapy* (3rd ed.). Baltimore: Johns Hopkins University Press.

Fraser, N. (1989). *Unruly practices: Power, discourse, and gender in contemporary social theory*. Minneapolis, MN: University of Minnesota Press.

Freedman, J., & Combs, G. (1996). *Narrative therapy: The social construction of preferred realities*. New York: Norton.

Freeman, A., Pretzer, J., Fleming, B., & Simon, K. M. (1990). *Clinical applications of cognitive therapy*. New York: Plenum.

Freeman, M. (1993). *Rewriting the self: History, memory, narrative*. New York: Routledge and Kegan Paul.

Freud, S. (1958). Recommendations to physicians practicing psycho-analysis. In J. Strachey (Ed. and Trans.), *The standard edition of the complete psychological works of Sigmund Freud* (Vol. 12, pp. 109–120). London: Hogarth Press. (Original work published 1912).

Friman, P. C., Allen, K. D., Kerwin, M. L. E., & Larzelere, R. (1993). Changes in modern psychology: A citation analysis of the Kuhnian displacement thesis. *American Psychologist, 48,* 658–664.

Furman, B., & Ahola, T. (1994). Solution talk: The solution-oriented way of talking about problems. In M. F. Hoyt (Ed.), *Constructive therapies* (pp. 41–66). New York: Guilford.

Gadamer, H.-G. (1975). *Truth and method*. New York: Seabury Press.

Gangaji (Speaker). (1994, July 18). *Satsang with Gangaji: Interviews with therapists*. [Cassette Recording]. (Available from Satsang Foundation and Press, 4855 Riverbend Road, Boulder, CO 80301).

Garfield, S. L. (1980). *Psychotherapy: An eclectic approach*. New York: Wiley.

Garfield, S. L. (1992). Eclectic psychotherapy: A common factors approach. In J. C. Norcross & M. R. Goldfried (Eds.), *Handbook of psychotherapy integration* (pp. 169–201). New York: Basic Books.

Garfield, S. L. (1998). Some comments on empirically supported treatments. *Journal of Consulting and Clinical Psychology, 66,* 121–125.

Garfield, S. L., & Bergin, A. E. (1994). Introduction and historical overview. In A. E. Bergin & S. L. Garfield (Eds.), *Handbook of psychotherapy and behavior change* (4th ed., pp. 3–18). New York: Wiley.

Garfield, S. L., & Kurtz, R. (1977). A study of eclectic views. *Journal of Consulting and Clinical Psychology, 45,* 78–83.

Geha, R. (1993). Transferred fictions. *Psychoanalytic Dialogues, 3,* 209–244.

Gergen, K. J. (1985). The social constructionist movement in modern psychology. *American Psychologist, 40,* 266–275.

Gergen, K. J. (1991). *The saturated self: Dilemmas of identity in contemporary life.* New York: Basic Books.

Gergen, K. J. (1993). Foreword. In S. Friedman (Ed.), *The new language of change: Constructive collaboration in psychotherapy* (pp. ix–xi). New York: Guilford.

Gergen, K. J. (1994). Exploring the postmodern: Perils or potentials? *American Psychologist, 49,* 412–416.

Gergen, K. J., & Kaye, J. (1992). Beyond narrative in the negotiation of therapeutic meaning. In S. McNamee & K. J. Gergen (Eds.), *Therapy as social construction* (pp. 166–185). Thousand Oaks, CA: Sage.

Gholson, B., & Barker, P. (1985). Kuhn, Lakatos, and Laudan: Applications in the history of physics and psychology. *American Psychologist, 40,* 755–769.

Gilford, P. (1996, August). *The normalizing effects of managed care on therapists and patients.* Paper presented at the annual meeting of the American Psychological Association, Toronto, Canada.

Gilligan, C. (1982). *In a different voice: Psychological theory and women's development.* Cambridge, MA: Harvard University Press.

Giorgi, A. (1970). *Psychology as a human science: A phenomenologically based approach.* New York: Harper and Row.

Glass, C. R., & Arnkoff, D. B. (1996). Psychotherapy integration and empirically validated treatments: Introduction to the special series. *Journal of Psychotherapy Integration, 6,* 183–189.

Godman, D. (Ed.). (1985). *Be as you are: The teachings of Sri Ramana Maharshi.* London: Arkana.

Goffman, E. (1961). *Asylums.* New York: Doubleday.

Gold, J. R. (1993). The sociohistorical context of psychotherapy integration. In G. Stricker & J. R. Gold (Eds.), *Comprehensive handbook of psychotherapy integration* (pp. 3–8). New York: Plenum.

Gold, J. R. (1995). Knowing and not knowing: Commentary on the roots of psychotherapeutic failure. *Journal of Psychotherapy Integration, 5,* 167–170.

Goldfried, M. R., & Wolfe, B. E. (1996). Psychotherapy practice and research: Repairing a strained alliance. *American Psychologist, 51,* 1007–1016.

Gonçalves, Ó. F. (1995). Hermeneutics, constructivism, and cognitive-behavioral therapies: From the object to the project. In R. A. Neimeyer & M. J. Mahoney (Eds.), *Constructivism in psychotherapy* (pp. 195–230). Washington, DC: American Psychological Association.

Greenberg, L., & Pascual-Leone, J. (1995). A dialectical constructivist approach to experiential change. In R. A. Neimeyer & M. J. Mahoney (Eds.), *Constructivism in psychotherapy* (pp. 169–191). Washington, DC: American Psychological Association.

Greenson, R. R. (1967). *The technique and practice of psychoanalysis.* New York: International Universities Press.

Groth-Marnat, G. (1990). *Handbook of psychological assessment* (2nd ed.). New York: Wiley.

Grünbaum, A. (1984). *The foundations of psychoanalysis: A philosophical critique.* Berkeley, CA: University of California Press.

Gutting, G. (1980). Introduction. In G. Gutting (Ed.), *Paradigms and revolutions: Appraisals and applications of Thomas Kuhn's philosophy of science* (pp. 1–21). Notre Dame, IN: University of Notre Dame Press.

Haber, H. F. (1994). *Beyond postmodern politics: Lyotard, Rorty, Foucault.* New York: Routledge and Kegan Paul.

Habermas, J. (1977). A review of Gadamer's *Truth and method.* In F. R. Dallmayr & T. A. McCarthy (Eds.), *Understanding and social inquiry* (pp. 335–363). Notre Dame, IN: University of Notre Dame Press.

Hall, C. S., & Lindzey, G. (1978). *Theories of personality* (3rd ed.). New York: Wiley.

Hall, D. L. (1994). *Richard Rorty: Prophet and poet of the new pragmatism.* Albany, NY: State University of New York Press.

Halleck, S. L. (1968). Psychiatry and the status quo: A political analysis of psychiatric practice. *Archives of General Psychiatry, 19,* 257–265.

Hampson, S. E. (1988). *The construction of personality: An introduction* (2nd ed.). New York: Routledge and Kegan Paul.

Hanna, F. J. (1994). A dialectic of experience: A radical empiricist approach to conflicting theories in psychotherapy. *Psychotherapy, 31,* 124–136.

Hanna, F. J., & Ottens, A. J. (1995). The role of wisdom in psychotherapy. *Journal of Psychotherapy Integration, 5,* 195–219.

Hanna, F. J., & Shank, G. (1995). The specter of metaphysics in counseling research and practice: The qualitative challenge. *Journal of Counseling and Development, 74,* 53–59.

Hanson, N. R. (1961). *Patterns of discovery: An inquiry into the conceptual foundations of science.* Cambridge: Cambridge University Press.

Harper, R. A. (1959). *Psychoanalysis and psychotherapy: 36 systems.* Englewood Cliffs, NJ: Prentice-Hall.

Harris, J. F. (1992). *Against relativism: A philosophical defense of method.* LaSalle, IL: Open Court.

Heidegger, M. (1966). *Discourse on thinking* (J. M. Anderson & E. H. Freund, Trans.). New York: Harper and Row.

Held, B. S. (1995). *Back to reality: A critique of postmodern theory in psychotherapy.* New York: Norton.

Henry, W. P., Strupp, H. H., Schacht, T. E., & Gaston, L. (1994). Psychodynamic approaches. In A. E. Bergin & S. L. Garfield (Eds.), *Handbook of psychotherapy and behavior change* (4th ed., pp. 467–508). New York: Wiley.

Herink, R. (Ed.) (1980). *The psychotherapy handbook: The A to Z guide to more than 250 different therapies in use today.* New York: New American Library.

Hermans, H. J. M., Kempen, H. J. G., & van Loon, R. J. P. (1992). The dialogical self: Beyond individualism and rationalism. *American Psychologist, 47,* 23–33.

Herrnstein, R. J., & Murray, C. (1994). *The bell curve: Intelligence and class structure in American life.* New York: Free Press.

Hixon, L. (1978). *Coming home: The experience of enlightenment in sacred traditions.* Burdett, NY: Larson.

Hoffman, I. Z. (1994). Dialectical thinking and therapeutic action in the psychoanalytic process. *Psychoanalytic Quarterly, LXIII,* 187–218.

Hoffman-Hennessy, L., & Davis, J. (1993). Tekka with feathers: Talking about talking (about suicide). In S. Friedman (Ed.), *The new language of change: Constructive collaboration in psychotherapy* (pp. 345–373). New York: Guilford.

Holzman, P. S. (1985). Psychoanalysis: Is therapy destroying the science? *Journal of the American Psychoanalytic Association, 27,* 725–770.

Honderich, T. (Ed.). (1995). *The Oxford companion to philosophy.* New York: Oxford University Press.

Hoshmand, L. T. (1994). *Orientation to inquiry in a reflective professional psychology.* Albany, NY: State University of New York Press.

Hoshmand, L. T., & Polkinghorne, D. E. (1992). Redefining the science-practice relationship and professional training. *American Psychologist, 47,* 55–66.

Howard, G. S. (1984). A modest proposal for a revision of strategies for counseling research. *Journal of Counseling Psychology, 31,* 430–441.

Howard, G. S. (1991). Culture tales: A narrative approach to thinking, cross-cultural psychology, and psychotherapy. *American Psychologist, 46,* 187–197.

Howard, G. S. (1993a). I think I can! I think I can! Reconsidering the place for practice methodologies in psychological research. *Professional Psychology: Research and Practice, 24,* 237–244.

Howard, G. S. (1993b). Is the scientific community ready to experiment with practice methodologies? *Professional Psychology: Research and Practice, 24,* 254–255.

Hoy, D. (1990). Jacques Derrida. In Q. Skinner (Ed.), *The return of grand theory in the human sciences* (pp. 41–64). Cambridge: Canto (Cambridge University Press).

Hoyt, M. F. (1994a). Introduction: Competency-based future-oriented therapy. In M. F. Hoyt (Ed.), *Constructive therapies* (pp. 1–10). New York: Guilford.

Hoyt, M. F. (Ed.). (1994b). *Constructive therapies.* New York: Guilford.

Hoyt, M. F. (1994c). On the importance of keeping it simple and taking the patient seriously: A conversation with Steve de Shazer and John Weakland. In M. F. Hoyt (Ed.), *Constructive therapies* (pp. 11–40). New York: Guilford.

Hoyt, M. F. (1996). Postmodernism, the relational self, constructive therapies, and beyond: A conversation with Kenneth Gergen. In M. F. Hoyt (Ed.), *Constructive therapies* (Vol. 2, pp. 347–368). New York: Guilford.

Hudson, L. (1972). *The cult of the fact: A psychologist's autobiographical critique of his discipline*. New York: Harper Torchbooks.

Imber, S. D., Pilkonis, P. A., Sotsky, S. M., Elkin, I., Watkins, J. T., Collins, J. F., Shea, M. T., Leber, W. R., & Glass, D. R. (1990). Mode-specific effects among three treatments for depression. *Journal of Consulting and Clinical Psychology, 58*, 352–359.

Ingleby, D. (1972). Ideology and the human sciences: Some comments on the role of reification in psychology and psychiatry. In T. Pateman (Ed.), *Counter course: A handbook for course criticism* (pp. 51–81). Middlesex, England: Penguin Books.

Jensen, J. P., Bergin, A. E., & Greaves, D. W. (1990). The meaning of eclecticism: New survey and analysis of components. *Professional Psychology: Research and Practice, 21*, 124–130.

Jones, S. L. (1994). A constructive relationship for religion with the science and profession of psychology: Perhaps the boldest model yet. *American Psychologist, 49*, 184–199.

Kahn, M. (1991). *Between therapist and client: The new relationship*. New York: Freeman.

Kaminstein, D. S. (1987). Toward a dialectical metatheory for psychotherapy. *Journal of Contemporary Psychotherapy, 17*, 87–101.

Karasu, T. B. (1992). The worst of times, the best of times: Psychotherapy in the 1990s. *Journal of Psychotherapy Practice and Research, 1*, 2–15.

Karasu, T. B. (1996). *Deconstruction of psychotherapy*. Northvale, NJ: Jason Aronson.

Katz, S. (1995). How to speak and write postmodern. In W. T. Anderson (Ed.), *The truth about the truth: De-confusing and re-constructing the postmodern world* (pp. 92–95). New York: Tarcher/Putnam.

Kazdin, A. E. (1996a). Validated treatments: Multiple perspectives and issues—Introduction to the series. *Clinical Psychology: Science and Practice, 3*, 216–217.

Kazdin, A. E. (1996b). Foreword. In A. Roth & P. Fonagy (Eds.), *What works for whom? A critical review of psychotherapy research* (pp. v–vii). New York: Guilford.

Kelly, G. A. (1955). *The psychology of personal constructs* (2 vols.). New York: Norton.

Kelly, G. A. (1963). *A theory of personality: The psychology of personal constructs*. New York: Norton Library.

Kelly, G. A. (1958a/1969). Man's construction of his alternatives. In B. Maher (Ed.), *Clinical psychology and personality: The selected papers of George Kelly* (pp. 66–93). New York: Wiley.

Kelly. G. A. (1958b/1969). Personal construct theory and the psychotherapeutic interview. In B. Maher (Ed.), *Clinical psychology and personality: The selected papers of George Kelly* (pp. 224–264). New York: Wiley.

Kelly, G. A. (1961/1969). A mathematical approach to psychology. In B. Maher (Ed.), *Clinical psychology and personality: The selected papers of George Kelly* (pp. 94–113). New York: Wiley.

Kelly, G. A. (1965 / 1969). The psychotherapeutic relationship. In B. Maher (Ed.), *Clinical psychology and personality: The selected papers of George Kelly* (pp. 216–223). New York: Wiley.

Kendall, P. C. (1998). Empirically supported psychological therapies. *Journal of Consulting and Clinical Psychology, 66,* 3–6.

Kiesler, D. J. (1966). Some myths of psychotherapy research and the search for a paradigm. *Psychological Bulletin, 65,* 110–136.

Kiesler, D. J. (1994). Standardization of intervention: The tie that binds psychotherapy research and practice. In P. F. Talley, H. H. Strupp, & S. F. Butler (Eds.), *Psychotherapy research and practice: Bridging the gap* (pp. 143–153). New York: Basic Books.

Kiev, A. (Ed.). (1964). *Magic, faith, and healing: Studies in primitive psychiatry today.* New York: Free Press.

Kitzinger, C. (1997). Lesbian and gay psychology: A critical analysis. In D. Fox & I. Prilleltensky (Eds.), *Critical psychology: An introduction* (pp. 202–216). Thousand Oaks, CA: Sage.

Koch, S. (Ed.). (1959–1963). *Psychology: A study of a science.* (Vols. 1–6). New York: McGraw-Hill.

Koch, S. (1959). Epilogue. In S. Koch (Ed.), *Psychology: A study of a science* (Vol. 3, pp. 729–788). New York: McGraw-Hill.

Koch, S. (1969, Sept.). Psychology cannot be a coherent science. *Psychology Today, 3,* 14, 64, 66–68.

Koch, S. (1985). The nature and limits of psychological knowledge: Lessons of a century qua "science." In S. Koch & D. E. Leary (Eds.), *A century of psychology as science* (pp. 75–97). New York: McGraw-Hill.

Koch, S. (1993). "Psychology" or "the psychological studies"? *American Psychologist, 48,* 902–904.

Kuhn, T. S. (1970a). *The structure of scientific revolutions* (2nd ed.). Chicago: University of Chicago Press.

Kuhn, T. S. (1970b). Logic of discovery or psychology of research? In I. Lakatos & A. Musgrave (Eds.), *Criticism and the growth of knowledge* (pp. 1–23). Cambridge: Cambridge University Press.

Kuhn, T. S. (1970c). Reflections on my critics. In I. Lakatos and A. Musgrave (Eds.), *Criticism and the growth of knowledge* (pp. 231–278). Cambridge: Cambridge University Press.

Kuhn, T. S. (1977). *The essential tension: Selected studies in scientific tradition and change.* Chicago: University of Chicago Press.

Kvale, S. (1992a). Introduction: From the archaeology of the psyche to the architecture of cultural landscapes. In S. Kvale (Ed.), *Psychology and postmodernism* (pp. 1–16). Thousand Oaks, CA: Sage.

Kvale, S. (1992b). Postmodern psychology: A contradiction in terms? In S. Kvale (Ed.), *Psychology and postmodernism* (pp. 31–57). Thousand Oaks, CA: Sage.

Laing, R. D. (1967). *The politics of experience.* New York: Pantheon Books.

Laing, R. D. (1969). *The divided self.* New York: Pantheon Books.

Laing, R. D. (l972). *The politics of the family and other essays*. New York: Vintage Books.

Lakatos, I. (1970). Falsification and the methodology of scientific research programmes. In I. Lakatos & A. Musgrave (Eds.), *Criticism and the growth of knowledge* (pp. 91–196). Cambridge: Cambridge University Press.

Lakatos, I., & Musgrave, A. (Eds.). (1970). *Criticism and the growth of knowledge*. Cambridge: Cambridge University Press.

Lakoff, G., & Johnson, M. (1980). *Metaphors we live by*. Chicago: University of Chicago Press.

Lambert, M. J. (1992). Psychotherapy outcome research: Implications for integrative and eclectic therapists. In J. C. Norcross & M. R. Goldfried (Eds.), *Handbook of psychotherapy integration* (pp. 94–129). New York: Basic Books.

Lambert, M. J., & Bergin, A. E. (1994). The effectiveness of psychotherapy. In A. E. Bergin & S. L. Garfield (Eds.), *Handbook of psychotherapy and behavior change* (4th ed., pp. 143–189). New York: Wiley.

Lather, P. (1992). Postmodernism and the human sciences. In S. Kvale (Ed.), *Psychology and postmodernism* (pp. 88–109). Thousand Oaks, CA: Sage.

Lawson, H. (1989). Stories about stories. In H. Lawson & L. Appignanesi (Eds.), *Dismantling truth: Reality in the post-modern world* (pp. xi–xxviii). New York: St. Martin's Press.

Lawson, H., & Appignanesi, L. (Eds.). (1989). *Dismantling truth: Reality in the post-modern world*. New York: St. Martin's Press.

Lazarus, A. A. (1971). *Behavior therapy and beyond*. New York: McGraw-Hill.

Lazarus, A. A. (1990). Foreword. In N. Saltzman & J. C. Norcross (Eds.), *Therapy wars: Contention and convergence in differing clinical approaches* (pp. xiii–xiv). San Francisco: Jossey-Bass.

Lazarus, A. A. (1992). Multimodal therapy: Technical eclecticism with minimal integration. In J. C. Norcross & M. R. Goldfried (Eds.), *Handbook of psychotherapy integration* (pp. 231–263). New York: Basic Books.

Lazarus, A. A. (1993). Theory, subjectivity, and bias: Can there be a future? *Psychotherapy, 30*, 674–677.

Lazarus, A. A., & Messer, S. B. (1991). Does chaos prevail? An exchange on technical eclecticism and assimilative integration. *Journal of Psychotherapy Integration, 1*, 143–158.

Leitenberg, H. (1976). Behavioral approaches to treatment of neuroses. In H. Leitenberg (Ed.), *Handbook of behavior modification and behavior therapy* (pp. 124–167). Englewood Cliffs, NJ: Prentice-Hall.

Lifton, R. J. (1993). *The protean self: Human resilience in an age of fragmentation*. New York: Basic Books.

London, P. (1986). *The modes and morals of psychotherapy* (2nd ed.). Washington, DC: Hemisphere.

Luborsky, L., Singer, B., & Luborsky, L. (1975). Comparative studies of psychotherapy: Is it true that "everybody has won and all must have prizes"? *Archives of General Psychiatry, 32*, 995–1008.

Lukoff, D., Turner, R., & Lu, F. G. (1993). Transpersonal psychology research review: Psychospiritual dimensions of healing. *Journal of Transpersonal Psychology, 25,* 11–28.

Lyddon, W. J. (1989). Personal epistemology and preference for counseling. *Journal of Counseling Psychology, 36,* 423–429.

Lyddon, W. J. (1995). Cognitive therapy and theories of knowing: A social constructionist view. *Journal of Counseling and Development, 73,* 579–585.

Lyotard, J.-F. (1984). *The postmodern condition: A report on knowledge.* Minneapolis, MN: University of Minnesota Press.

MacDonald, A. P. (1976). Homophobia: Its roots and meanings. *Homosexual Counseling Journal, 3,* 23–33.

Madison, G. B. (1991). Beyond seriousness and frivolity: A Gadamerian response to deconstruction. In H. J. Silverman (Ed.), *Gadamer and hermeneutics (Continental Philosophy—IV)* (pp. 119–135). New York: Routledge and Kegan Paul.

Mahalik, J. R. (1990). Systematic eclectic models. *The Counseling Psychologist, 18,* 655–679.

Maher, B. (Ed.). (1969). *Clinical psychology and personality: The selected papers of George Kelly.* New York: Wiley.

Mahoney, M. J. (1988a). The cognitive sciences and psychotherapy: Patterns in a developing relationship. In K. S. Dobson (Ed.), *The handbook of cognitive-behavioral therapies* (pp. 357–386). New York: Guilford.

Mahoney, M. J. (1988b). Constructive metatheory: II. Implications for psychotherapy. *International Journal of Personal Construct Psychology, 1,* 299–315.

Mahoney, M. J. (1991). *Human change processes: The scientific foundations of psychotherapy.* New York: Basic Books.

Mahoney, M. J. (1995a). Continuing evolution of the cognitive sciences and psychotherapies. In R. A. Neimeyer & M. J. Mahoney (Eds.), *Constructivism in psychotherapy* (pp. 39–67). Washington, DC: American Psychological Association.

Mahoney, M. J. (1995b). The psychological demands of being a constructive psychotherapist. In R. A. Neimeyer & M. J. Mahoney (Eds.), *Constructivism in psychotherapy* (pp. 385–399). Washington, DC: American Psychological Association.

Mahoney, M. J. (1996). Connected knowing in constructive psychotherapy. In N. R. Goldberger, J. M. Tarule, B. M. Clinchy, & M. F. Belenky (Eds.), *Knowledge, difference, and power: Essays inspired by Women's ways of knowing* (pp. 126–147). New York: Basic Books.

Marx, A. J., Test, M. A., & Stein, L. I. (1973). Extrohospital management of severe mental illness: Feasibility and effects of social functioning. *Archives of General Psychiatry, 29,* 505–511.

Maslow, A. H. (1968). *Toward a psychology of being* (2nd ed.). New York: Van Nostrand Reinhold.

Masterman, M. (1970). The nature of a paradigm. In I. Lakatos & A. Musgrave (Eds.), *Criticism and the growth of knowledge* (pp. 59–89). Cambridge: Cambridge University Press.

Masterson, J. F. (1988). *The search for the real self: Unmasking the personality disorders of our age.* New York: Free Press.

McNamee, S., & Gergen, K. J. (Eds.). (1992). *Therapy as social construction.* Thousand Oaks, CA: Sage.

McWhirter, E. H. (1998). Comment: Emancipatory communitarian psychology. *American Psychologist, 53,* 322–323.

Meichenbaum, D. (1993). Changing conceptions of cognitive behavior modification: Retrospect and prospect. *Journal of Consulting and Clinical Psychology, 61,* 202–204.

Messer, S. B. (1992). A critical examination of belief structures in integrative and eclectic psychotherapy. In J. C. Norcross & M. R. Goldfried (Eds.), *Handbook of psychotherapy integration* (pp. 130–165). New York: Basic Books.

Milan, M. A., Montgomery, R. W., & Rogers, E. C. (1994). Theoretical orientation revolution in clinical psychology: Fact or fiction? *Professional Psychology: Research and Practice, 25,* 398–402.

Miller, R. B. (1983). A call to armchairs. *Psychotherapy: Theory, Research, and Practice, 20,* 208–219.

Miller, R. B. (Ed.). (1992). *The restoration of dialogue: Readings in the philosophy of clinical psychology.* Washington, DC: American Psychological Association.

Mills, C. W. (1959). *The sociological imagination.* New York: Oxford University Press.

Mills, J. C., & Crowley, R. J. (1986). *Therapeutic metaphors for children and the child within.* New York: Brunner / Mazel.

Mischel, W. (1968). *Personality and assessment.* New York: Wiley.

Misra, G. (1993). Psychology from a constructionist perspective: An interview with Kenneth J. Gergen. *New Ideas in Psychology, 11,* 399–414.

Mitchell, S. A. (1988). *Relational concepts in psychoanalysis: An integration.* Cambridge, MA: Harvard University Press.

Mitchell, S. A. (1993). *Hope and dread in psychoanalysis.* New York: Basic Books.

Morrow-Bradley, C., & Elliott, R. (1986). Utilization of psychotherapy research by practicing psychotherapists. *American Psychologist, 41,* 188–197.

Mueller, G. E. (1953). *Dialectic: A way into and within philosophy.* New York: Bookman.

Natterson, J. M., & Friedman, R. J. (1995). *A primer of clinical intersubjectivity.* Northvale, NJ: Jason Aronson.

Neimeyer, G. J., & Morton, R. J. (1997). Personal epistemologies and preferences for rationalist versus constructivist psychotherapies. *Journal of Constructivist Psychology, 10,* 109–123.

Neimeyer, R. A. (1993). Constructivism and the cognitive psychotherapies: Some conceptual and strategic contrasts. *Journal of Cognitive Psychotherapy: An International Quarterly, 7,* 159–171.

Neimeyer, R. A. (1995). Constructivist psychotherapies: Features, foundations, and future directions. In R. A. Neimeyer & M. J. Mahoney (Eds.), *Constructivism in psychotherapy* (pp. 11–38). Washington, DC: American Psychological Association.

Neimeyer, R. A. (1996). Process interventions for the constructivist psychotherapist. In H. Rosen & K. T. Kuehlwein (Eds.), *Constructing realities: Meaning-making perspectives for psychotherapists* (pp. 371–411). San Francisco: Jossey-Bass.

Neimeyer, R. A. (1997). Problems and prospects in constructivist psychotherapy. *Journal of Constructivist Psychology, 10,* 51–74.

Neimeyer, R. A., & Mahoney, M. J. (Eds.). (1995). *Constructivism in psychotherapy.* Washington, DC: American Psychological Association.

Neisser, U. (1967). *Cognitive psychology.* Englewood Cliffs, NJ: Prentice-Hall.

Newton-Smith, W. H. (1989). Rationality, truth, and the new fuzzies. In H. Lawson & L. Appignanesi (Eds.), *Dismantling truth: Reality in the post-modern world* (pp. 23–42). New York: St. Martin's Press.

Norcross, J. C. (1995). Dispelling the Dodo bird verdict and the exclusivity myth in psychotherapy. *Psychotherapy, 32,* 500–504.

Norcross, J. C., & Newman, C. F. (1992). Psychotherapy integration: Setting the context. In J. C. Norcross & M. R. Goldfried (Eds.), *Handbook of psychotherapy integration* (pp. 3–45). New York: Basic Books.

Norcross, J. C., & Prochaska, J. O. (1988). A study of eclectic (and integrative) views revisited. *Professional Psychology: Research and Practice, 19,* 170–174.

Norcross, J. C., Prochaska, J. O., & Farber, J. A. (1993). Psychologists conducting psychotherapy: New findings and historical comparisons on the Psychotherapy Division membership. *Psychotherapy, 30,* 692–697.

Novak, M. (1971). *The experience of nothingness.* New York: Harper Colophon.

O'Donohue, W. (1989). The (even) bolder model: The clinical psychologist as metaphysician-scientist-practitioner. *American Psychologist, 44,* 1460–1468.

O'Donohue, W. (1993). The spell of Kuhn on psychology: An exegetical elixir. *Philosophical Psychology, 6,* 267–287.

Ofshe, R., & Watters, E. (1994). *Making monsters: False memories, psychotherapy, and sexual hysteria.* Berkeley, CA: University of California Press.

Ogden, T. H. (1994). *Subjects of analysis.* Northvale, NJ: Jason Aronson.

O'Hanlon, B., & Wilk, J. (1987). *Shifting contexts; The generation of effective psychotherapy.* New York: Guilford.

Olds, L. E. (1992). *Metaphors of interrelatedness: Toward a systems theory of psychology.* Albany, NY: State University of New York Press.

Oliver, W. D., & Landfield, A. W. (1962). Reflexivity: An unfaced issue of psychology. *Journal of Individual Psychology, 18,* 114–124.

Omer, H., & London, P. (1988). Metamorphosis in psychotherapy: End of the systems' era. *Psychotherapy, 25,* 171–180.

Omer, H., & Strenger, C. (1992). The pluralist revolution: From the one true meaning to an infinity of constructed ones. *Psychotherapy, 29,* 253–261.

Orange, D. M. (1995). *Emotional understanding: Studies in psychoanalytic epistemology.* New York: Guilford.

Outhwaite, W. (1990). Hans-Georg Gadamer. In Q. Skinner (Ed.), *The return of grand theory in the human sciences* (pp. 21–39). Cambridge: Canto (Cambridge University Press).

Parker, I. (1997). Discursive psychology. In D. Fox & I. Prilleltensky (Eds.), *Critical psychology: An introduction* (pp. 284–298). Thousand Oaks, CA: Sage.

Parker, I., Georgaca, E., Harper, D., McLaughlin, T., & Stowell-Smith, M. (1995). *Deconstructing psychopathology.* Thousand Oaks, CA: Sage.

Parloff, M. B. (1976, February 21). Shopping for the right therapy. *Saturday Review,* 14–20.

Parry, A., & Doan, R. E. (1994). *Story re-visions: Narrative therapy in the postmodern world.* New York: Guilford.

Persons, J. B., Gross, J. J., Etkin, M. S., & Madan, S. K. (1996). Psychodynamic therapists' reservations about cognitive-behavioral therapy: Implications for training and practice. *Journal of Psychotherapy Practice and Research, 5,* 202–212.

Persons, J. B., & Silberschatz, G. (1998). Are results of randomized controlled trials useful to psychotherapists? *Journal of Consulting and Clinical Psychology, 66,* 126–135.

Peterson, D. R., & Peterson, R. L. (1997). Ways of knowing in a profession: Toward an epistemology for the education of professional psychologists. In D. R. Peterson (Ed.), *Educating professional psychologists: History and guiding conception* (pp. 191–228). Washington, DC: American Psychological Association.

Pion, G. M., Cordray, D. S., & Anderson, S. (1993). Drawing the line between conjecture and evidence about the use and benefit of "practice" methodologies. *Professional Psychology: Research and Practice, 24,* 245–249.

Polanyi, M. (1964). *Personal knowledge: Towards a post-critical philosophy.* New York: Harper Torchbooks.

Polanyi, M. (1967). *The tacit dimension.* Garden City, NY: Anchor Books.

Polkinghorne, D. (1983). *Methodology for the human sciences: Systems of inquiry.* Albany, NY: State University of New York Press.

Polkinghorne, D. E. (1984). Further extensions of methodological diversity for counseling psychology. *Journal of Counseling Psychology, 31,* 416–429.

Polkinghorne, D. E. (1988). *Narrative knowing and the human sciences.* Albany, NY: State University of New York Press.

Polkinghorne, D. E. (1992). Postmodern epistemology of practice. In S. Kvale (Ed.), *Psychology and postmodernism* (pp. 146–165). Thousand Oaks, CA: Sage.

Popper, K. R. (1968). *Conjectures and refutations: The growth of scientific knowledge.* New York: Harper Torchbooks.

Popper, K. R. (1970). Normal science and its dangers. In I. Lakatos & A. Musgrave (Eds.), *Criticism and the growth of knowledge* (pp. 51–58). Cambridge: Cambridge University Press.

Popper, K. (1976). *Unended quest: An intellectual autobiography* (Rev. ed.). Glasgow: Fontana / Collins.

Pribram, K. H. (1990). From metaphors to models: The use of analogy in neuropsychology. In D. E. Leary (Ed.), *Metaphors in the history of psychology* (pp. 79–103). New York: Cambridge University Press.

Price, R. H. (1978). *Abnormal behavior: Perspectives in conflict* (2nd ed.). New York: Holt, Rinehart, and Winston.

Prilleltensky, I. (1989). Psychology and the status quo. *American Psychologist, 44,* 795–802.

Prilleltensky, I. (1997). Values, assumptions, and practices: Assessing the moral implications of psychological discourse and action. *American Psychologist, 52,* 517–535.

Prochaska, J. O., & Norcross, J. C. (1983). Contemporary psychotherapists: A national survey of characteristics, practices, orientations, and attitudes. *Psychotherapy: Theory, Research, and Practice, 20,* 161–173.

Prochaska, J. O., & Norcross, J. C. (1994). *Systems of psychotherapy: A transtheoretical analysis* (3rd ed.). Pacific Grove, CA: Brooks/Cole.

Protter, B. (1988). Ways of knowing in psychoanalysis: Some epistemic considerations for an autonomous theory of psychoanalytic praxis. *Contemporary Psychoanalysis, 24,* 498–526.

Protter, B. (1996). Classical, modern, and postmodern psychoanalysis: Epistemic transformations. *Psychoanalytic Dialogues, 6,* 533–562.

Psychiatrist faces penalty over memory therapy. (1998, August 14). *San Francisco Chronicle,* p. A4.

Rabten, G. (1983). *Echoes of voidness* (S. Batchelor, Ed./Trans.). London: Wisdom Publications.

Rainer, J. P. (1996). Introduction to the special issue on psychotherapy outcomes. *Psychotherapy, 33,* 159.

Rappaport, J., & Stewart, E. (1997). A critical look at critical psychology: Elaborating the questions. In D. Fox & I. Prilleltensky (Eds.), *Critical psychology: An introduction* (pp. 301–317). Thousand Oaks, CA: Sage.

Reese, H. W. (1982). A comment on the meanings of "dialectics." *Human Development, 25,* 423–429.

Reich, W. (1933a/1949). *Character analysis.* New York: Noonday.

Reich, W. (1933b/1973). *The mass psychology of fascism.* New York: Farrar, Straus, and Giroux.

Reich, W. (1948/1973). *The cancer biopathy.* New York: Farrar, Straus, and Giroux.

Rescher, N. (1995). *Pluralism: Against the demand for consensus.* Oxford: Clarendon.

Richardson, F. C. (1998). Beyond scientism and postmodernism? *Journal of Theoretical and Philosophical Psychology, 18,* 33–45.

Richardson, F. C., & Fowers, B. J. (1994, August). *Beyond scientism and constructionism.* Paper presented at the annual meeting of the American Psychological Association, Los Angeles, CA.

Richer, P. (1992). An introduction to deconstructionist psychology. In S. Kvale (Ed.), *Psychology and postmodernism* (pp. 110–118). Thousand Oaks, CA: Sage.

Riegel, K. F. (1979). *Foundations of dialectical psychology*. New York: Academic Press.

Robins, R. W., & Craik, K. H. (1994). Comment: A more appropriate test of the Kuhnian displacement thesis. *American Psychologist, 49*, 815–816.

Rogers, C. R. (1951). *Client-centered therapy*. Boston: Houghton Mifflin.

Rogers, C. R. (1959). A theory of therapy, personality, and interpersonal relationships, as developed in the client-centered framework. In S. Koch (Ed.), *Psychology: A study of a science* (Vol. 3, pp. 184–256). New York: McGraw Hill.

Rorty, R. (1979). *Philosophy and the mirror of nature*. Princeton, NJ: Princeton University Press.

Rorty, R. (1987). Pragmatism and philosophy. In K. Baynes, J. Bohman, & T. McCarthy (Eds.), *After philosophy: End or transformation?* (pp. 26–66). Cambridge, MA: MIT Press.

Rorty, R. (1989a). *Contingency, irony, and solidarity*. New York: Cambridge University Press.

Rorty, R. (1989b). Science as solidarity. In H. Lawson & L. Appignanesi (Eds.), *Dismantling truth: Reality in the post-modern world* (pp. 6–22). New York: St. Martin's Press.

Rorty, R. (1991). *Objectivity, relativism, and truth: Philosophical Papers* (Vol. 1). New York: Cambridge University Press.

Rosch, E. (Speaker). (1991, August). *Outside and inside the self: The convergence of cognitive science and the mindfulness tradition*. (Cassette Recording No. 91–047). Washington, DC: American Psychological Association.

Rosen, H. (1996). Meaning-making narratives: Foundations for constructivist and social constructionist psychotherapies. In H. Rosen & K. T. Kuehlwein (Eds.), *Constructing realities: Meaning-making perspectives for psychotherapists* (pp. 3–51). San Francisco: Jossey-Bass.

Rosenau, P. M. (1992). *Post-modernism and the social sciences: Insights, inroads, and intrusions*. Princeton, NJ: Princeton University Press.

Rosenhan, D. L. (1973). On being sane in insane places. *Science, 179*, 250–258.

Roth, A., & Fonagy, P. (Eds.). (1996). *What works for whom? A critical review of psychotherapy research*. New York: Guilford.

Roth, A., Fonagy, P., & Parry, G. (1996). Psychotherapy research, funding, and evidence-based practice. In A. Roth & P. Fonagy (Eds.), *What works for whom? A critical review of psychotherapy research* (pp. 37–56). New York: Guilford.

Royce, J. R. (1964). *The encapsulated man: An interdisciplinary essay on the search for meaning*. Princeton, NJ: Van Nostrand.

Royce, J. R., & Mos, L. P. (Eds.). (1981). *Humanistic psychology: Concepts and criticisms*. New York: Plenum.

Ruitenbeek, H. M. (Ed.). (1972). *Going crazy: The radical therapy of R. D. Laing and others*. New York: Bantam Books.

Ryan, W. (1976). *Blaming the victim* (Rev. ed.). New York: Vintage Books.

Rychlak, J. F. (1976). The multiple meanings of dialectic. In J. F. Rychlak (Ed.), *Dialectic: Humanistic rationale for behavior and development* (pp. 1–17). Basel, Switzerland: S. Karger AG.

Rychlak, J. F. (1977). *The psychology of rigorous humanism.* New York: Wiley.

Safran, J. D., & Messer, S. B. (1997). Psychotherapy integration: A postmodern critique. *Clinical Psychology: Science and Practice, 4,* 140–152.

Sass, L. A. (1992). The epic of disbelief: The postmodernist turn in contemporary psychoanalysis. In S. Kvale (Ed.), *Psychology and postmodernism* (pp. 166–182). Thousand Oaks, CA: Sage.

Schacht, T. E., & Black, D. A. (1985). Epistemological commitments of behavioral and psychoanalytic therapists. *Professional Psychology: Research and Practice, 16,* 316–323.

Scheff, T. J. (1966). *Being mentally ill: A sociological theory.* Chicago: Aldine.

Schön, D. A. (1963). *Displacement of concepts.* London: Tavistock.

Schön, D. A. (1983). *The reflective practitioner: How professionals think in action.* New York: Basic Books.

Schreiber, F. R. (1973). *Sybil.* New York: Warner.

Shapiro, D. A. (1996). "Validated" treatments and evidence-based psychological services. *Clinical Psychology: Science and Practice, 3,* 256–259.

Shoham, V., & Rohrbaugh, M. (1996). Promises and perils of empirically supported psychotherapy integration. *Journal of Psychotherapy Integration, 6,* 191–206.

Slife, B. D. (1987). Can cognitive psychology account for metacognitive functions of mind? *Journal of Mind and Behavior, 8,* 195–208.

Sloane, R. B., Staples, F. R., Cristol, A. H., Yorkston, N. J., & Whipple, K. (1975). *Psychotherapy versus behavior therapy.* Cambridge, MA: Harvard University Press.

Sluzki, C. E. (1992). Transformations: A blueprint for narrative changes in therapy. *Family Process, 31,* 217–230.

Smith, H. (1989). *Beyond the post-modern mind* (Rev. ed.). Wheaton, IL: Quest Books.

Smith, M., & Pazder, L. (1980). *Michelle remembers.* New York: Pocket Books.

Smith, M. B. (1994). Selfhood at risk: Postmodern perils and the perils of postmodernism. *American Psychologist, 49,* 405–411.

Smith, M. L., Glass, G. V., & Miller, T. I. (1980). *The benefits of psychotherapy.* Baltimore: Johns Hopkins University Press.

Soldz, S. (1996). Psychoanalysis and constructivism: Convergence in meaning-making perspectives. In H. Rosen & K. T. Kuehlwein (Eds.), *Constructing realities: Meaning-making perspectives for psychotherapists* (pp. 277–306). San Francisco: Jossey-Bass.

Spanos, N. P. (1996). *Multiple identities and false memories: A sociocognitive perspective.* Washington, DC: American Psychological Association.

Spence, D. P. (1982). *Narrative truth and historical truth: Meaning and interpretation in psychoanalysis.* New York: Norton.

Spence, D. P. (1987). *The Freudian metaphor: Toward paradigm change in psychoanalysis.* New York: Norton.

Spretnak, C. (1991). *States of grace: The recovery of meaning in the postmodern age*. San Francisco: Harper.

Stancombe, J., & White, S. (1998). Psychotherapy without foundations? Hermeneutics, discourse, and the end of certainty. *Theory & Psychology, 8,* 579–599.

Stiles, W. B., Shapiro, D. A., & Elliott, R. (1986). "Are all psychotherapies equivalent?" *American Psychologist, 41,* 165–180.

Stolorow, R. D., & Atwood, G. E. (1992). *Contexts of being: The intersubjective foundations of psychological life*. Hillsdale, NJ: Analytic Press.

Stolorow, R. D., Brandchaft, B., & Atwood, G. E. (1987). *Psychoanalytic treatment: An intersubjective approach*. Hillsdale, NJ: Analytic Press.

Stricker, G. (1996). Empirically validated treatment, psychotherapy manuals, and psychotherapy integration. *Journal of Psychotherapy Integration, 6,* 217–226.

Sue, D. W., & Sue, D. (1990). *Counseling the culturally different: Theory and practice* (2nd ed.). New York: Wiley.

Suler, J. R. (1993). *Contemporary psychoanalysis and eastern thought*. Albany, NY: State University of New York Press.

Sussman, M. B. (Ed.) (1995). *A perilous calling: The hazards of psychotherapy practice*. New York: Wiley.

Sutich, A. J. (1973). Transpersonal therapy. *Journal of Transpersonal Psychology, 5,* 1–6.

Sweet, A. A., Giles, T. R., & Young, R. R. (1987). Three theoretical perspectives on anxiety: A comparison of theory and outcome. In L. Michelson & L. M. Ascher (Eds.), *Anxiety and stress disorders: Cognitive-behavioral assessment and treatment* (pp. 39–61), New York: Guilford.

Szasz, T. S. (1960). The myth of mental illness. *American Psychologist, 15,* 113–118.

Szasz, T. S. (1970). *The manufacture of madness: A comparative study of the Inquisition and the mental health movement*. New York: Harper and Row.

Talley, P. F., Strupp, H. H., & Butler, S. F. (Eds.). (1994). *Psychotherapy research and practice: Bridging the gap*. New York: Basic Books.

Tansey, M. J., & Burke, W. F. (1989). *Understanding countertransference: From projective identification to empathy*. Hillsdale, NJ: Analytic Press.

Tart, C. T. (1975). *States of consciousness*. New York: E. P. Dutton.

Task Force on Promotion and Dissemination of Psychological Procedures (1995). Training in and dissemination of empirically-validated psychological treatments. *The Clinical Psychologist, 48,* 3–23.

Thurman, R. A. F. (Trans.). (1989). *The Speech of Gold: Reason and enlightenment in the Tibetan Buddhism*: Delhi, India: Motilal Banarsidass.

Tjeltveit, A. C. (1989). The ubiquity of models of human beings in psychotherapy: The need for rigorous reflection. *Psychotherapy, 26,* 1–10.

Tomlinson, H. (1989). After truth: Post-modernism and the rhetoric of science. In H. Lawson & L. Appignanesi (Eds.), *Dismantling truth: Reality in the post-modern world* (pp. 43–57). New York: St. Martin's Press.

Valentine, E. R. (1982). *Conceptual issues in psychology*. London: George Allen and Unwin.

VandenBos, G. R. (1996). Outcome assessment of psychotherapy. *American Psychologist, 51*, 1005–1006.

VandenBos, G. R., Cummings, N. A., & DeLeon, P. H. (1992). A century of psychotherapy: Economic and environmental influences. In D. K. Freedheim (Ed.), *History of psychotherapy: A century of change* (pp. 65–102). Washington, DC: American Psychological Association.

Varela, F. J., Thompson, E., & Rosch, E. (1993). *The embodied mind: Cognitive science and human experience*. Cambridge, MA: MIT Press.

Vasco, A. B. (1994). Correlates of constructivism among Portuguese therapists. *Journal of Constructivist Psychology, 7*, 1–16.

von Eckartsberg, R., & Valle, R. S. (1981). Heideggerian thinking and the Eastern mind. In R. S. Valle & R. von Eckartsberg (Eds.), *The metaphors of consciousness* (pp. 287–311). New York: Plenum.

Wachtel, P. L., & McKinney, M. K. (1992). Cyclical psychodynamics and integrative psychodynamic therapy. In J. C. Norcross & M. R. Goldfried (Eds.), *Handbook of psychotherapy integration* (pp. 335–370). New York: Basic Books.

Waldman, M. (1992). The therapeutic alliance, kundalini, and spiritual / religious issues in counseling: The case of Julia. *Journal of Transpersonal Psychology, 24*, 115–149.

Wallach, M. A., & Wallach, L. (1983). *Psychology's sanction for selfishness: The error of egoism in theory and therapy*. San Francisco: Freeman.

Walsh, R. N., & Vaughan, F. (1980). *Beyond ego: Transpersonal dimensions in psychology*. Los Angeles: Tarcher.

Warnke, G. (1987). *Gadamer: Hermeneutics, tradition, and reason*. Stanford, CA: Stanford University Press.

Watkins, J. G. (1978). *The therapeutic self: Developing resonance—Key to effective relationships*. New York: Human Sciences Press.

Watkins, J. W. N. (1970). Against "normal science." In I. Lakatos & A. Musgrave (Eds.), *Criticism and the growth of knowledge* (pp. 25–37). Cambridge: Cambridge University Press.

Watts, A. W. (1957). *The way of Zen*. New York: Vintage Books.

Weinberger, J. (1993). Common factors in psychotherapy. In G. Stricker & J. R. Gold (Eds.), *Comprehensive handbook of psychotherapy integration* (pp. 43–56). New York: Plenum.

Weisstein, N. (1968/1993). Psychology constructs the female, *or* the fantasy life of the male psychologist (with some attention to the fantasies of his friends, the male biologist and the male anthropologist). Reprinted 1993 in *Feminism & Psychology, 3*, 195–210.

Welwood, J. (1996). Reflection and presence: The dialectic of self-knowledge. *Journal of Transpersonal Psychology, 28*, 107–128.

WGBH Educational Foundation (1995, October 24). *The search for Satan*. [Online press release]. Available Internet: http://www.pbs.org/wgbh/pages/frontline

White, M., & Epston, D. (1990). *Narrative means to therapeutic ends*. New York: Norton.

Whitehead, A. N. (1929/1957). *Process and reality*. New York: Macmillan.

Winnicott, D. W. (1960/1965). Ego distortion in terms of true and false self. In *The maturational processes and the facilitating environment: Studies in the theory of emotional development* (pp. 140–152). New York: International Universities Press.

Wittgenstein, L. (1953). *Philosophical investigations*. New York: Macmillan.

Wittgenstein, L. (1967). *Zettel*. (G. E. M. Anscombe & G. H. von Wright, Eds.). Berkeley, CA: University of California Press.

Wolfe, B. E. (1995). Introduction: The treatment of panic disorder. *In Session: Psychotherapy in Practice, 1*, 1–6.

Wolpe, J. (1958). *Psychotherapy by reciprocal inhibition*. Stanford, CA: Stanford University Press.

Woolfolk, R. L. (1998). *The cure of souls: Science, values, and psychotherapy*. San Francisco: Jossey-Bass.

Woolfolk, R. L., Sass, L. A., & Messer, S. B. (1988). Introduction to hermeneutics. In S. B. Messer, L. A. Sass, & R. L. Woolfolk (Eds.), *Hermeneutics and psychological theory: Interpretive perspectives on personality, psychotherapy, and psychopathology* (pp. 2–26), New Brunswick, NJ: Rutgers University Press.

Woolgar, S. (Ed.). (1991). *Knowledge and reflexivity: New frontiers in the sociology of knowledge*. Thousand Oaks, CA: Sage.

Yalom, I. D. (1980). *Existential psychotherapy*. New York: Basic Books.

Zimmerman, J. L., & Dickerson, V. C. (1994). Tales of the body thief: Externalizing and deconstructing eating problems. In M. F. Hoyt (Ed.), *Constructive therapies* (pp. 295–318). New York: Guilford.

Zimmerman, M. E. (1981). *Eclipse of the self: The development of Heidegger's concept of authenticity*. Athens, OH: Ohio University Press.

Zweig, C. (1995). The death of the self in the postmodern world. In W. T. Anderson (Ed.), *The truth about the truth: De-confusing and re-constructing the postmodern world* (pp. 145–150). New York: Tarcher/Putnam.

Name Index

Subject Index

absolutism vs. nihilism, 176–77, 237, 281, 282

affirmative postmodernism, 88, 90, 102 (table), 162, 163; Critical mode and, 229; deconstruction and, 79, 235; defined, 77, 217; Dialogical mode and, 7, 216, 217, 222–23, 224–25; empowerment and, 229; narrative therapy and, 129, 140, 141, 142; Nihilistic mode and, 235, 237; relativism and, 78, 91–101; self in, 84. *See also* Dialogical mode

American Psychiatric Association, 244

American Psychological Association (APA), 7, 16, 24, 253; Task Force, 16, 17, 30

analogical reasoning, 199–200

anti-realism; defined, in relation to postmodernism, 5, 55, 75–78, 102 (table); vs. realism, 6, 53, 102 (table), 122–23, 174–75, 177; themes of: centrality of negation, 78–81; dissolution of

autonomous, coherent self, 83–84; end of metanarratives, 81–83; knowledge as non-foundational/non-representational, 80–81; knowledge as power, 85–87. *See also* postmodernism

behavior therapy, 20–22, 180–81, 207, 251 (*see also* empirical literature)

being and knowing, dialectic of, 274–84

belief, in psychotherapy. *See* certitude, therapeutic

Buddhism, 275, 289; on emptiness, 176–77, 276, 278, 284 (*see also* nondualism); on going beyond ego, 167, 277–78; on illusion of self, 90–91, 176, 279; vs. postmodernism, on transformation, 90–91, 289

calculative thinking, 168, 169, 172, 227, 275, 276, 279, 280, 282, 283, 284